ILLINOIS CENTRAL COLLEGE
PA6666.AI 1966
STACKS
Seneca, his tenne tragedies,
A12900 150015

W9-AQJ-671

Seneca: His Tenne Tragedies

SENECA
His Tenne Tragedies

TRANSLATED INTO ENGLISH

EDITED BY

Thomas Newton

ANNO 1581

WITH AN INTRODUCTION BY

T. S. Eliot

INDIANA UNIVERSITY PRESS
BLOOMINGTON & LONDON

THIS BOOK WAS ORIGINALLY PUBLISHED BY CONSTABLE AND CO., LTD., IN LONDON AND BY ALFRED A. KNOPF IN NEW YORK IN 1927. MR. ELIOT'S INTRODUCTION WAS LATER REPRINTED IN SELECTED ESSAYS, BY T. S. ELIOT, PUBLISHED IN 1932 BY FABER AND FABER IN LONDON AND BY HARCOURT IN THE UNITED STATES. IT IS REPRINTED HERE BY PERMISSION OF HARCOURT, BRACE & WORLD FROM SELECTED ESSAYS, NEW EDITION, BY T. S. ELIOT,

LIBRARY OF CONGRESS CATALOG CARD NUMBER: 66-12732
MANUFACTURED IN THE UNITED STATES OF AMERICA

INTRODUCTION

By T. S. Eliot

O author exercised a wider or deeper influence upon the Elizabethan mind or upon the Elizabethan form of tragedy than did Seneca. To present the Elizabethan translations of the tragedies in their proper setting, it is necessary to deal with three problems which at first may appear to be but slightly connected: (1) the character, virtues and vices of the Latin tragedies themselves; (2) the directions in which these tragedies influenced our Elizabethan drama; (3) the history of these translations, the part they played in extending the influence of Seneca, and their actual merit as translation and as poetry. There are here several questions which, with the greater number of important Tudor translations, do not arise. Most of the better known translations are of authors whose intrinsic merit is unquestioned, and the translations derive some of their prestige from the merit and fame of the author translated; and most of the better known prose translations have an easy beauty of style which arrests even the least prepared reader. But with the present translations (for they are by several hands) we are concerned first of all with a Latin poet whose

reputation would deter any reader but the most curious; with translations of unequal merit, because by different scholars; and with translation into a metre—the 'fourteener'—which is superficially a mere archaism, and which repels readers who have not the patience to accustom their ears and nerves to its beat. The translations have, as I hope to show, considerable poetic charm and quite adequate accuracy, with occasional flashes of real beauty; their literary value remains greater than that of any later translations of Seneca's tragedies that I have examined, either in English or French. But the appreciation of the literary value of these translations is inseparably engaged with the appreciation of the original and of its historical importance; so that although at first sight a consideration of the historical problems may appear irrelevant, it should in the end enhance our enjoyment of the translations as literature.

I

In the Renaissance, no Latin author was more highly esteemed than Seneca; in modern times, few Latin authors have been more consistently damned. The prose Seneca, the 'Seneca morale' of Dante, still enjoys a measure of tepid praise, though he has no influence; but the poet and tragedian receives from the historians and critics of Latin literature the most universal reprobation. Latin literature provides poets for several tastes, but there is no taste for Seneca. Mackail, for instance, whose taste in Latin literature is almost catholic, dismisses Seneca with half a page of his *Short History of Latin Literature*, and a few of the usual adjectives such as 'rhetorical.' Professor Mackail is inclined by his training and taste to enjoy the purer and more classical authors, and is inclined by his temperament to enjoy the more romantic: like Shenstone or some other eighteenth-century poets, Seneca falls between. Nisard, in his *Poètes Latins de la décadence*, devotes many pages and much patience to the difference of conditions which produced great tragedy in Athens, and only rhetorical declamation in Rome. Butler, after a more detailed and more tolerant examination from a more literary point of view (*Post-Augustan Poetry*), commits himself to the damaging statement that 'to Seneca more than to 'any other man is due the excessive predominance of de- 'clamatory rhetoric, which has characterised the drama 'throughout Western Europe from the Renaissance down 'to the latter half of the nineteenth century.' The most recent critic, Mr. F. L. Lucas (*Seneca and Elizabethan Tragedy*), admits 'the exasperatingly false rhetoric of the 'Senecan stage, with its far-fetched and frigid epigrams.' Yet this is a dramatist whom Scaliger preferred to Euripides, and whom the whole of Europe in the Renaissance delighted to honour. It is obviously a task of some difficulty to disentangle him from his reputation.

We must admit, first, that the tragedies of Seneca deserve the censure that has been directed upon them. On the other hand, it may be true—I think it is true—that the critics, especially the English critics, have been often biassed by Seneca's real and supposed bad influence upon the Renaissance, that they have included the demerits of his admirers in his own faults. But before we proceed to what redemption of his fame is possible, it is expedient to resume those universally admitted strictures and limitations which have become commonplaces of Senecan criticism. First, it is pretty generally agreed that the plays of Seneca were composed, not for stage performance, but for private declamation.[1] This theory attenuates the supposed 'horrors' of the tragedies, many of which could hardly have been represented on a stage, even with the most ingenious machinery, without being merely ridiculous; the Renaissance assumption to the contrary gave licence to a taste which would probably have been indulged even without Seneca's authority. And if the plays were written to be declaimed, probably by a single speaker ('elocutionist' is really the word), we can account for other singularities. I say 'account for,' I do not say without qualification that this peculiar form was the 'cause'; for the ultimate cause was probably the same Latin temper which made such an unacted drama possible. The cause lies in the Latin sensibility which is expressed by the Latin language. But if we imagine this unacted drama, we see at once that it is at one remove from reality, compared with the Greek. Behind the dialogue of Greek drama we are always conscious of a concrete visual actuality, and behind that of a specific emotional actuality. Behind the drama of words is the drama of action, the timbre of voice and voice, the uplifted hand or tense muscle, and the particular emotion. The spoken play, the words which

[1] I must admit, however, that this view has recently been contested with great force by Leon Herrmann: *Le Théâtre de Sénèque* (Paris, 1924). See p. 195 of that book.

we read, are symbols, a shorthand, and often, as in the best of Shakespeare, a very abbreviated shorthand indeed, for the acted and felt play, which is always the real thing. The phrase, beautiful as it may be, stands for a greater beauty still. This is merely a particular case of the amazing unity of Greek, the unity of concrete and abstract in philosophy, the unity of thought and feeling, action and speculation, in life. In the plays of Seneca, the drama is all in the word, and the word has no further reality behind it. His characters all seem to speak with the same voice, and at the top of it; they recite in turn.

I do not mean to suggest that the method of delivery of a play of Seneca was essentially different from that of Greek tragedy. It was probably nearer to the declamation of Greek tragedy than was the delivery of Latin comedy. The latter was acted by professional actors. I imagine that Seneca's plays were declaimed by himself and other amateurs, and it is likely that the Athenian tragedies were performed by amateurs. I mean that the beauty of phrase in Greek tragedy is the shadow of a greater beauty—the beauty of thought and emotion. In the tragedies of Seneca the centre of value is shifted from what the personage says to the way in which he says it. Very often the value comes near to being mere smartness. Nevertheless, we must remember that 'verbal' beauty is still a kind of beauty.

The plays were admirably adapted for declamation before an imperial highbrow audience of crude sensibility but considerable sophistication in the ingenuities of language. They would have been as unactable on the Greek

INTRODUCTION

stage as they are on the English. Superficially neat and trim, they are, for the stage, models of formlessness. The Athenians were accustomed to long speeches from Messengers, speeches which embarrass both the modern actor and the modern audience; this was a convention with practical advantages; their other long speeches usually have some dramatic point, some place in the whole scheme of the play. But the characters in a play of Seneca behave more like members of a minstrel troupe sitting in a semicircle, rising in turn each to do his 'number,' or varying their recitations by a song or a little back-chat. I do not suppose that a Greek audience would have sat through the first three hundred lines of the *Hercules Furens*. Only at the 523rd line does Amphitryon detect the sound of Hercules' tread, ascending from Hell, at which inopportune moment the chorus interrupt for two or three pages. When Hercules finally appears, he seems to be leading Cerberus, who presently evaporates, for he is not on the stage a few minutes later. After Amphitryon has in a rather roundabout way, but more briefly than might have been expected, explained to Hercules the pressing danger to his family and country, Hercules makes off to kill Lycus. While Hercules is thus engaged in a duel on the result of which everybody's life depends, the family sit down calmly and listen to a long description by Theseus of the Tartarean regions. This account is not a straight monologue, as Amphitryon from time to time puts leading questions about the fauna, the administration and system of justice, of the world below. Meanwhile, Hercules has (contrary to the usual belief that

Seneca murders all his victims in full view of the audience) despatched Lycus off-stage. At the end of the play, when Juno has stricken Hercules with madness, it is not at all clear whether he destroys his family on-stage or off. The slaughter is accompanied by a running commentary by Amphitryon, whose business it is to tell the audience what is going forward. If the children are slain in sight of the audience, this commentary is superfluous; Amphitryon also reports the collapse of Hercules; but presently Hercules comes to, certainly on-stage, and spies his dead wife and children. The whole situation is inconceivable unless we assume the play to have been composed solely for recitation; like other of Seneca's plays, it is full of statements useful only to an audience which sees nothing. Seneca's plays might, in fact, be practical models for the modern 'broadcasted drama.'

We need not look too closely into the conditions of the age which produced no genuine drama, but which allowed this curious freak of non-theatrical drama. The theatre is a gift which has not been vouchsafed to every race, even of the highest culture. It has been given to the Hindus, the Greeks, the Japanese (if anything so alien can be included), to the English, the French, and the Spanish, at moments; in less measure to the Teutons and Scandinavians. It was not given to the Romans, or generously to their successors the Italians. The Romans had some success in low comedy, itself an adaptation of Greek models, but their instinct turned to shows and circuses, as does that of the later race which created the Commedia dell' Arte, which still provides the best puppet shows, and which gives a home to Mr. Gordon Craig. No cause can be assigned, for every cause demands a further cause. It is handy to speak of 'the genius of the language,' and we shall continue to do so, but why did the language adopt that particular genius? At any rate, we should discourage any criticism which, in accounting for the defects and faults of the plays of Seneca, made much of the 'decadence' of the age of Nero. In the verse, yes, Seneca is unquestionably 'silver age,' or more exactly he is not a poet of the *first* rank in Latin, he is far inferior to Virgil; but for tragic drama, it would be a gross error to suppose that an earlier and more heroic age of Rome could have produced anything better. Many of the faults of Seneca which appear 'decadent' are, after all, merely Roman and (in the narrower sense) Latin.

It is so with the characterisation. The characters of Seneca's plays have no subtlety and, strictly speaking, no 'private life.' But it would be an error to imagine that they are merely cruder and coarser versions of the Greek originals. They belong to a different race. Their crudity is that which was of the Roman, as compared with the Greek, in real life. The Roman was much the simpler creature. At best, his training was that of devotion to the State, his virtues were public virtues. The Greek knew well enough the idea of the State, but he had also a strong traditional morality which constituted, so to speak, a direct relation between him and the gods, without the mediation of the State, and he had furthermore a sceptical and heterodox intelligence. Hence the greater efficiency of the Roman, and the greater interest of the Greek.

Hence the difference between Greek Stoicism and Roman Stoicism—the latter being the form through which Stoicism influenced later Europe. We must think of the characters of Seneca as offspring of Rome, more than we think of them as offspring of their age.

The drama of Antigone—which Seneca did not attempt—could hardly have been transposed for Roman sentiment. In the drama of Seneca there are no conflicts, except the conflict of passion, temper, or appetite with the external duties. The literary consequence, therefore, is the tendency which persists in modern Italy; the tendency to 'rhetoric'; and which, on such a large scale, may be attributed to a development of language exceeding the development of sensibility of the people. If you compare Catullus with Sappho, or Cicero with Demosthenes, or Thucydides with a Latin historian, you find that the genius is the genius of a different language, and what is lost is a gift of sensibility. So with Seneca and the Greek dramatists. Hence we should think of the long ranting speeches of Seneca, the beautiful but irrelevant descriptions, the smart stichomythia, rather as peculiarities of Latin than as the bad taste of the dramatist.

The congeniality of Stoicism to the Roman mind is no part of my duty to analyse; and it would be futile to attempt to decide what, in the dialogue and characterisation of Seneca's plays, is due to Stoicism, what due to the Roman mind, and what due to the peculiar form which Seneca elected. What is certain is the existence of a large element of Stoicism in the plays, enough to justify the belief that the plays and the prose are by the hand of the same Seneca. In the plays, indeed, the Stoicism is present in a form more quickly to catch the fancy of the Renaissance than in the prose epistles and essays. Half of the commonplaces of the Elizabethans—and the more commonplace half—are of Senecan origin. This ethic of sententious maxims was, as we shall see, much more sympathetic to the temper of the Renaissance than would have been the morals of the elder Greek dramatists; the Renaissance itself was much more Latin than Greek. In the Greek tragedy, as Nisard and others have pointed out, the moralising is not the expression of a conscious 'system' of philosophy; the Greek dramatists moralise only because morals are woven through and through the texture of their tragic idea. Their morals are a matter of feeling trained for generations, it is hereditary and religious, just as their dramatic forms themselves are the development of their early liturgies. Their ethics of thought are one with their ethics of behaviour. As the dramatic form of Seneca is no growth, but a construction, so is his moral philosophy and that of Roman Stoicism in general. Whether the Roman scepticism was, as Nisard suggests, the result of a too rapid and great expansion and mixture of races cancelling each other's beliefs, rather than the product of a lively inquiring intelligence, the 'beliefs' of Stoicism are a consequence of scepticism; and the ethic of Seneca's plays is that of an age which supplied the lack of moral habits by a system of moral attitudes and poses. To this the natural public temper of Rome contributed. The ethic of Seneca is a matter of postures. The posture which gives the greatest opportunity for effect, hence for the Senecan morality, is the posture of dying: death gives his characters the opportunity for their most sententious aphorisms—a hint which Elizabethan dramatists were only too ready to follow.

When all reserves have been made, there is still much to be said for Seneca as a dramatist. And I am convinced that the proper approach to his appreciation and enjoyment is not by comparison and contrast—to which, in his case, criticism is violently tempted—but by isolation. I made a careful comparison of the *Medea* and the *Hippolytus* of Seneca—perhaps his two best plays—with the *Medea* of Euripides and the *Phèdre* of Racine respectively; but I do not think that any advantage would be gained by reporting the results of this inquiry, by contrasting either the dramatic structure or the treatment of the title figures. Such comparisons have already been made; they magnify the defects and obscure the merits of the Senecan tragedy. If Seneca is to be compared, he should rather be compared for versification, descriptive and narrative power, and taste, with the earlier Roman poets. The comparison is fair, though Seneca comes off rather ill. His prosody is monotonous; in spite of a mastery of several metres, his choruses fall heavily on the ear. Sometimes his chorus rhythms seem to hover between the more flexible measures of his predecessors and the stiffer but more impressive beat of the mediaeval hymn.[1] But within the limits of his declamatory purpose, Seneca obtains, time after time,

[1] *E.g.* 'O mors amoris una sedamen mali,
O mors pudoris maximum laesi decus.
(*Hippolytus*, 1188-89).

magnificent effects. In the verbal *coup de théâtre* no one has ever excelled him. The final cry of Jason to Medea departing in her car is unique; I can think of no other play which reserves such a shock for the last word:

'Per alta vada spatia sublimi aethere;
testare nullos esse, qua veheris, deos.'[1]

Again and again the epigrammatic observation on life or death is put in the most telling way at the most telling moment. It is not only in his brief ejaculations that Seneca triumphs. The sixteen lines addressed by the chorus to the dead sons of Hercules (*Hercules Furens*, 1., 1135 ff.), which are exquisitely rendered by our translator, seem to me highly pathetic. The descriptive passages are often of great charm, with phrases which haunt us more than we should expect. The lines of Hercules,

'ubi sum? sub ortu solis, an sub cardine
glacialis ursae?'

must have lain long in the memory of Chapman before they came out in *Bussy d'Ambois* as

'fly where men feel
The cunning axle-tree, or those that suffer
Under the chariot of the snowy Bear.'

---

[1] Here, by the way, our translator (vol. ii. p. 98) seems to me to have hit on the sense:

'Bear witnesse, grace of God is none in place of thy repayre.'

A modern translator (Professor Miller, editing the Loeb Translation text) gives 'bear witness, where thou ridest, that there are no gods.' It seems to me more effective if we take the meaning to be that there are no gods *where (ever) Medea is*, instead of a mere outburst of atheism. But the old Farnaby edition observes 'testimonium contra deorum justitiam, vel argumento nullos esse in caelo deos.'

Though Seneca is long-winded, he is not diffuse; he is capable of great concision; there is even a monotony of forcefulness; but many of his short phrases have for us as much oratorical impressiveness as they had for the Elizabethans. As (to take an unworn example) the bitter words of Hecuba as the Greeks depart:

> 'concidit virgo ac puer;
> bellum peractum est.'

Even the most sententious sayings of stoical commonplace preserve their solemnity in that Latin language which carries such thoughts more grandly than could any other:

> 'Fatis agimur; cedite fatis.
> non sollicitae possunt curae
> mutare rati stamina fusi.
> quidquid patimur mortale genus,
> quidquid facimus venit ex alto,
> servatque suae decreta colus
> Lachesis nulla revoluta manu.
> omnia secto tramite vadunt
> primusque dies dedit extremum.'
>
> (*Œdipus*, 980 ff.)

But to quote Seneca is not criticism; it is merely to offer baits to a possible reader; it would indeed be bad criticism if we left the impression that these and such as these are moments in which Seneca excels himself, and which he could not sustain. An essential point to make about Seneca is the consistency of his writing, its maintenance on one level, below which he seldom falls and above which he never mounts. Seneca is not one of those poets who are to be remembered because they now and then rise to the tone and the vocabulary of greater poets. Seneca is wholly himself; what he attempted he executed, he created his own genre. And this leads us to a consideration which we must keep in mind in considering his later influence: whether we can treat him seriously as a *dramatist*. Critics are inclined to treat his drama as a bastard form. But this is an error which critics of the drama are in general apt to make; the forms of drama are so various that few critics are able to hold more than one or two in mind in pronouncing judgment of 'dramatic' and 'undramatic.' What is 'dramatic'? If one were saturated in the Japanese Noh, in Bhasa and Kalidasa, in Aeschylus, Sophocles and Euripides, Aristophanes and Menander, in the popular mediaeval plays of Europe, in Lope de Vega and Calderon, as well as the great English and French drama, and if one were (which is impossible) equally sensitive to them all, would one not hesitate to decide that one form is more dramatic than another? And Seneca's is definitely a 'form.' It does not fall within either of the categories of the defectively dramatic. There are the 'closet dramas' which are mostly simply inferior dramas: the plays of Tennyson, Browning, and Swinburne. (Whether a writer expected his play to be played or not is irrelevant, the point is whether it is playable.) And there is another, more interesting type, where the writer is trying to do something more or something different from what the stage can do, but yet with an implication of performance, where there is a mixture of dramatic and extra-dramatic elements. This is a modern and sophisticated form: it contains *The Dynasts*, Goethe's *Faust*, and possibly (not having seen it played I cannot speak with confidence) *Peer Gynt*. Seneca's plays do not belong to either of these types. If, as I confidently believe, they are intended for *recitation*, they have a form of their own ; and I believe that they were intended for recitation because they are perfectly adapted for recitation —they are better recited than read. And I have no doubt —though there is no external evidence—that Seneca must have had considerable practice himself in reciting the plays. He would have been, therefore, a playwright of as practical experience as Shakespeare or Molière. His form is a practical form ; it is even, I suggest, a form which might be interesting to attempt in our own time, when the revival of the theatre is obstructed by some of the difficulties which made the stage an impossibility in the age of Seneca.

What lessons the Elizabethans learnt from Seneca, and whether they were the same as those which we might learn ourselves, is the next subject to consider. But whether they profited by the study, or whether they admired him and pillaged him to their own detriment, we must remember that we cannot justly estimate his influence unless we form our own opinion of Seneca first, without being influenced by his influence.

II

The influence of Seneca upon Elizabethan drama has received much more attention from scholars than from literary critics. The historical treatment has been very thorough. The admirable edition of the works of Sir William Alexander, Earl of Stirling, by Kastner and Charlton (Manchester University Press, vol. I., 1921), has a full account of this influence both direct and through

Italy and France; in this introduction also will be found the best bibliography of the subject. Dr. F. S. Boas, especially in his edition of Kyd's Plays, has treated the matter at length. Professor J. W. Cunliffe's *Influence of Seneca on Elizabethan Tragedy* (1893) remains, within its limits, the most useful of all books, and Mr. Cunliffe has handled the question in a more general way in his *Early English Classical Tragedies.* Indirect Senecan influences have also been studied in detail, as in Professor A. M. Witherspoon's *Influence of Robert Garnier on Elizabethan Drama.* And work which is now being done on the earlier drama (cf. Dr. A. W. Reed's recent *Early Tudor Drama*, 1926) will enable us to understand better the junction of the Senecan influence with the native tradition. It is not fitting that a literary critic should retrace all this labour of scholarship, where either his dissent or his approval would be an impertinence; but we may benefit by this scholarship to draw certain general conclusions.

The plays of Seneca exerted their influence in several ways and to several results. The results are of three main types: (1) the popular Elizabethan tragedy; (2) the 'Senecal' drama, pseudo-classical, composed by and for a small and select body of persons not closely in touch or in sympathy with the popular drama of the day, and composed largely in protest against the defects and monstrosities of that drama; (3) the two Roman tragedies of Ben Jonson, which appear to belong between the two opposed classes, to constitute an attempt, by an active practising playwright, to improve the form of popular drama by the example of Seneca; not by slavish imitation but by adaptation, to make of popular drama a finished work of art. As for the ways in which Seneca influenced the Elizabethans, it must be remembered that these were never simple, and became more complicated. The Italian and the French drama of the day was already penetrated by Seneca. Seneca was a regular part of the school curriculum, while Greek drama was unknown to all but a few great scholars. Every schoolboy with a smattering of Latin had a verse or two of Seneca in his memory; probably a good part of the audiences could recognise the origin of the occasional bits of Seneca which are quoted in Latin in some of the popular plays (*e.g.* several times by Marston). And by the time that *The Spanish Tragedy* and the old *Hamlet* had made their success, the English playwright was under the influence of Seneca by being under the influence of his own predecessors. Here the influence of Kyd is of the greatest importance: if Senecan Kyd had such a vogue, that was surely the path to facile success for any hard-working and underpaid writer.

All that I wish to do in this Introduction is to consider certain misconceptions of the Senecan influence, which I believe are still current in our opinions of Elizabethan damra, although they do not appear in works of scholarship. For such a purpose these contemporary translations possess a particular value: whether they greatly affected the conception of Seneca, or greatly extended his influence, they give a reflection of the appearance of Seneca to the Englishman of the time. I do not suggest that the influence of Seneca has been exaggerated or diminished in modern criticism; but I believe that too much importance has been

INTRO-
DUCTION

attached to his influence in some directions, and too little to his influence in others. There is one point on which every one is agreed, and hardly more than one : the five-act division of the modern European play is due to Seneca. What I chiefly wish to consider are, first, his responsibility for what has been called since Symonds' day the Tragedy of Blood—how far Seneca is the author of the horrors which disfigure Elizabethan drama ; second, his responsibility for *bombast* in Elizabethan diction ; and third, his influence upon the *thought*, or what passes for thought, in the drama of Shakespeare and his contemporaries. It is the first which I think has been overestimated, the second misconstrued, the third undervalued.

Certainly, among all national dramas, the Elizabethan tragedies are remarkable for the extent to which they employ the horrible and revolting. It is true that but for this taste and practice we should never have had *King Lear* or *The Duchess of Malfy* ; so impossible is it to isolate the vices from the virtues, the failures from the masterpieces of Elizabethan tragedy. We cannot reprehend a custom but for which one great experiment of the human spirit must have been left unmade, even if we cannot like it ; nor can we wholly deplore anything which brings with it some information about the soul. And even leaving Shakespeare apart, the genius of no other race could have manipulated the tragedy of horror into the magnificent farce of Marlowe, or the magnificent nightmare of Webster. We must therefore reserve two measures of comparison : one, that between the baser tragedy of the time and the best tragedy of the time, the other (which is perhaps a moral measure, the application of which would lead us too far for the present discussion) between the tragedy of the time as a whole and another tragedy of horror—we think of Dante's Ugolino and the Œdipus of Sophocles—in which, in the end, the mind seems to triumph. Here, the question of Seneca's influence is capital. If the taste for horror was a result of being trained on Seneca, then it has neither justification nor interest; if it was something inherent in the people and in the age, and Seneca merely the excuse and precedent, then it is a phenomenon of interest. Even to speak of Seneca as offering a precedent and excuse is probably to falsify; for it implies that the Elizabethans would otherwise have been a little uneasy in conscience at indulging such tastes—which is ridiculous to suppose. They merely assumed that Seneca's taste was like their own—which is not *wholly* untrue; and that Seneca represented the whole of classical antiquity—which is quite false. Where Seneca took part is in affecting the type of plot; he supported one tendency against another. But for Seneca, we might have had more plays in the *Yorkshire Tragedy* mould; that is to say, the equivalent of the *News of the World* murder report; Seneca, and particularly the Italianised Seneca, encouraged the taste for the foreign, remote, or exotic. No doubt *The Jew of Malta* or *Titus Andronicus* would have made the living Seneca shudder with genuine aesthetic horror; but his influence helped to recommend work with which he had little in common.

When we examine the plays of Seneca, the actual horrors are not so heinous or so many as are supposed. The most unpleasantly sanguinary is the *Thyestes*, a subject which, so far as we know, was not attempted by a Greek dramatist. Even here, if the view that the tragedies were intended only for recitation is true, the cultivated Roman audience were listening to a story which was part of their Hellenic culture, and which is in fact a common property of folklore. The story was sanctified by time. The plots of Elizabethan tragedy were, so far as the audience were concerned, novelties. This plot of *Thyestes* is not employed by any Elizabethan, but the play has undoubtedly more in common with the Tragedy of Blood, especially in its early form, than any other of Seneca's. It has a particularly tedious Ghost. It has, more emphatically than any other, the motive of Revenge, unregulated by any divine control or justice. Yet even in the *Thyestes* the performance of the horrors is managed with conventional tact; the only visible horror is the perhaps unavoidable presentation of the evidence—the children's heads in a dish.

The most significant popular play under Senecan influence is of course *The Spanish Tragedy*, and the further responsibility of Kyd for the translation of the pseudo-Senecan *Cornelia* of Garnier has marked him as the disciple of Seneca. But in *The Spanish Tragedy* there is another element, not always sufficiently distinguished from the Senecan, which (though it may have relations among the Italian Renaissance progeny of Seneca) allies it to something more indigenous. The Senecan apparatus, it is true, is impressive. The Ghost, and Revenge, who replace the Tantalus and the Fury of the *Thyestes*, use all the infernal allusions—Acheron, Charon, and the rest—so dear to Seneca. Temporary insanity is an expedient well known to Seneca. But in the type of plot there is nothing classical or pseudo-classical at all. 'Plot' in the sense in which we find plot in *The Spanish Tragedy* does not exist for Seneca at all. He took a story perfectly well known to everybody, and interested his auditors entirely by his embellishments of description and narrative and by smartness and pungency of dialogue; suspense and surprise attached solely to verbal effects. *The Spanish Tragedy*, like the series of Hamlet plays, including Shakespeare's, has an affinity to our contemporary detective drama.[1] The plot of Hieronymo to compass his revenge by the play allies it with a small but interesting class of drama which certainly owes nothing essential to Seneca: that which includes *Arden of Feversham* [2] and *The Yorkshire Tragedy*. These two remarkable plays are both based on contemporary or recent crimes committed in England. Unless it be the hint of divine retribution in the epilogue to *Arden*, there is no token of foreign or classical influence in these two plays. Yet they are bloody enough. The husband in *The Yorkshire Tragedy* kills his two young sons, throws the servant downstairs and breaks her neck, and nearly succeeds in killing his wife. In *Arden of Feversham* the wife and her conspirators stab the husband to death upon the stage—the rest of the play being occupied by a primitive but effective police inquiry into evidence. It is only sur-

[1] I suggest also that besides *Hamlet*, *Macbeth* and to some extent *Othello* among Shakespeare's major tragedies have this 'thriller' interest, whilst it is not introduced into *King Lear*, *Antony and Cleopatra*, or *Coriolanus*.

[2] I dissent from Dr. Boas, and agree with that body of opinion which attributes *Arden* to Kyd, e.g. Fleay, Robertson, Crawford, Dugdale Sykes, Oliphant.

prising that there are not more examples of this type of play, since there is evidence of as lively a public interest in police court horrors as there is to-day. One of the pieces of evidence is associated with Kyd; it is a curious little account of a poisoning case, *The Murder of John Brewen.* (A little later, Dekkar was to supply the deficiency of penny journalism with his Plague Pamphlets.) In Kyd, whether *Arden* be by him or by an imitator, we find the union of Senecan with native elements, to the advantage of both For the Senecan influence is felt in the structure of the play—the structure of *The Spanish Tragedy* is more dramatic than that of *Arden* or *The Yorkshire Tragedy*; whilst the material of *The Spanish Tragedy*, like that of the other two plays, is quite different from the Senecan material, and much more satisfying to an unlettered audience.

The worst that can be urged against Seneca, in the matter of responsibility for what is disgusting in Elizabethan drama, is that he may have provided the dramatist with a pretext or justification for horrors which were not Senecan at all, for which there was certainly a taste, and the taste for which would certainly have been gratified at that time whether Seneca had ever written or not. Against my use of *The Yorkshire Tragedy*, it may be said that this play (the crime in question was committed only in 1603) and *Arden* also were written after the success of *The Spanish Tragedy*, and that the taste for horrors developed only after it had received Senecan licence. I cannot *prove* the contrary. But it must be admitted that the greater number of the horrors are such as Seneca himself would not have tolerated. In one of the worst offenders —indeed one of the stupidest and most uninspired plays ever written, a play in which it is incredible that Shakespeare had any hand at all, a play in which the best passages would be too highly honoured by the signature of Peele—in *Titus Andronicus* [1]—there is nothing really Senecan at all. There is a wantonness, an irrelevance, about the crimes of which Seneca would never have been guilty. Seneca's Œdipus has the traditional justification for blinding himself; and the blinding itself is far less offensive than that in *Lear*. In *Titus*, the hero cuts off his own hand in view of the audience, who can also testify to the mutilation of the hands and the tongue of Lavinia. In *The Spanish Tragedy*, Hieronymo bites out his own tongue. There is nothing like this in Seneca.

But if this is very unlike Seneca, it is very like the contemporary drama of Italy. Nothing could better illustrate the accidental character of literary 'influence'—accidental, that is, with reference to the work exercising the influence —than the difference between Senecan drama in Italy and in France. The French drama is from the beginning restrained and decorous; to the French drama, especially to Garnier, the Senecan drama of Greville, Daniel and Alexander is allied. The Italian is bloodthirsty in the extreme. Kyd knew both; but it was to the Italian that he and Peele yielded themselves with sympathetic delight. We must remember, too, that Italy had developed stagecraft and stage machinery to the highest point—for the

[1] See J. M. Robertson: *An Introduction to the Study of the Shakespeare Canon.*

most sumptuous masques in England, Italian managers, engineers and artists were brought over; that the plastic arts were much more important in Italy than elsewhere, and that consequently the spectacular and sensational elements of drama were insisted upon; that Italian civilisation had, in short, everything to dazzle the imagination of unsophisticated northerners emerging into a period of prosperity and luxury. I have no first-hand acquaintance with Italian plays of this epoch; it is a library which few readers would penetrate in pursuit of pleasure; but its character, and influence in England, are well attested. It is possible to say that Seneca hardly influenced this Italian drama at all; he was made use of by it and adopted into it; and for Kyd and Peele he was thoroughly Italianised.

The Tragedy of Blood is very little Senecan, in short, though it made much use of Senecan machinery; it is very largely Italian; and it added an ingenuity of plot which is native.

If we wished to find the reason for the sanguinary char acter of much Elizabethan drama—which persists to its end —we should have to allow ourselves some daring general isations concerning the temper of the epoch. When we consider it, and reflect how much more refined, how much more *classical* in the profounder sense, is that earlier popular drama which reached its highest point in *Everyman*, I cannot but think that the change is due to some funda mental release of restraint. The tastes gratified are always latent: they were then gratified by the drama, as they are now gratified by crime reports in the daily press. It is no more reasonable to connect Seneca with this aspect of Elizabethan drama than it is to connect Æschylus or Sophocles with *Jude the Obscure.* I am not sure that the latter association has not been made, though no one supposes that Mr. Hardy prepared himself by close application to the study of Greek drama.

It is pertinent to inquire, in this context, what was the influence of Seneca, in the way of horrors, upon the small body of 'Senecal' dramatists who professedly imitated him. But this collation is relevant also to the question of Seneca's influence upon language; so that before making the comparison we may consider this latter question next. Here, the great influence of Seneca is unquestionable. Quotation after quotation, parallel after parallel, may be adduced; the most conspicuous are given in Cunliffe's *Influence of Seneca*, others in Lucas's *Seneca and Elizabethan Tragedy.* So great is this influence that we can say neither that it was good nor that it was bad; for we cannot imagine what Elizabethan dramatic verse would have been without it. The direct influence is restricted to the group of Marlowe and to Marston; Jonson and Chapman are, each in his own way, more sophisticated and independent; the later or Jacobean dramatists, Middleton, Webster, Tourneur, Ford, Beaumont and Fletcher, found their language upon their own predecessors, and chiefly upon Shakespeare. But none of these authors hesitated to draw upon Seneca when occasion served, and Chapman owes much, both good and bad, of his dramatic style to his admiration for Seneca. No better examples can be found, however, of plays which, while not Senecan in form, and not containing any of the more obvious Senecan apparatus such as Ghosts, are yet deeply influenced by Seneca in language, than the *True Tragedy of Richard Duke of York*, and the Shakespearean *Richard II.* and *Richard III.* These, with the work of Kyd and that of Marlowe and of Peele, and several of the plays included in the Shakespeare Apocrypha, have a great deal in common.

The precise pilferings and paraphrases have been thoroughly catalogued by the scholars I have mentioned, and others ; hardly a dramatist between Kyd and Massinger who is not many times indebted to Seneca. Instead of repeating this labour, I prefer to call attention to his universal influence. Not only the evolution of the dramatic structure, but the evolution of the blank verse cadence, took place under the shadow of Seneca ; it is hardly too much to say that Shakespeare could not have formed the verse instrument which he left to his successors, Webster, Massinger, Tourneur, Ford, and Fletcher, unless he had received an instrument already highly developed by the genius of Marlowe and the influence of Seneca. Blank verse before 1600, or thereabouts, is a crude form of music compared to blank verse after that date ; but its progress in fifteen years had been astonishing. In the first place, I believe that the establishment of blank verse as the vehicle of drama, instead of the old fourteener, or the heroic couplet, or (what might have happened) a particular form of prose rhythm, received considerable support from its being obviously the nearest equivalent to the solemnity and weight of the Senecan iambic. A comparison of the trotting metre of our translations with Surrey's translation of Virgil will show, I think, that while the former has undeniable poetic charms of its own, the latter would reveal more resources to the ear of the dramatist. The pre-Marlowe versification is competent, but extremely monotonous; it is literally a *monotone*, containing none of the musical counter-rhythms which Marlowe introduced, nor the rhythms of individual speech which were later added.

> 'When this eternal substance of my soul
> Did live imprison'd in my wanton flesh,
> Each in their function serving other's need,
> I was a courtier in the Spanish court:'
> (Prologue, *Spanish Tragedy*, xxx.)

But to illustrate the early use of this metre under Senecan influence, a worse play serves our purpose better; the Senecan content justifies our quoting at some length from *Locrine*, an early play [1] of no merit whatever. Here is the Revival of Learning in the brain of a fourth-rate playwright:

HUMBER. Where may I find some desert wilderness,
Where I may breathe out curses as I would,
And scare the earth with my condemning voice;
Where every echo's repercussion
May help me to bewail mine overthrow,
And aid me in my sorrowful laments?
Where may I find some hollow uncouth rock,
Where I may damn, condemn, and ban my fill
The heavens, the hell, the earth, the air, the fire,
And utter curses to the concave sky,

---

[1] Usually attributed to Greene, and dated about 1585 (see Brooke, *Shakespeare Apocrypha*). Neither authorship nor date is important for my purpose: the play was obviously written by some one who had not yet experienced the influence of Marlowe.

Which may infect the airy regions,
And light upon the Brittain Locrine's head ?
You ugly sprites that in Cocytus mourn,
And gnash your teeth with dolorous laments :
You fearful dogs that in black Lethe howl,
And scare the ghosts with your wide open throats :
You ugly ghosts that, flying from these dogs,
Do plunge yourselves in Puryflegiton :
Come, all of you, and with your shriking notes
Accompany the Brittain's conquering host.
Come, fierce Erynnys, horrible with snakes ;
Come, ugly Furies, armed with your whips ;
You threefold judges of black Tartarus,
And all the army of you hellish fiends,
With new-found torments rack proud Locrine's bones !
O gods, and stars ! damned be the gods and stars
That did not drown me in fair Thetis' plains !
Curst be the sea, that with outrageous waves,
With surging billows did not rive my ships
Against the rocks of high Cerannia,
Or swallow me into her wat'ry gulf !
Would God we had arriv'd upon the shore
Where Polyphemus and the Cyclops dwell,
Or where the bloody Anthropophagi
With greedy jawes devours the wand'ring wights !

Enter the ghost of ALBANACT

But why comes Albanact's bloody ghost,
To bring a corsive to our miseries ?
Is 't not enough to suffer shameful flight,
But we must be tormented now with ghosts,
With apparitions fearful to behold ?

GHOST. Revenge ! revenge for blood !

HUMBER. So nought will satisfy your wand'ring ghost
But dire revenge, nothing but Humber's fall,
Because he conquered you in Albany.

Now, by my soul, Humber would be condemned
To Tantal's hunger or Ixion's wheel,
Or to the vulture of Prometheus,
Rather than that this murther were undone.
When as I die I 'll drag thy cursed ghost
Through all the rivers of foul Erebus,
Through burning sulphur of the Limbo-lake,
To allay the burning fury of that heat
That rageth in mine everlasting soul.

GHOST. *Vindicta, vindicta.* [*Exeunt.*

This is the proper Ercles bombast, ridiculed by Shakespeare, Jonson, and Nashe. From this, even to *Tamburlaine*, is a long way; it is too absurdly distorted to serve even as a burlesque of Seneca; but the metre has something Senecan about it. From such verse there is a long distance to the melodies of

' Now comes my lover tripping like a roe,
And brings my longings tangled in her hair.'

or

' Welcome, my son: who are the violets now
That strew the green lap of the new-come spring?'

or

' But look, the morn, in russet mantle clad,
Walks o'er the dew of yon high eastern hill:'

that is to say, to the *lyrical* phase of blank verse, before Shakespeare had analysed it into true dramatic differentiation; it belongs to the first or *declamatory* phase. But this declamation is in its impulse, if not in its achievement, Senecan; and progress was made, not by rejection, but by dissociating this type of verse into products with special properties.

The next stage also was reached with the help of a hint

from Seneca. Several scholars, Butler in particular, have called attention to a trick of Seneca of repeating one word of a phrase in the next phrase, especially in stichomythia, where the sentence of one speaker is caught up and twisted by the next. This was an effective stage trick, but it is something more ; it is the crossing of one rhythm pattern with another.

> ' — Sceptrone nostro *famulus* est potior tibi ?
> — Quot iste *famulus* tradidit *reges* neci.
> — Cur ergo *regi* servit et patitur iugum ? '
>
> (*Hercules.*)

Seneca also gets a kind of double pattern by breaking up lines into minimum antiphonal units :

> ' Rex est timendus.
> Rex meus fuerat pater.
> Non metuis arma ?
> Sint licet terra edita.
> Moriere.
> Cupio.
> Profuge.
> Paenituit fugae.
> Medea,
> Fiam.
> Mater es.
> Cui sim vides.'
>
> (*Medea*, 168 ff.)

A man like Marlowe, or even men with less scholarship and less genius for the use of words than he, could hardly have failed to learn something from this. At any rate, I believe that the study of Seneca had its part in the formation of verse like the following :

'— Wrong not her birth, she is of royal blood.
— To save her life, I 'll say she is not so.
— Her life is safest only in her birth.
— And only in that safety died her brothers.'

It is only a step (and a few lines further) to the pun :

'Cousins, indeed ; and by their uncle cozen'd.'

Some of the effects in such plays as *Richard II.* and *Richard III.* are indeed of pre-Marlowe origin, as :

'I had an Edward, till a Richard kill'd him ;
I had a Henry, till a Richard kill'd him ;
Thou hadst an Edward, till a Richard kill'd him ;
Thou hadst a Richard, till a Richard kill'd him.'

which is already in even *Locrine*, as :

'The boisterous Boreas thundreth forth Revenge,
The stony rocks cry out on sharp revenge,
The thorny bush pronounceth dire revenge,'

but in the following lines from Clarence's Dream we see an immense advance over *Locrine* in the use of infernal machinery :

'I pass'd, methought, the melancholy flood,
With that grim ferryman which poets write of,
Unto the kingdom of perpetual night.
The first that there did greet my stranger soul,
Was my great father-in-law, renowned Warwick ;
Who cried aloud, " What scourge for perjury
Can this dark monarchy afford false Clarence ? " '[1]

The 'kingdom of perpetual night' and the last two lines are a real approximation in English to the magnificence of Senecan Latin at its best ; they are far from being a mere

[1] I once expressed the opinion that these lines must be by Shakespeare. I am not so confident now. See J. M. Robertson : *The Shakespeare Canon*, Part II.

burlesque. The best of Seneca has here been absorbed into English.

In *Richard II.*, which is usually dated a little earlier than *Richard III.*, I find such interesting variations of versification that I am convinced that it is a slightly later play,[1] or else that there is more of Shakespeare in it. There is the same play of words :

> 'Give Richard leave to live till Richard die.
> A brittle glory shineth in this face ;
> As brittle as the glory is the face.'

but there is less stichomythia, less mere repetition, and a dexterity in retaining and developing the same rhythm with greater freedom and less obvious calculation. (See the long speeches of Richard in Act III., sc. ii. and sc. iii., and compare with the more carefully balanced verses of Queen Margaret's tirade in *Richard III.*, Act IV., sc. iv.)

When blank verse has reached this point, and passed into the hands of its greatest master, there is no need to look for fresh infusions of Seneca. He has done his work, and the one influence on later dramatic blank verse is the influence of Shakespeare. Not that later dramatists do not make great use of Seneca's plays. Chapman uses him, and employs the old machinery; but Seneca's influence on Chapman was chiefly on Chapman's 'thought.' Jonson uses Seneca deliberately ; the superb prologues of 'Envy' and 'Sylla's Ghost' are adaptations of the Senecan ghost-prologue form, not an inheritance from Kyd. Massinger,

[1] I do not deny that some parts, or some lines, of *Richard III.* are later than *Richard II.* Both plays may have undergone revision from time to time, and in any case must be dated near together.

a most accomplished dramatist and versifier, sometimes falls back most lamentably upon ghosts and spectacles. But the verse is formed, and Seneca no further responsible for its vices or virtues.

Certainly, Elizabethan bombast can be traced to Seneca; Elizabethans themselves ridiculed the Senecan imitation. But if we reflect, not on the more grotesque exaggerations, but on the dramatic poetry of the first half of the period, as a whole, we see that Seneca had as much to do with its merits and its progress as with its faults and its delays. Certainly it is all 'rhetorical,' but if it had not been rhetorical, would it have been anything? Certainly it is a relief to turn back to the austere, close language of *Everyman*, the simplicity of the mysteries; but if new influences had not entered, old orders decayed, would the language not have left some of its greatest resources unexplored? Without bombast, we should not have had *King Lear*. The art of dramatic language, we must remember, is as near to oratory as to ordinary speech or to other poetry. On the stage, M. Jean Cocteau reminds us, we must weave a pattern of coarse rope that can be apprehended from the back of the pit, not a pattern of lace that can only be apprehended from the printed page. We are not entitled to try fine effects unless we achieve the coarse ones. If the Elizabethans distorted and travestied Seneca in some ways, if they learned from him tricks and devices which they applied with inexpert hands, they also learned from him the essentials of declaimed verse. Their subsequent progress is a process of splitting up the primitive rhetoric, developing out of it subtler poetry and subtler tones of conversation, eventually mingling, as no other school of dramatists has done, the oratorical, the conversational, the elaborate and the simple, the direct and the indirect; so that they were able to write plays which can still be viewed as plays, with any plays, and which can still be read as poetry, with any poetry.

It is improper to pass from the questions of Seneca's influence upon the Tragedy of Blood and upon the language of the Elizabethans without mentioning the group of 'Senecal' plays, largely produced under the aegis of the Countess of Pembroke. The history of this type of play belongs rather to the history of scholarship and culture than to the history of the Drama: it begins in a sense with the household of Sir Thomas More, and therefore is doubly allied to the present subject by our translator Jasper Heywood; it is continued in the conversations at Cambridge of Mr. Ascham, Mr. Watson, and Mr. (later Sir John) Cheke. The first to attack openly the common stage was Sir Philip Sidney, whose words are well known:

'Our Tragedies and Comedies (not without cause cried out against), observing rules neither of honest civility nor of skilful Poetry, excepting *Gorboduc* (againe, I say, of those that I have seen), which notwithstanding, as it is full of stately speeches and well sounding Phrases, climbing to the height of Seneca his style, and as full of notable morality, which it doth most delightfully teach, and so obtain the very end of Poesie, yet in troth it is very defectious in the circumstances, which grieveth me, because it might not remain as an exact model of all Tragedies. For it is faulty both in place and time, the two necessary companions of all corporal actions. . . But if it be so in *Gorboduc*, how much more in all the rest, where you shall have Asia of the one side, and Afric of the other, and so many other under-kingdoms, that the Player, when he cometh in, must ever begin with telling where he is: or else the tale will not be conceived? Now ye shall have three Ladies walk to gather flowers, and then we must believe the stage to be a Garden. By and by, we hear news of shipwrack in the same place, and then we are to blame if we accept it not for a Rock.'

It was after Sidney's death that his sister, the Countess of Pembroke, tried to assemble a body of wits to compose drama in the proper Senecan style, to make head against the popular melodrama of the time. Great poetry should be both an art and a diversion; in a large and cultivated public like the Athenian it can be both; the shy recluses of Lady Pembroke's circle were bound to fail. But we must not draw too sharp a line of separation between the careful workman who laboured to create a classical drama in England and the hurried purveyors of playhouse successes: the two worlds were not without communication, and the work of the earlier Senecals was not without fruit.

With the part played by our *Tenne Tragedies* in this Senecan tradition I shall deal in the next section of this essay. Here, I wish only to call attention to certain characteristics of Senecal Tragedy in its final form, in the work of Greville, Daniel and Alexander. I would only remind the reader that these final Senecal plays were written after any real hope of altering or reforming the English stage had disappeared. In the early Elizabethan years appeared a succession of tragedies, mostly performed by the Inns of Court, and therefore not popular productions, which might in favourable circumstances have led to a living

Senecan drama. Notably, *Gorboduc* (mentioned by Sidney above), *Jocasta*, and *Gismond of Salerne* (three of the four plays contained in Cunliffe's *Early English Classical Tragedies*). When *The Spanish Tragedy* appeared (with, as I have suggested, its particularly non-classical element) these feeble lights were snuffed out. I pass on to the finished Senecal product, because I am only concerned to elicit the effect of Seneca upon his sedulous admirers and imitators who professed to be, and were, men of taste and culture.

The Monarchic Tragedies of Alexander, Earl of Stirling, are the last on our list, composed under the auspices of the scholarly King James I. They are poor stuff: I imagine that they are more important in the history of the Union than in the history of the Drama, since they represent the choice, by a Scotsman of accidental eminence, to write verse in English instead of in Scots. Their faults are the faults of the other plays of the group; but they have not the virtues of the others. The two plays of Fulke Greville, Lord Brooke, the friend and biographer of Sidney, have some magnificent passages, especially in the choruses; Greville had a true gift for sententious declamation. But they have much dullness also; and they do not imitate Seneca nearly so faithfully as either those of Alexander or those of Daniel. Greville not only cannot stick to one chorus, but will introduce, on one occasion, a chorus of 'Bashas or Caddies,' and after the next act, a chorus of 'Mahometan Priests'; he introduces the still more doubtful practice of supernatural figures, a 'dialogue of Good and Evil Spirits,' or even a chorus of two allegorical figures, 'Time and Eternity' (ending indeed with the fine line spoken by Eternity: *I am the measure of felicity*). The best, the best sustained, the most poetic and the most lyrical, are two tragedies of Samuel Daniel: *Cleopatra* and *Philotas*. They contain many lovely passages, they are readable all through, and they are well built.

Now, in comparison with the supposed influence of Seneca on the barbarity of Elizabethan tragedy, and his supposed bad influence upon the language, what do we find in the plays of those who took him as their model in their attack upon the popular stage, in that attack in which Daniel, in his dedication of *Cleopatra* to the Countess of Pembroke, declared himself the foe of 'Gross Barbarism'? Deaths there are, of course, but there is none of these tragedies that is not far more restrained, far more discreet and sober, not only than the Tragedy of Blood, but than Seneca himself. Characters die so decently, so remote from the stage, and the report of their deaths is wrapped up in such long speeches by messengers stuffed with so many moral maxims, that we may read on unaware that any one concerned in the play has died at all. Where the popular playwrights travestied Seneca's melodrama and his fury, the Senecals travesty his reserve and his decorum. And as for the language, that, too, is a different interpretation of Seneca. How vague are our notions of bombast and rhetoric when they must include styles and vocabularies so different as those of Kyd and Daniel! It is by opposite excesses that Senecals and popular dramatists attract the same reproach. The language of Daniel is pure and restrained; the vocabulary choice, the expression clear; there is nothing far-fetched, conceited, or perverse.

CLEOPATRA. What, hath my face yet power to win a Lover?
Can this torne remnant serve to grace me so,
That it can Caesar's secret plots discover
What he intends with me and mine to do?
Why then, poor beauty, thou hast done thy last,
And best good service thou could'st do unto me;
For now the time of death reveal'd thou hast,
Which in my life did'st serve but to undo me.

The first two lines are admirable; the rest are good serviceable lines; almost any passage from *Cleopatra* is as good, and some are far better. The whole thing is in excellent taste. Yet we may ponder the fact that it would not have made the slightest difference, to the formation of our Augustan poetry, if Daniel and his friends had never written a line; that Dryden and Pope are nearer allied to—Cowley; and that they owe more to Marlowe than to the purest taste of the sixteenth century. Daniel and Greville are good poets, and there is something to be learned from them; but they, and Sir John Davies who somewhat resembles them, had no influence. The only one of Lady Pembroke's heroes who endures is Edmund Spenser.

Within our limits it is impossible to do more than touch on the influence of Seneca upon the 'thought' of the Elizabethans, or more exactly, upon their attitude toward life so far as it can be formulated in words. I would only say enough, at this point, to remind the reader that Seneca's influence upon dramatic form, upon versification and language, upon sensibility, and upon thought, must in the end be all estimated together; they cannot be divided. How the influence of Seneca is related, in the Elizabethan mind, with other influences, perhaps those of Montaigne and Machiavelli, I do not know; and I think it is a subject still to be investigated. But the frequency with which a quotation from Seneca, or a thought or figure ultimately derived from Seneca, is employed in Elizabethan plays whenever a moral reflection is required, is too remarkable to be ignored; and when an Elizabethan hero or villain dies, he usually dies in the odour of Seneca. These facts are known to scholars; but if known, they are usually ignored by literary critics. In a comparison of Shakespeare with Dante, for instance, it is assumed that Dante leant upon a system of philosophy which he accepted whole, whereas Shakespeare created his own: or that Shakespeare had acquired some extra- or ultra-intellectual knowledge superior to a philosophy. This occult kind of information is sometimes called 'spiritual knowledge' or 'insight.' Shakespeare and Dante were both merely poets (and Shakespeare a dramatist as well); our estimate of the intellectual material they absorbed does not affect our estimate of their poetry, either absolutely or relatively to each other. But it must affect our vision of them and the use we make of them, the fact that Dante, for instance, had behind him an Aquinas, and Shakespeare behind him a Seneca. Perhaps it was Shakespeare's special rôle in history to have effected this peculiar union

—perhaps it is a part of his special eminence to have expressed an inferior philosophy in the greatest poetry. It is certainly one cause of the terror and awe with which he inspires us.

> 'Omnia certo tramite vadunt
> primusque dies dedit extremum.
> non illa deo vertisse licet
> quae nexa suis currunt causis.
> it cuique ratus prece non ulla
> mobilis ordo.
> multis ipsum timuisse nocet.
> multi ad fatum venere suum
> dum fata timent.'

Compare with *Edward III.*, Act IV., sc. iv. (see Cunliffe, *Influence of Seneca*, p. 87), and with *Measure for Measure*, Act III., sc. i. And

> 'Men must endure
> Their going hence, even as their coming hither :
> Ripeness is all.'

NOTE.—Mr. F. L. Lucas, in his *Seneca and Elizabethan Tragedy*, says (p. 122) : 'But it must be said once for all about the bulk of Shakespeare's supposed borrowings from Seneca, that one grows more and more sceptical.' What has been said once for all is not for me to dispute, but I would point out that I am not here concerned with Shakespeare's 'borrowings' (where I am inclined to agree) but with Shakespeare as the voice of his time, and this voice in poetry is, in the most serious matters of life and death, most often the voice of Seneca. I subscribe to the observation of Cunliffe (*op. cit.* p. 85): 'We have (in *King Lear*) Seneca's hopeless fatalism, not only in the catastrophe, but repeatedly brought forward in the course of the play.'

> 'As flies to wanton boys are we to the gods ;
> They kill us for their sport.'

III

The *Tenne Tragedies* were translated and printed separately over a space of about eight years, with the exception of the *Thebais*, which was translated by Newton in 1581 to complete the work for his edition of the whole. Copies of most of the first editions exist in the British Museum; the text which is here presented is that of the collected *Tenne Tragedies* produced by Newton. The order and dates of the several translations are of interest. The first and best of the translators was Jasper Heywood:[1] his *Troas* was printed in 1559, his *Thyestes* in 1560, his *Hercules Furens* in 1561. The *Œdipus* by Alexander Nevyle (translated 1560) was printed in 1563. In 1566 appeared the *Octavia* of Nuce, the *Agamemnon*, *Medea*, and *Hercules Œtaeus* of Studley in 1566, and the *Hippolytus* of Studley probably in 1567. About fourteen years then elapse before Newton produced his complete edition, and it may be presumed that he translated the *Thebais* for that purpose.[2]

It has never been supposed, in spite of the acid taunts of Nashe, that any of the Elizabethan dramatists owe any great debt to these translations.[3] Most of the playwrights, as I have intimated before, may be supposed to have had a smattering of Seneca at school; two of the popular

[1] Sometime Fellow of All Souls College, and later an eminent Jesuit; but chiefly remembered as the uncle of John Donne. Much information about Heywood and his family is contained in A. W. Reed's *Early Tudor Drama*.

[2] These facts are given succinctly in Cunliffe's *Influence of Seneca*. The slight textual differences between the early editions and that of 1581 are given by E. M. Spearing: *The Elizabethan Translations of Seneca's Tragedies*.

[3] See E. M. Spearing: *op. cit.*

INTRODUCTION

dramatists who exercised a decisive influence at an important moment—Kyd and Peele—were acquainted with several languages, and therefore themselves subjected to several influences. But if we look at the dates we cannot overlook the probability that these translations helped to direct the course of events. They (all but one) appeared between 1559 and 1566. The first plays of Senecan form which could be called popular were Sackville and Norton's *Gorboduc*, which appeared in 1561, Gascoyne's *Jocasta* in 1566, and *Gismond of Salerne* in 1567. We must also take account, of course, of the fact that plays of Seneca, and plays in imitation of Seneca, were being produced in Latin at the Universities.[1] The *Troades* was performed in Latin at Trinity College, Cambridge, in 1551. Trinity resumed its enterprise in 1559—the year of Heywood's *Troas*—and between 1559 and 1561 the College produced in Latin four plays of Seneca. And during the 'sixties the two Universities first, and the Inns of Court subsequently, composed and performed a number of Latin plays on the Senecan model. This would have occurred, no doubt, even had Heywood never translated Seneca at all. But there can be little doubt that his translations indicate a nascent interest in a new vernacular drama to vie with classical drama, and that they in turn stimulated the beginning of this drama. At the same busy moment took place another event of capital importance, which combined with this Senecan work to produce English tragedy. In 1557 came the publi-

[1] For a convenient summary of the Senecan movement throughout Europe, and particularly in England, see Kastner and Charlton's edition of Alexander, above mentioned.

cation of Surrey's translation of Book II. of the *Æneid*, in the new 'blank verse,' the instrument without which the Elizabethan drama would have been impossible. The firstfruits, *Gorboduc*, are inconsiderable; but this play marks a new epoch; there is no clearer division in the whole of English literature.

We have, in fact, within a period of about forty years, three distinct phases in the development of English tragedy: the first, from 1559 to some time in the early 'eighties, is announced by our translations of Heywood's; the second is the period in which flourished Kyd and Peele, both of whom came to be influenced by the sudden and soon extinguished genius of Marlowe; the third is the period of Shakespeare up to his culminating tragedies. Then follows a period of Jacobean drama which belongs not so much to Shakespeare, although Shakespeare's last plays fall within the first years of it, as to Beaumont and Fletcher: it is the period, not typically of tragedy, but of tragi-comic romance.

In the preceding section I insisted upon the difference between Seneca's influence upon popular drama and his influence upon those fastidious spirits, the Senecals, who tried to observe his dramatic laws. But this difference of tendency is hardly apparent in the first period, or until the appearance of Kyd and Peele. During this period the fashions set at the Universities were followed at the Inns of Court. The plays produced by the legal wits were sometimes acted at the Queen's Court, with which, indeed, the Inns had a kind of formal connection. And in turn the plays produced at the Royal Court affected the more popular drama.[1] *Gorboduc* is followed by *Gismond of Salerne*, and *Gismond* later by the popular and atrocious *Locrine* (in which Peele almost certainly had at least a heavy hand); *The Misfortunes of Arthur* was probably too tardy to play much part in the transition. Another play of importance, which shows the persistence of the influence from the Universities upon popular drama, is Legge's *Richardus Tertius*, a Latin chronicle play acted at St. John's College, Cambridge, in 1573, and apparently repeated in 1579 and 1582. This play is the parent of *The True Tragedy of Richard III.*, and consequently of the entire brood of chronicle plays.

Another point which I have already considered, but which must be mentioned here in a different context, is the relation of Seneca to *Italian* Seneca, and of both to the native tendencies of the time. Italian Seneca is not conspicuous until the period of Kyd and Peele; but even among the translations of Heywood we can find evidence that he was to be by no means unwelcome. Besides other peculiarities of these translations which we must examine, there is an interesting addition made by Heywood to the *Troas*. In the play of Seneca Achilles' Ghost makes no appearance; it is merely mentioned as having been seen. The play was the first to be translated, and there is some reason for believing that the translation was intended to be played. The 'divers and sundrye' additions which Heywood invents render this supposition all the more plausible; for they are such as a translator would be much

[1] See J. M. Manly's introduction (p. v.) to F. S. Miller's translation of *The Tragedies of Seneca* (1907).

more likely to make if he had a performance in view, than if his translation were intended only for reading; in the latter event he might be expected to stick pretty closely to the text. Between the second and third acts of the *Troas* Heywood allows himself the liberty of interpolating a new scene of his own invention, which is a long soliloquy in thirteen stanzas by the Ghost of Achilles. And this independent 'Sprite' rants in a tone which hardly Peele could outdo:

> 'From burning lakes the furies wrath I threate,
> And fire that nought but streames of bloud may slake
> The rage of wind and seas their shippes shall beate,
> And Ditis deepe on you shall vengeance take,
> The sprites crye out, the earth and seas do quake,
> The poole of Styx ungratefull Greekes it seath,
> With slaughtred bloud revenge Achilles death.'

It is to be observed that Nevyle and Studley both joined Inns of Court; that Nevyle came there to know Gascoyne, the author of *Jocasta*; and that Heywood knew, or at least knew of, Sackville and Norton before they had written *Gorboduc*. The impulse toward the Tragedy of Blood is already present in these translators, and they do not hesitate to add or to alter; the distortion of Seneca begins with his translation.

It is not only as an embryonic form of Elizabethan tragedy that these translations have documentary interest. They represent the transformation of the older form of versification into the new—consequently the transformation of language and sensibility as well. Few things that can happen to a nation are more important than the invention of a new form of verse. And at no other time, and to no other country than England at that time, has such an achievement as that of Henry Howard, Earl of Surrey, had greater consequences. To the French or to the Italians it could not have mattered so much. Their sensibility had already learned to express itself in large part in prose: Boccaccio and Machiavelli in one country, and the chroniclers—Froissart, Joinville, Commines—in the other, had already done a great work in forming the local mind. But the Elizabethan mind, far more than the contemporary mind in any other country, grew and matured through its verse rather than through its prose. The development of prose between Elyot and Bacon is certainly remarkable; but a comparison of styles between, say, Latimer and Andrewes shows a slower rate of change than the same space of time in verse, or the same space of time in prose in the next century. On the other hand, a study of the styles, the syntax, and the cadences of blank verse from *Gorboduc* to Shakespeare, and even after Shakespeare in the work of Webster and Tourneur, brings to light a process which is wholly astonishing.

The *Tenne Tragedies* must have shown conclusively to the most sensitive contemporary ears that the fourteener had had its day; it was certain that the verse of Surrey's *Æneid* was in every way the verse in which to render the dignity and pomposity of the Senecan rhythm. And the slower iambic pentameter brought with it an alteration in vocabulary. The fourteener had served very well in rough comedy; it runs jollily in *Roister Doister* and *Gammer Gurton*. It is no vehicle for solemn tragedy, and the miracle is that Heywood and Studley made as good a job with it as they did. The fourteener, and the kindred loose metres of the interlude, are not adapted to a highly Latinised vocabulary; they are adapted to a vocabulary containing a large proportion of short words and monosyllables of Germanic origin; a vocabulary which must have come to seem, as it seems to us, *naif* and 'countrified,' if fresh and vigorous. The language of early Tudor times is indeed in some ways a deterioration from the language of Chaucer. One reason for this is no doubt the change in pronunciation, the suppression of syllables; the melody of the older tongue had gone, and with this melody much of its dignity; new rhythms, and new infusions from abroad, were very much needed. At first, in fact, the innovations overpowered the language; the Elizabethan bombast was a verbal even more than an emotional debauch; it was not until the prose of Dryden and Hobbes that English settled down to something like sobriety.

In the *Iliad* of Chapman we see new wine bursting old bottles; the poem is a magnificent *tour de force* in which Chapman sometimes succeeds in fitting the new vocabulary to the old 'stretched' metre. But it is, consequently, a poem of brilliant passages rather than sustained success. Heywood and Studley—particularly Studley—make no such attempt: their fourteener is early, not late Tudor; it is a different thing from Chapman's. Only in the pentameter rhymed choruses does their sensibility become more modern; the contrast between their dialogue and their chorus verse is most interesting. Here is a random bit of Studley:

'O *wanny* jaws of Blacke Averne, *eake* Tartar dungeon *grim*,
O Lethes Lake of woful Soules the joy that therein swimme,
And *eake* ye *glummy* Gulphes destroy, destroy me wicked wight
And still in *pit of pangues* let me be plunged day and night.
Now, now, come up ye Goblins grim from water *creekes* alow . . .'

The majority of the rhyme words are monosyllables. The most sonorous and canorous Latin names are truncated (it remained for Marlowe to discover, and Milton to perfect, the musical possibilities of classical names almost to the point of *incantation*). Alliteration, in as primitive a form as that of *Piers Plowman*, is constant. For instance, Heywood has

'*s*hal *S*isyphus his *s*tone
That slipper *r*estles *r*ollyng payse uppon my *b*acke be *b*orne,
Or shall my lymmes with *s*wifter *s*winge of *w*hirling *w*hele be torne ?
Or shal my *p*aynes be Tytius *p*anges th' encreasing liver still,
Whose *g*rowing *g*uttes the *g*nawing *g*ripes and *f*ylthy *f*oules do *f*yll ?'

To examine such lines under the microscope is not to do them justice ; the vigorous vocabulary and swinging metre appear at their best when we read through a long descriptive or narrative passage : in the same play (the *Thyestes*) the messenger's account of the crime of Atreus (Act IV.) is admirably rendered.

In their handling of the choruses our translators are less scrupulous. When they translate the dialogue they are literal to the best of their ability—occasional inaccuracies or mistranslations being admitted—but in the choruses they will sometimes lengthen or shorten, sometimes omit altogether, or substitute an invention of their own. On the whole, their alterations tend to make the play more dramatic; sometimes they may be suspected of adding a political innuendo to the Senecan moralising on the vanity of place and power. And it is especially in the choruses that we find, now and then, flashes of that felicity which is present in Tudor translation more perhaps than in the translations of any period into any language. For example, the whole of the chorus at the end of Act IV. of Heywood's *Hercules Furens* is very fine, but the last six lines seem to me of singular beauty; and as the original, too, is a lovely passage, it is both fair and interesting to quote both original and translation. The persons addressed are the dead children of Hercules, whom he has just slain in his madness.

> 'ite ad Stygios, umbrae, portus
> ite, innocues, quas in primo
> limine vitae scelus oppressit
> patriusque furor;
> ite, iratos visite reges.'

And Heywood:

> 'Goe hurtles soules, whom mischiefe hath opprest
> Even in first porch of life but lately had,
> And fathers fury goe unhappy kind
> O litle children, by the way ful sad
> Of journey knowen.
> Goe see the angry kynges.'

Nothing can be said of such a translation except that it is perfect. It is a last echo of the earlier tongue, the language of Chaucer, with an overtone of that Christian piety and pity which disappears from Elizabethan verse. The greater part of the chorus work has not this purity: one feels a curious strain on the old vocabulary to say new things; the fluctuation, the shades of variation between the old world and the new deserve inquisitive study; the ambiguity probably contributes to give these translations a unique mood, which is only to be extracted and enjoyed after patient perusals. They are not translations to be read in a hurry; they do not yield their charm easily.

> 'Such friendship finde wyth Gods yet no man myght,
> That he the morowe might be sure to lyve.
> The God our things all tost and turned quight
> Rolles with a whyrle wynde.'

Volume One

SENECA

HIS TENNE TRAGEDIES

TRANSLATED INTO ENGLISH

Mercury nutrices horae

1581

To The Right Worshipful,

SIR THOMAS HENNEAGE KNIGHT,

Treasurer of Her Maiesties Chamber
Thomas Newton wisheth all
abundaunce of Felicitie, and Spiritual
benedictions in Christe.

OU may think Sir, some want of discretion in mee, for thus boldly presuminge to thrust into your handes these Tragedies of Seneca, From whych boldnesse, the very conscience of myne own unworthynes, might easely haue dissuaded mee, had not certayne learned Gentlemen of good credite and worship thereunto persuaded and animated mee. Assuring me [where of I thought my selfe afore assured] that your Worship [such is your loue to learning, and the generosity of your Heroicall mynde] would daygne not only to dispence with my temerity, but also take in worth my affectionate simplicity. And yet [all this notwithstandinge] well durst I not haue geuen the advēture to approch your presence,

ORIGINAL DEDICATION

upon trust of any singularity, that in this Booke hath unskilfully dropped out of myne owne penne, but that I hoped the perfection of others artificiall workmãship, that haue trauayled herein aswell as my selfe should somewhat couer my nakednesse and purchase my pardon. And hard were the dealing, if in payment of a good round gubbe of Gold of full wayght and poyse, one poore peece somewhat clypped and lighter then his fellowes may not be foysted in amõg the rest, and passe in pay for currant coigne.

Theirs I know to be deliuered with singuler dexterity: myne, I confesse to be an unflidge nestling, unable to fly: an unnatural abortion, and an unperfect Embroyon: neyther throughlye laboured at Aristophanes and Cleanthes candle, neither yet exactly waighed in Critolaus his precise ballaũce. Yet this dare I saye, I haue deliuered myne Authors meaning with as much perspicuity, as so meane a Scholler, out of so meane a stoare, in so smal a time, and upon so short a warning was well able to performe. And whereas it is by some squeymish Areopagites surmyzed, that the readinge of these Tragedies, being enterlarded with many Phrases and sentẽces, literally tending [at the first sight] sometime to the prayse of Ambition, sometyme to the mayntenaũce of cruelty, now and then to the approbation of incontinencie, and here and there to the ratification of tyranny, cannot be digested without great daũger of infection; to omit all other reasons, if it might please thē with no forestalled judgmēt, to mark and consider the circumstaunces, why, where, and by what manner of persons such sentences are pronoũced, they cānot in any equity otherwise choose, but find good cause ynough to leade thē to a more fauourable and milde resolutiō. For it may not at any hād be thought and deemed the direct meaning of Seneca himselfe, whose whole wrytinges [penned with a peerelesse sublimity and loftinesse of Style,] are so farre from countenauncing vice, that I doubt whether there bee any amonge all the Catalogue of Heathen wryters, that with more grauity of Philosophicall sentences, more waightynes of sappy words, or greater authority of soũd matter beateth down sinne, loose lyfe, dissolute dealinge, and unbrydled sensuality: or that more sensibly, pithily, and bytingly layeth doune the guedon of filthy lust, cloaked dissimulation and odious treachery: which is the dryft, whereunto he leueleth the whole yssue of ech one of his Tragedies. Howsoeuer and whatsoeuer it be, your Worships curteous acceptaũce shal easily counterpoyse any of our imperfections. Unto whose learned Censure, wee humbly submit these the exercises of our blushing Muses. The Lord God in mercy long preserue you in health and dignity, with daily encrease of many his gracious gyfts, already rychly abounding in you: to the propagation, and aduauncement of his truth [whereof yee are a zealous Professor,] to the honoure of her Maiestye, to whom you are a most loyall seruitour, and to the generall benefite of your Countrey, whereof you are a rare and most worthy Ornament.

From Butley in Chesshyre the
24. of Aprill.
1581.

Your Worshippes most
humble,

THOMAS NEWTON.

THE FIRST TRAGEDIE OF SENECA
ENTITULED HERCULES FURENS

THE ARGUMENT OF THIS TRAGEDY

Juno the Wyfe and sister of Jupiter, hating his bastard broode, cometh downe from heaven, complayning of all his injuries done to her, devising also by what despight she may vexe his base Sonne Hercules. And having by experience proved, no toyles to be to hard for him, findeth the meanes to make his owne hand his owne vengeance. Hercules therefore returning now from Hell (from whence he was enjoyned to set Cerberus) and finding that the Tyrant Lycus had invaded his countrey, destroieth the tyrant. For the which victory as hee sacrificeth to his Goddesse, wrathfull Juno strikes him into a sodayne frensy: Wherewith he beinge sore vexed, thynking to flea the Children and Wyfe of Lycus, in steede of them, killeth his owne Wyfe and Children in his madnes. This done hee sleapeth. Juno restoreth to him agayne his Wits. He being wakt, seing his Wyfe and Children slayne by his owne hand, at last also would kill himselfe.

THE SPEAKERS

Juno.	Lycus.
Chorus.	Hercules.
Megara.	Theseus.
Amphitrion.	

THE FIRST ACTE

JUNO alone

I SYSTER of the Thunderer, (for now that name alone
Remaynes to me) Jove evermore as though devorst and gone,
And temples of the highest ayre as wydowe shunned have,
And beaten out of skyes above the place to Harlots gave.
I must go dwell beneath on ground, for Whoores do hold the sky,
From hence the Beare in parte above of ycy poale full hy,
A haughty starre the greekish shyps by Seas doth guyde about:
From this way, whence at spring time warme the day is loased out,
Europaes bearer through the waves of Tyria shynes full bright.
From thence, their stormy fearefull flocke to Ships, and seas affright,
The wandring daughters here and there of Atlas upward sway.
With staring bush of hayre from hens Orion Gods doth fray:
And Perseus eke his glitteryng starres of golden glosse hath here.
From hence the twynnes of Tyndars stocke do shine, a signe full clere:
And at whose byrth first stode the grounde that erst went to and fro.
Nor onely Bacchus now himselfe, or Bacchus mother Io,
Have clymd to Gods: least any parte should from rebuke be free,
The skies the Gnossian strumpets crownes do beare in spight of mee,
But I of old contemptes complayne: me, one dire, fierce, and shrewde,
Thebana land with wicked broode of Joves base daughters strewde,
How oft hath it a stepdame made? though up to heaven should ryse,
The conqueryng drabbe Alcmena now, and hold my place in skyes,

And eke her sonne to promisd starres obtayne the worthy way,
At byrth of whom the staying worlde so long dèferd the day,
And Phœbus slow frome morning sea began to glister bright,
Commaunded long in th' Ocean waves to hyde his drowned lyght
Yet shall my hates not leave them so, a wrathful kindled rage
His mynd in madnes shall stirre up, and yre that may not swage
Shall evermore (all peace layd downe) wage warres eternally.
What warres ? what ever hideous thinge the earth his ennemy
Begets, or what soever sea or ayre hath brought to syght
Both dredfull, dire, and pestilent, of cruel fiercest might,
'Tis tierd and tam'd : he passeth all, and name by ills doth rayse
And all my wrath he doth injoy and to his greater prayse
He turnes my hates : whyle tedious toyles to much I him behest,
He proves what father him begot : both thence where light opprest
Hath sea, and where it showde agayne, where Titan day doth trayne,
And with his brand approaching nere doth dye those Aethiops twaine,
His strength untamde is honoured : and God eche where is hee
Now calde : in worlde, and now more store of monsters want to mee,
And laboure lesse to Hercles is t'acomplish all my will,
Then me to bydde : at ease he doth myne imperies fulfyl.
What cruel bestes of tyrante now so fyerce a yong man may
Prevayle to hurt ? for lo he beares for weapons now awaye
What once he fearde, and put to flight : he armed comes at syde
With Lyon fyerce and Hydra both : nor land suffiseth wyde,
But broake he hath the threshold loe of that infernall Jove,
And spoyls with him of conquerd king he drawes to Gods above.
But thats but light, broke is the league of sprites that there do dwell
I saw my selfe, I saw him lo (the night now gone, of hell
And Ditis tamde) throw out abroade before his fathers sight
His brothers spoyles. Why drawes he not opprest and bound by might
Hymselfe in chaynes that equall thynges to Jove by lot doth hold ?
And beare the rule of captive hel, and way to Styxe unfolde ?
Up opened is from lowest ghostes the backward way to skye,
And sacred secrets of dire death in open sight do lye.
But he (the dredful den of sprites brake up ful fierce and stout
Even over mee doth tryumph lo, and with proude hand about

THE FIRST ACTE

The foule blacke dogge by Grekish townes he leades from hel away.
When seene was ugly Cerberus I saw the fading day,
And fearefull sunne : even me lykewyse a trembling dread opprest,
And looking on the fylthy neckes of conquerd monstruous beast,
I feared much myne owne behestes : but light things I complayne
For heaven I may be frayde, lest he may get the highest rayne,
That lowest wonne, the sceptors from his father wil he take,
Nor hee to starres (as Bacchus dyd) his way wil gently make :
The way with ruine will he seeke, and hee in empty skyes
Wil reygne alone with force displayd hys haughty hart doth ryse,
And he that heaven it selfe by force of his might gotted bee,
It bearyng learnd : quite underneth the world his head set hee.
Nor once his shoulders bowde the prayse of such a mighty mas :
And midst of heaven on Hercles necke alone (loe) setled was.
His necke unwryde the starres above and skyes did only stay :
And me likewyse oppressyng him, to Gods he seekes the way.
Goe ire, goe on, and beate hym downe that great things doth invent
Match thou with him, and with thy handes now thou thy selfe him rent.
Such hates why dost thou meditate ? let all wyld beastes now go :
And weary Euristheus now be free from greving charges mo.
The Tytans daryng once of Jove to breake the impery
Send out : let loase the denne abroade of mount of Sicilye.
The Doricke land that with the turne of gyant quakes afrayd,
Let it bring forth the dredful neckes of monster under layd.
Let yet the haughty moone above some other beastes beget,
But these he overcame. Seekes thou a match t'Alcides yet ?
Thers none, except hymselfe : let him agaynst himselfe rebell.
Let present be from bottome deepe upraysd of lowest hell
Th' Eumenides, let flaming lockes of theyrs the fires out flinge,
And furious hands bestowe aboute the stroakes of vipers fling.
Go now ful prowde, and scale the skyes to seates of gods make waye.
Now must thy battels wages be ful cleere loe shynes the daye.
Despyse mans workes thinkst thou fierce wight that hell and soules alow
Thou hast escapt ? nay here I will another hel thee show.
In deepe miste hid I wil call up from bottome low of hell
Beyond the wayes of gylty ghostes debateful goddesse fell.

THE FIRST TRAGEDY

Wheras the roaring dreadful den resoundes with cryes about,
From depest bond of Ditis raygne beneath I wil set out,
What so is left. Let hateful hurt now come in anger wood,
And fierce impyety imbrew himselfe with his owne bloud,
And errour eke, and fury arm'd agaynst it selfe to fight.
This meane, this meane, let wrath of myne now use to shewe my might.
Beginne ye servantes now of hell: the fervent burning tree
Of Pyne shake up: and set with snakes her dreadful flocke to see.
Let now Megæra bring to sight, and with her mournful hand
For burning rage bring out of hell a huge and direful brand.
Do this, require you vengeance due, and paynes of hel his spoyle,
Strike through his breast, let fyercer flame, within his bosome boyle.
Then which in Aetna fornace beates, so furiously to see.
That mad of mind and witles may Alcides driven bee
With fury great through pearced quight, my selfe must first of all
Be mad. Wherfore doth Juno yet not into raging fall?
Mee, me, ye Furyes, systers three throwne quite out of my wit
Tosse fyrst, if any thing to do, I do endevour yet
For stepdame meete: let now my hates be turnd another way,
Let him (returnd) his babes behold in safety I you pray.
And strong of hand come home, I have now found the day at length,
In which may greatly mee avayle the hated Hercles strength.
Both mee and eke hym selfe let him subdue and wish to die
Returnd from hel, yea let it here be my commodity,
That he of Jove begotten is: here present wil I stand,
And that his shaftes goe streyght from bow, I wil direct his hand,
The mad mans weapons will I guide, even Hercles fyghtyng, lo,
At length Ile ayde. This gylt once done then leefull is that so
His father may admit to skies those gylty handes of his.

CHORUS

The fading starres now shyne but seelde in sighte
In stipye skye, night overcome with day
Plucks in her fyres, while spronge agayne is light.
The day starre drawes the cleresome beames theire waye,

HERCULES FURENS

THE FIRST ACTE

The ycye signe of haughtye poale agayne,
With seven starres markt, the Beares of Arcadye,
Do call the light with overturned wayne.
With marble horse now drawne, hys waye to hye
Doth Titan toppe of Oetha over spred
The bushes bright that nowe with berryes bee
Of Thebes strewde, by daye do blushe full redde.
And to returne doth Phœbus syster flee.
Now labor harde beginnes, and everye kynde
Of cares it styrres, the Shepehearde doth unfolde :
His flockes unpende, do grase their foode to fynde,
And nippes the grasse with hoary frost full colde.
At will doth play in open medow faire
The Calfe whose brow did damme yet never teare,
The empty Kyne their udders doe repayre.
And lyght with course uncertayne here and there,
In grasse full soft the wanton kidde hee flynges.
In toppe of boughe doth sitte with chaunting songe,
And to the Sunne newe rose to spreade her wynges,
Bestirres herselfe her mourneful nestes amonge
The Nightingall : and doth with byrdes aboute
Confuse resound with murmure mixed ryse
To witnes day, his sayles to wynde set out
The shypman doth committe in doubt of lyfe,
Whyle gale of wynde the slacke sayles filles full strayte
He leaning over hollow rocke doth lye,
And either his begiled hookes doth bayte,
Or els beholdes and feeles the pray from hye with paised hand
The trembling fish he feeles with line extent.
This hope to them to whom of hurtles lyfe,
Is quiet rest, and with his owne content,
And lytle, house, such hope in fieldes is ryfe
The troblous hopes with rolling whirlewynd great
And dredful feares their wayes in cityes keepe.
He proude repayre to prince in regall seate,
And hard court gates without the rest of sleepe
Esteemes, and endless happynes to hold
Doth gather goods, for treasure gaping more,

And is ful pore amid his heaped gold.
The peoples favour him (astonied sore)
And commons more unconstant then the sea,
With blast of vayne renoume liftes up full proude.
He selling at the brawling barre his plea,
Full wicked, sets his yres and scoulding loud
And woordes to sale, a fewe hath knowne of all
The careles rest, who mindfull how doth flitte
Swift age away, the tyme that never shall
Returne agayne do holde : while fates permitte,
At quiet live : the lyfe full quickly glydes
With hastned course, and with the winged day
The wheele is turnde of yere that hedlong slides,
The sisters hard perfourme their taskes alway,
Nor may agayne untwist the threede once sponne
Yet mankind loe unsure what way to take
To meete the greedy destenyes do thronne
And willingly wee seke the Stigian lake.
To much Alcides thou with stomacke stoute
The sory sprites of hell dost hast to see.
With course prefixt the fates are brought aboute
To none once warnd to come may respite bee
To none to passe their once appointed day,
The tombe all people calde by death doth hyde
Let glory him by many landes awaye
Display, and fame throughout all cityes wyde
Full babling praise, and even with skye to stande
Avaunce and starres : let him in chariot bright
Ful haughty goe : let me my native land
In safe and secrete house keepe close from sight
To restful men hoare age by course doth fall,
And low in place, yet safe and sure doth lye,
The poore and base estate of cottage small :
The prowder pompe of minde doth fall from hye
But sad here comes with losed lockes of heare
Loe Megara with litle company,
And slowe by age drawes Hercles father neare

HERCULES FURENS

THE SECOND ACTE

MEGARA

GUIDER great of heaven, and of the world O Judge full hie,
Yet now at length apoinct a meane of carefull miserie,
And ende of our calamitie. To mee yet never day
Hath careles shin'de : the ende of one affliction past away
Beginning of an other is : an other ennemy
Is forthwith founde, before that hee his joyfull family
Retourne unto : an other syght hee taketh by behest :
Nor any respite given is to him nor quiet rest :
But whyle that he commaunded is : straight him pursueth shee
The hatefull Juno. Was yet once from toyle and labour free
His infants age ? the monsters (lo) he vanquisht hath and slayne,
Before he knew what monsters ment. The skaled serpents twayne
Their double neckes drew on toward him, agaynst the which to ryse,
The infant crept to meete with them, the serpents glittring eyes
Lyke fyre, with quiet carelesse brest he looking fast upon,
With countnance cleere, hard wrested knots of them he caught anon :
And strangling then the swelling throates of them with tender hand,
To Hydra prelude made, the beast so swyfte of Mænale land,
That with much Golde bare up full bright his beautified head,
Is caught in course, of Nemey wood likewise the greatest dread
The Lyon prest with Hercles armes hath roarde with dreadfull crie.
What should I speake of stables dyre, of steedes of Bystonye ?
Or King cast out himselfe for foode his horses fierce to fill ?
And bristled beast in thicke tops woont of Erymanthus hill ?

THE FIRST TRAGEDY

The boare of Mænalye, the woods of Arcady to shake ?
And Bull that did no litle dread to hundred peoples make ?
Among the flocks of Hesper lande that hence farre distant bee,
The sheepherde of Cartesian coast of triple shape to see
Is slayne, and driven is the pray from farthest parte of weast,
Citheton quak't when by him past to sea the well knowne beast.
He being bid to make by coastes of sommer sunne his way,
And parched landes which sore with heate doth boyle the middell day,
The mountaynes brake on either side and rampiers all undoon,
Even unto swyft and raging sea hath made a way to roon.
Then entring in of plenteous wood, the pleasant gardeins gay,
The waking dragons golden spoyles with him he brought away.
The Lerna monsters numerous ill what neede to tell have I ?
Hath he not him with fyre at length subdewde, and taught to dye ?
And which were woont with wings abrode to hyde the day from sight,
Even from the cloudes he sought and drave the Stimphale birdes to flight.
Not him subdewde who ever lyes in bed unmatcht at night
The widdowe queene of them that tooke to Thermodont their flight.
Nor handes that well durst enterprise his noble travayles all
The filthy labour made to shrynke of foule Augias hall.
What vayle all these ? he wants the world which oft defended he.
And th' earth well knowes the worker of his quietnes to be
Away from earth : the prosperous gilt that beareth happy sway,
Is vertue callde, and now the good to wicked doe obay.
The right doth stand in might of armes, feare treadeth downe the lawe.
Before my face with cruell hand, even presently I sawe
Revengers of theyr fathers reygne, the sonnes with sworde downe cast,
And of the noble Cadmus eke himselfe the offspring last
Then slayne : I sawe his regall crowne at once from him away
With head bereft. Who Thebes alas enough bewayle nowe may ?
The fertile land of Gods, what lorde now quakes it for to knowe ?
Out of the fieldes of which somtime, and fruictfull bosome lowe,
The youth upsprong with sworde in hand preparde to battell stoode :
And walls of which Amphion one of mighty Jove his broode,

Hath built with sounding melody in drawing to the stones :
To towne of whom the parent chiefe of Gods not onely ones
Heaven being left hath come, this land that Gods above alway
Receiv'de, and which hath made them Gods, and (leefull beete to say)
Perhaps shall make, with lothsome yoake of bondage is prest downe.
O Cadmus stocke, and citezens of olde Amphions towne,
Whereto are yee nowe fall'ne ? dread yee a cowardly exull thus,
His coastes to dwell in, lacking, and to ours injurious ?
Who through the worlde pursues the gilts and wrong by sea and land,
And cruell sceptors broken hath with just and ryghtfull hand,
Nowe absent serves, and what he eal'de in other doth sustayne :
And now doth bannysht Lycus holde of Hercles Thebes the rayne.
Yet shall he not : he shall come home, and him with vengeaunce quight,
And sodaine rise to starres : he will soone finde the way to light,
Or make it ells, returne thou safe, repayre to thine in haste :
And conquerour to conquer'de house yet come agayne at laste
Ryse up my spouse, and darknes deepe repell'de of helly shade
Breake up with hand, if no way may for thee kept backe bee made,
And passage be shut up, returne with world uprent by might.
And what soever li'the possest byneath in darkest night,
Send out with thee, as when the tops of haughty hylles undoon
A headlong passage making through for hasty floude to roon
Thou somtime stoodst, what with great might of thyne a sunder broake
The Tempye woods wyde open lay : and beaten with thy stroake
The mount, now here, now there fell downe : and rampier rente of stay,
The raging brooke of Thessaly did roon a newe found way.
Thy parentes so, thy sonnes, thy land repayring home to see,
Breake out, and lowest bonde of things out bringing thence with thee,
And what soever greedy age in all these long yeares race
Hath hid, shew forth, and ghosts that have forgot theyr former case,
And people up before thee drive that fearefull are of light.
Unworthy spoyles for thee they are, if thou but bring to sight

What hidden is, great thinges, but farre to much I speake for mee,
Unwotting of myne owne estate, when shall I hap to see,
The day when thee, and thy right hand, I may embrace agayne,
And slowe returnes, nor yet of me once myndefull, may complayne ?
To thee for this O guide of Gods, untamed Bulls shall bring
Their hundred necks : to thee O Queene of fruits on earth that spring
I'le geve thee secret sacrifice : to thee with much sayth loe
Long fyre brands at Eleusis towne full silent wyll I throe.
Then to my brethren shall I thinke to bee restoarde agayne
Theyr soules, and eke himselfe alive and guiding of his rayne
My father for to flouryshe yet, if any greater might
Doe keepe thee shet, we followe thee : with thy returne to sight
Defend us all, or els to hell drawe downe us all to thee.
Thou shalt us drawe, no God shall rayse us up that broken bee.

AMPHITRYON, MEGARA

O Faythfull fellowe of our bloud, with chaste true faythfulnes
The Bridebed keeping, and the sonne of haughty Hercules,
Conceive in mynde some better thinges, and take good heart to thee :
He will come home, as after all his labours woonteth hee,
Of more renowne. Me. What wretches doe most chiefly wishe of all,
They soone beleve. Am. Nay what they feare to much lest it may fall,
They thinke it never may bee shoon'de, nor rid by remedy.
Me. Beleefe is ready still to dreade the woorser mysery.
Deepe drown'de, and whellm'de, and farthermore with all the world full lowe :
Oppressed downe, what way hath he to light agayne to goe ?
Am. What way I pray you had he then when through the burning coste,
And tumbling after maner of the troubled Sea up toste
He went by sands : and freate that twyse with ebbe away doth slip,
And twyse upflowe : and when alone with his forsaken ship,

Fast caught he stucke in shallowe foordes of shelfye Syrtes sande,
And (nowe his ship on grounde) did passe through seas a foote to land ?
ME. Injurious fortune vertue most of men most stout and strong
Doth seldome spare : no man alyve himselfe in safety long
To perills great and daungers may so often times out cast,
Whom chaunce doth often overslip, the same it findes at last.
But cruell loe, and greevous threats even bearing in his face,
And such as he of stomacke is, doth come even such of pace,
Proude Lycus who the sceptors shakes in hande of other king,
The plentuous places of the towne of Thebes governing,
And every thinge about the whych with fertile soyle doth goe
Sloape Phocis, and what ever doth Ismenus overfloe,
What ever thing Cithæron seeth with haughty top and hye,
And slender Isthmos Ile, the which betweene two seas doth lye.

LYCUS, MEGARA, AMPHITRION

NOT I of native countrey bowres possesse the auncient right
Unworthy heir, nor yet to me are noble men of might
The grandfathers, nor stocke renownd with titles hie of name,
But noble vertue : who so boastes of kinred whence he came,
Of others vertue makes his vaunt, but got with fearful hand
My sceptors are obtaynd : in sword doth all my safety stand.
What thee thou wotst agaynst the will of cytesyns to get,
The bright drawne sword must it defend : in forrayne countrey set
No stable kingdome is. But one my pompe and princely might
May ratify once joynd to me with regall torche ful bright,
And chambers Megara : of stocke of such nobility
Let upstart state of myne take shape. I do not thinke that shee
Refuse it will, or in the bed with mee despyse to lye.
But if with proude unbridled mynde shee stubburn do denye,
Then quite I purpose to destroy the house of Hercules
The hate of men will then my pryde, and peoples speach oppres.
Chiefe knacke of kingdome is to beare thy subjectes hates eche one
Lets prove her then, chaunce geven hath to us a place alone.
For shee her head in fold of vayle ful sad and wofully
Enwrapt the Gods that are her guides for succour standes fast by,

And at the syde of her doth leane Alcides father trewe.
MEG. What thing doth this destroyer of our stocke agayne anew
Prepare ? what proveth he ? LY. O Queene that name renowmed hye
And tytle takste of regall stocke ful gentle and easily
A litle whyle receive and heare my wordes with pacient eare,
If alwayes men eternal hates should one to th' other beare,
And rage be gone out of the hart should never fall away,
But th' happy still should armour holde, th' unhappy stil obay,
Then shall the battayles nothing leave : with wide fieldes then the lande
Shall lie untild, with underlayd to housen fiery brand
Then ashes deepe shal overwhelme the buried people all.
Expedient is to conquerour to wish that peace befall :
To conquerd nedefull partner of the kingdome come to me :
Let 's joyne our myndes, take here this pledge of fayth and truth to thee.
My right hand touch. Why whishtest thou with cruell face and moode ?
MEG. Should I abyde, that I the hand sprinkt with my fathers bloud,
Should touch, and double death imbrewd of both my brethren ? nay
Fyrst shall sunne ryse extinguish quite, and West shal bring the day :
First faythful peace betweene the snowes and fiers there shalbe tryde,
And Scilla shall t'Ausonius fyrst joyne his Sicilian syde :
And fyrst, the fleetyng floud that with swift turnes of course doth flowe
Euripus with Euboik waur shall stand ful stil and slow.
My father, th' empire, bretherne, house, thou hast me cleare bereft,
My countrey to : what may be more ? one thing to me is left,
Then brother, father, kingdome, house, that dearer is to mee
The hate of thee, the which to me with people for to be
In commune woe I am : how great is myne alonly part ?
Rule on ful proude, beare up ful hye thy sprites and haughty hart :
Yet God the proude behynd theyr backes doth follow them to wreake.
I know the Thebane kingdomes : what should I the mothers speake,

Both suffring, and adventring gyltes? what double mischiefe done?
And mixed name of spouse at once, of father and of sonne?
What brether as double tentes? or what as many roages also?
The mother proude of Tantals brood congeald in mourning loe,
And sory stone yet flowes with teares in Phrygian Sipylye.
Himselfe likewyse erected up his scaled heade awrye.
Even Cadmus measuring throughout th' Illyrian lands in flight,
Behynd him left of body drawne long slymy markes in sight.
All these examples wayte for thee: rule thou as likes thy will,
Whyle thee our kingdomes wonted fates do call and oft hap yll.
LY. Goe to, these fierce and furious wordes thou woman mad refraine,
And imperyes of princes learne of Hercles to sustayne.
Though I the scepters gotten by the force of war do beare,
In conquering hand and all do rule without the law his feare.
Which armes subdue, a few wordes yet to thee now speake I shall
For this my cause thy father did in bloudy battel fall:
Thy brethren fell, the weapons kepe no measurable stay.
For neither easily tempred be, nor yet repressed may
The drawne swordes yre, the battels doth the bloud delite out shedde.
But he yet for his kingdome fought, wee altogether led
With wicked lust: yet th' end of war is now complayned, loe,
And not the cause, but now let all remembraunce therof goe:
When conquerour hath weapons left, the conquerde part should be
To leave his hates. Not I that thou with lowly bended knee
Mee raygning worship should'st, require: even this doth mee delight,
That thou thy myseries do'st beare with mynde so stout upright.
Thou for a king a spouse art meete, let's joyne our beds anone.
ME. A trembling colde doth run throughout my bloudles lims ech one.
What hainous thinge comes to myne eares? I fear'de not then at all,
When (all peace broake) the noyse of warre did by the city wall
Resounde about, I bare all that unfearefully to see,
I feare the wedding chambers: nowe I captive seeme to mee.

THE FIRST TRAGEDY

Let heavy chaynes my body greeve, and eke with hunger long
Let lingring death be slowly brought, yet shall no force full strong
My truthe subdue : for even thine owne Alcides will I dye.
Ly. Doth then thy husband droun'de in hell geve thee this stomack hie ?
Me. The hells alowe he toucht, that he the height againe might get.
Ly. The heavy paise oppresseth him of all the earth full great.
Me. Hee with no burdein shall be prest, that heaven it selfe sustayn'de.
Ly. Thou shalt be forst. Me. He wots not how to die, that is constrain'd.
Ly. Speake, what may rather I prepare then wedding newe for thee
More royall gyft ? Me. Thine owne death els, or els the death of mee.
Ly. Thou shalt mad woman die. Me. I shall then to my husbande go.
Ly. More then my Sceptors is to thee a servaunt loved so ?
Me. How many hath this servant slayne of kings with handy stroake ?
Ly. Why doth he yet a king then serve, and still sustayne his yoake?
Me. Take once away the hard behests, what's vertue then at last ?
Ly. Do'st thou it vertue counte, to bee to beasts, and monsters cast ?
Me. T'is vertues part, to tame the things, that all men quake to know.
Ly. Him great things braggig, darknes deepe of tartare presse ful low.
Me. There never may from ground to stars an easy passage be.
Ly. Of whom begot, the housen then of Gods through pearceth he ?
Am. O wretched wife of Hercles great, thy words a whyle now spare.
My parte it is, the father of Alcides to declare,
And his true stocke, yet after all of man so stoute as this
So famous deedes, and after all appeas'de with hand of his
What ever Titan rysen up, doth see, or els at fall,
And after all these monsters tam'de, and Phlegrey sprinkled all
With wicked bloud, and after Gods defended all on hye,
Is not his father yet well knowne ? or Jove doe we beelye ?

Beleeve it yet by Junoes hate. Ly. Why do'ste thou sclaunder
Jove ?
No mortall kinred ever may be mixt with heaven above.
Am. To many of the Gods in skyes is this a common trade.
Ly. But were they ever servauntes yet, before they Gods were
made ?
Am. Of Delos Ile the sheepherde loe the flocks of Pherey fed.
Ly. But through all coasts he wandred not abroade as banished.
Am. Whom straying mother first brought forth in wandring land
to sight.
Ly. Yet Phœbus did no monsters feare, or beasts of cruell might.
Am. First Dragon with his bloud embrew'd the shafts of Phœbus lo.
Howe greevous ills even yet full yong he bare, doe you not knoe ?
From mothers wombe the babe out thrown with lightning flame
from hie,
Even next his lightning Father stoode forthwith above in skye.
What ? he him selfe that guides the starres, and shakes the clouds
at will,
Did not that Infant lurke in Den of hollowe caved hill ?
The byrthes so great full troublous pryce to have loe alwayes ought :
And ever to be borne a God, with coste full great is bought.
Ly. Whom thou a miser see'st, thou mai'st know him a man to bee.
Am. A miser him deny yee may, whom stout of heart yee see.
Ly. Call we him stout, from shoulders hye of whom the Lyon
throwne
A gift for mayden made, and eke his Club from hand fell downe,
And paynted side with purple weede did shyne that he did weare ?
Or may we him call stout of heart, whose staring lockes of heare
With ointment flowde ? who hands renownde and knowne by
prayses hye
To found unmeete for any man of timber did applye,
With barbarous mytar cloasing in his forhead rounde about ?
Am. The tender Bacchus did not blushe abroade to have layde out
His brayded heares, nor yet with hand full soft the Thyrsus light
For to have shooke, what time that he with pace unstout in sight
His long train'de barbarous garment drew with golde full fayre to
see.
Still vertue after many workes is woont releast to bee.

Ly. Of this the house of Euritus destroyde doth witnesse beare,
And virgins flockes that brutishly by him oppressed weare.
No Juno did commaunde him this, nor none Eurystheus loe.
But these in deede his owne workes are. Am. Yet all yee doe not knoe.
His worke it is, with weapons of his owne hand vanquished
Both Eryx, and to Eryx joyn'de Antæus Lybian ded :
And aulters which with slaughter of the straungers flowing fast,
Busyris well deserved bloud likewise have drunke at last.
His deede it is, that he that met the wounde, and sworde is slayne
Constrain'de to suffre death before those other Geryons twayne.
Nor one all onely Geryon doth with one hand conquer'de lye.
Thou shalt among these be which yet with none adulterye
Have wedlocke hurt. Ly. What is to Jove, to king is leefull thyng :
To Jove thou gav'ste a wyfe, thou shalt nowe geve one to a kyng.
And even of thee shee shall it learne to bee a thing not newe,
Her husband even approving it the better man t'ensewe.
But if shee stubberne to be matcht with me deny it still,
Then even by force a noble childe of her beget I will.
Me. O Creons ghosts and all yee Gods of th' house of Labdacus,
And wedding torches blasing bryght, of wicked Oedipus,
To this my wedding geve yee nowe our wonted destenyes.
Now, now yee bloudy daughters all of Ægypts king likewyse,
Bee here whose hands defyled are with so much bloud out spilt :
One daughter lacks of Danaus, I wyll fyll up the gylt.
Ly. Because that stubburnely thou do'st refuse my wedding so,
And fear'ste a king, thou shalt know what the Scepters now may do.
Embrace thyne aulters, yet no God shall ever take away
Thee from my hands : no not although with world upturned, may
Alcides victor yet agayne to Gods above returne.
The woods on heapes together cast, let all their temples burne
Even throwne upon theyr heads : his wyfe, and all his flocke at laste
With underlayed fyre, let one wood pyle consume and waste.
Am. This only bowne I father of Alcides aske of thee,
Which well may me beseeme to crave, that I fyrst slayne may bee.
Ly. Who all appoyncts with present death to have their punishment,
He tyrant wots not how to be : more sundry greeves invent.

Restrayne the wretched man from death, commaunde that th' happy dye.
I, while with beames prepar'de to burne the pyle encreaseth hye,
Will him with vowing sacrifyce that rules the seas entreate.
AM. Oh chiefest powre of Gods, and oh of heavenly things so great
The guyde, and parent eke, with whose throwne thunderbolts do shake
All things humane throughout the world of king so cruell slake
The wicked hande : but why do I to Gods in vayne thus cry ?
Where ever thou be, heare me soone, why start so sodaynely
The temples thus with mooving shakte ? Why roareth out the ground ?
The noyse of Hell from bottome deepe byneathe hath made a sound :
Wee herde are, loe it is the sound of Hercules his pace.

CHORUS

O Fortune hating men of stoutest brest,
How ill rewards dost thou to good devyde ?
Eurystheus raynes at home in easy rest,
Alcmenaes sonne in every battayle tryde,
To Monsters turnes hys hande that Skyes dyd stay :
And cruell Neckes cuts of, of hydous Snake,
And Apples brynges from Systers mokt away,
When once to sleepe hys watchefull Eyes beetake,
Dyd Dragon set ryche fruicte to oversee.
Hee past the Scythian bowres that straye abroade,
And those that in their countreys straungers bee
And hardned top of frosen freate hee troade,
And sylent Sea with bankes full dumme about.
The Waters hard want there their floudes to floe.
And where before the Shyps full Sayles spred out
Is worne a pathe for Sarmates wylde to goe.
The Sea doth stande to moove in course agayne,
Nowe apt to beare the Ship, nowe horsemen bolde

The Queene that there doth over Wydowes rayne,
That gyrds her Wombe wyth gyrth of glittring gold,
Her noble spoyle from body drawne hath shee
And shyelde, and bandes of breast as whyte as snowe,
Acknowledging the Conquerour with Knee.
Wyth what hope drawne to headlong Hell alowe,
So bolde to passe the unreturned wayes
Saw'ste thon Proserpines rayne of Sicylye?
Wyth Southern wynde, or Western there no seas
Aryse wyth wave and swellinge Surges hye.
Not there of Tyndars stocke the double broode
Two starres the fearefull Shyps doe ayde and guide,
Wyth gulph full blacke doth stande the slouthfull floode
And when pale death with greedy teeth so wyde,
Unnumbred Nations hath sent downe to sprightes
Wyth one Boateman all over feryed bee.
God graunt thou maist of Hell subdue the rightes
And unrevoked webs of Systers three.
There kyng of many people raygneth hee,
Who when thou did'st wyth Nestors Pylos fight,
Pestiferous handes appli'de to matche with thee
And weapon bare with triple mace of might:
And prickt with litle wounde he fled away,
And lorde of death hymselfe did feare to dye.
Breake Fate by force: and let the sight of day
To sorry sprightes of Hell apparant lye
And porche unpast shew way to Gods above.
The cruell lordes of sprightes wyth pleasaunt song
And humble bowne full well could Orpheus move,
Whyle he Eurydicen them craves among.
The Arte that drew Woods, Byrds, and stones at will:
Which made delay to Floudes of flitting flight
At sound whereof the savage Beastes stoode still
With tunes unwont doth Ghosts of hell delight
And clearer doth resounde in darker place:
And weepe wyth teares did Gods of cruell brest:
And they which faultes with to severe a face
Doe seeke, and former gylt of Ghosts out wrest:

The Thracian Daughters wayls Eurydicen.
For her the Judges weeping sit also.
Wee conquer'de are, chyefe kyng of death sayd then
To Gods (but under this condition) goe,
Behynde thy husbandes backe keepe thou thy way,
Looke thou not backe thy Wyfe before to see.
Than thee to sight of Gods hath brought the day
And gate of Spartane Tœnare present bee.
Love hates delay, nor coulde abyde so long.
His gyft, hee lost, while hee desires the syght.
The place that coulde bee thus subdew'de with song
That place may soone bee overcome by myght.

THE THYRDE ACTE

HERCULES

COMFORTABLE guyde of light, and honour of the skye,
That compassing both Hemyspheres with flaming chariot hye
Thy radiant head to joyful lands about the world dost bring,
Thou Phœbus pardon geve to me, if any unlawful thing
Thyne eyes have seene : (commaunded) I have here to light
The secretes of the worlde : and thou of heaven o guider gret, (out set)
And parent eke, in flashe out throwne of lightning hide thy syght.
And thou that governest the seas with seconde sceptors myght,
To bottome synke of deepest waves : who so from hye doth see,
And dreading yet with countnaunce newe the earth defil'de to bee,
Let him from hence turne backe his sight, and face to heaven upholde,
These monstrous sights to shun : let twayn this mischiefe great behold,
Hee who it brought, and shee that bad, for paynefull toyles to mee,
And laboures long, not all the earth thought wide inough may bee
For Junoes hate : things uncome to all men I did see,
Unknowne to sonne, and spaces wyde that darke and shadefull bee
Which woorser poale geves dyrer Jove to raygne and rule therein.
And yet if thyrde place pleased more for mee to enter in,
I there coulde raygne, the Chaos of eternall nyght of hell,
And woorse then night, the dolefull Gods I have that there doe dwell,

And Fates subdu'de, the death contemn'de I am return'de to light.
What yet remaynes ? I sawe and show'de the spryghts of hell to sight :
Appoynct, if ought be more, do'ste thou my hands so long permit
Juno to ceasse ? what thing byd'st thou to be subdued yet ?
But why doe cruell souldiars holde the holy temples wyde ?
And dread of armour sacred porche beset on every syde ?

AMPHITRYON, HERCULES, THESEUS

Do eyther els my great desyres delude and mocke myne eyes ?
Or hath the tamer of the world and Greekes renowme likewyse,
Forsooke the silent howse, besette with cloude full sadde to see ?
Is this my sonne ? my members loe for joy amased bee.
Oh sonne, the sure and savegard late of Thebes in misery,
See I thy body true indeede ? or els deceiv'de am I
Mockt with thy sprite ? art thou the same ? these brawnes of armes I know
And shoulders, and thy noble handes from body hie that grow.
HER. Whens (father) happes this uglines, and why in mourning clad
Is thus my wyfe ? how happes it that with filth so foule bestad
My children are ? what misery doth thus my house oppresse ?
AM. Thy father in law is slayne : the kingdome Licus doth possesse.
Thy sonnes, thy parent and thy wyfe to death pursueth hee.
HER. Ungrateful land, doth no man come that will an ayder bee
Of Hercles house ? and this behelde so great and haynous wronge
Hath th'ayded world ? but why were I the day in playnt so long ?
Let then my dye and this renoume let strength obtayne in haste,
And of Alcides enmies all let Lycus be the last.
I driven am to goe to shedde the bloud of enmye out.
Watch Theseu that no sodayne strength beset us here aboute :
Me warres require, embracing yet deferre O father deare,
And wyfe deferre them : Lycus shall to hell this message beare

That I am now returnd. TH. Shake of O Queene out of thyne eyes
This weping face, and thou synce that thy sonne is safe likewyse
Thy dropping teares refrayne : yf yet I Hercles ever knew
Then Lycus shall for Creon paye the paynes to him ful due.
T'is lyght, he shal, he doth and that's to light he hath it done.
AM. Now God that can them bring to passe, spede wel our wishes soone,
And come to helpe our weary woes. O noble harted mate
Of my stout sonne, of his renowne declare us all the rate :
How long away doth leade to place where sory sprites doth dwell,
And how the hard and heavy bondes the dog hath borne of hell.
TH. The deedes thou dost constrayne to tell, that even to mynde secure
Are dredful yet and horrible, scant yet the trust is sure
Of vitall ayre, sore blunted is the sharpnesse of my sight,
And dulled eyes do scant sustayne to see th' unwoonted light.
AM. Yet Theseus throughly overcome what ever feare remaynes
In bosome deepe, nor do thou not of best fruict of thy paynes
Beguilde thy selfe. What thing hath once to suffre beene a care,
To have remembred it is sweete, those dredful haps declare.
TH. All ryght of worlde, and thee lykewise I praye that bearst the rayne
In kingdome wyde, and thee, for whom all round about in vayne
Thy mother throughout Ætna sought, that secret things alowe
And hid in ground, it freely may bee lawfull for to showe.
The Spartane land a noble toppe of hyll advaunceth hye,
Where Tænarus with woods full thick the Sea doth overly.
The house of hatefull Ditis here his mouth doth open set,
And rocke of hyll above doth gape, and with a denne full gret
A huge and gaping cleft of ground with Jawes full wyde doth lye,
And way full broade to people all doth spred to passe thereby.
Not straight with darkenes both begin the way that blindes the sight.
A litle lingring brightnes loe behinde of late left light,
And doubtfull glittring yet of sonne afflicted falles alowe,
And mocks the sight : such light is wont undoubtedly to showe

The dawne of day, or twylight els at edge of evening tyde.
From hence to hollowe places voyde are loaste the spaces wyde,
To which needes peryshe must all kinde of men that once are throwne.
Nor it a labour is to goe, the way it selfe leades downe.
As oft the ships agaynst theyr willes doth tosse the swelling surge,
So downward doth that headlong way, and greedy Chaos urge :
And backe agayne to drawe thy pace thee never doe permit
The sprits who what they catch hold fast, alowe within doth flit
In chanell wyde with silent foorde the quiet lake of lethe,
And cares doth rid : and that there may to scape agayne from death
No meane be made, with many turnes and windings every way
Foldes in his floude, in such sorte as with wave unsure doth play
Mæander wandring up and downe, and yeldes himselfe unto,
And doubtfull stands, if he toward banke, or backe to spryng may goe.
The foule and filthy poole to see of slowe Cocytus lyes.
On th' one the Grype, on th' other side the mournefull Howlet cries,
And sad lucke of th' unhappy Strix likewise resoundeth there.
Full uglily in shady bowes blacke Locks of lothsome heare,
Where Taxus tree doth over leane, which holdeth slouthfull sleepe,
And hunger sad with famisht Jawe that lyes his place to keepe,
And shame to late doth hide his face that knowes what crimes it hath,
Both feare, and quaking, funerall, and fretting raging wrath,
And mourning dyre doth follow on, and trembling pale disease,
And boystrous battayles set with sworde : and hid beyond all thease
Doth slouthfull age his lingring pace help forth with staffe in hand.
AM. Of corne and wyne in hell alowe is any fertile land ?
TH. No joyfull Meades do there bring forth with face so greene and fayre,
Nor yet with gentill Zephyrus wagges ripened corne in th' ayre.
Nor any tree hath there such bowes as doe bryng apples out.
The barrayne compasse of deepe soyle full filthy lyes about,
And withred with eternall drought the lothsome land doth waste
And bond full sad of thinges, and of the worlde the places laste :
The ayre unmoved stands, and night sits there full darke to see
In slouthfull world, all thinges by dread full horrible there bee.

And even farre worse then death it selfe, is place where death doth bide.
AM. What? he that doth those places darke with regall sceptor guide,
In what seate set, doth he dispose and rule those peoples light?
TH. A place there is in turne obscure of Tartarus from sight,
Which mist full thick with fearefull shade doth holde and overgoe.
From hence a double parted streame from one wellspring doth floe:
The tone, much like a standing poole (by this the gods doe sweare)
The which the sacred Stygian lake with silent floude doth beare:
The t'other fierce with tumult great is drawen his course to goe,
And Acheron with raging floud the stones dryves to and froe
Unsaylable, with double foorde is rounde about beset
Agaynst it Ditis pallace dyre, and mansion house full gret
In shadefull woode is covered: from wide den here the posts
And thresholds of the tyrant hang, this is the walke of ghosts:
This of his kingdome is the gate: a fielde about it goes,
Where sitting with a countnaunce proude abroade he doth dispose
Newe soules, a cruell majesty is in the God to knowe:
A frowning forehead, which yet of his brethren beares the showe,
And so great stocke: there is in him of Jove the very face,
But when he lightens: and great part of cruell kingdomes place,
Is he himselfe the lorde thereof: the sight of whom doth feare,
What ever thing is fear'de. AM. Is fame in this poynct true, that there
Such rygours are, and gilty Ghosts of men that there remayne
Forgetfull of theyr former faulte, have there deserved payne?
Who is the rector there of ryght, and judge of equity?
TH. Not onely one extorter out of faultes in seate set hye
The judgements late to trembling soules doth there by lot awarde:
In one appoyncted judgement place is Gnossian Minos harde,
And in an other Radamanthe: this crime doth Aeac heare.
What eche man once hath done, he feeles: and guilt to th' author theare
Returnes, and th' hurtfull with their owne example punisht bee.
The bloudy cruell captaynes I in pryson shet did see,
And backe of tyrant impotent even with his peoples hande
All torne and cut, what man of might with favour leades his lande,

And of his owne lyfe lorde reserves his hurtlesse handes to good,
And gently doth his empyre guide without the thyrst of blood,
And spares his soule, he having long led forth the lingring dayes
Of happy age, at length to heaven doth eyther finde the wayes,
Or joyfull happe places ells of fayre Elysius woode.
Thou then that here must be a judge abstayne from man his bloode,
Who so thou be that raygnest kyng : our gyltes are there acquit
In greater wyse. Am. Doth any place prescript of lymite shit
The gylty Ghosts, and as the fame reportes, doth cruell payne
The wicked men make tame that in eternall bondes remayne ?
Th. Ixion roll'de on whyrling wheele is tost and turned hye :
Upon the necke of Sisyphus the mighty stone doth lye.
Amyd the lake with thyrsty Jawes olde Tantalus therein
Pursues the waves, the water streame doth wet and washe his chin,
And when to him nowe ofte deceyv'de it doth yet promise make,
Straight flits the floud : the fruicte at mouth his famyne doth forsake.
Eternall foode to fleeing foule doth Tytius hart geve still :
And Danaus daughters doe in vayne theyr water vessels fill.
The wicked Cadmus daughters all goe raging every way :
And there doth greedy ravening byrde the Phiney tables fray.
Am. Nowe of my sonne declare to me the noble worthy sight.
Brings he his willing unckles gyft, or Plutoes spoyles to sight ?
Th. A dyre and dredfull stone there is the slouthfull foordes fast bye,
Where sluggish freat with wave aston'd full dull and slowe doth lye :
This lake a dredfull fellow keepes both of attire and sight,
And quaking Ghosts doth over beare an aged ugly wyght :
His Bearde unkempt, his bosome foule deform'de in filthy wyse
A knot byndes in, full lothesome stand in head his hollowe eyes :
He Feary man doth steare about his Boate with his long Ore.
He driving nowe his lightned Ship of burden towarde the Shore,
Repayres to waves : and then his way Alcides doth requyre,
The flocke of Ghosts all geving place : alowde cryes Charon dyre,
What way attemptest thou so bolde ? thy hastening pace here stay.
But Nathales Alcmenaes sonne abyding no delay,
Even with his owne poale bet he dothe full tame the shipman make,
And clymes the ship : the barke that coulde full many peoples take,

Did yelde to one : he sat, the boate more heavy like to breake
Whith shyvering joyntes on eyther syde the lethey floud doth leake.
Then tremble all the monsters huge, the Centaures fierce of myght,
And Lapithes, kindled with much wyne to warres and bloudy fight,
The lowest Chanelles seeking out of Stygian poole a downe,
His Lerney labour sore affright his fertile heads doth drowne.
Of greedy Ditis after this doth then the house appere.
The fierce and cruell Stygian dogge doth fray the spirites there,
The which with great and roaring sounde his heads upshaking three,
The kingdome keepes his ugly head with filth full foule to see
The serpentes licke : his hayres be fowle with vypers set among,
And at his crooked wrested tayle doth hysse a Dragon longe :
Lyke yre to shape, when him he wyst his pace that way to take,
His bristle hayres he lifteth up with fierce up bended snake :
And sounde sent out he soone perceyves in his applyed eare,
Who even the sprits is wont to sent as soone as stoode more neare
The sonne of Jove, the doubtfull dogge strait couched downe in denne,
And eche of them did feare, beholde with dolefull barking then
The places dumme he makes a dred, the threatning serpent stout
Through all the fieldes about doth hysse : the bawling noyse sent out
Of dredfull voyce from triple mouth, even sprits that happy bee
Doth make afrayde, from left side then strayte way undoeth hee
The cruell Jawes, and Lyons head once slayne in Cleon fielde
Agaynst him sets, and cover doth himselfe with mighty shielde.
And bearing in his conquering hande a sturdy club of Oke,
Nowe here, now there he rolleth him about with often stroke :
His stripes he doubles : he subdew'de his threates asswaged all,
And all his heads the weary dogge at once full lowe let fall,
And quite out of the denn he fled, full greatly feared (set
In regall throne) both king and queene, and bad him to bee set
And me likewyse they gave for gyft to Hercles craving mee.
The monsters heavy neckes with hand then strooking downe all three,
In lynked chayne he byndeth faste forgetting then his strength
The dogge the watchefull keeper of the kingdome darke at length

Layth downe his eares full sore affray'de : and suffring to be led,
And eke acknowledging his lorde, following wyth lowly hed,
With tayle that snakes theron doth beare he both his sides doth smight.
But after that to Tænare mouth we came, and clearenes bright
Had strooke his eyes of light unknowne, good stomacke yet agayne
He takes although once overcome, and now the happy chayne
He raging shakes : he had almost his leader pluckt from place,
And headlong backward drawne to hell, and moved from his pace.
And even to my handes Hercles then his eyes did backward cast,
Wee both with double joyned strength the dogge out drawne at last
For anger woode, and battells yet attempting all in vayne,
Brought up to world, as soone as he the cleere ayre sawe agayne,
And spaces pure of bryght fayre poale had once behelde with eye,
The nyght arose : his sight to ground he turned by and by,
Cast downe his eyes, and hatefull day forthwith he put to flight,
And backward turnd away his looke, and streight with all his might
To th' earthe he falles : and underneath the shade of Hercles then
He hyd his head, therewith there came a great resorte of men
With clamour glad, that did the bay about theyr forheads bryng :
And of the noble Hercules deserved prayses sing.

CHORUS

Eurystheus borne with swiftned birth in hast,
Did bid to bottome of the Worlde to go :
This only lackt of labours all at last,
To spoyle the Kyng of thyrde estate also.
The dongeons darke to enter ventred hee,
Where as the way to sprits farre of doth bring
Full sadde, and woode so blacke and fear'de to bee :
But full with flocke full great him following.
As great a preasse as flocke in cyties streetes,
To see the Playes of Theatre newe wrought :

As great as at Eleus thundrer meetes,
When Sommer fift the sacred game hath brought :
As great as when comes houre of longer night,
And willing quiet sleepes to bee extent,
Holdes equall Libra Phœbus Chariots light,
A sorte the secrete Ceres doe frequent,
And from their howsen left doe hast to comme,
The Atticke priestes the nyghte to celebrate :
Such heape is chaste beneath by fieldes so dumme.
With age full slowe some taking forth their gate
Full sad, and fillde with life so long now led :
Some yet doe runne the race of better yeares,
The virgins yet unjoynde to Spowses bed,
And yonglings eke on whom grow yet no heare ;
And Infant lately taught his mothers name.
To these alone, (that they the lesse might feare)
Is graunted night to ease with foreborne flame.
The rest full sad by darke doe wander theare :
As is our mynde, when once away is fled
The lyght, when eche man sorry feeles to bee
Deepe overwhelmde with all the earth his hed.
Thick Chaos standes, and darknesse fowle to see,
And colour ill of night, and slouthfull state
Of silent World, and divers Cloudes about.
Let hoary age us thyther bring full late.
No man comes late to that, whence never out,
When once hee is come, turne agayne he may.
To hast the hard and heavy Fate what vayles ?
This wandring heape in wyde landes farre away,
Shall goe to Ghostes : and all shall geve their sayles
To flowe Cocytus all is to thee enclinde,
Both what the fall, and rise of sonne doth see :
Spare us that comme, to thee wee death are signde :
Though thou be slow, our selves yet haste doe wee.
Fyrst houre, that gave the lyfe, it loast agayne.

To Thebes is come the joyfull day,
Your Aulters touch yee humbylly,
The fat fayre Sacrifices slay,
Maydes myxte with men in company
Let them in solempne Flockes goe royle :
And nowe wyth yoake layde downe let cease
The Tillers of the fertile Soyle.
Made is wyth hande of Hercles peace
Betweene the morne and Hespers Glade,
And where Sonne holding myddle seate,
Doth make the Bodyes caste no Shade.
What ever grounde is overweate
Wyth compasse longe of Seas abought,
Alcydes laboure taemde full well.
Hee over Foordes of Tartare brought
Returnde appeased beeinge Hell.
There is remayning nowe no feare,
Nought lyes beyonde the Hell to see.
O Priest thy staring Lockes of heare
Wrappe in wyth loved Poplar tree.

THE FOURTHE ACTE

HERCULES, THESEUS, AMPHITRYON, MEGARA

ITH my revenging right hand slayne now Lycus loe the ground
With groveling face hath smit : then who soever fellow found
Of Tyraunt was, partaker of his paynes did also lye.
Nowe to my father sacrifice and Gods victor will I,
And aulters that deserve it, with slayne offrings reverence.
Thee, thee O mate of all my toyles I pray and my defence
O warrefull Pallas, in whose left hand the cleare shielde Ægis shakes
Fierce threats, with head that eche thing stone that lookes upon it makes.
Let tamer of Lycurgus nowe, and of red Sea be heare,
That poynct of speare with Ivye greene in hand doth cover'de beare :
And two Gods powre, both Phœbus, and his Syster to I pray
The sister meeter for her shaftes, but hee on th' harpe to play :
And what soever brother ells of myne doth dwell in sky,
Not of my stepdame brother, bring yee hyther by and by
Your plentuous flocks, what ever have all th' Indians fruicts brought out,
And what sweete odours th' Arabickes doe get in trees about,
To th' aulters bring : let vapour fat and fume smoke up full hye,
Let rounde about the Poplar tree my hayres now beautifye
Let th' olive bowe thee hyde with braunche accustom'de in our lande
Theseu : for foorthwith reverence the thundrer, shall my hande.
TH. O Gods the builders of the towne, and which of Dragon fell,
The wilde woods dens, and noble waves likewise of Dirces well,

And Tyrian house enhabite eke of straunger wandring king.
HE. Cast into fyres the frankencense. AM. Sonne fyrst thy hands flowing
With bloudy slaughter, and the death of enmy purify.
HER. Would God the bloud of hatefull head even unto Gods on hye
I might out shed, for lycour loe more acceptable none
Myght th' aulters stayne : nor sacrifice more ample any one
Nor yet more plentyfull may bee to Jove above downe cast,
Then king unjust. AM. Desyre that now thy father ende at last
Thy labours all : let quietnes at length yet gieven bee,
And rest to weary folke. HER. I will thee prayers make, for mee
And Jove ful meete in this due place let stand the haughty skye,
And land, and ayre, and let the starres dryve forth eternally
Their course unstayde : let restful peace kepe nations quietly,
Let labour of the hurtles land all yron now occupye,
And swordes lye hyd : let tempest none ful vyolent and dyre
Disturbe the sea : let from the skyes no flash of lightning fyre
Fall downe whyle Jove ful angry is : nor yet with winter snowe
Encreased flood the ground upturnde, and field quyte overthrowe.
Let poysons cease : and from hensforth let up from ground aryse
No greevous hearbe with hurtful sappe : nor fierce and fell lykewyse
Let tyrantes raygne but if to sight some other mischiefe bringe
The ground yet shall, let it make hast : and any monstruous thinge
If it prepare let it be myne, but what meanes this ? myd day
The darkenes have incloas'd aboute lo Phœbus goeth his way
With face obscure without a clowde who dryves the day to flight,
And turnes to east ? from whence doth now his dusky hed the night
Unknowne bring forth ? whence fil the poale so many rownde about
Of daytyme starres ? lo here behold my laboure first ful stout
Not in the lowest parte of heaven the Lyon shyneth bryght,
And fervently doth rage with yre, and byttes prepares to fyght.
Even now loe he some star wil take, with mouth full wyde to see
He threatning standes, and fires out blowes and mane up rustleth he
Shaking with necke the harvest sad of shape, what ever thinge,
And what soever winter colde in frosen tyme doth bring,
He with one rage wil overpasse, of spring tyme bull he will
Both seeke and breake the neckes at once. AM. What is this sodayne yll ?

Thy cruel count'naunce whether sonne dost thou cast here and there ?
And seest with troubled daseld syght false shape of heaven appere.
HER. The land is tam'de the swelling seas their surges did asswage,
The kingdomes lowe of hell lykewyse have felt and knowne my rage,
Yet heaven is free, a labour meete for Hercules to prove.
To spaces high I wil be borne of haughty skies above
Let th' ayre be skaeld, my father doth me promise starres t' obtayne.
What if he it denyde ? all th' earth can Hercles not contayne,
And geeves at length to gods, me calles of one accorde beholde
The whole assembly of the gods, and doth their gates unfolde,
Whyle one forbyddes, receyv'st thou mee, and openest thou the skye,
Or els the gate of stubburne heaven draw after me do I ?
Do I yet doubt ? I even the bondes from Saturne wyll undoe,
And even agaynst the kingdome prowde of wicked father loe
My graundsyre loase. Let Titans now prepare agayne their fight
With me theyr captaine raging : stones with woods I will down smight
And hye hilles tops with Centaures full in right hande will I take.
With double mountayne now I will a stayre to Gods up make.
Let Chyron under Ossa see his Pelion mountayne gret :
Olympus up to heaven above in thyrd degree then set
Shall come it selfe, or ells be cast. AM. Put farre away from thee
The thoughts that ought not to be spoake : of mynde unsounde to see,
But yet full great, the furious rage asswage and lay away.
HER. What meaneth this ? the Gyauntes doe pestiferous armes assay,
And Tityus from the sprights is fled, and bearing torne to see
And empty bosome, loe howe neere to heaven it selfe stoode hee ?
Cythæron falles, the mountayne hie Pallene shakes for feare,
And torne are Tempe, he the tops of Pindus caught hath here,
And Oethen he, some dredfull thing threatning doth rage about
Erynnis bringing flames : with stripes she soundes nowe shaken out,

And burned brandes in funeralles, loe yet more neare and neare
Throwes in my face : fearce Tisyphone with head and ugly heare
With serpentes set, nowe after dogge set out with Hercles hand,
That empty gate shee hath shut up, with bolte of fyry brande.
But loe the stocke of enmious king doth hidden yet remayne,
The wicked Lycus seede : but to your hatefull father slayne
Even now this right hande shall you sende let nowe his arrowes light
My bowe out shoote : it seemes the shaftes to goe with such a flight
Of Hercles. Am. Whether doth the rage and fury blinde yet goe ?
His mighty Bowe he drewe with hornes together driven loe,
And quiver loaste : great noyese makes with violence sent out
The shaft, and quight the weapon flewe his middle necke throughout,
The wound yet left. Her. His other broode I overthrow will quight,
And corners all. What stay I yet ? to me a greater fyght
Remaynes then all Mycenes loe, that rockye stones should all
Of Cyclops being overturn'de with hande of myne, downe fall.
Let shake both here, and there the house, with all stayes overthrowne,
Let breake the poasts : and quight let shrinke the shaken piller downe :
Let all the Pallace fall at once. I here yet hidden see
The sonne of wycked father. Am. Loe his flattring handes to thee
Applying to thy knees dooth crave his lyfe with piteous mone.
O wicked gylt, full sad, and eike abhorde to looke upone,
His humble right hand caught he hath, and raging rounde about
Him rolled twyse, or thryse hath cast, his head resoundeth out,
The sprinkled houses with the brayne of him throwne out are wet.
But shee poore wretch her little sonne in bosome hyding yet
Loe Megara, like one in rage doth from the corners flee.
Her. Though runagate in bosome of the thundrer hid thou bee,
This right hand shall from every where thee seeke, and bring to sight.
Am. Wher goest thou wretch ? what lurking dens, seekst thou to take, or flight ?
No place of savegarde is if once bee Hercles styrde with yre :
But doe thou rather him embrace, and with thy meeke desyre

Assay t' asswage him. Me. Husband spare us I beseech thee nowe,
And knowe thy Megara, this sonne thy countenaunce doth showe,
And bodyes pytche : behould'st thou howe his hands up lyfteth hee?
Her. I holde my stepdame : followe on due penaunce paye to mee,
And bounden Jove from fylthy bonde deliver free away :
But I before the mother will this litle monster slay.
Me. Thou mad man whither goest thou ? wylt thou thine owne bloude sheade ?
Am. Th' infant with fathers fyry face astonnied all for dread,
Died even before the wounde : his feare hath tooke away his lyfe.
And now likewise his heavy club is shaken towarde his wyfe :
He broaken hath the bones, her head from blocklyke body gone
Is quight, nor any where it stayes, dar'ste thou this looke upone
To long lyv'de age ? if mourning doe the greeve, thou hast then loe
The death preparde. Doe thou thy breast uppon his weapons throe,
Or ells this club with slaughter stayn'de of monsters slayne that bee,
Nowe hyther turne, thy parent false, unfit for name of thee
Ryd hence away, least he should be to thy renowne a let.
Th. Which way the father toward thy death dost thou thy selfe cast yet ?
Or whyther goest thou mad man ? flee and lye thou cloasely hid,
And yet from handes of Hercules this onely myschiefe rid.
Her. T'is well, the house of shameful king is now quight overthrowne.
To thee O spouse of greattest Jove I have loe beaten downe
This offred flocke : I gladly have fulfill'de my wyshes all
Full meete for thee, and Argos now geve other offrings shall.
Am. Thou hast not sonne yet all perform'de, fill up the sacrifise.
Loe th' offring doth at th' aultars stande, it waytes thy hand likewyse
With necke full prone : I geve my selfe, I roon, I follow loe.
Mee sacrifice. What meaneth this ? his eyes rolle to and froe,
And heavines doth dull his sight, see I of Hercules
The trembling hands ? downe falles his face to sleepe and quietnes,
And weary necke with bowed head full fast doth downeward shrynke,
With bended knee : nowe all at once he downe to ground doth sinke,
As in the woods wylde Ashe cut downe, or Bulwarke for to make
A Haven in Seas. Liv'ste thou ? or els to death doth thee betake

The selfe same rage, that hath sent all thy famyly to death ?
It is but sleepe, for to and fro doth goe and come his breath.
Let tyme bee had of quietnesse, that thus by sleepe and rest
Great force of his disease subdew'de, may ease his greeved brest.
Remove his weapons servants, least he mad get them agayne.

CHORUS

Let th' ayre complayne, and eke the parent great
Of haughty Sky, and fertile land throughout,
And wandring wave of ever moving freat.
And thou before them all, which lands about
And trayn of Sea thy beames abroade dost throe
With glittring face, and mak'st the night to flee,
O fervent Titan : bothe thy settinges loe
And rysing, hath Alcides seene wyth thee :
And knowne lykewise hee hath thy howsen twayne.
From so great ills release yee nowe hys brest,
O Gods release : to better turne agayne
His ryghter mynde, and thou O tamer best
O sleepe of toyles, the quietnesse of mynde,
Of all the lyfe of man the better parte,
O of thy mother Astrey wynged kynde,
Of hard and pyning death that brother arte,
With truth mingling the false, of after state
The sure, but eke the worste foreteller yet :
O Father of all thynges of Lyfe the gate,
Of lyght the rest, of nyght and fellowe fyt,
That com'st to Kyng, and servaunt equally,
And gently cherysshest who weary bee,
All mankynde loe that dreadfull is to dye,
Thou doost constrayne long death to learne by thee.
Keepe him fast bounde wyth heavy sleepe opprest,
Let slomber deepe his Limmes untamed bynde,
Nor soner leave his unright raginge breaste
Then former mynd his course agayne may fynd.

Loe layd on ground with full fierce hart yet still
His cruel sleepes he turnes : and not yet is
The plague subdude of so great raging yll
And on great club the weary head of his
He wont to laye, doth seeke the staffe to fynde
With empty handes his armes out casting yet
With moving vayne : nor yet all rage of minde
He hath layd downe, but as with Sowthwind greate
The wave once vext yet after kepeth still
His raging long, and though the wind now bee
Asswaged swelles, shake of theis madde and yll
Tossinges of mynde, returne let piety,
And vertue to the man, els let be so
His mynde with moving mad toste every waye :
Let errour blynd, where it begun hath, go,
For naught els now but only madnes maye
Thee gyltles make : in next estate it standes
To hurtles handes thy mischiefe not to know.
Now stroken let with Hercules his handes
Thy bosome sounde : thyne armes the worlde allow
Were wonte to beare, let grevous strypes now smyte
With conquering hande, and lowde complayning
cryes,
Let th' ayre now heare, let of darke pole and nighte
The Queene them hear, and who ful fyercely lyes
That beares his neckes in mighty chaynes fast bounde,
Low lurking Cerberus in deepest cave.
Let Chaos all with clamour sad resound,
And of broad sea wide open wasting wave.
And th' ayre that felt thy weapons beter yet, but felt
them though.
The breastes with so great yls as these beset,
With litle stroake they must not beaten bee.
Let kingdomes three sound with one playnt and crye,
And thou neckes honour and defence to see,
His arrowe strong longe hanged up on hye,
And quivers light the cruell stripes now smyte
On his fierce backe his shouldars strong and stout

Let oken club now strike, and poast of might
With knots ful hard his brestee load all aboute.
Let even his weapons so great woes complayne
Not you pore babes mates of your fathers praise,
With cruell wound revenging kinges agayne :
Not you your lims in Argos barriars playes,
Are taught to turne with weapons strong to smite
And strong of hand yet even now daring loe
The weapons of the Scithian quiver light
With stedy hand to paise set out from bow.
And stags to perce that save them selves by flight
And backes not yet ful maend of cruel beast.
To Stigian havens goe ye of shade and night
Goe hurtles soules, whom mischiefe hath opprest
Even in fyrst porch of lyfe but lately had,
And fathers fury goe unhappy kind
O litle children, by the way ful sad
Of journey knowen.
Goe see the angry kynges.

THE FIFTHE ACTE

HERCULES, AMPHITRYON, THESEUS

HAT place is this ? what region ? or of the world what coast ?
Where am I ? under ryse of sunne or bond els uttermost
Of th' ycy beare or els doth here of sea of Hespery
The fardest ground appoynt a bond for th' ocean sea to lye ?
What ayre draw we ? to weary wight what ground is underset ?
Of truth we are returnd from hell whence in my house downe bet
See I these bloudy bodyes ? hath not yet my mynd of cast
Th' infernall shapes ? but after yet returnd from hel at last
Yet wander doth that helly heape before myne eys to see ?
I am asham'de to graunt, I quake, I know not what to me,
I cannot tell what greevous yll my mynde before doth know.
Where is my parent ? where is shee with goodly childrens show
My noble harty stomackt spouse why doth my left syde lacke
The lyons spoyle ? which way is gone the cover of my backe ?
And selfe same bedde ful soft for slepe of Hercules also ?
Where are my shaftes ? where is my bow ? then from my living who
Could plucke away ? who taken hath the spoyles so great as these
And who was he that feared not even sleepe of Hercules ?
To see my conquerour me lykes, yt lykes me hym to know
Ryse victor up, what new sonne hath my father gotten now
Heaven beynge left ? at byrth of whom myght ever stayd bee
A longer night then, was in myne ? what mischiefe do I see ?
My children loe do lye on ground with bloudy slaughter slayne :
My wyfe is kild : what Lycus doth the kingdome yet obtayne ?

Who durst so haynous giltes as these at Thebes take in hand
When Hercles is returnd ? who so Ismenus waters land,
Who so Acteons fieldes or who with double seas beset
The shaken Pelops kingdomes dost of Dardan dwell on yet
Helpe me : of cruel slaughter show who may the author bee.
Let rage my yre and all : my foe he is who so to me
Shewes not my foe dost thou yet hyde Alcides victorly ?
Come forth, even whether thou revenge the cruel charyots hye
Of Bloudy Thracian king or yf thou Gerions catell quight
Or lordes of Lybia, no delay there is with thee to fight.
Beholde I naked stande, although even with my weapons loe
Thou me unarmed sette uppon. Wherfore fleeth Theseus soe,
And eke my father from my sight ? theyr faces why hyde they ?
Deferre your weepings, and who did my wyfe and children sley
Thus all at once, me tell. Wherfore O father dost thou whusht ?
But tell thou Theseu, but Theseu with thy accustom'd truste.
Ech of them sylent hydes away their bashefull count'naunces,
And privily they shed their teares in so great ils as these,
Of what ought wee asham'de to be ? doth ruler yet of might
Of Argos towne, or hateful band of sowldiars apt to sight
Of Lycus dying, us oppresse with such calamity ?
By prayse of all my noble actes I do desyre of thee
O father, and of thy great name approv'de to me alway
The prosperous powre declare to mee, who did my houshold slay ?
Whose pray lay I ? AM. Let thus thyne ylles in sylens overpas.
HER. That I should unrevenged bee ? AM. Revenge oft hurtful was.
HER. Did ever man so greevous yls without revenge sustayne ?
AM. Whos'ever greater fearde. HER. Then these O father yet agayne
May any greater thing, or els more grevous feared be ?
AM. How great a part is it thou wotst of thy calamity ?
HER. Take mercy father, lo I lift to thee my humble hands.
What meaneth this ? my hand fleeth backe, some privy gylt their standes
Whence comes this bloud ? or what doth mean flowing with death of child
The shaft imbrewd with slaughter once of Lerney monster kilde ?

I see my weapons now, the hand I seeke no more to witte.
Whose hand could bend this bow but myne ? or what right arme but it
Could string the bow that unto mee even scantly doth obay ?
To you I turne : O father deare, is this my gylt I pray ?
They held their peace : it is myne own. AM. Thy grevous woe is there,
The cryme thy stepdames : this mischaunce no falt of thyne hath here.
HER. From every part now father throw in wrath thy thunders mighte,
And of thy sonne forgetful now with cruel hand requighte
At least thy nephewes, let the world that beares the starres sounde out.
And let both th' one and th' other poale, flyng downe thy flames aboute :
And let the bankes of Caspyan sea my bounden body teare,
And gredy foule. Wherfore do of Prometheus lacke heare
The rockes ? with huge and haughty top let now prepared be,
Both feeding beastes and foules, the syde of Caucas turne to see,
And bare of woods, the yle that bridge of Scithe that therby standes
Simplegas joynes, both here and there let it my bounden handes
Stretch out abroade : and when with course return'de accustomd'ly
They shall togeather dryve, and shall the rockes tosse up to skye
With bankes togeather beyng thrust, and eke the middle seay,
Let me betweene the mountaynes lye unquiet restlesse stay
But building up with wood throwne on a heaped pile on hie
My body thus with wicked bloud besprinct, why burne not I ?
So, so yt must be done : to hell I Hercles will restore.
AM. Not yet his hart astonied lackes his ragyng tumult sore,
But wrathe hath turnd : and which of rage is property and yre
Agaynst himselfe he rageth now. HER. The furies places dire
And dungeon depe of sprites in hell and place of tormentry
To gylty ghostes and banishment yf any yet do lye
Beyond Erebus, yet unknowen to Cerberus and mee,
There hyde me ground to farthest bond of Tartarus to see.
To tary there Ile goe O brest of myne to fierce and stoute :
Who you my children thus disprest through all my house about,

May worthely enough bewayle ? in all my evils yet
This countnaunce hard can never weepe, a sword now hether set :
My shaftes reach hether, hyther reach my mighty club also :
To thee my weapons breake I will, to thee my sonne a two
Ile knappe my bowes, and eke my clubbe, this blocke of heavy waygths
Shal to thy sprites be burned loe : this selfe same quiver frayght
With Lerney shaftes to funerall of thyne shall likewyse goe.
Let all my weapons penance pay and you unhappy to
Even with my weapons burne I wil, O stepdames handes of myne.
TH. Who ever yet to ignoraunce hath geven name of cryme ?
HER. Ful oftentymes did errour greate the place of gylt obtayne.
TH. T'is neede to be a Hercles now, this heape of yll sustayne.
HER. Not so, hath shame yet geven place with fury drowned quight :
But peoples all I rather should dryve from my wicked sight,
My weapons, weapons Theseus, I quickly crave to mee
Withdraw to be restoard agayne : if sound my mynd now bee,
Restore to me my weapons : if yet last my rage of mynd,
Then father flee : for I the waye to death my selfe shal fynde.
AM. By sacred holy kynreds rightes, by force and duty all
Of both my names, if eyther me thy brynger up thou call,
Or parent els, and (which of good men reverenced are)
By these hoare hayres, I the besech my desert age yet spare,
And wery yeares of house laine downe the one alonly stay,
One onely light to mee, with yls afflicted every way
Reserve thy selfe : yet never hath there happ'ned once of thee
Fruite of thy toyles : still eyther I the doubtful sea to see
Or monsters feard : who ever yet hath bene a cruell king
In all the world to ghostes allow, and aulters both hurtinge,
Of me is feard : the father of thee absent stil to have
The fruite, the touching, and the sight of thee at length I crave.
HER. Wherfore I longer should sustayn my life yet in this light,
And linger here no cause there is, all good lost have I quighte,
My mynd, my weapons, my renoume, my wife, my sonnes, my handes,
And fury to no man may heale and lose from gylty bandes
My mynd defyeld : needes must with death be heald so haynous yll.
TH. Wilt thou thy father slay ? HER. Least I shoulde do it die I will.

TH. Before thy fathers face ? HER. I taught him mischief for to see.
TH. Thy deedes marking rather that should of al remembred bee,
Of this one only cryme I do a pardon of thee crave.
HER. Shall he geve pardon to himselfe, that to none els it gave ?
I beeing bidden prayse deserv'd, this deede mine owne doth prove.
Helpe father now, if eyther els thy piety thee move,
Or els my heavy fate, or els the honour and renowne.
Of stained strength, my weapons bringe, let fortune be throwen downe.
With my right hand. TH. The prayers which thy father makes to thee
Are stronge enough, but yet likewyse with weeping loe of me
Be moved yet : aryse thou up, and with thy wonted myght
Subdue thyne yls : now such a mynde unmeete to beare upright
No evill hap, receyve againe, loe now with manhode gret
Thou must prevayle, even Hercules forbyd with yre to fret.
HER. Alyve, I hurt : but if I dye I take the gylt also.
I hast to ridde the world of cryme even now before me lo
A wicked monster cruel, and untamed fierce and stout
Doth wander : now with thy ryght hand beginne to goe aboute
A greate affayre, yea more then all thy twyse sixe labours long.
Yet stayst thou wretch, that late agaynst the children wast so stronge,
And fearful mother now except restoard my weapons bee
Of Thracian Pindus eyther I wil teare downe every tree,
And Bacchus holly woods and tops of mount Cythæron hye
Burne with my selfe, and al at once with all their housen I
And with the Lordes therof the roofes with goddes of Thebes all
The Thebane temples even uppon my body will let fall :
And wyl be hyd in towne upturnd : if to my shoulders might
The walles themselves all cast theron shall fall a burden light,
And coverd with seven gates I shall not be enough opprest,
Then all the wayght wheron the worlde in middle part doth rest,
And partes the Goddes uppon my head Ile turne and overthrow
My weapons geve. AM. This word is meete for Hercles father lo
With this same arrow slaine behold thy sonne is tombled downe,
This weapons cruell Juno lo from handes of thyne hath throwne,

This same will I now use, loe see how leaps with feare afright
My wretched harte, and how it doth my careful body smight.
The shaft is set therto thou shalt a mischiefe lo do now
Both willing it and wotting : tel, what thing commaundest thou ?
I nothing crave my doloure loe in saf'ty standeth now,
To kepe my sonne alyve to mee that onely do canst thou
O Theseu, yet I have not scapte great'st feare that happen can
Thou canst mee not a miser make, thou mayst a happy man
So order every thyng thou dost, as all thy cause in hand,
And fame thou mayst wel know in strayght and doubtful case to stande
Thou liv'st, or diest : this slender soule that light is hence to flee,
Weried with age, and no lesse bet with grevous ils to see,
In mouth I holde so slowly to a father with such staye
Doth any man geve lyfe ? I wil no longer bid delay,
The deadly sword throughout my breast to strike I wil apply,
Here, here the gylt of Hercules even sound of mynd shall lye.
HER. Forbeare O father now forbeare, withdraw thy hand againe.
My manhood yeld thy fathers will, and impery sustaine.
To Hercles labours now likewyse, let this one labour goe,
Let me yet live, lift up from ground th' afflicted lims with woe
O Theseu of my parent : for whom Godly touch doth flee
My wicked hand. AM. I gladly do this hand embrace to mee.
By this I beyng slayed will goe, this moving to my brest
Ile slake my woes. HER. What place shall I seeke ronnagate for rest ?
Where shall I hyde my selfe ? or in what land my selfe engrave ?
What Tanais, or what Nilus els, or with his Persyan wave
What Tygris violent of streame, or what fierce Rhenus flood,
Or Tagus troublesome that flowes with Ibers treasures good
May my ryght hand now wash from gylt ? although Mæotis cold
The waves of all the Northen sea on me shed out now wolde,
And al the water therof shoulde now pas by my two handes,
Yet wil the mischiefe deepe remayne, alas into what landes
Wilt thou O wicked man resort ? to East or westerne coste ?
Ech where wel knowen, all place I have of banishment quight loste
From me the worlde doth flee a back, the starres that sydelyng rone
Do backwarde dryve their turned course, even Cerberus the sone

With better count'naunce did behold O faythfull friend I saye,
O Theseu seeke some lurking place, farre hence out of the way
O thou awarder of mens gyltes what ever Judge thou bee
That hurtful men dost love, repay a worthy thanke to me :
And my desertes. I thee beseech, to ghostes of hell againe
Send me that once escaped them : and subject to thy raine
Restore me yet to those thy bandes, that place shal me wel hyde :
And yet even that place knowes me wel. TH. Our land for thee doth bide
There Mars his hande acquite agayne and made from slaughter free
Restoard to armoure, loe that land (Alcides) calles for thee,
Which wontes to quite the gods, and prove them Innocent to be.

Here endeth the First Tragedye of Seneca, called Hercules furens, translated into Englishe by Jasper Heywood studente in Oxenforde.

THE SECOND TRAGEDIE OF SENECA
ENTITULED THYESTES

FAYTHFULLY ENGLISHED BY JASPER HEYWOOD

FELOW OF ALSOLNE COLLEDGE IN OXENFORDE

THE ARGUMENT OF THIS TRAGEDIE

MEGÆRA one of the Hellish furies raising up Tantalus from Hell, incited him to set mortall hatred betweene his two nephewes Thiestes, and Atreus being brothers, and raining as Kinges over Mycenæ by enterchangeable turnes, that is to witte Thiestes to raine the one yere, and Atreus the other. Now Atreus enraged with furie against his brother partly for defiling and deflouring his wife Ærope by pollicie, and partly for taking from him a Ram with a golden fleese, practised with his servant how to be revenged of his brother. This Atreus therfore dissembling a reconciliation and inviting Thyestes to Mycenæ secretly and unknowne to him, set before him at a banquet the flesh of his owne children to eate. Afterward Atreus having also geven to his said brother the bloud of his children in a goblet to drinke, did lastly commaund the heads also to be brought in, at the doleful sight wherof Thiestes greatly lamenting knowing that he had eaten his owne children, was wonderfully anguished. But Atreus for that he had thus revenged himselfe, toke therin great pleasure and delectation.

THE SPEAKERS

TANTALUS.
MEGÆRA.
ATREUS.
SERVANT.
THIESTES.
PHILISTENES.
MESSENGER.
CHORUS.

THE FIRST ACTE

TANTALUS, MEGÆRA

WHAT furye fell enforceth mee to fle, th' unhappy seat,
That gape and gaspe with greedye jawe, the fleeyng food to eate
What God to Tantalus the bowres wher breathing bodyes dwel
Doth shew agayne ? is ought found worse, then burning thyrst of hel
In lakes alow ? or yet worse plague then hunger is there one,
In vayne that ever gapes for foode ? shal Sisyphus his stone,
That slipper restles rollyng payse uppon my backe be borne,
Or shall my lymmes with swifter swinge of whirling whele be torne ?
Or shal my paynes be Tytius panges th' encreasyng liver still,
Whose growing guttes the gnawing gripes and fylthy foules do fyll ?
That styl by nyght repayres the panch that was devourd by day,
And wondrous wombe unwasted lieth a new prepared pray
What ill am I appoynted for ? O cruell judge of sprites,
Who so thou be that tormentes new among the fowles delytes
Stil to dispose, ad what thou canst to all my deadly woe,
That keeper even of dungeon darke would sore abhorre to knowe.
Or hel it selfe it quake to se : for dread wherof likewyse
I tremble wold, that plague seke out : lo now there doth aryse
My broode that shal in mischiefe farre the grandsyers gilt out goe,
And gyltles make : that first shall dare unventred ills to do.
What ever place remayneth yet of all this wicked land,
I wil fill up : and never once while Pelops house doth stand
Shall Minos idle be. ME. Go forth thou detestable sprite
And vexe the Goddes of wicked house with rage of furyes might.

Let them contend with all offence, by turnes and one by one
Let swordes be drawne : and meane of ire procure there may be none,
Nor shame : let fury blynd enflame theyr myndes and wrathful will,
Let yet the parentes rage endure and longer lasting yll
Through childrens children spreade : nor yet let any leysure be
The former fawte to hate, but still more mischiefe newe to see,
Nor one in one : but ere the gylt with vengeance be acquit,
Encrease the cryme : from brethren proud let rule of kingdom flyt
To runnagates : and swarving state of all unstable thinges,
Let it by doubtfull dome be toste, betwene thuncertaine kyngs.
Let mighty fall to misery, and myser clime to might,
Let chaunce turne thempyre upsydowne both geve and take the right.
The banyshed for gylt, when god restore theyr country shall.
Let them to mischiefe fall a fresh as hatefull then to all,
As to themselves : let Ire thinke nought unlawfull to be doon,
Let brother dread the brothers wrath, and father feare the soon,
And eke the soon his parents powre : let babes be murdered yll,
But worse begot ? her spouse betrapt to treasons trayne to kyll,
Let hatefull wyfe awayte, and let them beare through seas their warre,
Let bloodshed lye the lands about and every field a farre :
And over conqueryng captaynes greate, of countreys far to see,
Let lust tryumphe : in wicked house let whoredome counted be
The light'st offens : let trust that in the breasts of brethren breedes,
And truth be gone : let not from sight of your so heynous deedes
The heavens be hyd, about the poale when shyne the starres on hye,
And flames with woonted beames of light doe decke the paynted skye.
Let darkest night bee made, and let the day the heavens forsake.
Dysturbe the godds of wicked house, hate, slaughter, murder make.
Fyll up the house of Tantalus with mischieves and debates,
Adorned be the pillers hygh with bay, and let the gates
Be garnysht greene : and worthy there for thy returne to sight,
Be kyndled fyre : let mischyefe done in Thracia once, theyr lyght

More manyfolde, wherefore doth yet the uncles hand delaye ?
Doth yet Thyestes not bewayle his childrens fatall day ?
Shall he not finde them where with heat of fyres that under glowe
The cawderne boyles ? their limmes eche one a peeces let them go
Disperste : let fathers fires, with blood of chyldren fyled bee :
Let deynties such be drest : it is no mischiefe newe to thee,
To banquet so : behold this day we have to thee releast,
And hunger starved wombe of thyne we send to such a feast.
With fowlest foode thy famyne fyll, let bloud in wyne be drownd,
And dronke in sight of thee : loe now such dishes have I found,
As thou wouldst shonne, stay whither doste thou hedlong way now take ?
TAN. To pooles and floods of hell agayne and styll declining lake,
And flight of tree ful frayght with fruite that from the lippes doth flee,
To dungeon darke of hateful hell let leeful be for me
To goe : or if to light be thought the paynes that there I have,
Remove me from those lakes agayne : in midst of worser wave
Of Phlegethon, to stand in seas of fyre beset to bee.
Who so beneath thy poynted paynes by destenyes decree
Dost stil endure who soo thou bee that underliest alow
The hollow denne, or ruyne who that feares and overthrow
Of fallyng hyl, or cruel cryes that sound in caves of hell
Of greedy roaryng Lyons throats or flocke of furyes fell
Who quakes to know or who the brandes of fyre in dyrest payne
Halfe burnt throwes of harke to the voyce of Tantalus : agayne
That hastes to hel, and, whom the truth hath taught beleeve wel mee
Love wel your paynes, they are but small when shall my hap so bee
To flee the light ? ME. Disturbe thou fyrst thys house with dire discord
Debates and battels bring with thee, and of th' unhappy sworde
Ill love to kinges : the cruel brest stryke through and hateful hart,
With tumult mad. TAN. To suffer paynes it seemeth wel my part,
Not woes to worke : I am sent forth lyke vapoure dyre to ryse,
That breakes the ground or poyson like the plague in wondrouse wyse

That slaughter makes, shall I to such detested crymes, applye
My nephewes hartes ? o parentes great of Gods above the skie
And myne (though sham'de I be to graunt) although with greater pain
My tongue be vext, yet this to speake I may no whit refrayne
Nor hold my peace : I warne you this least sacred hand with bloud
Of slaughter dyre, or fransie fell of frantike fury wood
The aulters slayne, I wil resist : And garde such gylt away.
With strypes why dost thou me affryght ? why threatst thou me to fraye
Those crallyng snakes ? or famine fyxt in empty wombe, wherfore
Dost thou revyve ? now fries within with thyrst enkindled sore
My harte : and in the bowels burnt the boyling flames do glow.
ME. I follow thee : through all this house now rage and fury throwe
Let them be driven so, and so let eyther thirst to see
Each others blood ful wel hath felt the comming in of thee
This house, and all with wicked touch of the begune to quake.
Enough it is, repayre agayne to dens and loathsome lake,
Of floud well knowen, the sadder soyle with heavy fote of thyne
Agreeved is, seest thou from springes how waters do declyne
And inward sinke ? or how the bankes lye voyde by drughty heate ?
And hoatter blast of fyery wynde the fewer cloudes doth beate ?
The treese be spoyld, and naked stand to sight in withred woddes,
The barayne bowes whose fruites are fled : the land betwene the floods
With surge of seas on eyther syde that wonted to resound,
And nearer foordes to seperat sometyme with lesser ground,
Now broader spred, it heareth how aloofe the waters ryse.
Now Lerna turnes agaynst the streame Phoronides likewyse
His poores be stopt, with custom'd course Alphéus dryves not still,
His hollie waves, the trembling tops of high Cithæron hill,
They stand not sure : from height adowne they shake their sylver snowe,
And noble fieldes of Argos feare, theyr former drought to know.
Yea Tytan doubtes himselfe to rolle the worlde his wonted way,
And drive by force to former course the backward drawing daye.

THYESTES

THE FIRST ACTE

CHORUS

This Argos towne if any God be founde,
And Piseyboures that famous yet remayn,
Or kingdomes els to love of Corinthes ground,
The double havens, or sundred seas in twayne
If any love of Taygetus his snowes,
(By Winter which when they on hils be cast :
By Boreas blastes that from Sarmatia blowes,
With yerely breath the sommer meltes as fast)
Where clere Alphéus runnes with floude so cold,
By playes wel knowen that there Olimpiks hight :
Let pleasaunt powre of his from hense withholde
Such turnes of stryfe that here they may not light :
Nor nephew worse then grandsier spring from us,
Or direr deedes delyght the yonger age.
Let wicked stocke of thirsty Tantalus
At length leave of, and wery be of rage.
Enoughe is done, and naught prevaild the just,
Or wrong : betrayed is Mirtilus and drownde,
That did betray his dame, and with like trust
Borne as he bare, himselfe hath made renound
With chaunged name the sea : and better knowne
To mariners therof no fable is.
On wicked sword the litle infant throwne
As ran the childe to take his fathers kisse.
Unrype for thaulters offring fell downe deade :
And with thy hand (O Tantalus) was rent,
With such a meate for Gods thy boordes to spread.
Eternall famine for such foode is sent,
And thyrst : nor for those daynty meats unmilde,
Might meeter payne appoynted ever bee
With empty throate standes Tantalus begylde,
Above thy wicked head their leanes to thee,
Then Phineys fowles in flight a swifter pray.
With burned bowes declynd on every syde,

And of his fruites all bent to beare the sway,
The tree deludes the gapes of hunger wyde
Though hee full greedy feede theron would fayne.
So oft deceyv'de neglectes to touch them yet :
He turnes his eyes, his jawes he doth refrayne,
And famine fixt in closed gummes doth shet.
But then each braunch his plenteous ritches all,
Lets lower downe, and apples from on hie
With lither leaves they flatter like to fall
And famine styrre : in vayne that bids to trye
His handes : which when he hath rought forth anone
To be beguyld, in higher ayre againe
The harvest hanges and fickle fruite is gone,
Then thirst him greeves no lesse then hungers payne :
Wherwith when kindled is his boyling bloud
Lyke fyre, the wretch the waves to him doth call,
That meete his mouth : which straight the fleeyng floud
Withdrawes, and from the dryed foorde doth fall :
And him forsakes that followes them. He drinkes
The dust so deepe of gulfe that from him shrinkes.

THYESTES

THE SECONDE ACTE

ATREUS, SERVAUNT

DASTARD, cowrde, O wretche, and (which the greatest yet of all
To Tyrantes checke I compte that maye in waighty thinges befall)
O unrevenged: after guyltes so great and brothers guyle,
And trewth trode downe dost thou provoke with vayne complaynts the whyle
Thy wrath? already now to rage all Argos towne throughout
In armoure ought of thyne, and all the double seas about
Thy fleete to ryde: now all the fieldes with fervent flames of thyne,
And townes to flash it wel beseemde: and every where to shyne,
The bright drawne sword: all under foote of horse let every syde
Of Argos lande resound: and let the woundes not serve to hyde
Our foes, nor yet in haughty top of hilles and mountaynes hye,
The builded towers. The people all let them to battel crye
And clere forsake Mycenas towne who so his hateful head
Hides and defendes, with slaughter dire let bloud of him be shed.
This princely Pelops palace proude, and bowres of high renowne,
On mee so on my brother to let them be beaten downe,
Go to, do that which never shall no after age allow,
Nor none it whisht: some mischefe greate ther must be ventred now,
Both fierce and bloudy: such as woulde my brother rather long
To have bene his. Thou never dost enough revenge the wronge,
Exept thou passe. And feercer fact what may be done so dyre,
That his exceedes? doth ever he lay downe his hateful yre?
Doth ever he the modest meane in tyme of wealth regard
Or quiet in adversity? I know his nature harde

Untractable, that broke may be, but never wil it bend.
For which ere he prepare himselfe, or force to fight entend,
Set fyrst on him, least while I rest he should on me aryse.
He wil destroy or he destroyd in midst the mischiefe lyes,
Prepard to him that takes it first. SER. Doth fame of people naught
Adverse thee feare ? ATRE. The greatest good of kingdom may be thought
That still the people are constraynd their princes deedes as well
To prayse, as them to suffer all. SER. Whom feare doth so compell
To prayse, the same his foes to bee, doth feare enforce agayne :
But who indeede the glory seekes of favour trew t'obtayne
He rather would with hates of each be praysd, then tounges of all.
ATRE. The trewer prayse ful oft hath hapt to meaner men to fall :
The false but unto myghty man what nill they let them will.
SER. Let first the king will honest thinges and none the same dare nill.
ATRE. Where leeful are to him that rules but honest thinges alone,
There raynes the kyng by others leave. SER. And where the shame is none,
Nor care of ryght, fayth, piety, nor holines none stayeth,
That kingdome swarves. ATRE. Such holines, such piety and fayth,
Are private goods : let kinges runne one in that that likes their will.
SER. The brothers hurt a mischiefe count though he be nere so ill.
ATRE. It is but right to do to hym, that wrong to brother were.
What heynous hurt hath his offence let passe to prove ? or where
Refraynd the gylt, my spouse he stale away for lechery,
And raygne by stelth : the auncient note and sygne of impery,
By frawde he got : my house by fraud to vexe he never ceast :
In Pelops house there fostred is a noble worthy beast
The close kept Ramme : the goodly guyde of rych and fayrest flockes.
By whom throughout on every syde depend adowne the lockes
Of glittering gold, with fleece of which the new kinges wonted were
Of Tantals stocke their sceptors gylt, and mace of might to beare.
Of this the owner raygneth he, with him of house so great
The fortune fleeth, this sacred Ramme aloofe in safety shet

In secret mead is wont to grase, which stone on every syde
With rocky wall incloseth rounde the fatall beast to hyde.
This beast (adventryng mischiefe greate) adjoyning yet for pray
My spoused mate, the traytour false hath hence convayde away
From hence the wrongs of mutuall hate, and mischiefe all upsprong :
In exile wandred he throughout my kingdomes all along :
No part of myne remayneth safe to mee, from traynes of hys.
My feere deflourde, and loyalty of empyre broken is :
My house all vext, my bloud in doubt, and naught that trust is in,
But brother foe. What stayst thou yet ? at length lo now beginne.
Take hart of Tantalus to thee, to Pelops cast thyne eye :
To such examples well beseemes, I should my hand applye.
Tell thou which way were best to bring that cruell head to death.
SER. Through perst with sword let him be slayne and yelde his hatefull breath.
ATRE. Thou speak'st of th' end : but I him would opres with greter payne.
Let tyrants vexe with torment more : should ever in my rayne
Be gentle death ? SER. Doth piety in thee prevayle no whit ?
ATRE. Depart thou hence all piety, if in this house as yet
Thou ever wert : and now let all the flocke of furies dyre,
And full of strife Erinnis come, and double brands of fyre
Megæra shaking : for not yet enough with fury great
And rage doth burne my boyling brest : it ought to bee repleate,
With monster more. SER. What mischiefe new do'ste thou in rage provide ?
ATRE. Not such a one as may the meane of woonted griefe abide.
No guilt will I forbeare, nor none may be enough despight.
SER. What sword ? ATRE. To litle that. SER. What fire ? ATRE. And that is yet to light.
SER. What weapon then shall sorrow such finde fit to worke thy will ?
ATRE. Thyestes selfe. SER. Then yre it selfe yet that's a greater ill.
ATRE. I graunt : a tombling tumult quakes, within my bosomes loe,
And round it rolles : I moved am and wote not whereunto.
But drawen I am : from bottome deepe the roryng soyle doth cry
The day so fayre with thunder soundes, and house as all from hy

Were rent, from roofe, and rafters crakes : and lares turnde abought
Have wryde theyr sight : so bee'te, so bee'te, let mischiefe such be sought,
As yee O Gods would feare. Ser. What thing seek'st thou to bring to pas
I note what greater thing my mynde, and more then woont it was.
Atre. Above the reache that men are woont to worke, begins to swell :
And slayth with slouthfull hands. What thinge it is I cannot tell :
But great it is. Bee'te so, my mynde now in this feate proceede,
For Atreus and Thyestes bothe, it were a worthy deede.
Let eche of us the crime commit. The Thracian house did see
Such wicked tables once : I graunt the mischiefe great to bee,
But done ere this : some greater guilt and mischiefe more, let yre
Fynde out. The stomacke of thy sonne O father thou enspyre,
And syster eke, like is the cause : assist me with your powre,
And dryve my hand : let greedy parents all his babes devowre,
And glad to rent his children bee : and on their lyms to feede.
Enough, and well it is devis'de : this pleaseth me in deede.
In meane time where is he ? so long and innocent wherefore
Doth Atreus walke ? before myne eyes alredy more and more
The shade of such a slaughter walkes : the want of children cast,
In fathers Jawes. But why my mynde, yet dreadst thou so at last,
And faint'st before thou enterprise ? it must bee done, let bee.
That which in all this mischiefe is the greatest guilt to see,
Let him commit. Ser. But what disceit may wee for him prepare,
Whereby betrapt he may be drawne, to fall into the snare ?
He wotes full well we are his foes. Atre. He could not taken bee,
Except himselfe woulde take : but now my kingdomes hopeth hee.
For hope of this he woulde not feare to meete the mighty Jove,
Though him he threatned to destroy, with lightning from above.
For hope of this to passe the threats of waves he will not fayle,
Nor dread no whit by doubtfull shelves, of Lybike seas to fayle,
For hope of this (which thing he doth the woorst of all beleeve,)
He will his brother see. Ser. Who shall of peace the promise geeve ?

Whom will he trust ? ATRE. His evill hope will soone beleve it well.
Yet to my sonnes the charge which they shall to theyr unckle tell,
We will commit : that whom he would from exile come agayne,
And myseries so : kingdome chaunge, and over Argos raygne
A king of halfe : and though to hard of heart our prayers all
Him selfe despise, his children yet nought woting what may fall,
With travels tier'de, and apte to be entys'de from misery,
Requests will move : on th' one side his desyre of Imperie,
On th' other syde his poverty, and labour hard to see,
Will him subdue and make to yeelde, although full stoute he bee.
SER. His travayles now the time hath made to seeme to him but small.
ATRE. Not so : for day by day the griefe of ill encreaseth all.
T'is light to suffer miseries, but heavy them t' endure.
SER. Yet other messengers to send, in such affayres procure.
ATRE. The yonger sorte the wrose precepts do easely harken to.
SER. What thing agaynst their buckle now, you them enstruckt to do,
Perhaps with you to worke the like, they will not be a dread.
Such mischiefe wrought hath oft return'de upon the workers head.
ATRE. Though never man to them the wayes of guile and guilt have taught,
Yet kingdome will. Fear'st thou they should be made by counsel naught ?
They are so borne. That which thou cal'ste a cruell enterpryse,
And dyrely deemest doone to be, and wickedly likewise,
Perhaps is wrought agaynst me there. SER. And shall your sons of this
Disceipt beware that worke you will ? no secretnes there is
In theyr so greene and tender yeares : they will your traynes disclose,
ATRE. A privy counsell close to keepe, is learnde with many woes.
SER. And will yee them, by whom yee woulde he should beguiled bee,
Them selves beguil'de ? ATRE. Nay let them both from fault and blame be free.
For what shall neede in mischiefes such as I to woorke entende,
To mingle them ? let all my hate by mee alone take ende.

Thou lean'ste thy purpose ill my mynde : if thou thine owne forbeare,
Thou sparest him. Wherefore of this let Agamemnon heare
Be mynister : and Client eke of myne for such a deede,
Let Menelaus present bee : truth of th' uncertayne seede,
By such a pracktise may be tri'de : if it refuse they shall,
Nor of debate will bearers be, if they him unckle call,
He is their father : let them goe. But much the fearefull face
Bewrayes it selfe : even him that faynes the secret wayghty case,
Doth oft betray : let them therefore not know, how great a guyle
They goe about. And thou these things in secret keepe the whyle.
SER. I neede not warned bee, for these within my bosome deepe,
Both fayth, and feare, but chiefely fayth, doth shet and closely kepe.

CHORUS

The noble house at length of high renowne,
The famous stocke of auncient Inachus,
Apeasd and layd the threats of brethren down.
But nowe what fury styrs and drives you thus
Eche one to thyrst the others bloud agayne,
Or get by guylt the golden Mace in hande?
Yee litle wote that so desyre to raygne,
In what estate or place doth kyngdome stande.
Not ritches makes a kyng or high renowne,
Not garnisht weede wyth purple Tyrian die,
Not lofty lookes, or head encloasde with crowne,
Not glyttring beames with golde and turrets hie.
A Kyng he is that feare hath layde aside,
And all affects that in the breast are bred :
Whom impotent ambition doth not guide,
Nor fickle favour hath of people led.
Nor all that west in mettalls mynes hath founde,
Or chanell cleere of golden Tagus showes,
Nor all the grayne that thresshed is on grounde,
That with the heate of libyk harvest glowes.

Nor whom the flasshe of lightning flame shall beate,
Nor eastern wynde that smightes upon the seas,
Nor swelling surge with rage of wynde repleate,
Or greedy Gulphe of Adria displease.
Whom not the pricke of Souldiers sharpest speare,
Or poyncted pyke in hand hath made to rue,
Nor whom the glympse of swoorde myght cause to feare,
Or bright drawen blade of glyttring steele subdue.
Who in the seate of safty sets his feete,
Beholdes all haps how under him they lye,
And gladly runnes his fatall day to meete,
Nor ought complaynes or grudgeth for to dye.
Though present were the Prynces everychone,
The scattered Dakes to chase that wonted bee,
That shyning seas beset with precious stone,
And red sea coastes doe holde, lyke bloud to see :
Or they which els the Caspian mountaynes hye,
From Sarmats strong with all theyr power withholde :
Or hee that on the floude of Danubye,
In frost a foote to travayle dare bee bolde :
Or Seres in what ever place they lye,
Renownde with fleece that there of sylke doth spring,
They never might the truth hereof denye,
It is the mynde that onely makes a king.
There is no neede of sturdie steedes in warre,
No neede with armes or arrowes ells to fight,
That Parthus woonts with bowe to fling from farre,
Whyle from the fielde hee falsely fayneth flight.
Nor yet to siege no neede it is to bringe
Great Guns in Carts to overthrowe the wall,
That from farre of theyr battring Pellets flyng.
A kyng hee is that feareth nought at all.
Eche man him selfe this kyngdome geeves at hand.
Let who so lyst with mighty mace to raygne,
In tyckle toppe of court delight to stand
Let mee the sweete and quiet rest obtayne.
So set in place obscure and lowe degree,
Of pleasaunt rest I shall the sweetnesse knoe.

My lyfe unknowne to them that noble bee,
Shall in the steppe of secret sylence goe.
Thus when my dayes at length are over past,
And tyme without all troublous tumult spent,
An aged man I shall depart at last,
In meane estate, to dye full well content.
But greevuous is to him the death, that when
So farre abroade the bruite of him is blowne,
That knowne hee is to much to other men :
Departeth yet unto him selfe unknowne.

THYESTES

THE THYRDE ACTE

THYESTES, PHYLISTHENES

Y countrey bowres so long wisht for, and Argos rytches all,
Chiefe good that unto banisht men, and Mysers may befall,
The touch of soyle where born I was, and gods of native land,
(If gods they be,) and sacred towres I see of Cyclops hand :
That represent then all mans woorke, a greater majesty.
Renowned stadies to my youth, where noble sometime I
Have not so seelde as once, the palme in fathers chariot woon.
All Argos now to meete with me, and people fast will roon :
But Atreus to, yet rather leade in woods agayne thy flight,
And bushes thicke, and hid among the brutyshe beastes from sight,
Lyke lyfe to theyrs : where splendent pompe of court and princely pryde,
May not with flattring fulgent face, allure thine eyes aside.
With whom the kingdome geven is, behold, and well regarde,
Beset but late with such mishaps, as all men counte full harde,
I stoute and joyfull was : but now agayne thus into feare
I am returne, my mynde misdoubtes, and backeward seekes to beare
My body hence : and forthe I draw my pace agaynst my will.
PHY. With slouthfull step (what meaneth this ?) my father standeth still,
And turnes his face and holdes him selfe, in doubt what thing to do.
THY. What thing (my minde) considrest thou ? or els so long whereto

Do'st thou so easie counsayle wrest ? wilt thou to thinges unsure
Thy brother and the kingdome trust ? fearst thou those ills t' endure
Now overcome, and mielder made ? and travayls do'st thou flee
That well were plaste ? it thee avayls, a myser now to bee.
Turne hence thy pace while leefull is, and keepe thee from his hande.

PHY. What cause thee drives (O father deere) thus from thy native lande,
Now seene to shrynk ? what makes thee thus from things so good at last
Withdrawe thy selfe ? thy brother comes whose ires be overpast,
And halfe the kyngdome geves, and of the house Dylacerate,
Repayres the partes : and thee restores agayne to former state.

THY. The cause of feare that I know not, thou do'st require to heare.
I see nothing that makes mee dread, and yet I greatly feare.
I would goe on, but yet my limmes with weary legges doe slacke :
And other way then I would passe, I am withholden backe.
So oft the ship that driven is with wynde and eke with Ore,
The swelling surge resisting both beates backe upon the shore.

PHY. Yet overcome what ever stayes, and thus doth let your mynde,
And see what are at your returne, prepar'de for you to finde.
You may O father raygne. THY. I may but then when die I mought.

PHY. Chiefe thing is powre. THY. Nought worth at al, if thou desyre it nought.

PHY. You shall it to your children leave. THY. The kingdome takes not twayne.

PHY. Who may be happy, rather would he myser yet remayne ?

THY. Beleve me well, with titles false the great thinges us delight :
And heavy haps in vayne are fearde, while high I stoode in sight,
I never stinted then to quake, and selfe same sworde to feare,
That hanged by myne owne side was. Oh how great good it were,
With none to strive, but careles foode to eate and rest to knowe ?
The greater gyltes they enter not in cotage set alowe :
And safer foode is fed upon, at narrowe boorde alway,
While drunke in golde the poyson is by proofe well taught I say,

That evill haps before the good to love it likes my will.
Of haughty house that standes aloft in tickle top of hyll,
And swayes asyde, the cyty lowe neede never be affright:
Nor in the top of roofe above, there shynes no Ivery bright,
Nor watchman none defendes my sleepes by night, or gardes my rest:
With fleete I fishe not, nor the sees I have not backwarde prest,
Nor turn'de to flight with builded wall: nor wicked belly I
With taxes of the people fed: nor parcell none doth lie,
Of ground of myne beyonde the Getes: and Parthians farre about:
Nor worshiped with frankinsence I am, nor (Jove shet out)
My Aulters decked are: nor none in top of house doth stande
In garden treese, nor kindled yet with helpe of eche mans hande,
The bathes doe smoake: nor yet are dayes in slouthfull slumbers led,
Nor nightes past forth in watche and wyne, without the rest of bed.
Wee nothing feare, the house is safe without the hidden knyfe,
And poore estate the sweetnes feeles, of rest and quiet lyfe.
Greate kindome is to be content, without the same to lyve.
PHY. Yet should it not refused be, if God the kingdome give.
THY. Not yet desierd it ought to be. PHY. Your brother byds you rayne.
THY. Bids he? the more is to be fearde: there lurketh there some trayne.
PHY. From whence it fell, yet piety is woont to turne at length:
And love unfaynde, repayres agayne his erst omitted strength.
THY. Doth Atreus then his brother love? eche Ursa fyrst on hye,
The Seas shall washe, and swelling surge of Seas of Sicylye
Shall rest and all asswaged be: and corne to rypenes growe
In bottome of Ionian seas, and darkest night shall showe
And spreade the light about the soyle: the waters with the fyre,
The lyfe with death, the wynde with seas, shall friendship first requyre,
And be at league. PHY. Of what deceipte are you so dreadfull here?
THY. Of everychone: what ende at length might I provide of feare?
In all he can he hateth me. PHY. To you what hurt can he?
THY. As for my selfe I nothing dread you litle Babes make mee

Afrayde of him. PHY. Dread, yee to be beguilde when caught yee are :
To late it is to shoon the trayne in middle of the snare.
But goe we on, this (father) is to you my last request.
THY. I follow you. I leade you not. PHY. God turne it to the best
That well devised is for good : passe forth with cherefull pace.

THE SECOND SCENE

ATREUS, THYESTES

ENTRAPT in trayne the beast is caught and in the snare doth fall :
Both him, and eke of hated stocke with him the offspring all,
About the fathers syde I see : and nowe in saufety stands
And surest ground my wrathfull hate : nowe comes into my hands
At length Thyestes : yea hee comes and all at once to mee.
I scant refrayne my selfe, and scant may anger brydled bee.
So when the Bloudhound seekes the beast, by step and quick of sent
Drawes in the leame, and pace by pace to wynde the wayes hee went,
With nose to soyle doth hunt, while he the Boare aloofe hath founde
Farre of by sent, he yet refraynes and wanders through the grounde
With silent mouth : but when at hand he once perceives the pray,
With all the strength he hath he strives, with voyce and calls away
His lingring maister, and from him by force out breaketh hee.
When Ire doth hope the present bloud, it may not hydden bee.
Yet let it hydden be, beholde with ugly hayre to sight
How yrkesomely deform'de with filthe his fowlest face is dight,
How lothsome lyes his Bearde unkempt : but let us friendship fayne.
To see my brother me delights : geve now to me agayne
Embracing long desyred for : what ever stryfe there was
Before this time betwene us twayne, forget and let it pas :

Fro this day forth let brothers love, let bloud, and lawe of kinde
Regarded be, let all debate be slakte in eythers mynde.
THY. I coulde excuse my selfe, except thou wert as now thou art.
But (Atreus) now I graunt, the faulte was myne in every part:
And I offended have in all, my cause the worse to bee,
Your this dayes kindnes makes: in deede a guilty wight is hee,
That would so good a brother hurt as you, in any whit.
But now with teares I must entreate, and first I me submit.
These handes that at thy feete doe lye, doe thee beseeche and pray,
That yre and hate be layde aside, and from thy bosome may
Be scraped out: and cleere forgot, for pledges take thou these
O brother deere, these guiltles babes. ATRE. Thy hands yet from my kneese
Remove, and rather me to take in armes, upon me fall
And yee O aydes of elders age, yee litle infants all,
Mee clyp and coll about the necke: this fowle attyre forsake,
And spare myne eyes that pity it, and fresher vesture take
Lyke myne to see, and you with joy, the halfe of emperie
Deere brother take: the greater prayse shall come to mee thereby,
Our fathers seate to yelde to you, and brother to releeve.
To have a kingdome is but chaunce, but vertue it to geeve.
THY. A just reward for such deserts, the Gods (O brother deare)
Repay to thee: but on my head a regall crowne to weare,
My lothsome lyfe denyes: and farre doth from the sceptor flee
My hand unhappy: in the mydst let leefull be for mee
Of men to lurke. ATRE. This kingdome can with twayne full well agree.
THY. What ever is (O brother) yours, I count it myne to bee.
ATRE. Who would dame fortunes gifts refuse, if shee him rayse to reigne?
THY. The gyfts of hir eche man it wotes, how soone they passe againe.
ATRE. Yee me depryve of glory great, except yee th' empyre take.
THY. You have your prayse in offring it, and I it to forsake.
And full perswaded to refuse the kingdome, am I still.
ATRE. Except your part yee will susteine myne owne forsake I will.
THY. I take it then, and beare I will the name thereof alone:
The ryghts and armes, as well as myne they shall be yours eche one.

ATRE. The regall crowne as you beseemes upon your head then take:
And I th' appoyncted sacrifice for Gods, will now goe make.

CHORUS

Woulde any man it weene? that cruell wight
Atreus, of mynde so impotent to see
Was soone astonied with his brothers sight,
Mo greater force then pietye may bee:
Where kynred is not, lasteth every threat,
Whom true love holdes, it holdes eternally.
The wrath but late with causes kyndled great
All favour brake, and did to battayle cry,
Whan horsemen did resounde one every syde,
The swoordes eche where, then glystred more and more:
Which raging Mars with often stroke did guide
The fresher bloud to shed yet thyrsting sore.
But love the sworde agaynst theyr wills doth swage,
And them to peace perswads with hand in hand.
So sodeyne rest, amid so great a rage
What God hath made? throughout Mycenas land
The harnesse clynkt, but late of cyvill strife:
And for their babes did fearefull mother quake,
Her armed spouse to leese much fearde the wyfe,
When sworde was made the scabberde to forsake,
That now by rest with rust was overgrowne.
Some to repayre the walles that did decay,
And some to strength the towres halfe overthrowne,
And some the gates with gyns of Yrne to stay
Full busie were, and dredfull watch by nyght
From turret high did overlooke the towne.
Woorse is then warre it selfe the feare of fight.
(Nowe are the threats of cruell sworde layde downe,
And nowe the rumour whists of battayles sowne,
The noyse of crooked trumpet silent lyes,
And quiet peace returnes to joyfull towne.
So when the waves of swelling surge aryse,

Whyle Corus wynde the Brutian seas doth smight,
And Scylla soundes from hollowe Caves within,
And Shipmen are with wasting waves affright,
Charybdis casts that erst it had drunke in :
And Cyclops fierce his father yet doth dred,
In Ætna banke that fervent is with heates,
Least quenched be with waves that overshed
The fire that from eternall Fornace beates :
And poore Laërtes thinkes his kyngdomes all
May drowned be, and Ithaca doth quake :
If once the force of wyndes begin to fall,
The sea lyth downe more mylde then standing lake.
The deepe, where Ships so wyde full dredfull were
To passe, with sayles on eyther syde out spred
Now fallne adowne, the lesser Boate doth beare :
And leysure is to vewe the fyshes ded
Even there, where late with tempest bet upon
The shaken Cyclades were with Seas agast.
No state endures, the payne and pleasure, one
To other yeldes, and joyes be soonest past.
One howre sets up the thinges that lowest bee.
Hee that the crownes to prynces doth devyde,
Whom people please with bending of the knee,
And at whose becke theyr battayles lay aside
The Meades, and Indians eke to Phebus nye,
And Dakes that Parthyans doe with horsemen threat,
Him selfe yet holdes his Sceptors doubtfully,
And men of might he feares and chaunces great
(That eche estate may turne) and doubtfull howre.
O yee, whom lorde of lande and waters wyde,
Of Lyfe and death grauntes here to have the powre,
Lay yee your proude and lofty lookes aside :
What your inferiour feares of you amis,
That your superiour threats to you agayne.
To greater kyng, eche kyng a subject is.
Whom dawne of day hath seene in pryde to raygne,
Hym overthrowne hath seene the evening late.
Let none rejoyce to much that good hath got,

Let none dispayre of best in worst estate.
For Clotho myngles all, and suffreth not
Fortune to stande : but Fates about doth drive.
Such friendship finde wyth Gods yet no man myght,
That he the morowe might be sure to lyve.
The God our things all tost and turned quight
Rolles with a whyrle wynde.

THE FOURTHE ACTE

MESSENGER, CHORUS

HAT whirlwynde may me headlong dryve and up in ayre mee fling,
And wrap in darkest cloude, whereby it might so heynous thing,
Take from myne eyes? O wicked house that even of Pelops ought
And Tantalus abhorred bee. CH. What new thing hast thou brought?
ME. What lande is this? lythe Sparta here and Argos, that hath bred
So wicked brethern? and the ground of Corinth lying spred
Betweene the seas? or Ister else where woont to take their flight,
Are people wylde? or that which woonts with snowe to shyne so bright
Hircana lande? or els doe here the wandring Scythians dwell?
CH. What monstrous mischiefe is this place then guilty of? that tell,
And this declare to us at large what ever be the ill.
ME. If once my mynde may stay it selfe, and quaking limmes I will.
But yet of such a cruell deede before myne eyes the feare
And Image walkes: yee raging stormes now far from hence me beare
And to that place me drive, to which now driven is the day
Thus drawen from hence. CH. Our myndes yee holde yet still in doubt: full stay.
Tell what it is yee so abhorre. The author thereof showe.
I aske not who, but which of them that quickly let us know.
ME. In Pelops Turret high, a part there is of Pallace wyde
That towarde the south erected leanes, of which the utter syde

With equall top to mountayne standes, and on the City lies,
And people proude agaynst theyr prynce if once the traytors rise
Hath underneath his battring stroke : there shynes the place in sight
Where woont the people to frequent, whose golden beames so bright
The noble spotted pillers gray, of marble doe supporte,
Within this place well knowen to men, where they so oft resorte,
To many other roomes about the noble court doth goe.
The privie Palaice underlieth in secret place aloe,
With ditch ful deepe that doth enclose the wood of privitee,
And hidden parts of kyngdome olde : where never grew no tree
That chereful bowes is woont to beare, with knife or lopped be,
But Tare, and Cypresse, and with tree of Holme ful blacke to see
Doth becke and bende the wood so darke : alofte above all theese
The higher oke doth over looke, surmounting all the treese.
From hens with lucke the raigne to take, accustom'd are the kyngs,
From hens in daunger ayd to aske, and doome in doubtfull things.
To this affixed are the gifts, the sounding Trumpets bright,
The Chariots broke, and spoyles of sea that now Mirtôon hight,
There hang the wheeles once won by crafte of falser axel tree,
And every other conquests note, here leeful is to see
The Phrygian tyre of Pelops head : the spoyle of enmies heere,
And of Barbarian triumphe left, the paynted gorgeous geere.
A lothsome springe stands under shade, and slouthfull course doth take,
With water blacke : even such as is : of yrkesome Stygian lake
The ugly wave whereby art wont, to sweare the gods on hye.
Here all the night the grisly ghosts and gods of death to crie
The fame reportes : with clinkyng chaynes resounds the wood ech where
The sprights cry out : and every thinge that dredfull is to heare,
May there bee seene : of ugly shapes from olde Sepulchres sent
A fearefull flocke doth wander there, and in that place frequent
Worse things then ever yet were knowwne : ye all the wood full ofte
With flame is woont to flash, and all the higher trees alofte

Without a fyre do burne : and ofte the wood beside all this
With triple barkyng roares at once : ful oft the palaice is
Affright with shapes, nor lighte of day may on the terrour quell.
Eternall night doth hold the place, and darknes there of hell
In mid day raignes : from hens to them that pray, out of the ground
The certayne answers geven are, what tyme with dredful sound
From secret place the fates be tolde, and dungeon roares within
While of the God breakes out the voyce : whereto when entred in
Fierce Atreus was, that did wyth him his brothers children trayle,
Dekt are the aulters : who (alas) may it enough bewayle ?
Behynde the infants backs anone he knyt theyr noble hands,
And eke theyr heavy heads about he bound with purple bands :
There wanted there no Frankensence, nor yet the holy wine,
Nor knyfe to cut the sacrifice, besprinkt with levens fine,
Kept is in all the order due, least such a mischiefe gret
Should not be ordred well. Ch. Who doth his hand on sword then set ?
Me. He is him selfe the priest, and he himselfe the deadly verse
With prayer dyre from fervent mouth doth syng and oft reherse.
And he at th' aulters stands himselfe, he them assygn'de to dye
Doth handle, and in order set, and to the knyfe applye,
He lights the fyres, no rights were left of sacrifice undone.
The woode then quakt, and all at once from trembling grounde anone
The Pallace beckt, in doubt which way the payse thereof woulde fall,
And shaking as in waves it stoode : from th' ayre and there-withall
A blasing starre that foulest trayne drew after him doth goe :
The wynes that in the fyres were cast, with chaunged licour floe,
And turne to bloud : and twyse or thryse th' attyre fell from his hed,
The Iverye bright in Temples seem'de to weepe and teares to shed,
The sights amas'de all other men, but stedfast yet alway
Of mynde, unmoved Atreus stands, and even the Gods doth fray
That threaten him and all delay forsaken by and by
To th' aulters turnes, and therewithall a syde he lookes awry.

THE SECOND TRAGEDY

As hungry Tygre wonts that doth in gengey woods remayne
With doubtfull pace to range and roame betweene the bullocks twayne,
Of eyther pray full covetous and yet uncertayne where
She fyrst may byte, and roaring throate now turnes the tone to teare
And then to th' other strayght returnes, and doubtfull famyne holdes :
So Atreus dyre, betwene the babes doth stand and them beholdes
On whom he poynctes to slake his yre : first slaughter where to make,
Hee doubts : or whom he shoulde agayne for second offring take,
Yet skills it nought, but yet he doubtes and such a cruelty
It him delights to order well. Ch. Whom take he fyrst to dy ?
Me. First place, least in him thinke yee might no piete to remayne
To graundsier dedicated is, fyrst Tantalus is slayne.
Ch. With what a minde and count'nesice, could the boy his death sustayne ?
Me. All careles of him selfe he stoode, nor once he would in vayne
His prayers leese. But Atreus fierce the sword in him at last
In deepe and deadly wound doth hide to hilts, and gryping fast
His throate in hand, he thrust him through. The sword then drawne away
When long the body had uphelde it selfe in doubtfull stay,
Which way to fall, at length upon the unckle downe it falles.
And then to th' aulters cruelly Philisthenes he tralles,
And on his brother throwes : and strayght his necke of cutteth hee.
The Carcase headlong falles to ground : a piteous thing to see,
The mourning head with murmure yet uncertayne doth complayne.
Chor. What after double death doth he and slaughter then of twayne ?
Spares he the Child ? or gilt on gilt agayne yet heapeth he ?
Mess. As long maynd Lyon feerce amid the wood of Armenie,
The drove pursues and conquest makes of slaughter many one,
Though now defyled be his jawes with bloud and hunger gone
Yet slaketh not his yreful rage with bloud of Bulles so great,
But slouthful now with weary tooth the lesser Calves doth threate

None other wyse doth Atreus rage, and swelles with anger straynd,
And holding now the sword in hand, with double slaughter staynd,
Regarding not where fell his rage, with cursed hand unmild
He strake it through his body quite, at bosome of the Child
The blade goeth in, and at the backe agayne out went the same,
He falles and quenching with his bloud the aulters sacred flame,
Of eyther wound at length he dieth. CHOR. O heynous hateful act.
MESS. Abhorre ye this ? ye heare not yet the end of all the fact,
There followes more. CHOR. A fiercer thing, or worse then this to see
Could Nature beare ? ME. Why thinke ye this of gylt the end to be ?
It is but part. CHOR. What could he more ? to cruel beastes he cast
Perhappes their bodyes to be torne, and kept from fyres at last.
ME. Would God he had : that never tombe the dead might over hyde,
Nor flames dissolve, though them for food to foules in pastures wyde
He had out throwen, or them for pray to cruell beastes would flinge.
That which the worst was wont to be, were here a wished thing,
That them their father saw untombd : but oh more cursed crime
Uncredible, the which denye will men of after tyme :
From bosomes yet alive out drawne the trembling bowels shake,
The vaynes yet breath, the feareful hart doth yet both pant and quake :
But he the stringes doth turne in hand, and destenies beholde,
And of the guttes the sygnes each one doth vewe not fully cold.
When him the sacrifyce had pleasd, his diligence he puttes
To dresse his brothers banquet now : and streight a sonder cuttes
The bodyes into quarters all, and by the stoompes anone
The shoulders wyde, and brawnes of armes he strikes of everychone.
He layes abroad their naked lims, and cuts away the bones :
The onely heads he kepes and handes to him committed once.
Some of the guttes are broacht, and in the fyres that burne full sloe
They drop, the boyling licour fome doth tomble to and froe
In moorning cawderne : from the flesh that overstandes aloft
The fyre doth flye, and skatter out and into chimney ofte

Up heapt agayne, and there constraynd by force to tary yet
Unwilling burnes : the liver makes great noyse upon the spit,
Nor easely wot I, if the flesh, or flames they be that cry,
But crye they do : the fyre like pitch it fumeth by and by :
Nor yet the smoke it selfe so sad, like flithy miste in sight
Ascendeth up as wont it is, nor takes his way upright,
But even the Gods and house it doth with fylthy fume defile.
O pacient Phœbus though from hence thou backeward flee the whyle,
And in the midst of heaven above dost drowne the broken day,
Thou fleest to late : the father eats his children, well away,
And limmes to which he once gave life, with cursed jaw doth teare.
He shynes with oyntment shed ful sweete all round about his heare,
Replete with wyne : and oftentymes so cursed kynd of food
His mouth hath held, that would not downe, but yet this one thing good
In all thy yls (Thyestes) is that them thou dost not knoe,
And yet shal that not long endure, though Titan backward goe
And chariots turne agaynst himselfe, to meete the wayes he went,
And heavy night so heynous deede to kepe from sight be sent,
And out of tyme from East aryse, so foule a fact to hyde,
Yet shall the whole at length be seene : thy ylles shall all be spide

CHORUS

Which way O Prince of landes and Gods on hie,
At whose uprise eftsones of shadowd night
All beawty fleeth, which way turnst thou awrye ?
And drawest the day in midst of heaven to flight ?
Why dost thou (Phœbus) hide from us thy sight ?
Not yet the watch that later howre bringes in,
Doth Vesper warne the Starres to kindle light.
Not yet doth turne of Hespers whele begin
To loase thy chare his well deserved way.
The trumpet third not yet hath blowen his blast
Whyle toward the night beginnes to yeld the day :
Great wonder hath of sodayne suppers hast

The Plowman yet whose Oxen are untierd.
From woonted course of Heaven what drawes thee back?
What causes have from certayne race conspierd
To turne thy horse? do yet from dongeon black
Of hollow hell, the conquerd Gyantes prove
A fresh assaut? doth Tityus yet assay
With trenched hart, and wounded wombe to move
The former yres? or from the hil away
Hath now Typhœus wound his syde by might?
Is up to heaven the way erected hie
Of phlegrey foes by mountaynes set upright?
And now doth Ossa Pelion overlye?
The wonted turnes are gone of day and night,
The ryse of Sunne, nor fall shal be no more,
Aurora dewish mother of the light
That wontes to send the horses out before,
Doth wonder much agayne returne to see,
Her dawning light: she wots not how to ease
The weary wheeles, nor manes that smoaking be
Of horse with sweate to bathe amid the seas.
Himselfe unwonted there to lodge likewise,
Doth setting sonne agayne the morning see,
And now commaundes the darkenes up to ryse,
Before the night to come prepared bee.
About the Poale yet glowth no fyre in sight.
Nor light of Moone the shades doth comfort yet.
What so it be, God graunt it be the night.
Our hartes do quake with feare oppressed gret,
And dreadfull are least heaven and earth and all
With fatall ruine shaken shall decay:
And least on Gods agayne, and men shall fall
Disfigurde Chaos: and the land away
The Seas, and Fyres, and of the glorious Skife
The wandring lampes, least nature yet shal hide.
Now shall no more with blase of his uprise,
The Lord of starres that leades the world so wyde,
Of Sommer both and Winter geve the markes,
Nor yet the Moone with Phœbus flames that burnes,

Shall take from us by night the dreadful carkes,
With swifter course or passe her brothers turnes,
While compasse lesse the fets in croked race :
The Gods on heaps shal out of order fall,
And each with other mingled be in place.
The wryed way of holy planets all,
With path a slope that doth devide the Zones.
That beares the sygnes, and yeares in course doth brynge
Shall see the starres with him fall downe at ones.
And he that first not yet with gentle spring,
The temperate Gale doth geve to sayles, the Ramme
Shall headlong fall adowne to Seas agayne,
Through which he once with fearefull Hellen swam.
Next him the Bull that doth with horne sustayne
The systers seven with him shall overturne
The twins and armes of croked Cancer all,
The Lyon hoat that wontes the soyle to burne
Of Hercules agayne from heaven shall fall.
To landes once left the Virgin shall be throwne,
And leveld payse of balance sway alow,
And draw with them the stinging Scorpion downe.
So likewyse he that holdes in Thessale bowe
His swift wel fethred arrowes Chiron old,
Shal breake the same and eke shal lese his shotte
And Capricorne that bringes the winter cold
Shall overturne and breake the water pot
Who so thou be : and downe with thee to grounde,
The last of all the sygnes shal Pisces fall
And monsters eake in seas yet never drounde,
The water gulph shal overwhelme them all.
And he which doth betwene each ursa glyde,
Lyke croked flood the slipper serpent twynde :
And lesser Beare by greater Dragons syde,
Full cold with frost congealed hard by kinde,
And carter dull that slowly guides his waine
Unstable shall Boôtes fall from hye.
We are thought meete of all men whom agayn
Should hugy heape of Chaos overly.

And world oppresse with overturned masse
The latest age now falleth us uppon.
With evil hap we are begot alas
If wretches we have lost the sight of sonne,
Or him by fraught enforced have to flye
Let our complayntes yet goe and feare be past :
He greedy is of life, that wil not die
When all the world shall end with him at last.

THE FIFTE ACTE

ATREUS *alone*

OWE equall with the Starres I goe, beyond each other wight,
With haughty heade the heavens above, and highest Poale I smite.
The kingdome nowe, and seate I holde, where once my father raynd :
I nowe lette goe the gods : for all my wil I have obtaynde
Enoughe and well, ye even enough for me I am acquit
But why enough ? I wil procede and fyl the father yet
With bloud of his least any shame should me restrayne at all,
The day is gone, go to therfore whyle thee the heaven doth call.
Would God I could agaynst their wils yet hold the Goddes that flee
And of revenging dish constrayne them witnesses to bee :
But yet (which wel enough is wrought) let it the father see.
In spighte of al the drowned day I will remove from thee
The darknesse all, in shade wherof do lurke thy miseryes.
And guest at such a banquet now to long he careles lyes,
With mery face : now eate and drunke enough he hath at last.
T'ys best him selfe should know his ylls, ye servauntes all in hast
Undoe the temple dores : and let the house bee open all :
Fayne would I see, when loke uppon his childrens heads he shal
What countenaunce he then would make, or in what woordes break out
Would first his griefe, or how would quake his body round about
With spright amased sore : of all my worke the fruite were this
I would him not a miser see, but while so made he is,
Behold the temple opened now doth shyne with many a light :
In glitteryng gold and purple seate he sittes hymselfe upright,

And staying up his heavy head with wyne uppon his hand,
He belcheth out, now chiefe of goddes in highest place I stand,
And king of kinges : I have my wish, and more then I could thinke
He filled is, he now the wyne in silver bolle doth drinke
And spare it not : there yet remaynes a worser draught for thee
That sprong out of the bodyes late of sacrifyces three,
Which wyne shall hyde let therwithall the boordes be taken up.
The father (mingled with the wyne) his childrens bloud shall sup,
That would have dronke of myne. Behold he now beginnes to
strayne
His voyce, and synges, nor yet for joy his mynde he may refrayne.

THE SECONDE SCEANE

THIESTES *alone*

O BEATEN bosomes dullde so longe with woe,
Laie down your cares, at length your greves relent
Let sorowe passe, and all your dread let goe,
And fellow eke of fearefull banishment,
Sad povertye and ill in misery
The shame of cares, more whense thy fall thou haste,
Then whether skylles, great hap to him, from hye
That falles, it is in surety to be plast
Beneath, and great it is to him agayne
That prest with storme of evylls feeles the smart,
Of kyngedome loste the payses to sustaine
With necke unbowde nor yet detect of heart
Nor overcome, his heavy haps alwayes
To beare upright but now of carefull carkes
Shake of the showres, and of thy wretched dayes
Away with all the myserable markes.
To joyfull state returne thy chearefull face.
Put fro thy mynde the olde Thyestes hence.
It is the woont of wight in wofull case,
In state of joy to have no confidence.
Though better haps to them returned be,
Thafflicted yet to joy it yrketh sore.

Why calst thou me abacke, and hyndrest me
This happy day to celebrate ? wherefore
Bidst thou me (sorrow) wepe without a cause ?
Who doth me let with flowers so fresh and gay,
To decke my hayres ? it lets and me withdrawes.
Downe from my head the roses fall away :
My moysted haire with oyntment over all,
With sodayne mase standes up in wondrous wyse,
From face that would not weepe the streames do fall.
And howling cryes amid my wordes aryse.
My sorrowe yet thaccustomd teares doth love
And wretches stil delyght to weepe and crye.
Unpleasant playntes it pleaseth them to move :
And florisht fayre it likes with Tyrian die
Their robes to rent, to waile it likes them still
For sorrow sendes (in signe that woes draw nie)
The mind that wots before of after yll.
The sturdy stormes the shipmen over lye.
When voyd of wynd thasswaged seas do rest.
What tumult yet or countenaunce to see
Makste thou mad man ? at length a trustful breast
To brother gene, what ever now it be,
Causeles, or els to late thou art a dred.
I wretch would not so feare, but yet me drawes
A trembling terrour : downe myne eyes do shed
Their sodayne teares and yet I know no cause.
Is it a greefe, or feare ? or els hath teares great joy it selfe.

THE THIRDE SCEANE

ATREUS, THYESTES

Lette us this daye with one consente (O brother celebrate)
This daye my sceptors may confyrme, and stablish my estate,
And faythfull bonde of peace and love betwene us ratifye.
Thy. Enough with meate and eke with wyne, now satisfyed am I.

But yet of all my joyes it were a great encrease to mee,
If now about my syde I might my litle children see.
Atr. Beleeve that here even in thyne armes thy children present be.
For here they are, and shalbe here, no part of them fro thee
Sal be withhelde : their loved lookes now geve to thee I wil,
And with the heape of all his babes, the father fully fyll.
Thou shalt be glutted feare thou not : they with my boyes as yet
The joyful sacrifyces make at borde where children sit.
They shalbe cald, the frendly cup now take of curtesy
With wyne upfylde. Thy. Of brothers feast I take ful willingly
The fynal gyft, shed some to gods of this our fathers lande,
Then let the rest be dronke, what's this ? in no wyse wil my hand
Obeye : the payse increaseth sore, and downe myne arme doth
sway.
And from my lippes the wasting wyne it selfe doth flye away,
And in deceived mouth, about my jawes it runneth rounde.
The table to, it selfe doth shake and leape from trembling ground.
Scant burnes the fyre : the ayre it selfe with heavy chere to sight
Forsooke of sonne amased is betweene the day and night.
What meaneth this ? yet more and more of backward beaten skye
The compas falles, and thicker myst the world doth overly
Then blackest darkenes, and the night in night it selfe doth hyde.
All starres be fled, what so it bee my brother God provyde
And soones to spare : the Gods so graunt that all this tempest fall
On this vyle head : but now restore to me my children all.
Atr. I wil, and never day agayne shal them from thee withdraw.
Thy. What tumult tumbleth so my guttes, and doth my bowels
gnaw ?
What quakes within ? with heavy payse I feele my selfe opprest,
And with an other voyce then myne bewayles my doleful brest :
Come nere my sonnes, for you now doth thunhappy father call :
Come nere, for you once seene, this griefe would soone asswage and
fall.
Whence murmure they ? Atr. With fathers armes embrace them
quickly now
For here they are loe come to thee : dost thou thy children know ?
Thy. I know my brother : such a gylt yet canst thou suffer well
O earth to beare ? nor yet from hence to Stygian lake of hell

Dost thou both browne thy selfe and us ? nor yet with broaken ground
Dost thou these kingdomes and their king with Chaos rude confounde ?
Nor yet uprenting from the soyle the bowres of wicked land,
Dost thou Micenas overturne with Tantalus to stand,
And aunciters of ours, if there in hel be any one,
Now ought we both : now from the frames on eyther syde anone
Of ground, all here and there rent up out of thy bosome depe :
Thy dens and dungeons set abrode, and us enclosed keepe,
In bottome low of Acheront above our heds aloft
Let wander all the gylty ghostes, with burning frete ful oft
Let fyry Phlegethon that drives his sands both to and fro
To our confusion overroon and vyolently flow.
O slothful soyle unshaken payse unmoved yet art thou ?
The Gods are fled. Atr. But take to thee with joy thy children now,
And rather them embrace : at length thy children all of thee
So long wisht for (for no delay there standeth now in mee)
Enjoy and kisse embracing armes devyde thou unto three.
Thy. Is this thy league ? may this thy love and fayth of brother bee ?
And doost thou so repose thy hate ? the father doth not crave
His sonnes alive (which might have bene without thy gylt) to have
And eke without thy hate, but this doth brother brother pray :
That them he may entoombe restore, whom see thou shalt strayght waye,
Be burnt : the father naught requires of thee that have he shall,
But soone forgoe. Atr. What ever part yet of thy children all
Remaynes, here shalt thou have : and what remayneth not thou hast.
Thy. Lye they in fieldes, a food out flong for fleeyng fowles to wast ?
Or are they kept a pray, for wyld and brutish beastes to eate ?
Atr. Thou hast devourd thy sonnes and fyld thy selfe with wicked meat.
Thy. Oh this is it that sham'de the Gods and day from hence did dryve
Turn'd back to east, alas I wretch what waylinges may I geve ?

Or what complayntes ? what woeful woordes may be enough for mee ?
Their heads cut of, and handes of torne, I from their bodyes see,
And wretched feete from broken thighes I here behold agayn
Tys this that greedy father could not suffer to sustayne.
In belly roll my bowels round, and cloased cryme so great
Without a passage stryves within and seekes away to get.
Thy sword (O brother) lend to me much of my bloud alas
It hath : let us therwith make way for all my sonnes to passe.
Is yet the sword from me withheld ? thy selfe thy bosoms teare,
And let thy brestes resound with stroakes : yet wretch thy hand forbeare
And spare the deade : who ever saw such mischiefe put in proofe ?
What rude Heniochus that dwels by ragged coast aloofe,
Of Caucasus unapt for men ? or feare to Athens, who
Procustes wyld ? the father I oppress my children do
And am opprest, is any meane of gylt or mischiefe yet ?
Atr. I meane in mischiefe ought to be when gylt thou dost commit,
Not when thou quytst : for yet even this to litle seemes to me.
The blood yet warme even from the wound I should in sight of thee
Even in thy jawes have shed, that thou the bloud of them mightst drinke
That lyved yet : but whyle to much to hast my hate I thinke
My wrath beguyled is my selfe with sword the woundes them gave
I strake them downe, the sacred fyres with slaughter vowde I have
Wel pleasd, the carcase cutting then, and liveles lymmes on grounde.
I have in litle parcels chopt, and some of them I drounde
In boyling cauderns, some to fyres that burnte ful slow I put,
And made to droppes their synewes all, and limmes a two I cut
Even yet alyve and on the spitte, that thrust was through the same
I harde the liver wayle and crye, and with my hand the flame
I oft kept in : but every whit the father might of this
Have better done, but now my wrath so lightly ended is.
He rent his sonnes with wicked gumme, himselfe yet wotting naught,
Nor they therof. Thy. O ye encloas'd with bending bankes abought
All seas me heare, and to this gylt ye Gods now harken well
What ever place ye fled are to here all ye sprites of hel,

And here ye landes, and night so darke that them dost overly
With clowde so blacke: to my complayntes do thou thy selfe apply.
To thee now left I am, thou dost alone me miser see,
And thou art left without thy starres: I wil not make for me
Peticions yet, nor ought for me require may ought yet bee
That me should vayle? for you shal all my wishes now foresee.
Thou guyder great of skyes above, and prince of highest might,
Of heavenly place now all with cloudes ful horrible to sight,
Enwrap the worlde, and let the wyndes on every syde breake out:
And send the dredfull thunderclap through al the world about
Not with what hand thou gyltles house and undeserved wall
With lesser bolt are wonte to beate, but with the which did fall
The three unheaped mountaynes once and which to hils in height
Stoode equall up, the gyantes huge: throuw out such weapons streight,
And flyng thy fires: and therwithall revenge the drowned day.
Let flee thy flames, the light thus lost and hid from heaven away,
With flashes fyll: the cause (lest long thou shouldst doubte whom to hit)
Of ech of us is ill: if not at least let myne be it.
Me strike with tryple edged toole thy brande of flaminge fyre
Beate through this breast: if father I my children do desyre
To lay in tombe or corpses cast to fyre as doth behove,
I must be burnt if nothing now the gods to wrath may move,
Nor powre from skies with thunderbolt none strikes the wicked men
Let yet eternall night remayne, and hyde with darknes then
The world about: I Titan naught complayne as now it standes,
If stil thou hyde thee thus away. ATR. Now prayse I well my handes,
Now got I have the palme. I had bene overcome of thee,
Except thou sorrow'dst so but now even children borne to mee
I compt and now of bridebed chast the fayth I do repayre.
THY. In what offended have my sons: ATR. In that, that thyne they were.
THY. Setst thou the sonnes for fathers foode? ATR. I do and (which is best)
The certayne sonnes. THY. The gods that guyde all infantes I protest.

ATR. What wedlock gods? THY. Who would the gilt with gylt so quite again?
ATR. I know thy greefe prevented now with wrong thou dost complayne:
Nor this thee yrkes, that fed thou art with food of cursed kind,
But that thou hadst not it prepard for so it was thy mynd,
Such meates as these to set before thy brother wotting naught,
And by the mothers helpe to have likewyse my children caught:
And them with such like to slay: this one thing letted thee,
Thou thought'st them thine. THY. The gods shall al of this revengers be
And unto them for vengeance due my vowes thee render shall.
ATR. But vext to be I thee the whyle, geeve to thy children all.

THE FOURTH SCENE

Added to the Tragedy by the Translatour

THYESTES *alone*

O KYNG of Dytis dungeon darke, and grysly Ghosts of hell,
That in the deepe and dredfull Denne, of blackest Tartare dwell.
Where leane and pale dyseases lye, where feare and famyne are,
Where discord stands with bleeding browes, where every kynde of care,
Where furies fight in beds of steele, and heares of crauling snakes,
Where Gorgon grimme, where Harpyes are, and lothsome Lymbo lakes,
Where most prodigious ugly thinges, the hollowe hell doth hyde,
If yet a monster more myshapt then all that there doe byde,
That makes his broode his cursed foode, yee all abhorre to see,
Nor yet the deepe Averne it selfe, may byde to cover mee,
Nor grisly gates of Putoes place, yet dare them selves to spred,
Nor gaping grounde to swallowe him, whom Gods and day have fled:
Yet breake yee out from cursed seates, and heere remayne with mee,
Yee neede not now to be affrayde, the Ayre and Heaven to see.

Nor triple headed Cerberus, thou needst not bee affryght,
The day unknowne to thee to see or els the lothsome lyght.
They both be fled : and now doth dwell none other count'naunce heere,
Then doth beneath the fowlest face, of hatefull hell appeere.
Come see a meetest match for thee, a more then monstrous wombe,
That is of his unhappy broode, become a cursed tombe.
Flocke here yee fowlest fiendes of hell, and thou O graundsyre greate,
Come see the glutted guts of myne, with such a kinde of meate,
As thou didst once for Gods prepare. Let torments all of hel
Now fall uppon this hatefull head, that hath deservde them well.
Yee all be plagued wrongfully, your guiltes be small, in sight
Of myne, and meete it were your pange on me alone should light.
Now thou O graundsier guiltlesse arte, and meeter were for mee,
With fleeing floud to be beguilde, and fruite of fickle tree.
Thou slewst thy sonne, but I my sonnes, alas, have made my meate.
I coulde thy famyne better beare, my paunch is now repleate
With foode : and with my children three, my belly is extent.
O filthy fowles and gnawyng gripes, that Tytius bosome rent
Beholde a fitter pray for you, to fill your selves uppone
Then are the growing guts of him : foure wombes enwrapt in one
This paunche at once shall fill you all : if yee abhorre the foode,
Nor may your selves abide to bathe, in such a cursed bloode :
Yet lend to me your clinching clawes, your pray a while forbeare,
And with your tallons suffer mee, this monstrous mawe to teare.
Or whirling wheeles, with swinge of which Ixion still is rolde,
Your hookes upon this glutted gorge, would catche a surer holde.
Thou filthy floud of Lymbo lake, and Stygian poole so dyre,
From choaked chanell belche abrode, Thou fearefull freate of fyre,
Spue out thy flames O Phlegethon : and overshed the grounde.
With vomit of thy fyry streame, let me and earth be drownde,
Breake up thou soyle from bottome deepe, and geve thou roome to hell,
That night, where day, the ghosts, where Gods were woont to raigne, may dwel.
Why gapst thou not ? Why do you not O gates of hell unfolde ?
Why do yee thus thinfernall fiendes, so long from hence withholde ?

Are you likewyse affrayde to see, and knowe so wretched wight,
From whom the Gods have wryde theyr lookes, and turned are to flight ?
O hatefull head, whom heaven and hell, have shoonde and left alone,
The Sunne, the starres, the light, the day, the Gods, the ghosts be gone.
Yet turne agayne yee Skyes a while, ere quight yee goe fro mee,
Take vengeance fyrst on him, whose faulte enforceth you to flee.
If needes yee must your flight prepare, and may no longer bide,
But rolle yee must with you forthwith, the Gods and Sunne a syde,
Yet slowly flee : that I at length, may you yet overtake,
While wandring wayes I after you, and speedy jorney make.
By seas, by lands, by woods, by rocks, in darke I wonder shall :
And on your wrath, for right rewarde to due deserts, will call.
Yee scape not fro me, so yee Gods, still after you I goe,
And vengeaunce aske on wicked wight, your thunder bolte to throe.

FINIS

THE

THYRD TRAGEDY OF L. ANNAEUS SENECA

ENTITULED THEBAIS

TRANSLATED OUT OF LATIN INTO ENGLISHE

BY THOMAS NEWTON

1581

THE ARGUMENT

Laius King of Thebes, hadde by his Wyfe and Queene Jocasta, a Sonne named Oedipus: Who being yet in his Mothers Wombe, Apollo his Oracle pronounced, that by the handes of that childe, King Laius the father should bee murthered. The feare whereof caused the King to commaund him to be put to death. The Kinges heardman, who had the charge to see this done, on thone side mooved with compassion over a tender weakeling: and on the other side, afraid to incurre the King his maisters displeasure, contented himselfe onely to boare two hoales through the Infants two feete, and with certayne plyable Twigges beinge thrust through the same, hong him up on a tree by the Heeles: supposing that heereby hee should commit a lesse crime in suffring the childe to perishe by famine, then in playing the Butcher himselfe. It fortuned, that one Phorbas heardman to Polybius King of Corynth, passing by that way and hearing a yong Childe crye, went and cut him downe, and caryinge him to Corynth, it so fell out that at length hee was given for a present or gyft to Merope, Wyfe to the said King Polybus. This Oedipus afterward going to Thebes, in a certayne sedicious hurly burly in the countrey there, unawares and unwitting slewe King Laius his Father. About which tyme the City of Thebes, and Countrey there about was mervelously infested with a monster called Sphinx: who propounding a certaine Riddle, or obscure question to such as passed that way, and devouringe as many, as coulde not assoyle the same. To him that coulde assoile it, and so rid the Countrey from that so ugly and daungerous a monster, the mariage of Queene Jocasta, and the kingdome of Thebes was promysed as a recompence: Oedipus after many others, taking the matter in hand, assoyled the Ryddle, and slew the monster. Whereupon marying the Queene, not knowing her to bee his owne Mother, had by her foure Chyldren: Etheocles, Polynices, Antigone, and Ismene.

THEBAIS

In the end, having knowledge, how first hee had kylled his Father, and then incestuously maryed his Mother, hee forsooke his kingdome being continually infested wyth the plague, and (as one ashamed to loke any man in the face) pulled out his own Eyes, and hid himselfe in corners and solitary places. His Sonnes Etheocles and Polynices agreed to raigne enterchaungeably, that is to wit, Etheocles, one yeare, and Polynices the other. Etheocles having raigned his yeare, refused according to the articles of agrement, to resigne the Crowne to his brother for the next yeare. Whereupon they fel to mortal warres, and in the end meaning by combat to ende the matter, they mutually slew one the other. And note that this Tragedy, was left by the Authour unperfect, because it neyther hath in it, Chorus, ne yet the fifth Acte.

THE NAMES OF THE SPEAKERS

ŒDIPUS.	ANTIGONE.
NUNTIUS.	JOCASTA.

THE FIRST ACTE

ŒDIPUS, ANTIGONE

EARE Daughter, unto Father blynde a Staffe of steady stay,
To weary Syre, a comfort greate, and Guide in all his way :
And whom to have begotten, I may glad and joyfull bee :
Yet leave me now, thy haplesse Syre, thus plungde in misery.
Why seekst thou meanes, still to direct my stalking steppes aright ?
Let mee I pray thee headlong slyde in breaknecke tumbling plight.
I better shall and sooner fynde a way my selfe alone
To rid mee out of all the thrall wherein I now am throwne.
Whereby both heaven shall eased bee, and earth shall want the sight
Of mee vile wretch, whom guilt hath made a most abhorred wight.
Alas, what litle triffling tricke hath hitherto bene wrought
By these my hands ? what feate of worth or maistry have I sought ?
In deede, they have me helpt to pull myne eyes out of my head :
So that ne Sunne, ne Moone I see, but life in darknesse lead.
And though that I can nothing see, yet is my guilt and cryme
Both seene and knowne, and poyncted at, (woe worth the cursed tyme,)
Leave of thy hold, let lose thy hand, good daughter, let mee goe :
Let foultring foote light where it will, let it (this once) be so.
Ile trudge, and runne, Ile skudde, and raunge, Ile hasten to the hill
Of craggy stiepe Cytheron, there I hope to worke my will.
Where earst Acteon lost his lyfe by straunge, and uncouth death,
Whom bawling Dogges, and hunting Hounds bereft of vitall breath :

THEBAIS

THE FIRST ACTE

Where once Agave (bedlemitke) raunged up and downe the woode
With Systers hers, enspired all with Bacchus raging moode.
And pleasing well her selfe in that her fact and mischiefe donne,
Pitcht on a Poale the grisly head of him that was her Sonne.
Where Zethus with his ruffling Crew of Gallantes young and stoute
Dragd, hald, and puld, the hateful corps of Dirce, all aboute.
Where bushie bloudied brambles show which way the Bull her drew :
Nere where dame Ino from a Rocke her selfe in Sea downe threw.
So that poore mother though she ment t' avoyde one fault by flight :
Yet she therby a worse procur'd, while like a seely wight
She both her selfe and eke her sonne from Scyron hurled downe
Entending both her selfe and him in foaming Sea to drowne.
Oh happy, yea thryse happy they, that had so good an hap :
And whom such mothers pitiful earst dandled in theyr lap.
Yea yet there is in these same woods an other place to mee
Thats due by right, and rightly may me challenge as his fee.
Where I an Infant out was layed, at Fortunes to abide :
I thyther wil direct my course to try what may bëtyde.
Ile neither stop ne stay til that I be arryved there,
For guyde I recke not, neyther force for Stumbling any where.
Why stay I thus like dastard drudge to hasten unto it ?
Sith wel I know it lotted is to be my grave and Pit ?
Let me myne owne Cytheron mount enjoy in quiet state,
It is myne old and auncient bower, appoynted me by fate.
I pray thee be not discontent that I should (aged) die,
Even there, where life I should have lost in pueling infancy.
I yeild me heere with willing hart unto those tortures all
That earst to me were due, and which to others have befall :
To thee I speake O bloudy mount, fierce, cruel, slyepe and fell,
As well in that thou sparest some, as that thou some dost quell.
This carion corps, this sinful soule, this carcasse here of myne
Long tyme agone by right good Law and propertye is thine.
Now yet at length perfourme the hest that earst enjoyned was
To thee by those my parentes both, now bring their doome to passe.
My hart even longeth till I may so fully satisfy
By this my death that their decree, that glad I am to die.

Ah Daughter, Daughter, why wouldst thou thus keepe mee gaynst my mynd ?
In this so vile incestuous love ? thou art but now to kind.
Oh stay me not I thee desire, behold, behold, I heare
My Fathers ghost to bidde me come apace, and not to feare.
O Father myne I come, I come, now father ceasse thy rage :
I know (alas) how I abus'd my Fathers hoary age :
Who had to name King Laius : how hee doth fret and frye
To see such lewd disparagement : and none to blame but I.
Wherby the Crowne usurped is, and he by murther slayne.
And Bastardly incestuous broode in Kingly throne remayne.
And loe, dost thou not playnly see, how he my panting Ghost
With raking pawes doth hale and pull, which grieves my conscience most ?
Dost thou not see how he my face bescratcheth tyrant wyse ?
Tel mee (my Daughter) hast thou seene Ghostes in such griesly guyse ?
ANTIG. I see and marke each thing ful well. Good father leave this mind,
And take a better if you can : from this your selfe unwynd.
ŒD. O what a beastly cowardise is in this breast of myne ?
Was I so stout and venturous in pulling out myne Eyen ?
And shall all courage be employd agaynst one onely part
Of Body, and from other partes shall valour wholly start ?
Let none of all these puling trickes nor any faint excuse
Thus daunt thy sprites, let no delay to basenes thee enduce :
Dispatch at once, why lingre I, as one thats loth to dye ?
Why live I ? ist because I can no longer mischieves trye ?
Yes that I can, wretch though I be : and therfore tel I thee,
Deare Daughter, that the sooner thou mightst hence depart from mee.
Depart a mayd and Virgin hence, for feare of afterclaps :
Since villany to Mother shewde, its good to doubt mishaps.
ANTIG. No force, no power, no violence, shall make me to withdraw
My duty unto thee my Syre, to whom I vow myne awe.
I will not be dissevered, ne pulled from thy syde
I will assist thee, whyle that breath shal in this Breast abyde.

THEBAIS

THE FIRST ACTE

My Brothers twayne let them contend, and fight for Princelye swaye
Of wealthy Thebes: where whilom raignd King Labdacke many a day.
The greatest share and portion that I do loke to have
Out of my Fathers Kingdome, is my Fathers lyfe to save.
Him neither shall Etheocles my elder brother take
Away from mee, who now by force the Thebane realme doth rake.
Ne Polynices, who as now is Mustring men apace
From Argos Land: with ful entent his brother to displace.
No, though the world went all on wheeles: though Jove should from above
Hurle flashing flakes upon the Earth, all shall not quayle my love.
No, though his thumping thunderbolt (when wee togeather stand)
Should light betweene us, where as we are plighted hand in hand)
Yet wil I never thee forsake, but hold my handfast still:
Therefore its booteles father deare, to countermaund my will
In this my full resolved mynd. Forbid me if you please,
But surely I will be your guide in weale, woe, dole, and ease.
And maugre al your sharpe reprofes (though much against your mind)
I wil direct your steppes and gate, that you your way may fynd:
Through thick and thinne, through rough and smoth I wil be at an ynch
In hill and dale, in wood and grove, Ile serve at ev'ry pinch.
If that you goe where daunger lies, and seeke your owne annoy,
You shall wel prove, that I to leade the daunce wil not be coy.
Advyse your selfe therfore, of twayne to which I guyde shall be:
My count is cast, I am ful bent with you to live and die.
Without me perish can you not: but with me, wel you may,
It booteth not, in other sort to move me ought to saye.
Here is an huyge Promontory that elboes into Sea
Let us from thence throw downe our selves, and worke our last decay,
If that ye wil. Here also is a flinty Rocke besyde,
Which if you please shal serve our turnes: Heere beaten with the tyde

Bee craggy Cliffes, let 's goe to them : Here runnes a gulphy streame
With force afore it dryving stones as bigge as mountaine beame.
What say you ? shall wee drench our selves within this fomy Flood ?
Goe where you wil, take which you list, do as you deeme it good.
Conditionally that I may first receyve the wound of death :
I recke no whit, I ready stand to yeld up vitall breath.
I neyther draw you to nor froe : but even as best you thinke
So doe, so deale. Would you so fayne Deathes bitter cup to drinke ?
My lord and Father, take you death so greate a boone to bee ?
If that you dye (this I assure) die first you shall me see.
If life in shew more pleasaunt seme, if so you rather chuse,
I am to wayte upon you still and never wil refuse.
But chaunge this mynde wherein you rest, take hart a grace, and show
The noble magnanimity that earst in you did flow :
Resist these panges, subdue these dumpes by valour of the mynd,
Let manly courage qualify these your affections blynd.
Tis great dishonor thus to yeeld your selfe to dolor thrall,
No storme of adverse hap thus ought a Princes hart t' appall.
ŒD. This geare surmounteth far the reach of my capacity :
I am astonn'd, I feele my selfe rapt with an extasie,
Is this not wonder of so lewd, and of so curst a tree
Such fruite to grow ? of graceles Syre so good a child to see ?
Is it not straunge that in a house distaynd in villany
Such noble shew of towardnes and vertuous gyftes should lye ?
Let me some speach to thee direct, dame Fortune : how haps this
That here my daughter so unlike to wretched father is ?
Degenerating from his steps, and with such vertue fraught,
As in her Fathers cursed house she never yet was taught ?
Is it (I pray thee) credible, that out of me should spring
Such Yssue, as should geven be to any honest thinge ?
No truely, no : it cannot bee (my fates ful wel I know)
None such, (unlesse to doe me scath and mischiefe) would be so.
T' encrease the heape of myne annoy no straunge effect shall want :
Dame Nature in her Creatures wil new effectes emplant.

THEBAIS

THE FIRST ACTE

The Ryver shall returne his course to Fountayne backe agayne,
Dan Phœbus Lamp shall bring the Night, and Night shal day remain,
So that my grievous miseryes with surplusage may grow,
But be as tis : I for a whyle wil play my part also,
And shew some sparke of piety, my fault to countervayle :
With murtdrous knife, my woeful dayes to end I wil not fayle,
The onely helpe for Oedipus, the onely safety is
To ridde himselfe, and so redeeme that Hellish fact of his.
Let mee take vengeance on my selfe for wronges to father donne,
Whose Death is yet unexpiate, by mee his cursed sonne.
Why dost thou shake and tremble thus thou hand, not good for ought ?
Why staggrest thou to stabbe him in, who Syre to spoyle hath brought ?
That punishment which hetherto by pulling out myne eyes
Thou hast inflicted on me, is but as a sacrifyce,
Or guerdon due for villany which I committed have
With mother-myne. Now Daughter stoute, leave of pretences brave,
Alledge no gloses : but with speede let goe thy Fathers hand :
Thou mak'st me die a lingring death within this loathed land.
Thou thinkst I am alive, but I am dead long while agoe :
To this my hateful Corps at length the rytes of Buriall show.
Thou meanest well, (I know) but yet therin thou dost offend :
Though colour for thy piety I see thou dost pretend.
But piety it canot be, to dragge thus up and downe
Thy Fathers Corpes unburied through City, Field, and Towne.
For hee that doth enforce a man agaynst his will to dye :
And he that stayeth him that would fayne dye, most willingly,
Are both alike in equall fault, and stand in egallt plight.
To hinder one that would be dead is murthring him outright.
Yet not so great as thother is. I would be more content
To have my death commaunded me, then from me to be bent.
Desist from this thy purpose (Mayd) my lyfe and death both are
To dispose at my liberty, with choyse to spill or spare,
I willingly resignd the Crowne of Thebane soyle : yet I
Do still retaine upon my selfe the entyre Soveraygntye.

If I may make accompt of thee as of a trusty feere,
And true compagnion at assayes : deliver even heere
Into thy Fathers hand a Sweard : but tell me, dost thou reach
The Sword embrewd in fathers bloud, wherewith my sonnes empeach
The course of Law, possessing it and kingdome all by force ?
Where so it is, doubt is there none, but cleane without remorse
There bee the Floudgates opned wyde, to al licencious lust,
And thriftlesse trades : I al my clayme therein do rake in dust,
And cleane forsake. Let both my Sonnes by Legacy enjoy
The same, wherewith they surely shall contrive no smal annoy.
For mee pyle rather up a stacke of wood set all on fyre,
That I therein may thrust my selfe : that is my chiefe desyre :
And make an end at once of all this carrion Carkasse vyle.
Where is the surging wavous Sea ? why stay I all this whyle ?
Bring mee to some stiepe breaknecke fall : bring me where Ismene flood
With swift and horned course doth runne, bring me wheras my blood
With goaryng push of savage beastes may out be let at once.
To some Gulfe bring me, where the fall and tide may crush my Bones.
If needes thou wilt my guyde remayne, as oft thou dost me tell,
Bring me that am dispos'd to dye, where Sphinx that Monster fell
With double shape apposed them that passed by the way,
Propounding Riddles intricate, and after did them slay.
There would I bee, that place I seeke : thy Father thyther bring
Into that Monsters Cabin dire thy Monstrous Father fling.
That though that Monster be dispatcht, the place may bee supplyde
With one as badde or worse then hee : there wil I farre and wyde
In tearmes obscure report and tell my heavy lucklesse lot,
The misteries whereof the hearers understandeth not.
Geve eare to that which I shal speake, marke thou Assyrian borne,
Consider this thou Thebane, where Duke Cadmus men were torne
And slayne in wood by Serpentes rage : where Dirce seely trull
In humble sort at Aulter lies : advert my tale at full
Thou, that in Lacedæmon dwelles, and honorst Castors grace,
And Pollux eake, two brethren twynnes. Fynd out this doubtful case.

THEBAIS

THE FIRST ACTE

Or thou that dwelst in Elis towne or by Parnassus hill,
Or thou that till'st Bæotia ground, there reaping gayne at wil.
Hearke, listen well, and flatly say, if ever heretofore
That murdrous monster Sphinx of Thebes that men in peeces tore,
In all his riddles askt the like, or of so straunge a sort ?
Or whether so insolubly his termes he cold report ?
The Sonne in Law to Graundfather, the Rival of his Syre :
The Brother of his litle Babes : to Brethren, father dire :
The Graundmother at every byrth to Husband (graceles Elfe)
Brought forth a Sonne or Daughter, which was Nephew to her selfe
How say you Syrs, in Ryddle darke, who hath so good insight,
That able is the sense hereof t' unfold and tell aryght ?
As for my selfe, although the Sphinx I whylome put to foyle :
Yet myne owne heavy destenie I scarcely can assoyle.
Why dost thou (Daughter) labour loose in usyng further speech ?
To alter this my stony hart why dost thou mee beseech ?
I tell thee playne, I fully meane this bloud of myne to spill,
That long with Death hath struggling kept : and thereupon I will
Descend to darke infernall Lake : for this same darknes blynd
Of both myne eyes is nothing such, as fact of myne should fynd.
It were my Blisse to bee in Hell in deepest dungeon fast :
Now that which should long since have bene, I wil perfourme at last.
I cannot be debard from Death : wilt thou deny me glave
Or Sword, or knife ? wilt thou no toole for mischiefe let me have ?
Wilt thou both watch and ward each way, where daunger lies in wayte ?
Shall such a sinful Caytife wretch as I, be kept so straite ?
Wilt thou not suffer me with Coard to breake my hatefull Necke ?
Canst thou kepe mee from poysonous herbes ? hast thou them al at beck ?
What shall it thee prevayle to take for mee such earnest care ?
Death ech where is : and wayes to death in thousand corners are.
Herein hath God good order tane, that every selie Foe,
May take away an others life : but Death hee cannot so.
I seeke not anye toole to have : this desprate mynd of myne
Can use the service of my hand, my threede of lyfe t' untwine.

Now hand, thy maister at a pinch assist to worke his feate,
Helpe him with all thy power and strength, t' exployt his purpose great.
I poynt thee not in this my Corps unto one place alone :
Alas, each part of me with guilt is plaunch and overgrowne.
In which soever part thou wilt, thy Massacre beginne,
And seeke to bring me to my death which way thou mayst it winne.
In pieces crush this body all, this hart that harbors sinne
Pluck out, out all my entrailes pull, proceede, and never linne
To gash and cut my wezand pype. My vaynes asonder scratch,
And make the Bloud come spowting out, or use that other match,
Which heretofore thou used haste : digge where myne eyes earst stood :
And let these woundes gush out apace much mattry filth and blood.
Hale out of mee this loathed soule that is so hard and stout :
And thou deare father Laius stand up and looke about :
Behold where ever that thou standst : I Umpyre doe the make,
And eyed Judge of all my plagues that justly heere I take.
My fact so lewde, so horrible, so loathsome to bee tolde
I never thought with any pryce or tormentes manifolde
Could have full expiation : ne thought I it inough
To die this death : or in one part to be beslashed through.
By piecemeale I am well content to suffer tormentes all
And even by piecemeale for to die : for plagues to plague mee call,
Exact the punishment that 's due : I heere most ready stand
To satisfie with any death that law and righte hath scand.
My former smartes, when as mine eyes I raked out with pawes,
Were but as tastes of sacrifice, somewhat to helpe my cause.
Come therefore (Father) neare to mee, and thrust this hand of myne
More nearer into every wound. It swerv'de and did decline
For feare, when first it tooke th' assay mine eyes to ransacke out.
I beare it still in memory, my eyes then star'de about
And seemed to disswade the hand from doing of the charge
Whereto it was enjoyned tho, and had Commission large.
Thou shalt well thinke that Œdipus dissembleth not a whit
But what his word hath warranted, his deede hath firmely quit.

Thy stoutnes then was not so great when eyes thou pulledst out
As was thy manhoode, when thou threwst them from thee round about.
Now, by those Eyeholes thrust thy hand into the very braine :
That part where death attempted was, let death be sought againe.
AN. Undaunted Prynce, most noble Syre, with humble mynde I sue
That I your Daughter may be bolde to use some speech to you :
And that you would with patience digest my poore advise :
My suite is not to draw your minde to thinges, that earst in price
You highly held, ne to the view of glittring Pallace olde,
Ne bravery of your noble Realme, scarce able to bee tolde :
But that you would these yrefull fittes, by tract of time now quailde,
With patient minde sustayne and beare : this vertue never faylde
In any Prynce of such a spright as in your noble Grace
Appeareth bryght : it fitteth not that such should once abase
Themselves as thralles to Sorrowes checke, or once the conquest yeelde
To adverse hap : or courage loose lyke dastardes in the fielde.
It is no prayse, syr, though perhappes you so your reckening cast
To make of lyfe so small accoumpt, and thus to bee agast
At every wagging of a leafe, and combersome myschaunce :
No, no, tis vertue in such case high courage to advaunce.
And when thinges are at worst, to shew true magnanimitie :
Not lyke a Meycocke, cowardly at eche alarme to flee.
Hee that hath tride all fortunes spight and worldly wealth despisde,
And constantly hath borne all bruntes that are to be devisde,
Mee thinks no cause hath, why he needes to ende his breathing dayes
Or wish himselfe in grave : for why, starcke cravens use such wayes.
But as for him thats drencht in dole and wrapt in carking care,
Whose pensive plight can be no worse, nor tast of sowrer fare,
That man hath cause well pleasde to be : sith hee in safety standes,
And pykes hath past, and now is free from feare of further bandes.
Put case the Gods would weave the webbe of further woe to thee,
What more can any of them doe thy grieves to amplifie ?
Nay, thou thy selfe, (although thou wouldst) canst adde thereto no more,
Unlesse thou thinke thy selfe to have deserved death therefore.

And yet, thou arte not worthy death : my reason is, because
Through ignoraunce thou didst a fact contrary to the lawes.
And therefore Father thinke your selfe most guiltlesse in the case,
And (maugre Gods) stand on your guarde, my counsell sound embrace :
For doubtlesse you an innocent are deem'de and thought to bee,
And are in deede : what makes you thus in dumpes and dolefull glee ?
What cause so great should so enchaunt your conscience, and your wits,
To seeke your owne decay and spoyle ? what meane faint hearted fits ?
That thus in hast you would so faine abandon this your lyfe
And goe to hell, where torment dwelles and grisly ghostes be ryfe.
You would not see Sun, Moone, ne Starre : no more you can : your eyes
Are blynd : you faine would leave your Court, and Countries miseries.
Why so you may, and so you doe. These all are put to sacke,
That now alyve, aswell as dead you feele of these the lacke.
You flee from Mother, Wyfe, and Chylde, you see no man alyve :
What more can death dispatch away but life doth now deprive ?
Your lords, your knights, your courtly traine, your kingly state and crowne
Your graund Affaires, your waighty charge is gone and brought adowne.
From whom, from what, do you thus flee. ŒD. From none but from my selfe
Who have a breast full fraught with guilte : who, wretched caitiffe Elfe
Have all embrude my hands with blood. From these apace I flee
And from the heavens and Gods therein : and from that villanie
Which I most wicked wretch have wrought. Shall I treade on thys ground ?
Or am I worthy so to doe, in whom such trickes abound ?
Am I to have the benefite of any Element ?
Of Ayre for breath, of water moyst, or Earth for nourishment ?
O Slave forlorne, O beastly wretch, O Incestmonger vyle,
O Varlet most detestable, O Paysaunte full of guile.

THEBAIS

THE FIRST ACTE

Why doe I with polluted Fyst, and bloudy pawes presume
To touch thy chast and comely hand ? I foame, I fret, I fume
In hearing any speake to mee. Ought I heare any tell
Or once of Sonne or Father speake, syth I did Father quell ?
Would God it were within my power my Senses all to stop,
Would God I could these Eares of myne, even by the stumps to crop.
If that might bee, then (daughter) I should not have heard thy voyce.
I, I thy Syre, that thee begot by most incestuous choise.
Beegetting of thee, makes my crymes moe then they were before :
Remorse thereof doth gnaw and grype my conscience more and more.
Ofttymes that which myne Eyes not see, with Eares that doe I heare,
And of my Facts afore time done the inward wound I beare.
Why is there stay made of my doome ? Why am I spard so long ?
Why is not this blind head of myne throwne damned ghosts among ?
Why rest I on the Earth, and not among infernall Sprightes ?
Why pester I the company of any mortall Wightes ?
What myschiefe is there more behind ? to aggravate my care ?
My Kingdome, Parents, Children, Wit and Vertue quayled are
By sturdy stormes of froward Fate : nothing remaynde but teares,
And they bee dryde, and Eyes be gon : my hardned heart forbeares
Such signes of grace : leave of therefore, and make no more adoe :
A minde so mated with dispayre no suytes will stowpe unto.
I practize some straunge punishments agreeing to my deede :
But what proportion can bee found of plagues unto my meede ?
Whose Fortune ever was so bad ? I was no sooner borne,
But seely Infant Judged I was in peeces to be torne.
My mother in whose wombe I lay, forth had not mee yet brought
And yet even then I feared was : and straight my death was sought.
Some Babes soone after they bee borne, by stroke of death depart :
But I poore soule, before my byrth adjudged was to dart
Of death : some yet in Mothers wombe, ere any light they see
Doe taste the dint of hasty Fate, while Innocents they bee.
Apollo by his Oracle pronounced sentence dyre
Upon mee being yet unborne, that I unto my Syre

Should beastly parricide commit: and thereupon was I
Condemned straight by Fathers doome. My feete were by and by
Launcde through and through with yron Pins: hangde was I by the Heeles
Upon a Tree: my swelling plants the printe thereof yet feeles:
As pray to Beastes, cast out also, to cramme theyr greedy Jawes
In Mount Cytheron, and to fill the griping Vulturs Mawes.
Such Sauce to tast full lyke was I, as others heeretofore
Descended of the royall Sangue, with smart (perforce) have bore.
But see the chaunce: I thus condemn'de by Dan Apollos hest
And cast to beasts by Fathers doome, and every way distrest,
Coulde finde no death: no death on mee durst seyze his lordly Pawe,
But fled from mee, as though I had not beene within his Lawe.
I verified the Oracle, with wicked hand I kilde
Myne owne deere Father, and unwares his guiltlesse bloud I spilde.
Shall any satisfaction redeeme so vile an Acte?
May any kinde of Piety purge such a shamefull fact?
I rested not contented thus. For Father beeing slayne,
I fell in linkes of lawlesse Love with Mother: Oh what payne
And grudge of minde sustaynde I there? in thinking on the same,
To tell our wicked wedlocke Yoake, I loath, I blush, I shame.
I may not well this geare conceale, Ile tell it: out it shall:
Though to my shame it much redound, it may augment my thrall.
I will display straunge villanies, and them in number many,
Most beastlike parts, most lewde attempts, to bee abhorr'de of any.
So filthy, and so monstruous, that (sure I thinke) no Age
Will them believe to have bene done: so cruell was my rage,
That even ech cutthroate Parricide thereat may be ashamde
To heare it nam'de: and with disdaine straight wayes will be enflamde.
My handes in Fathers bloud embrude to Fathers Bed I brought.
And have with Mother myne, his Wife, incestuous practyse sought.
To myschiefe adding mischiefe more: I wis my fault to Sire
Is slender in comparison: my gracelesse fond desire
Could not bee staide, till solemnely the mariage knot was knit
Twixt mee and Mother myne, alas for want of grace and wit.

THEBAIS

THE FIRST ACTE

How plungde am I in myschiefe still ? how is the measure full
Of horrours vile, which doe my minde and heart asunder pull ?
And least the heape of these my woes might seeme to bee too skant,
My Mother (she my Wyfe that is) yong issue doth not want.
Can any crime in all the World more haynous be surmisde ?
If any may : by wicked Impes the same I have devisde.
My Realme and Crowne I have resignde, which I received as hyre
For murdring most unnaturally the king, my Lord, and Syre,
Which Crowne now since, twixt both my sonnes hath kindled mortall war,
And all the countrey by the ears remains at deadly jarre.
I know ful wel what destenies to this same Crowne belonges.
None without Bloud the same shall weare, and most accursed wrongs.
This mynd of myne (who Father am) presageth many ills :
And gloomy dayes of slaughter dyre : the plot that murther willes,
Already is contriv'd and cast : all truth of word and deede
Is quight exild, al promise broke of pactes afore decreed.
Etheocles, thone of my sonnes who now in princely throne
Beares all the sway, meanes stil to keepe the Diademe alone.
Poore Polynices th' other sonne, thus beyng dispossest,
And kept by force from Kingly rule his humble sute addrest
Unto the Gods this wrong to wreake, this breach of league and oth
T' avenge and plague : he Argos soyle and Greekish Cittyes both
Perswades t' assist him in this warre, this quarel to mayntayne :
That he in Thebes (as promise was) might have his turne to raygne.
The ruyne that to wearied Thebes shall greevously befall,
And bring the pompous state therof adowne, shall not be small.
Fire, sword, glave, wounds, and thwacking thumps, shal light unto their share,
And that ere long : and mischieves worse (if any worse there are)
And this shall hap, that all the worlde may know it is the race
And yssue of a cursed Syre that darraygnes such a case.
Though other causes none there were to move you (sir) to live,
Yet is this one sufficient, that you by awe may dryve
Your sonnes my Brethren jarring thus to unity and peace :
For you their Father only may theyr furies cause to cease.

You and none els may turne away thoccasions of this warre :
These bransicke youthes from further rage you onely may debarre,
By this your meanes the countrey shall their quiet peace enjoy
And Brethren joyntly reconcild shal worke no more annoy.
If you therefore this mortall life thus to your selfe deny :
You many thousandes shal undoe, whose states on you relye.
ŒD. What ? canst thou make me to beleve, that any sparke of grace
Or love to Syre, or honesty in them hath any place,
Which thirst for one an others bloud, which after kingdomes gape,
Whose whole delight is villany, warre, murther, guile and rape ?
Such hateful ympes on mischiefe set, such wicked Termagauntes,
As to be sonnes of such a Syre with shame may make their vauntes.
At one bare woord to tel thee all : thy brethren two are bent
Uppon all mischiefe, wayghing not what loosenes they frequent.
When flingbrayne rage ensots their heades, they care not they a rush
Upon what Develish vile attemptes they geve the desprat push.
And as they are conceav'd and borne in most abhorred sort,
So still devoyde of Grace they thincke all villany but sport.
Theyr Fathers shame and wretched state moves them no whit at all,
To Countrey they no reckning make what massacre befall.
Their myndes are ravisht with desyre ambitiously to raygne.
I know their driftes, and what they hope at length by shiftes to gayne.
And therefor sith the case so standes I leyfer had to die
With poasting speede whyle in my house there is none worse then I.
Ahlas, deare Daughter what adoe dost thou about me make ?
Why liest thou prostrate at my knees ? why dost thou travaile take,
To conquere my resolved mynd with this thy spiced phraze
Of fayre entreatie ? these thy wordes my flynty hart amaze.
Dame Fortune hath none other bayte to bryng me to her lure
Then this alone : til now I still unvanquisht did endure.
No Creatures words but thyne alone could pearce this hart of myne,
Ne from a purpose resolute my setled mynd untwyne.
Thou conquere canst thaffections fond that in my breast do boyle,
Thou teachest grace to fathers house, and zeale to native soyle.

Each thing to me delightful is which jumpeth with thy wil :
Commaund me (Daughter) I thy hestes am ready to fulfill.
Old Œdipus if thou enjoyne, wil passe th' Ægæan Sea :
And flashing flakes of Aetna Mount, with mouth he dare assay.
He boldly dare object himselfe to raumping Dragons claw
Which rag'd, and sweld and venime spit apace, when as he saw
Dan Hercules away to steale his golden Aples all
In Gardens of Hesperides. At thy commaund, he shall
His entrails offer unto jobbe of greedy Vulturs Byll :
At thy commaund, content he is in life to linger still.

THE SECONDE ACTE

NUNTIUS, ŒDIPUS, ANTIGONE, JOCASTA

ENOWMED Prynce, of royall Race and Noble lygne yspronge :
The Thebans dreading much the drift of this your childrens thronge,
And warlicke garboyle now in hand, most humbly pray your Grace
For Countreys safety, downe to set some order in the case.
They bee not threates and menacies that thus their mindes affright :
The mischiefe is more neere then so : the Enmy is in sight.
For Polynices he that is your younger sonne of twayne,
Doth clayme the crowne, and in his turne in Thebes requires to raigne
According unto covenaunts made : which quarrell to decide
Hee purposeth the dent of sword, and martiall force t' abide.
With him he brings a mighty Troupe from ev'ry part of Greece,
Sir, seven Dukes, besieging Thebes are minded it to fleese.
Helpe noble King, els are wee lyke to perishe man and chylde,
These bloudy broyles of civill warre from us protect and shyelde.
ŒD. Am I one like to stop the rage of any wicked act ?
Am I one like to cause these Youthes to leave their bloudy fact ?
Am I a maister like to teach what lawes of love do meane ?
Should I not then from former guise digresse in nature cleane ?
They treade their Fathers steps aright, they play my lawlesse prankes :
Like Syre, like Sonnes, like Tree, like fruite : I con them harty thanks :

By this I know them for my Sonnes, and praise their towardnesse :
I would they should by peevish partes, whose Sonnes they be, expresse.
Shew forth you noble Gallante ympes, what metled minds you beare,
Shew forth by deedes your valor great, let lofty sprights appeare.
Surmount and dimme my prayses all, Eclypse my glory quight :
Attempt some enterprise in which your Syre may have delight
To have till now remaynd in life : hereof I have no doubt :
For well I know your practise is straunge feates to bring about.
Your byrth and signe from whence you spronge, assures me of no lesse
Such noble Bloudes must needes atchive some doughty worthinesse.
Your Weapons and Artillery for warre bring out with speede,
Consume with flame your native Soyle, and desolation breede
In ev'ry house within the Land : a hurly burly make
Confusedly of ev'ry thinge. Make all the Realme to quake,
And in exile theyr dayes let end : make levell with the ground
Eche fenced Fort and walled Towne : The Gods and all confound,
And throw their Temples on their heads : Their Images deface,
And melt them all : turne upsidowne eche house in ev'ry place.
Burne, spoyle, make havocke, leave no jote of City free from fyre,
And let the flame begin his rage within my Chamber dyre
AN. Syr, banish these unpatient panges, let plagues of Common wealth
Entreate your Grace, sith upon you stayth all their hope and health.
Procure your sonnes to reconcile themselves, as brothers ought,
Establishe peace betweene them both, let meanes of love be sought.
ŒD. Oh daughter, see and well beholde howe I to peace am bent ?
And how to end these garboyles all I seeme full well content ?
My minde (I tell thee) swelles with yre : within my entrailes boyles
Abundaunt stoare of Choller fell : such restlesse rage turmoyles
My inward Soule, that I must yet some greater matter brew :
Which may the Realme enwrap in bale, and cause them all to rue.
That which my rashe and heady sonnes have hitherto begon
Is nothing in respect of that wich must by me be don.
This civill warre is nothing like to that which I devise :
These trifling broyles for such a Sea of harmes cannot suffice.

Let brother cut the brothers throate with murthrous knife in hand :
Yet is not this ynough to purge the mischieves of this land.
Some haynous Fact, unheard of yet, some detestable deede
Must practisde bee : as is to mee, and myne by Fates decreed.
Such custome haunts our cursed race : such guise our house hath caught :
My vile incestuous Bed requires, such pageaunts to be wrought.
To me your Father Weapons reach, my selfe heere let me shrowde
In covert of these queechy wooddes : and let me be allowde
To lurke behinde this Craggy Rocke, or els my selfe to hyde
On backside of some thickset hedge : where lying unespide,
I hearken may what marketfolkes in passing to and froe
Do talke : and what the countrey Clownes speake, as by way they goe.
There (syth with eyes I cannot see) with eares yet may I heare
How cruelly my Sonnes by warre do one the other teare.
Joc. A fortunate and happy Dame Agave may be thought,
Who (though with bloudy hands) her sonne to fatall death she brought,
And from the shoulders chopt his head, and bore the same about
In bloudy hand, at Bacchus feast with all th' inspired rout
Of sacrificers, quartering poore Pentheus mangled lymmes :
Though this her cruell facte, somewhat her commendation dymmes :
Yet even in these her phrantick fits shee stayde her selfe in time
From further harme, not adding more to aggravate her crime.
My guilt were light, if I had not some others guilty made :
And yet is this but matter light : I tooke a viler trade.
For, Mother I am unto those that in all vice excell,
And who in most abhorred sinnes condignely beare the bell.
To all my woes and myseries there wanted onely this,
That I should love my Countreyes foe, who Polynices is.
Three snowy Wynters passed are, and Sommers three be gone,
Synce he an exilde wretch abroade hath lead his lyfe in moane :
And sought his bread among the fremmd : till now compell'de perforce
Hee craves reliefe of Greekish Kings, on him to have remorse.
Hee maried hath the Daughter of Adrastus, who at becke
Rules Argive people, swaying them with awe of Princely checke :

And he t'advaunce his sonne in law to his most lawfull right
Hath with him brought from seven Realmes a warlike Crue to fight.
What doome I should in this case geve, which syde I wish to winne,
I cannot tell: my minde amazde, yet doubtfull rests therein.
Th' one of my Sonnes (as right it is) requyres the Crowne as due:
I knowe it so accorded was: his cause is good and true.
But in such sort, by force of Armes to redemaunde the same,
Is ill and most unnaturall, herein he is to blame.
What shall I doe, what may I say? I mother am to both:
And thus my Sonnes at deadly fewde to see I am full loth.
Without the breach of mother zeale I can no way devise:
For what good hap I wishe to th' one, thence th' others harme doth rise.
But though I love them both alyke, yet sure my heart enclynes
To him that hath the better cause: though wronged thus, he pynes:
As one by frowning fortune thrilde from pillar unto post:
His Credite, Countrey, friendes, and wealth, and treasure being lost.
The weaker side I will support, and further al I can,
Most mercy alwayes should be shewde unto th' oppressed man.
Nu. While (Madame) you waymenting here your heavy plaints declare:
And waste the time, my Lords your Sonnes in raunged battayle are:
Eche Captaine bright in Armour standes, the Trumpet sounds amain,
And Standard is advanc'de, amid the thronge of eyther traine.
In marshall ray full prest to fight stand seven worthy Kynges:
And eche of them a warlicke troupe of valiaunt Souldiers bringes.
With courage not behynd the best, the Thebanes marche apace:
And like right ympes of Cadmus brood, do flash at Enmies face.
The Souldiers force and willingnes on eyther side to fyght,
Appeares: in that they nothing lesse pretend them shameful flight.
See how their trampling to and froe, the dust to Skies doth reare,
And what a Cloud of Smoke in Campe the horses make t' appeare.
And if my feare dismay me not: If all be true I see:
Me thinkes I view their glittering glaves begoard with bloud to bee.

Me thinkes I see the Voward thrill and shake their Pikes in hand :
Me thinkes I see the Gydons gay, and Streamers where they stand :
Wherein is wrought by curious skill, in Letters all of Gold
The Scotchton, Poesie, Name and Armes of every captayne bold.
Make hast, be gone, dispatch, (Madame) Cause Brethren to agree :
Betwyxt them stay this quarell, least a slaughter great ye see.
So shall you to your Children love, to each syde peace restoare :
The mothers mediation may heale up all the Soare.

THEBAIS

THE THIRDE ACTE

ANTIGONE, JOCASTA, NUNTIUS

OAST, poast, be gone, and trudge for life:
Queene mother make no stay:
That twixt my Brothers, perfect league and truce continue may.
You that be Mother to them both, use your auctority:
Out of their handes their weapons wrest, and make them warres defye.
Your bared Breastes which once they suckt, hold out amid their Swordes:
Beare of the brunt of all their blowes, or end this warre with wordes.
Joc. Thy talke I like, I wil be gone: Ile goe with might and mayne:
This head of myne I jeopard wil, betwene them to be slayne.
In thickest thronge of all the Troupes I purposd am to stand,
And try what grace, or curtesy remaynes in eyther Bande.
If Brothers beare malicious myndes each other to subdue,
Let them first onset geve on mee, and me to death pursue.
If eyther of them be endude with any sparke of grace,
Or Natures lawes or Filiall awe doth any whit embrace,
Let him at mothers suite lay downe his Pikes and glaves of warre,
And weapons of hostility let him abandon farre.
And he that cancard stomacke beares his Brother there to quell,
Forgetting Nature, let him first with me his Mother mell.
These headdy youthes from further rage I seely Trot wil staye:
I wittingly will not behold such mischiefe cary sway.
Or if I live to see the same, it shal not bee alone.
An. The Standardes are displayd in field, the Ennemyes are prone

To fall to fight : the clashing noyse of weapons heare you may.
Much murther, death, and dreadfull dule, cannot be far away.
Their stony hartes goe mollify, with sugred termes perswade
Their wilful myndes O Queene, before they furiously invade
The one the other : yonder see how they in armour bright
Bestirre themselves from place to place : (O dire and dismall sight.)
My trickling teares, my blubbring Eyes, may put you out of doubt
That all is true which I have sayd : looke, looke, how al the route
Of eyther part doth slowly march as loth (belike) to trye
By dent of Sword so straunge a case : But both my brothers hie
Apace, to grapple force to force, and joyne with handy blowes :
This day wil breede the bitter smart of ever during woes.
Joc. What whirlewynd swift might I procure to beare me through the ayre ?
What monstruous flying Sphinx wil helpe, that I were quickly there ?
Of all the Byrdes Stimphalides (with winges so huge and large
That Phœbus rayes they shadowed quight) wil any take the charge
To cary mee to yonder place ? what ravenous Harpye Burd
With ugly talantes all with filth, and dirty dung befurde,
(Which hungrestarvd King Phineus, that had put out the Eyes
Of children his) wil at this pinch a meane for me devyse,
That I aloft may hoysed bee, and with al spede be set,
Where yonder cruel armies two in open field be met ?
Nunt. Shee runnes apace, like one of wit and senses all distract :
No Arrow swifter out of Bow : no Ship with Sayle ful thwacke
With wynd at will more way can make : with motion such shee flyes
As glyding Star whose leames do drawe a Furrow longe in Skyes.
As much agast she trottes apace : and now in Campe she standes :
Her presence and arrivall there hath parted both the Bandes.
At mothers great entreaty made, the bloudy broyle is husht :
And where before with goring Glave the one at th' other pusht,
With ful entent to kill and slay, appeas'd is now their yre
And they well pleasd to bend to peace, as she doth them require.

The Sword agayne in sheath is put, that lately out was drawne
To pash out Braynes of Brothers Scull : she ceaseth not to fawne
Upon them both, their strife to stint : her gray and hoary haires,
Her Snow whyte lockes with tears besprent in ruthful sort she teares.
She Motherlike seekes how to linke their hartes in one assent,
With brynish teares she wettes the cheekes of him thats malcontent.
That Child that staggryng longe doth stand, with mother to dispute,
May seeme unwilling mynd to beare to yeeld to Mothers sute.

THE FOURTH ACTE

JOCASTA, POLYNICES

GAYNSTE mee onely turne the force of wreckful Sword and Fyre:
Let all the Youthes with one accord repay to me that hyre,
That earnde I have by due deserte: let both the gallant Band
Of them that come from Argos soyle, and them of Thebane Land
Come runne upon me all at once: let neither freend ne foe
Refrayne a whit his bloudy blade at this my wombe to throw.
This wombe, this wombe, wherein I bare these wilful Brethren here
Begot by hym that was my sonne, and eke my wedded fere.
Dismembre this my Body vyle: cast all my lymmes abrode:
I am their mother: child wyfe throwes for them I once abode.
You two, my sonnes, neede I to speake, to wil you leave your yre?
Ist not your partes, in such a case t' accomplish my desyre?
Wil you not plight the faythful league of true and perfect love?
Wil you not joyntly quarrels all at Mothers sute remove?
That this shalbe as I request, come, geve me both your handes
While they yet undystayned be, and cleane from murther standes.
What cryme you heretofore have done, agaynst your wil it was.
And al that spot which staynes your fame, by Fortune came to passe.
This haynous Act, this franticke coyle you can no wise excuse.
But wittingly and willingly sound counsell yee refuse.
It resteth free within your choyse: of these take which yee list:
If peace delight, for mothers sake this brabling broyle untwist.

If such a lewde outrage as this more pleasaunt seeme to bee :
Behold, the same and greater too yee may commit on mee.
Who beeing mother, heere oppose my selfe betwene you twayne :
Ere you do one an other kill, I needes must first be slayne.
Take either therefore quight away this straunge ungodly jarre,
Or if you will not : mee dispatch, who stay your wished warre ?
Ahlas in this my pensive plight to whom should I dyrect
My piteous plaint, and earnest suyte ? to whom might I detect
Myne inward griefe and throbbed heart ? which of them were I best
T' encounter first and fast embrace, to breede my surest rest ?
I love them both even equally, affection like I beare
To either party : mother fond and parciall els I weare.
The one of them these three yeares space hath liv'de in banishment.
But if all covenaunts may be kept, as at the first was ment,
The other now as turne doth fall, must trudge an other while,
And learne to know what tis to live so long in like exile.
Woe worth this haplesse heavy hap : shall I not live the day,
To see my sonnes together once in one selfe place to stay ?
Shall never I behold them both to better concord bent ?
Is all affection naturall within them both so spent ?
Then, Polynices, come thou fyrst, embrace thy Mother deare ?
Thou that hast travaild many a myle, and languisht many a yeare.
That many a storme abidden haste, and many a brunt sustainde,
And wearied long with sharpe exile, from Mothers sight bene wainde :
Come unto mee, and neerer stand, put up thy Sword againe
Into thy sheath : thy shyvering Speare (that out of hand so faine
Would be dischargd at Brothers throate) within this ground sticke fast.
This Shielde of thine lay also downe. It makes mee sore agast.
It is so bigge, it will not let this loving breast of myne
To joyne and debonairely meete with that sweete heart of thine :
Take of thy helmet from thine head, the Thonge thereof unty,
That I thy Visage may behold, and all thy face descry.
Why dost thou backward turne thy head ? and glauncest still thine Eye,
And takest keepe of brothers hand for feare of villany ?

Thy body all with these myne Armes I will defend and hyde :
If hee attempt thy bloud to spill, his murthrous blade shall glyde
First through these tender sydes of myne : why standst thou so amazd ?
Dost thou distrust thy Mothers love ? thinkst thou her kindnes razd ?
POLY. I feare in deede, distrusting sore, Syre, Damme and all my kinne :
And thinke that truthles treachery in hartes of all hath bin.
Dame Natures lawes are flung at heele, and naught esteemed be :
No fayth in kinred planted is, ne true syncerity.
Synce I by proofe have seene and felt what hurly burly growes
Betwixt us Brethren : and from thence what Sea of mischiefe flowes :
I may suspect no faster fayth in Mother to remayne :
Its not unlike, but shee likewyse wil prankes as bad mayntaine.
JOC. Thy sword in hand fast clasped keepe : On heade thy Basnet tye :
On Left Arme holde thy Targat sure, and on thy Gard relye.
At all poyntes armd prepared stand : all future doubtes prevent :
Be sure to see thy Brother first t' unarme himselfe content.
And now to thee Etheocles some speech I am to use :
Thou first wast cause of all this warre, doe not therfore refuse
Downe first to lay thy brawling Blade, and yeld to Reasons lore :
If name of peace so hateful be, if that thou any more
Entendst this warre to prosecute, in this so savage sort,
Let mother yet this curtesy from thee (her sonne) extort
That some small tyme of trusty truce thou wilt with willing mynd
Consent unto : til I my Sonne thy Brother most unkind
May after flight goe kisse and col, now first or last of all.
Whyle I for peace entreaty make, you men unarmd I call
To listen unto that I say : thy Brother feareth thee :
And thou fearst him : and I feare both. But this my feare you see
Is nothing for my selfe at all, but for th' avayle of both.
Why seemest thou thy naked sword to put in sheath so loth ?
Be glad to take the benefyte of any litle stay :
In matters lewde tis wysedome good to stand upon delay.

You enter into such a warre, wherein he speedeth best
That vanquisht is : both of you feare to be by fraud distrest
Through practisd meanes and subtil plots of Brothers spitefull drift,
Or overreacht by pollicy of some devysed shift.
But if deceive or be deceyv'd by him that is our Frend
Wee needes must be : in such a case wee shall the lesse offend
In suffring wrong then doyng harme : But feare thou not a whit,
You both from ambusht treacheryes your Mother wil acquit.
What say you Sonnes : shall this request of myne with you prevayle,
Or shall I curse my luckelesse fate, and on my Fortune rayle.
And judge your Sire an happy man, in that he liveth blinde
And cannot see the thing which I beholde with pensive minde ?
In comming unto you, did I bring with mee this intent,
To ende these broyles ? or did I come to see some dyre event ?
Etheocles, somewhat appeasde, hath pitcht his Speare in ground,
And not a weapon bloud to sheed, in hand of his is found.
Now Polynices, unto thee my former suite I bring,
Regard thy Mothers mournefull plight, and yeelde unto the thing
That shee with teares entreates to have. O Sonne, at length I see,
I hold with hands, I kisse with mouth, I touch with joyfull glee
This Face of thyne, the sight whereof I wanted have so longe :
And have more often wished for, then can bee tolde with tonge.
Thou hast from native Soyle bene chasde to Coaste of forraigne King,
And crossed bene with frouncing force of frowning Fortunes sting.
Thou many a Storme, and many a brunt in many a foming Sea,
In Wandring sort and banisht guise, didst oftentimes assay.
Thy Mother at thy Spousall feast was absent farre away,
And could not doe such nuptiall Rytes as fell for such a day.
Into thy wedding Chamber shee brought thee, ne yet thy Bryde,
Ne yet in solemne sorte the house with herbes and odours plide :
Ne yet did with a Ryband white the wedding Torches tye,
As use and custome willes to bee at such solempnitie.
Adrastus, Father to thy Wife, and father in lawe to thee,
With Daughter his, hath not defraide much store of golde or Fee.
No Dower hath he bestowde on her, her wealth was very small,
Of Citties, Landes, and Revenewes hee gave her none at all.

Warre, Warre, is it thou onely hadst, by taking her to Wyfe :
In lew of other gyfts, hee helpes to kindle all this Stryfe.
Thou Sonne in lawe arte unto him, that is our Countreyes Foe :
Thy Native soyle thou leavest, and to forraigne Courts doth goe.
Thou feedest now at Straungers boarde, and makest more accoumpt
Of new acquaintaunce got abroade : as though it did surmount
The friendship of thy country heere : thou art a banisht wight,
And liv'st in exile, for no fault, but through thy brothers spight.
In thee appeares resemblaunce playne of all thy Fathers Fate,
In which there lacketh not so much as choyse of wedded Mate.
Whom with as ill mischaunce and hap as ever Fathers was,
Thou haste in lucklesse houre and time of mariage brought to passe.
O Sonne, thy mothers onely hope, for whom such care I take :
Whose sight, now after many yeares, doth mee most joyfull make.
For whom I have full many a time to Gods devoutly praide :
Whereas in deede, thy new retourne to mee, may well bee saide
To take away as great a joye, and bring as great a griefe,
As it to these myne aged yeares is comfort and reliefe.
I prostrate at the Oracle, besought Apollos Grace
To tell mee, when I should not neede to further feare thy case.
Who flowting this my fond demaund, anone did flatly tell,
And spake these words, which yet (I trow) I doe remember well.
Thou fearst thy son, least harme he take, as is a mothers guise :
But thou I say more cause shalt have, to feare him otherwise.
For if this warre unraisde had bene I should thy presence lacke :
And if thou wert not, Thebane Land might free remayne from Sacke.
The sight of thee doth cost us all a hard and nipping price,
Yet doth it like thy mother well : so that her sound advice
In this one thing thou follow wilt. Dispatch these Armies hence :
Even presently, whyle yet of bloud there hath not bene expence.
So foule a Fact to bee so neere, is haynous out of doubt :
I shake, I quake to thinke thereon, in every Joynt throughout.
My hayre stands upright even for feare, two brethren thus to see
Aloofe, and ready one to chop at th' other, cruelly.
How neere was I (poore Mother theirs, a bloudier act t' have seene.)
Then father blind yet ever saw, or ever yet would weene ?

And though my feare be overpast, and th' act unbrought to passe :
My selfe yet doe I wretched thincke, that done so neere it was.
By all the throwes for tenne months space, in wombe when I thee bare,
And for thy Sisters sake both twaine, which shine in vertue rare :
And by those Eyehoales of thy Syre, for which with wrekefull Pawe
Hee pulld his Eyes, because (unwares) hee stained Natures lawe,
I thee beseech from Thebane Walles send backe these armed Bandes,
Which threatning all our throates to cut, against our Countrey stands :
Yea though you presently depart : yet are you much to blame,
And there is due unto you both, a blot of during shame :
Because this Countrey round about hath pestred bene with powre,
And troupes of Souldiours stout and brave, it ready to devowre.
With pensive hearts and mourning minds, these Eyes of ours have seene
Your prauncing coursers with their Feete, spoile Theban Medowes greene.
Wee oft have seene your haulty Peeres in warlike Chariot ride :
And oft our houses to have brunt with wildfier have bene spide.
And last of all. An act wee sawe (which even to Thebes is straung.)
Two Brethren warring mortally, all Natures bondes to chaung.
Ech one in th' Army sawe this sight, the people witnesse bee.
Your Systers two, and Mother I this all did plainly see.
Your Father, hee may thanke himselfe : that he did not behold
This lamentable spectacle and havockes manifold.
Call now to thy remembraunce heere, thy Father Œdipus,
Whose doome, did Facts (by errour done) even plague, and punishe thus.
With Fyre, and sword subvert not cleane (good Sonne) thy countrey deare,
And Thebes (whereof thou wouldst be king) surcease with force to teare.
What Bedlem pang enchaunts thy mind ? what might thy meaning bee ?
Thou claymst a Realme, which to subvert thou geevest lycence free.

In seeking thus a countryes rule : a countrey thou destroyest :
Which thou thine own would make, thou marr'st, and (as twere none) annoyest.
Heereby thou hindrest much thy selfe, in that thou makest spoyle,
And burnest up both Corne and Grasse, and keep'st a shamefull coyle,
In chasing men out of their homes : (O desprate witlesse parte)
What man alive, to waste his owne, can thus find in his harte ?
These thinges that thou commaundest thus by rage of sword and flame
To bee consum'de : an other man thou thinkst doth owe the same.
If thus for princely Chayre you twayne by th' Eares your title try :
The state of Realme and Commonwealth will totter soone awry.
Seeke it, while yet your Countrey standes unblemisht by decay :
It so t' enjoy, and so to raigne, I coumpt the better way.
Ah, canst thou finde in heart to burne, and spoyle these houses brave ?
The lyke whereof in all the worlde besides, thou canst not have :
Canst thou destroy and ruinate the noble Thebane wall,
To whose first building stones apace at Dan Amphions call
Came dauncing of their owne accord, through tunes of warbling harpe ;
And coucht themselves in order right upon the Turrets sharpe,
Without all helpe of worckmans hand, or Pully up to draw
Such pieces as most waighty were ? Wilt thou by lawlesse law
Throw downe these worthy Monuments ? wilt thou from hence convey
And cary with thee all these spoyles ? wilt thou such pageaunts play ?
Thy Fathers old acquainted mates, wilt thou by force surpryze
And leade as captive where thou goest in proude triumphing wise ?
Shall these thy cutthroate Souldiors dragge and hale the mothers old ?
Shal they, graund Matrons tied in chaines, from husbands armes unfold ?
Shall Thebane Maydes, and Damselles chaste of freshe and lusty Age,
Bee mingled with the raskal rout, and hamperd bee in Cage ?

Shall they as presents, forced bee in dabbling dirt to toyle
Unto the mynsing Mistresses, and Trulles of Argos Soyle ?
Shall I thy seely Mother trudge with Pinyond hands behinde ?
Shall I this triumph of my Childe to furnish bee assignde ?
Canst thou with grudgelesse minde, behold thy Countreyfolkes arow,
Slayne, mangled, spoylde, in peeces hewen, thus to their deathes to goe ?
Canst thou bring in a deadly Foe, thy Countrey to subdue ?
Shall streates of Thebes runne all with bloud ? shall all the Countrey rue
Thy comming home with flame and fyre ? hast thou an heart so hard ?
A breast so tipt with flint ? a mynde to rage so well preparde ?
If thus thou fare, and swell with yre whiles yet thou art no King :
What wilt thou bee in Princely throne, if thou shouldst win the King ?
Surcease therefore and qualifie this outrage of thy mynde :
In thee let all thy Countrey, grace and Princely myldnes finde.
Pol. Would you me have, my selfe so much to loyall duties yeeld,
As that I should a Pylgrims life like wandring Beast in field
Skud up and downe from place to place, without both house and home,
And fleeing native soyle, bee forst in forraigne Landes to roame ?
What other plagues could you award in justice unto mee,
If I my fayth or sacred Oath had broken caytifly ?
Shall I beare all the punishment for that vile villains guile ?
And shall hee false deceiptfull wretch at my misfortunes smyle ?
Shall hee in wealth still flaunt it out, and keepe this jolly coyle ?
Shall hee for sinnes rewarded bee ? and I still put to foyle ?
Well, well, goe to, bee as bee may : you bid mee wander hence :
I am content : your hard decree t' obay is my pretence.
But tell mee whyther shall I goe ? Assigne mee to some place :
Bylike, you would that brother myne should still with shamelesse face
Possesse my stately Pallaces, and revell in his ruffe,
And I thereat to holde my peace, and not a whit to snuffe,

THE THIRD TRAGEDY

But like a Countrey Mome to dwell in some poore thatched Cot :
Allow mee poore Exyle such one : I rest content, God wot.
You know, such Noddyes as I am, are woont to make exchaung
Of Kingdomes, for poore thatched Cots, beelike this is not straung
Yea more : I, matcht now to a Wyfe of noble ligne and race
Shall like a seely Dottipoll live there in servile case,
At becke and checke of queenely Wyfe, and like a kitchin drudge
Shall at Adrastus lordly heeles, (my Wyves owne Father) trudge.
From Princely Port to tumble downe into poore servile state,
Is greatest griefe that may betyde by doome of frouncing fate.
Joc. If that thou gape so greedely a Kingly Crowne to weare :
And that thou canst not rest content, till thou a Scepter beare :
Behold ech quarter of the world affoordeth Kingdomes store.
No doubt thou mayst winne some of them, if that thou seke therfore.
On one syde here, lies Tmolus mount, a soyle bethwact with Wines :
There runnes Pactolus noble streame with golden Sand and mynes,
On that syde crookt Meander glydes through midst of Phrygia fieldes :
On this syde Hebrus swift of course much fruict to Thracia yeldes.
Nere thereunto lies Gargarus, renoumd each where for Corne,
And Trojan Xanthus swelling floud, that pricke and price hath borne.
There Seftos and Abidus stand in mouth of Ionian Sea,
Which now is called Hellespont : and here an other waye
Are countreys, which more Eastward lye. There Lycia full of Creekes
And Havens strong is situate : these kingdomes, he that seekes,
Is like to winne : these would I have thee conquere with thy Sword :
These, these to winne let King Adrast to thee his ayd affoorde.
In some of these, let him thee make a King : in Thebes as yit,
Suppose thy father Œdipus in seat of King to sit.
Thy banishment much better is to thee, then this returne,
Sith all thy drift is cruelly to wast, to spoyle, and burne.
Thy banishment reputed is to grow through others crime :
This thy retourne, in such a sort to Kingly state to clyme,
Is ill and faulty every way : with this thy warlicke crue
Thou shalt do better Realms to seeke, where bloudy guilt ne grue.

Yea, this thy Brother, whom thou dost pursue with deadly hate
Whose life, whose health, whose house thou dost with curses dire rahate
Wil ayde thee with all powre he canne : himselfe will also goe
And serve in field for thyne avayle, gaynst him that is thy foe.
Advaunce thy powre, march boldly forth to take this warre in hand:
Wherein thy parentes wish thee good, and wil thy helpers stand.
A Kingdome got mischievously, and snatcht with grudge of mynd,
More greevous is then exiles al, of what soever kind.
Of warre, the doubtful hazardes all set downe before thy syght,
And throughly weigh thuncertayne chaunce, that longes to martial fight.
Though al the power of Grece thou bring thy quarel to mayntayne,
And though great armed multitudes of Souldiours thou retayne :
Yet chaunce of warre stil doubtful hanges, and hard it is to know,
Who cary shal the victory, thou or thy vowed foe.
Mars no party tyed is : what he decrees, shal be,
As chaunce allots, so falles it out : this dome abydeth free.
Sword, hope and feare makes equall those, betwene whom otherwyse
Great oddes there is : blynd Fortunes lot the case betweene them tryes.
Thy rash attempt with cryme begonne, gropes after doubtful gayne:
And fond devyses enterprisd oft reape deserved payne.
Admit that all the Gods in heaven did further thy request,
And to promote thy hoat desyre both willing were, and prest:
Yet al thy frendes are fled away, and al recoyled backe,
And Souldiours here and there in Fieldes are come to deadly wracke.
Although thou joy hereat receyve, although the spoyles thou take
Of vanquisht Brother, yet the palme of victory must slake,
And not to thee be geven whole. What kind of warre (alas)
Is this, thinkst thou ? ist not more straunge then ever any was ?
Wherin if he that victor is, joy therein any whyt,
Most execrable wickednes he (doubtles) doth commit.
This Brother thyne, whom now so faine thou wouldst bereave of breath,
I wis, if he were once dispatcht, thou wouldst bewale his death.
And therfore make no more adoe, but cease from wicked bral,
Ridde countrey out of trembling feare, and parentes dole forestal.

POLY. What, shal my Brother for this vyle and shamefull breach of pacte
Goe skotfree thus? shal he receyve no guerdon for his fact?
Joc. Feare not my Sonne, he shall be payd, and payd agayne, I trow:
He shalbe King and raygne in Thebes, his payne shal even be so.
A payne in grayne I warrant him. And if thou doubtful be,
Let Graundsyre Laius and thy Syre examples be to thee.
Sir Cadmus wil the same display, and Cadmus ofspring all
Can witnes be that none in Thebes yet raygnd without a fall.
None yet the Theban Scepter swayd, that hath not felt the whippe.
And promise breach made most of them from regall Crowne to skippe.
Now if thou wilte, thou mayst insert within this bedroll heere
Thy Brother. POLY. Mary, that I wil, in shame hath he no peere.
And unto mee it seemes a world of blisse to bee a king
And dye with Kings. Joc. Thy case doth thee in rank of exiles bring.
Raygne Kinge, but yet a loathed wight unto thy Subjectes all.
POLY. For that I neyther recke ne care what shall to me befall.
That Prince that feares disdaynful hate, unwilling seemes to raygne.
The God that swayes the Golden Globe, together hath these twayne
Conjoynd and coupled Hate and Rule: and him do I suppose
To be a noble King indeede, that can supplant his foes,
And Subjectes cancred hate suppresse. A King is often stayed
From doyng many thinges he would, when Subjectes love is wayed.
But unto them that do repyne to se him sit aloft,
He may more rigour boldly shew, and pare their pates more oft.
He that will love of Subjectes winne, with Clemency must raygne:
A King that 's hated, cannot long in Kingly seate remayne.
For Kingdomes Kinges can best describe, what preceptes needfull are.
Mell thou in cases of Exile: for Kingdomes take no care.
POLY. To be a King, I would engage to force of flaming Fire,
Both Countrey, house, land, Wyfe, and Chyld, to compasse my desyre.
No Fee, to purchase Princely seate, ne labour coumpt I lost:
A Kingly Crowne is never deare, what ever price it cost.

Thomas Newtonus, Cestreshyrius.

FINIS

THE FOURTH, AND MOST RUTHFUL TRAGEDY OF L. ANNAEUS SENECA

ENTITULED HIPPOLYTUS

TRANSLATED INTO ENGLISHE BY JHON STUDLEY

THE ARGUMENT

Hippolytus, the Sonne of Theseus and Antiopa Quene of the Amazons, renouncing al Worldly pleasures, and carnall delightes, lyved a Batcheler, forbearing all Womens company, and amorous allurements: and only vowed himselfe to the service of chaste Diana, pursuing the Gentlemanly pastime of hunting. In the absence of Theseus his Father, it chaunced that his Stepmother Phædra ardently enamored with his beawty and lusty age, enveigled him by all meanes shee coulde, to commit wyth her filthy, and monstruous adultry. Whych her beastly, unchaste, and undutifull practise, hee dutifully loathinge, shee turned hir former love into extreame hatred, and told her husband Theseus at his returne home, that his Sonne Hippolytus woulde have unlawfully layne with her. Theseus believing his Wyves most untrue accusation, meant to have put his sonne to death. Hippolytus understanding thereof, got up into his Chariot and fled. Theseus being therewith tickeled, and after some pursuite, not overtaking him, went to his Father Ægæus beeing a God of the Sea, desiring him to graunt him three Wishes: the last whereof was, the destruction and Death of Hippolytus: whereupon Ægæus sent out certaine great Sea-monsters, or Whirlepooles, which affrighting the Horses in Hippolytus Charyot, made them to overturne the Charyot, and to runne through thick and thinne till they had dismembred true Hippolytus in pieces. The remorse of which villany so strake Phædra in Conscience, that with a Sword shee stabbed herselfe into the Entrailes, and died upon the body of Hippolytus.

THE SPEAKERS NAMES

Hippolytus. Chorus.
Phædra. Theseus.
Nuntius. Nutrix.

HIPPOLYTUS

THE FIRST ACTE

HIPPOLYTUS

OE raunge about the shady Woods, beset on every side
With Nets, with Hounds, and toyles, and running out at randon ride
About, about, the craggy crests of high Cecropes hill,
With speedy foote about the Rockes, with coursing wander still.
That under Carpanetus Soyle, in Dale below doth lurke,
Whereas the Rivers running swift, their flapping waves doe worke,
And dashe against the beaten Banks of Thrias valley low,
And clamber up the slimy clives, besmeard with hory Snow,
(That falleth, when the Westerne winde from Riphes Mounts doth blow.)
Heere, heere away, let other wend, whereas with lofty head,
The Elme displayes his braunched armes, the wood to overspread.
Whereas the Meadowes greene doe lye, where Zephyrus most milde
Out brayes his baumy breath so sweete, to garnish up the field
With lusty springtide flowers fresh whereas Elysus slow
Doth fleete upon the Ysie flakes, and on the Pastures low.
Mæander sheds his stragling streame, and sheares the fruitlesse sand
With wrackfull wave : yee whom the path on Marathons left hand,
Doth lead unto the leavened launds, whereas the heirde of beast
For Evening forrage goe to graze, and stalke unto their rest.
The rascall Deare trip after fast, you thither take your way,
Where clottered hard Acarnan forst warme Southerne windes t' obay

Doth slake the chilling colde, unto Hymerus Ysie clive
To Alphids litle Villages, now let some other drive :
That plot where Sunion surges high doe beate the sandy bankes,
Whereas the marble Sea doth fleete with crooked compast crankes,
Unhaunted lies too long, withoutten race of any wight.
Who set agog with hunting brave, in woods doth take delyght,
Philippis him allures : her hauntes a fomy bristled Bore
That doth annoy with gastly dread the husbandmen full sore :
We know him well for he it is foyld with so many woundes,
But ere they do begin to ope, let slip, let slip your Houndes.
But in your leashes Syrs keepe up your eiger Mastifs yet,
Keepe on their Collers still, that doe their galled neckes yfret :
The Spartayne Dogges eiger of pray and of couragious kynd
That sone can single out their game, wherto they be assygnd,
Tye shorter up within your leash : to passe tyme shall it bring,
That with the youlping noyse of houndes the hollow rockes shal ring.
Now let the Houndes goe fynd of it with Nosthrell good of sent,
And trace unto the uglye den ere dawning day be spent.
Whyle in the dewish stabby ground the pricke of cleaze doth sticke.
One bear the toyle on cumbred necke, and some with nettes ful thicke
Make speede : some with the arming coard by pensell paynted red
By sleight, and subtill guyleful feare shall make the Beastes adred :
Loke thou to pitch thy thirling dart, and thou to trye thy might,
Shalt cope him with broad Boarespeare : thrust with hand both lefte and right,
Thou standing at receipt shalt chase the roused beastes amayne
With hallowing : thou with limere sharpe undoe him beyng slayne.
Graunt good successe unto thy mate, Virago, thou Divyne,
That secret desartes chosen hast for noble Empire thyne :
Whose thirled Dartes with leavel right do gore the Beast with Bloud
That lappes the lukewarme licour of Arexis fleeting Floud.
And eke the Beast that sportes it selfe on frosen Isters strand.
The ramping Lyons eake of Geate are chased by thy hand.
And eke the wyndy heeled Hart in Candie thou dost chase.
Now with more gentle launce thou strikst the Doe that trippes apace.

To thee the Tygar fierce his divers spotted breast doth yeeld,
The rough shaghatry Bugle turnes on thee his backe in field,
Eke salvage Buffes with braunched hornes: all thinges thy quarelles feare,
That to the needy Garamas in Affricke doth appeare.
Or els the wyld Arabian enriched by his wood,
Or what the Brutish roches at Pyrene understood,
Or else what other Beastes do lurcke in wyld Hyrcanus grove,
Or else among Sarmatians in desert fieldes that rove:
If that the Ploughman come to field, that standeth in thy grace,
Into his nettes the roused beast full sure he is to chase.
No feete in sunder breake the coardes and home he bringes the Bore
In jolting wayne, when as the houndes with gubs of clottered gore,
Besmeared have their grymed snoutes: and then the Countrey rout
To Cottages repayre in rankes, with triumph all about.
Lo, Goddesse graunt us grace: the hounds already opened have,
I follow must the Chase: this gainer way my paynes to save,
I take into the woods.

THE SECOND SCEANE

PHÆDRA, NUTRIX

O Countrey Crete that beares the sway, upon the Seas so vast,
Whose Ships so thicke in every Shore, the Seas doe overcast,
What ever coast as farre as is Assyria lande doth lye,
Where Nereus doth the piked Stemme to cut his course deny,
Why force ye mee that yeelded am, a pledge to those I hate?
And gieven in Bridall bed to bee my enmies Spousall mate,
To languish out my time in teares, in woe to leade my lyfe?
My husband lo, a runnagate is gon from mee his Wyfe,
Yet Theseus still performes his Othe alike unto his Spouse
As earst to Ariadne, when hee falsifide his Vowes:
Hee champion stoute dare enterprise the darkenesse deepe to passe
Of lothsome Lake, whence yet found out, no way returning was.

A souldier of the Wooer bolde Proserpin home to bring,
Out pullde perforce from grisly throne of Dire infernall King.
Accompanide with fury fierce hee marcheth forward still,
Whom neither dread nor shame could force forbeare his wicked will.
With lawlesse wedlocks ravishments Hippolytus his Sire
Doth in the boyling bottom deepe of Acheron require,
But yet another greater griefe swayes on my pensive brest,
No silent night, nor slumber deepe can set my heart at rest.
My sorrow still is nourished, and still encreaseth it,
And ranklesse in my boyling breast, as out of Ætnaes pit.
The stifling vapour upward flies and Pallas Web, it standes
At rest, my dropping distaffe downe doth drop betweene my handes.
My luskish minde it hath no lust my vowed gifts to pay
Unto the Temples of the Gods that live my Theseus may :
Nor rigging with Th'athenian Dames among the aulters proude
To tosse the fiery brands, unto the sacrifice aloude,
Nor yet devoutly praying at the Aares with godly guise
To Pallas president in earth to offer sacrifice :
It doth delight me to pursue the chased beasts in flight,
And tosse my flashing Faucon fierce with nimble hand full light,
What ayles thou minde this mad to take conceypte in freight and fell ?
My wretched mothers fatall vice a breeding now I smell :
To cloake our crime, our lust doth knowe, woods are the fittest place,
Alas good Mother, I lament the heavy lucklesse case :
Thou rashe attaint with lothsome lust enamored is thy breast.
Even with the cruell head of al the herd of salvage beast,
That churlish angry roaring Bull no yoake can hee sustayne,
And hee among the wilde, and eke untamed Neat doth raygne.
Yet was enclinde to love : what God can graunt mee my desire ?
Or Dedalus with curious craft can ease my flaming fire ?
Not if hee might returne, whom Ariadne hath instruct
From crooked compast Laberinth by thred that out hee pluckt
Among the lurcking corners close, and wily winding way,
To grope his footing backe agayne, and did deprive of day

Our monstrous Minotaur enclosde in Maze and Dungeon blinde :
Although hee promise to our sore, no salve yet can hee finde :
Through mee Apollos Progeny doth Venus quite agayne,
The filthy shame that shee and Mars together did sustayne.
Whom Phœbus taking at their taske all naked in the Skie,
Hung up in Nets, a laughing stocke to every gasing Eye :
For this all Phœbus stocke, with vile and foule reproche she staynes,
In some of Minos family still lothsome lusting raygnes :
One mischiefe brings another in. Nu. O Theseus wyfe, and Chylde
Of Jove, let vyce be soone out of thine honest breast exilde :
And quench the raging heat : to dire dispayre doe not up yeeld,
Who at the first repulseth love, is safe and winnes the field,
Who doth by flattring fancy fonde feede on his vitious vayne,
To late doth grudge agaynst the yoake which earst hee did sustayne :
Nor yet doe I forget how hard, and voyde of reason cleane :
A Princes stately stomacke yeeldes unto the golden meane :
Ph. That ende I will accept, whereto by Fortune I can leade
The neighbors weale great comfort brings unto the horie heade.
Nu. The first redresse is to withstand, not willingly to slide,
The second is to have the fault by meane and measure tride :
O wicked wretch what wilt thou doe ? why dost thou burden more
The stayned stocke and dost excell thy mothers fault afore ?
More haynous is thy guilt than yet thy mothers Monster was :
For monsters mayst thou thinke are brought by destiny to passe :
But let the cause of sinne, to blame of maners lewde redounde :
And if bicause thy husband doth, not breath above the grounde.
Thou thinkst thou mayst defend thy fault, and make thy matter good
And free from feare : thou arte beguilde, yet thinke the Stygian flood
In griefly gaping gulfe for aye hath drenched Theseus deepe,
But yet thy Syre, whose Kingdomes large the Seas at will do keepe :
Whose dredfull doome pronounceth panges, and due deserved payne,
Two hundreth wayling soules at once. Will he thinkst thou maintayne

So haynous crime to couche ? the care of tender Parents breast
Full wise, and wary is to bring their children to the best.
Yet shall we thinke by subtill meane, by craft and divelish guile,
In hugger mugger close to keepe our trechery so vile.
What shall thy mothers father Phœbe, whose beames so blasing bright,
With fiery gleede on every thing, doth shed his golden light ?
Or Jove the Grandsire great of Gods that all the world doth shake,
And brandisheth with flaming Fist, his fiery lightnings flake :
That Vulcane doth in Fornace hoate, of dusky Ætna make
Thinkst thou thys may be brought to passe, so haynous crime to hide ?
Among thy Grandsire all that have eche privy thing espide ?
But though the favor of the Gods conceale the second time
Thy lothsome lust (unworthy name) and to thy baudy crime,
Sure faythfulnesse annexed be, that ever barred was.
Ech great offence, what will this worke ? a present plague, alas
Suspicion lest the guilty night bewray thy deede unjust :
And conscience burdned sore with sinne that doth it selfe mistrust.
Some have commit offence full safe from any bitter blame,
But none without the stinging pricks of conscience did the same :
Asswage the boyling flames of this thy lewde ungratious love,
Such monstrous mischiefe horrible from modest minde remove.
Which never did Barbarian commit unto this day,
No not the Gadding Gothes that up and downe the fyeldes do stray.
Nor craggy crested Taurus mount whose hoary and frosty face
With numming cold abandons all inhabitors the place.
Nor yet the scattered Scithian, thy mother have in mynd,
And feare this forrayne venery, so straunge agaynst thy kind :
The Fathers wedlocke with the sonnes thou seekst to be defylde,
And to conceive in wicked womb a Bastard Mungrell Child :
Go too, and turne thy Nature to the flame of burning breast.
Why yet do Monsters cease ? why is thy Brothers cave in reast.
That Mynotaurus hideous hole and ugly couching den
Without an other greedy fyend to mounch up flesh of men ?
Mishapen, lothly monsters borne so oft the world shall heare,
So oft rebels agaynst her selfe confused Nature deare,

As love entangles Nimphes of Crete. Ph. I know the truth ye teach
O Nurce, but fury forceth mee at worser thinges to reach :
My mynd even wittingly to vyce falles forward prone and bent
To holesome counsell backe agayne in vayne it doth relente :
As when the Norman tugges and toyles to bring the fraighted Barke
Agaynst the striving streame, in vayne he loseth al his carke
And downe the shallow streame perforce the Shyp doth hedlong yeeld,
Where reason preaseth forth, there fighting fury winnes the field,
And beares the swinging sway, and cranke Cupidoes puissant might
Tryumpheth over all my breast this flighty winged wight
And puissant potestate throughout the world doth beare the stroke,
And with unquenched flames doth force Joves kindled breast to smoake,
The Battelbeaten Mars hath felt these bitter burning brandes,
And eke the God hath tasted these whose fervent fierye handes,
The thumping thunder bouncing boltes three forked wyse doth frame,
And he that ever busied is about the furious flame,
In smoltring Fornace raging hoat on dusky top so hie
Of foggye Aetna mount : and with such slender heat doth frie,
And Phœbe himselfe that weldes his dart upon his twanging string,
With aymed shaft directlie driven the wimpled Ladde doth sting.
With powre he scoures along the Earth and Marble Skye amayne.
Lust favoring folly filthily did falsely forge and fayne
Love for a God : and that he might hys freedome more attayne.
Ascribes the name of fayned God to shittel bedlame rage.
Erycina about the world doth send her roving page,
Who glyding through the Azure skies with slender joynted arme
His perlous weapons weildes at will, and working grievous harme,
Of bones and stature beyng least great might he doth display
Upon the Gods, compelling them to crouch and him obey.
Some Brainsicke head did attribute these thinges unto himselfe,
And Venus Godhead with the bow of Cupid little else.
Who cockred is, tryumphing much in fauning fortunes lap,
And flotes in welth, or seekes and sues for thinges that seldome hap,

Lust (mighty fortunes mischeous mate) assaulteth straight his breast,
His tooth contempneth wonted fare and victuals homly drest.
Nor hansome houses pleaseth him, why doth this plague refuse
The simple sort, and to annoy doth stately bowers chuse ?
How haps it matrimony pure to byde in Cottage base ?
And honest love in middle sort of men doth purchase place ?
And thinges that be of meane estate themselves restraine ful wel,
But they that wallow in their luste whose stately stomackes swell,
Puft up and bolstred bigge with trust of Kingly scepter proude
Do greater matters enterprise then may be well alowde.
Hee that is able much to do, of powre wil also bee
To do these thinges he cannot doe. Now Lady dost thou see
What thinges do thee beseeme thus staid on stately throne on hie ?
Mistrust the scepter of thy spouse returning by and by.
PH. In me I beare a violent and mighty payse of love,
And no mans comming home againe to terrour may me move.
He never stepped backe agayne, the welkin skie to touch,
That swallowed once and sunke in gulfe and glummy cave did couch
Shut up in shimering shade for ay. NU. Yet do not thou suppose,
Though dreadful Ditis lock with barres, and bolt his dongeon close :
And though the hideous hellicke hounde do watch the griesly gates,
Not Theseus alone shal have his passage stopt by fates.
PH. Perhaps he pardon wil the cryme of loves procuring heate.
NU. Nay churlishly hee would of old his honest wyfe entreate.
Antiope his bobbing buffets felt and heavy cuffe :
Suppose, yet thou can qualifye thy husbandes raging ruffe :
Yet who can move Hippolytus most stony stubborne mynd ?
He wil abhorre the very name detesting womankind,
And faring frantickly, wil gyve himselfe to single life,
And shunne the hated spousall bedde of every marride wife,
Then shal ye playnly understand his brutish Scithian blood.
PH. To follow him even through the hilles, the Forrest thycke and wood,
That keepes among the clottred clives besmeard with silver Snow,
Whose nimble heeles on craggy rockes are frisking to and froe :

I wysh. Nu. He wil resist and not be dalyed with nor coyd,
Nor chaunge his chast estate, for lyfe of chastity devoyd,
And turne perhaps his cankred hate to light on thee alone,
That now he beares to all. Ph. Wil not he moved be with mone ?
Nu. Stark wilde he is. Ph. And I have learnd wilde thinges by love to tame.
Nu. Hee 'le runne away. Ph. If by the Seas he flie, I on the same
Will follow him. Nu. Remember then thy father may thee take.
Ph. I may remember myne offence, my mother eake wil slake.
Nu. Detesting womankinde, he drives and courseth them away.
Ph. No strumpets bashful feare agaynst my breast doth hold at bay :
Nu. Thy husband wil be here. Ph. I wis he comes I warrant him
Pyrothous companion in hellicke dungeon dimme.
Nu. Thy Father also he wil come. Ph. A gentle hearted Syre
Forgeving Ariadnes fault, when she did him require.
Nu. For these my silver shining lockes of horie drouping age,
And breast beduld with cloying cares restrayne thy furious rage,
I humbly thee beseech even by these tender teats of myne,
Succor thy selfe, much health it is, if will to health encline.
Ph. Not every jote of honesty exiled is my breast,
I yeeld me Nurse, love that denies thus under rule to rest
In quietnes, let him, let him perforce be battered downe.
I wil not let my fleeting fame and glorious bright renoume
With stayne to be dishonoured, this onely is the gap,
To shunne the perlous path that leades to vices trayning trap.
My spouse let mee ensue with death this sinne I shall subvert.
Nu. Deare daughter slake the ramping rage of thy unruly heart.
Plucke downe thy stomacke stout, for this I judge thee worthy breath,
In that thou dost confesse thy selfe to have deserved death.
Ph. Condemde I am to die, what kind of death now would I know,
As eyther strangled with a rope shal I my life forgoe ?
Or runne uppon a bloudy blade, with gory wound to dye ?
Or topste turvy headlong hurld downe Pallas turret hie,
In quarrel just of Chastity. Nu. Now strengthen we our hand,
Alas shal not my feble age thy despret death withstand,

Forbeare the sway of furye fierce. PH. No reason can restrayne
Him that desireth death, when death he hath determind playne
And ought to die. NU. Sweete Lady myne (thou comfort of my age
And feeble yeares) if in thy breast prevayles such mighty rage
Have not regard what sounding blast in trompe of fame be blowne
Whereby thy name in stayned stock of blacke reproch be sowne,
Or graft in spotlesse honesty : for fame doth favour small
The most upright, to better worse, to worse shee 's best of al,
Let us assay the froward mynd of yonder stubborne Child
It is my part to set uppon the clubbish youngman wilde
And to compell the sturdy lad with stony hart to yeeld.

CHORUS

O Goddesse great that art the wondrous seede
Of frothie surge in stormy raging seas
Whom flamy Cupid armd with scorching gleed,
And Shaftes, to call his Mother it doth please :
This wanton Elfe forth putting sappy might
From stedfast Bowe how surely doth he throwe
His venimd shaftes, through all thy marrow right
The foystring fyre doth rankle in and glowe
The secret flame that boyleth in each vayne
The strype layd on shewes not in open marke :
But inward marrow he sucketh out amayne,
This boy to sound of peace doth never harke.
His scattered shaftes ful nimble every where
He dartes aboute, the East that doth behold
The dawning sunne himselfe aloft to reare,
From purple bed, and whether late he rold.
With ruddy lamp, in Westerne wade doth glyde :
If any coast lye under scorching clawes
Of burning Crab, or people do abyde,
Beneath the clyme of Isy frosen pawes,
Of ougly gargle faced bigger Beare,
That wandring still from place to place doth goe

HIPPOLYTUS

THE FIRST ACTE

The fervent Fumes, and stoving heate eche where
That issues out from Cupid's burning bow,
The flashing flames of Yongmens burning brest,
Hee stirreth up, enkindling new the heate
Of quenched coales, that wonted was to rest
In drouping age : and virgins hearts doe beate
Wyth straunge untasted brandes : and doth compell
The Gods descending downe from starry Sky,
Wyth counterfeited Vysages, to dwell
Upon the Earth to blinde the Lovers Eye.
Sir Phoebus whilome forst in Thessail Land
To Sheepeherds state Admetus Heirdes did drive,
His mourning Harp deprivde of heavenly Hand
With orderd Pipe his Bullockes did revive.
Even hee that trayles the dusky riding rack,
And wieldes the swaying Poles with swinging swift
How oft did hee faynde fourmes put on his back
And heavenly Face with baser countenaunce shift.
Sometime a Byrde with silver shining wings,
He fluttering flusht, and languishing the death
With sweete melodious tuned voyce hee sings,
When silly Cygnus gave up gasping breath.
Sometime also wyth curled forhead grim
A dallying Bull, he bent his stouping backe
To maydens sport, through deepest Seas to swim
Whyle horny hove made shift like Ore slacke
Through waters wyld his brothers perlous cost
Wyth forward glauncing breast the stream he brake,
And least he should his tender pray have lost,
Her troublus thought did cause his heart to quake
Diana bright that swayes in circle murke,
Of darkened Sky, with frying fits did burne,
And leaving of the Evening watch her worke
Her fulgent Chariot bright, eke did shee turne.
To Phoebus charge, to weelde it otherwise
Her Evening Wayne Apollo learnde to guide,
And take his turne in lesser compast sise :
The dampish nights watcht not their wonted tyde

And late it was ere that Aurora fayre
Set forth the morning Sunne with golde aray,
Whyle that the Marble axell tree in th' ayre
The shogging Carte made crake with swagging sway,
Alcmenas boystrous Impe did lay aside
His clattering shafts, and also did refuse
To weare the ramping Lyons hairy Hyde
And Emraudes for his fingers did hee chuse,
And brayded kept his rufled staring Locks,
Ware Garters wrought on knee with seames of Golde
And on his feete his durty dabled Socks,
And with the hand where whilome hee did holde
His Clubbish bat, a thred hee nimbly spun :
Both Persia and fertile Lidia knew
(Where golden sanded Pactolus doth run)
Alcydes bid the Lyons case adew
And thunderpropping brawny shoulderd sier
That heaved and bolstred up the Welkin throne,
In slender Kirtell wrought by Web of Tyre
Did jet about to please his Love alone.
This flame (beleve the heart that feeles the wound)
Enspirde with holines excels in might,
Whereas the Land by Seas embraced round,
Where twinkling Starres doe start in Welkin bright
This peevish Elfe the Countreys all doth keepe,
Whose quarrels sting the Marble faced rout
Of water Nimphes, that with the Waters deepe
The brand that burnes in breast cannot quench out,
The flying fowle doth feele the foystring flames.
What cruell Skirmish doe the Heyffers make ?
Prickt up by lust that nice Dame Venus frames
In furious sorte for all the Cattels sake ?
If fearefull Hearts their Hindes doe once mistrust,
In love disloyall then gladly dare they fight,
And bellowings out, they bray to witnesse just
Their angry moode, conceyv'de in irefull spright
The paynted coast of India then doth hate
The spotty Hyded Tygar, then the Bore

Doth whet his Tuskes to combat for his mate,
And fomes at mouth : the ramping Lyons rore
And shake their Manes, when Cupids corsies move :
Wyth grunts and grones the howling frythes doe murn :
The Dolphin of the raging Sea doth love :
The Elephants by Cupids blaze doe burn :
Dame nature all doth challeng as her owne,
And nothing is that can escape her lawes :
The rage of wrath is quencht and overthrowne,
When as it pleaseth Love to bid them pawes :
Blacke hate that rusting frets in cankred breast,
And all olde grudge is dasht by burning love.
What shall I make discourse more of the rest
Stout Stepdames doth this gripe to mercy move.

THE SECOND ACTE

PHÆDRA, NUTRIX, HIPPOLYTUS

ECLARE what tidings bringst thou Nurce, where is Hippolitus ?
NU. To cure this puissant breach of illes no hope there is in us :
Nor yet to quench his flashing flame : his furies fretting ire,
Doth fry in secret boyling breast, and though the smothering fire
Be coverte close, yet bursting forth in welked face it fryes :
The sparkling flakes doe glowing flash from bloudred rowling eyes.
She hanging downe her pouched groyne, abhors the lothsome light,
Her skittish wits and wayward minde can fancy nothing right :
Her faltring legs doe fayle her now, downe squatting on the ground
With sprauling lims her shittell griefe doth cast her in a swound :
Now scant shee on her lithy necke holdes up her giddy hed,
Nor can commit her selfe to couche in rest upon her bed.
Nor harbring quietnes in heart wyth drery dewle and plaint
She languisheth through out the night, and now her body faynt
She biddes them up to lift : and now her downe agayne to lay,
And now hir crispen locks undone abroade shee biddes display :
And strayt to wrap them up agayne. Thus fickle fansie still
Doth fleete, nor is contented with his wayward wandring will.
No care she casteth on her health nor eates one crum of breade,
With feeble fumbling foote upon the floore eke doth she treade,
Her strength alas is quight consumde, her savor sweete doth faynt :
Nor ruddy sanguine purple deye her cherry cheekes doth paynt :
Wyth greedy gripes of gnawing griefe her pinched limmes doe pyne :
Her foltring legs doe stagger now : the glosse of beauty fyne

In body Alabaster bright is shronke away and wast.
Those Cristall Eyes that wonted were resemblance cleare to cast
Of radiant Phœbus gold arayes, now nothing gentry shyne :
Nor beare a sparke of Phœbus bright her fathers beams devyne :
The trickling teares tril down her chekes, dew dampish dropping still,
Doth wet her watrye plantes, as on the toppe of Taurus hill
The watry snowes with lukewarme shoures to moisture turnd do drop
But lo the Princes pallace is set open in the top :
She lying downe upon her golden bed of high estate
Hurles of hir wonted royal robes which wounded hart doth hate :
PH. Maydes, have our purple garmentes hence, and vestures wrought with gold,
These crimson robes of scarlet red let not myne eyes behold.
And damaske weedes, wheron the Seres embrauder braunches brave,
Whose Silken substaunce gatherd of their trees aloofe they have,
My bosome shalbe swadled in with cuttied gaberdine,
No golden coller on my necke nor Indian jewels fyne,
The precious pearles so whyte shal hang no more now at myne eares,
Nor sweete perfumes of Siria shal poulder more my heares.
My flaring ruffled lockes shal dagling hang my necke aboute
And shoulder poyntes : then then apace it shattring in and out.
Let wyndes even blow it where it list, in left hand wil I take
A quiver of shaftes, and in my right a Boarespere wil I shake,
To cruell child Hippolitus such one his mother was,
As fleeting from the frosen Seas those countrey costes did passe,
And drave her heerdes that bet with trampling feete Th' Athenian soyle
Or like the trull of Tanais, Or like her wil I toyle,
Of Meotis that on a knot wounde up her crispen lockes :
Thus wil I trot with moonelike targe among the wodes and rockes.
NU. Leave of thy bitter languishing unto the silie sort
(That walter thus in waves of woe) griefe gives not resting port
Is any measure to be found in thy tormenting fire :
Some grace at wyld Dianaes hand with sacrifyce require

O Goddesse greate of Woods, in hilles that onely setst thy throne,
And Goddes that of the craggy clyves at worshipped alone,
Thy wrathful threatninges on us all now turne to better plight
O Goddesse that in forestes wyld and groves obtaynest might,
O shyning lampe of heaven, and then the Diamon of the Night,
O threefold shapen Heccate that on the world his face
Dost render light with torch by turnes, vouchsafe to graunt thy grace
To further this our enterprise and helpe our piteous case,
O mollify Hippolytus his stubborne hardned hart,
And let him learne the pangues of love and tast like bitter smart :
And yeeld his light allured eares : entreate his brutish breast,
And chaunge his mynd, in Venus boundes compel him once to rest.
So froward and untoward now so crabbed curst and mad :
So shalt thou be with blandishing and smyling countnaunce clad.
Thy shimering clowde cleane fading hence then brightly shalt thou bear
And glisteryng hornes, then whyle by night upon the whirling sphere,
Thy cloudy heeled steedes thou guydes, the raging witches charme
Of Thessal, shal not draw thee from the heavens nor do thy harme
No Shepherd purchase shal renoume. Thou comst at our request :
Now favour dost thou graunt unto the prayers of our Breast :
I do espye him worshipping the solemne Sacrifyce,
Both place and tyme convenient by Fortune doth arise :
We must go craftely to worke : for feare we quaking stand,
Ful hard it is the buysy charge of guylt to take in hand :
But who of Princes standes in awe, let him defye all right,
Cast of the care of honesty from mind exiled quight,
A man unfit is for the hest of King a bashful wight.

HIP. O Nurse, how chaunce thy limping limmes do crepe into this place ?
With blubbred Cheekes, and leaden lookes, with sad and mourning face ?
Doth yet my Father Theseus with health enjoy his life ?
Doth Phædra yet enjoy her health my stepdam and his wyfe.

NU. Forgoe these feares, and gently come thy blessed hap to take,
For care constrayneth me to mourne with sorrow for thy sake,

That hurtfully thou looudes thy selfe with pangues of plunging payne:
Let him rubbe on in misery whom destny doth constrayne:
But if that any yeld himselfe to waves of wilful woe,
And doth torment himselfe, deserves his weale for to forgoe
The which he knowes not how to use: tush, be not so demure,
Considering how thy yeares do runne, take part of sport and play,
Let mirry Bacchus cause thee cast these clogging cares away,
And reape the fruite of sweete delyght belonging to thy yeares,
For lusty youth with speedy foote ful fast away it weares.
Earst tender love, earst Venus feedes the young mannes appetite,
Be blyth my Boy, why Widow like liest thou alone by night?
Shake of thy sollem sadnesse man that harty youth doth spill:
Huff, royst it out couragiously, take bridle at thy will.
Let not the flowre of plooming yeares all fruitles fade away.
God poynteth every tyme his taske, and leades in due aray
Each age by order just, as mirth the sappy youthfull yeares,
A forehed frayte with gravity becommeth hoary hayres.
Why dost thou bridle thus thy selfe, and dulles thy pregnant wit?
The corne that did but lately sproute above the ground, if it
Be rancke of roote, yet in the huske, with enterest at large
Unto the hoping husbandman shall travel all discharge.
With braunched bough above the Wood the tree shall raise his top,
Whom rusty hand of canckred hate, did never spill nor lop.
The pregnant Wittes are evermore more prone to purchase prayse,
If noble heartes by freedome franckt be nourisht from decayes.
Thou churlish countrey Clowne Hodgelike not knowing Courtly life,
Delight in drousy doting youth without a loving wyfe.
Dost thou suppose that to this end Dame Nature did us frame,
To suffer hardnes in this world and to abyde the same?
With courses and kerereyes set the prauncing Steedes to tame?
Or bicker els with battails fierce, and broyls of bloudy warre?
That soveraygne Syre of heaven and earth, when fates do us detarre,
With signes and plagues prognosticate provided hath with heede,
For to repayre the damage done with new begotten seede.
Go to, let bedding in the world be used once no more
(That stil mankind from age to age upholdes and doth restore).

The filthy world deformd would lie in yrksome ugly stay,
No floting ships on wambling Seas should hoysted Sayles display,
No Foule should skoare in azur Skie, ne Beast to woods repayre,
And onely whisking windes should whirle amid the empty ayre.
What divers dreery deathes drive one mankind to dumpish grave ?
The Seas, the sword and trayterous traynes whole countries wasted have :
Yet for to limit forth our league there is no destny thincke,
So downe to blackefast Stigian dampes we of our selves do sincke.
Let youth that never felt the joyes, in Venus lap which lie,
Alow the solitary life, what ever thou espye,
An hurliburly shall become for tearme of one mans life,
And worke it one destruction by mutuall hate and strife.
Now therfore follow natures course, of life the soveraygne guyde,
Resort unto the towne : with men delight thee to abyde.
HIP. No life is more devoyd of sinne, and free from grievous thralles,
And keeping fashions old, then that which leaving Townish walles,
Doth take delight in pleasant Woods, he is not set on fyre,
Enraged sore with burning Byle of covetous desyre.
Who hath addict himselfe among the mountaynes wilde to live,
Not prickt with pratling peoples bruite, no credit doth he geve.
To th' Vulgar sort disloyall still, unto the better part
Nor cankred rancour pale doth gnaw his blacke and fretting hart.
Nor fickle favour forceth he, he bound doth not obay
The payse of Scepter proude : but weildes the massy scepter sway
At ebbing honours gapes he not, nor moyles for fleeting mucke,
Removed farre from hovering hope and dread of backward lucke,
Not bitter gnawing Envy rancke teares him with tooth unkind,
Not quaynted with the mischiefe that in Cittyes and in mynd
Of people presseth thicke : nor quakes at every blast that flies
With guilty conscience to himselfe, nor frames himselfe to lies.
Nor covets rich with thousand pillers close his head to shroude,
Nor guildes his beams with glisteryng gold for fancy fond and proude,
Nor gushing streames of bloud upon his innocent Alters flow.
Nor Bullockes bright their hundred heads as whyte as flakie Snow,
Do yeeld to Axe, whyle scattered is on thaulter sacred grayne,
But al the quiet countrey round at wil he doth obtayne.

And harmles walketh too and froe amid the open ayre,
And onely for the brutish Beast contrives a trapping snare.
Another whyle uppon the swift Alpheus banckes he walkes
Now up and downe the breary Brakes of bushy woods he stalkes
Where lukewarme Lernas christall floud with water cleare doth shine,
And chaunging course his Channell out another way doth twyne :
And heare the piteous plaining Birds with chirping charmes do chide,
And Braunches trembling shake whereon soft windye puffes do glyde.
And spreading Beches old do stand, to fast and shake my shankes :
To stampe and daunce it doth me good on running Rivers bankes :
Or els upon a withred clod to steale a nap of sleepe,
Whereas the fountayne flowes amayne with gushing waters deepe.
Or els among the baulmy flowres out braying savours sweete,
Wheras with pleasant humming noise the bubbling brooke doth fleete.
The Apples beaten of the tree do ravening hunger staunch,
An Strawberyes gathered of the bush soone fill with hungry paunch.
He shoons assaultes, that doth himselfe from regall royall hold.
Estates do quaffe theyr dreadful drinke in Bolles of massye Golde :
How trimme it is water to lap in palme of naked hand :
The sooner drowsye Morpheus byndes thy Browes with sleepy bande :
The carelesse corpes doth rest at ease upon the hardest Couch :
The Cabin base hauntes not by Nookes, to prig and filch a pouch :
In house of many corners blynd his head he doth not hyde,
He loves to come abroade and in the light to be espyde :
The Heavens beare witnesse of his life, they lived in this wise.
I thinke, that scattred did of Gods in alder time arise.
No doting covetous blinde desire of Golde in them was found :
No stones nor stakes set up in field did stint the parted ground :
The sayling Ship with brazen Stem cut not the waltring wave,
But every man doth know his coast and how much he should have.
No hugy Rampires raysed were, nor Ditches delved deepe,
Nor countermured Castle strong the walled Townes to keepe.

The Souldier was not busied his blunted Tooles to whet,
Nor rapping Pellets, Cannon shot the barred Gates downe bet,
Nor soyle with yoaked Oxe was strainde to beare the cutting share,
The field even fertill of it selfe did feede the World with fare,
The plentifull aboundant Woods great wealth by nature gave :
A house of nature eake they had a dimme and darksome Cave :
The covetous minde to scrape up wealth, and despret furious ire,
And greedy Lust (that eggeth on the minde all set on fire.)
First brake the bands, and eger thirst of bearing sway stept in,
To be the strongers ravening pray the weaker did begin,
And might went for oppressed right : the naked Fist found out
To scratch and cuffe, to box and bum, with dealing blowes about.
The knarrie Logs, and snaggie shive were framed weapons strong,
The gatten Tree ungrayned was with Pikes of Yron long.
No nor the rusty Fawchon then did hang along the side,
Nor Helmet crest upon the head stood percking up for pride,
Pale spightfull griefe invented Tooles, and warlick Mars his braine
Contriv'de new sleights, a thousand kinde of deathes he did ordaine :
By meanes hereof eche Land is fild with clottred gore yshed,
With streames of bloud the Seas are dyde to hue of sanguine red,
Then Mischiefe wanting measure gan through every house to passe,
No kinde of vitious villany that practise wanted was.
By Brother, Brother reft of Breath, and eake the Fathers Life
By hand of Childe, eake murthred was the husband of his Wyfe,
And Mother lewde on mischiefe set destroyde their bodies seede.
I overpasse the Stepdame with her guilt and haynous deede.
And no where pitty planted is, as in the brutish beast :
But womankinde in mischiefe is ringleader of the reast,
The instrument of wickednesse enkindling first desire,
Whose vile uncesteous whoredome set so many Townes on fire.
So many Nations fall to warre, eake Kingdomes overthrowne,
And raysed from the ground, to crushe so many people downe.
Let other passe : by Jasons Wyfe Medea may wee finde
By her alone, that Women are a plaguy crabbed kinde.
NU. Why, for one womans fault of blame shall every one have part ?
HIP. I hate, detest, abhore, I loth, I curse them from my heart.
Bee 't reason, right, or Natures law, or vengeance fury fell,
It likes me to abhorre them still : the burning fire shall dwell,

And bide with quenching water first, the daungerous quick Sand
Shall promise Ships with safetinesse upon the shold to land,
And Western Thetis soonke aloofe and drencht in deepest nooke,
Shall force the ruddy Morning Sunne from scarlet Skies to looke,
The Woolfe shall yeelde his fleering Chaps to suck the Tet of Do
Ere woon by womans love, to her I crouch and stoupe alow.
NU. Love bridles oft with snaffling bits the stubborne wayward heart,
Beholde thy Mothers native land in Scythia every part,
The salvage women feele the force of Venus yoaking band.
Thou onely Childe thy Mother had dost this well understand.
HIP. This onely comfort of my Mother must I keepe behinde,
That leefull unto me it is to hate all Womankinde.
NU. Even as the stiffe and sturdy Rocks have waltring waves wythstoode,
And dasheth backe from shore aloofe the fomy flapping floode :
So lightly he contemnes my talke : but Phædra runneth mad
Because of this my long delay with crushing cares yclad :
What will she doe ? Aye me alas how shall she now be spead ?
Her breathlesse body to the ground drops sodenly downe dead.
A sallow hue like gastly death overstrikes her frenzy Face,
Looke up and speake beholde thy deare sweete heart doth thee embrace.

PHÆDRA, NUTRIX, HIPPOLYTUS

ALAS to flote in Waves of woe who mee revives agayne ?
To pinch my minde with pining pangues and bitter brunts of payne.
What ease to mee it was, when as I lay in traunce at rest ?
Why dost thou thus the pleasure of renued lyfe detest :
O heart be bolde, assay and seeke thy purpose to attayne,
Be not abasht, nor faced out with churlish wordes agayne.
Who faintly craveth any boone, gives courage to deny :
The greatest portion of my crime dispacht ere now have I :
Shame seekes to late to purchase place within our bashfull brow,
Sith that in foule and lothsome love wee have delight ere now,
If I obtayne my will, then shall our wedlocke cloake the crime :
Successe corrupteth honesty with wickednesse sometime :

HIP. Behold this secret place is voyde from any witnesse bye.
PH. My foltring tong doth in my mouth my tale begun denye.
Great force constrayneth mee to speake, but greater holde my peace,
O heavenly Ghostes I you protest, tis this that doth me please.
HIP. Cannot the minde that covers talke in wordes at will out brast?
PH. Light cares have words at will, but great doe make us sore agast.
HIP. Mother the griefe that galles your heart come whisper in mine eare.
PH. The name of Mother is to proude a name for me to beare,
Importing puissant power too much: the fancy of my minde
It doth behove, a baser name of lesse renowne to finde.
Mee (if thou please) Hippolytus thy Loving Sister call,
Or wayting Maide, and rather so: no drudgry spare I shall,
If thou through thicke and thin in snowes to travaile me desire,
Or else commaunde mee for to runne through Coales of flaming fire,
Or set my foote on Pindus frosen Rocks, it yrkes mee not.
Or if thou will me rashly runne thorow scorching fire hot,
Or ravening routes of salvage beastes I will not slowly rest,
With gory Launce of naked blade my bowels to unbrest.
These Kingdomes left to mee in charge weild thou of them the sway,
And take mee as thy humble Mate, it fits mee to obay,
And thee to give commaundement, it is no womans feate,
To claime her Title to the Crowne, to raigne in Parents seate.
Thou flourishing amid the pryde of lusty youthfull race
Supply a valiant Prynces roome with Fathers golden Mace,
Protect thy humble suppliant, defend thy lowly Maide
Embrast in mercies bosome, at thy Feete so meeklye layde.
Take pitty on a siely Widdowes wo, and wretched plight.
HIP. The God that raignes aloft, forbid such lucklesse lot to light.
My Father Theseus safe in health will straight returne againe.
PH. The lowring Lord that deepe in strong infernal Gaile doe raigne,
And damned up alwayes to passe from Stygian Puddle glum,
Whereby to breathing bodies left alone the ground to cum,

Shall he let scape the Cloyner of his joyes from spousall bed,
Unlesse that Plutos fancy fond by doting love be led ?
HIP. The righteous Gods will make for him a right retourning way,
But while through feare our wavering wils in hovering Ballance sway,
Upon my brethren will I cast a due and earnest care,
And thee defend : beleve not that in Widdowes plight yee are :
And I my selfe will unto the supply my Fathers place.
PH. O Love (alas) of credit light, O Love of flickring Face,
Is this inough that hee hath sayd ? entreatance will I try,
Deare chylde rue on my wretched woe, doe not my suite deny,
That lurcking close doth couch in secret mourning breast of mee,
Faine would I speake : yet loth I am. HIP. What mischiefe may this bee ?
PH. Such mischief as ye would not think, could light in Mothers minde.
HIP. With mumbling voyce perplext yee waste your words against the winde.
PH. A vapor hoate, and Love doe glow within my bedlem brest :
It raging ranke no inwarde juyce undried leaves in rest :
The fier sonk in skalded guts through every vayne doth frie,
And smothering close in seething bloud as flashing flame doth flie,
With egar sweeping sway along up burning beames on hie.
HIP. Enamorde thus with Love entiere of Theseus dost thou rage ?
PH. Even so it is : the lovely lookes of Theseus former age
Which hee a sweete welfavorde Boy did beare with comly grace,
When prety dapper cutted Beard on cleare complexionde Face
Can sproute, on naked Chin, when hee the kennels clottred bloode
Beheld of mongrell Minotaur, and crooking Maze withstoode
By groping long untwined thredes the beames of bewty bright
That shone then in his Face, his crispen lockes with labels dight,
Smooth stroked lay, his scarlet Cheekes by nature paincted bright
Pouldred with spots of golden glosse, and sharpe assaults of Love
Prevayled in his fleshly armes : what grace doth shine above
In the Dianaes Face, or fiery crested Phœbus myne,
Or else in comely count'naunce of this lovely face of thine,
Such Theseus had when Ariadnaes Eye he did delight :
Thus portly pacing did he beare his noble head upright.

It is no counterfeyted glosse that shineth in thy Face,
In thee appeares thy manly Fathers sterne and lowring Grace.
Thy Mothers crabbed count'naunce eake resembled in some part
Puts in full well a seemelynesse, to please the Lookers hart.
The Scythian awfull Majesty with Greekish favour sweete
Appeares : if thou had with thy Syre attempt the Seas of Creete,
(One of those seaven from Athens sent elect by lucklesse lot
To pay such bloudy tribute, which King Minos of them got.
The ravening and bloudthirsty Minotaurus fowle to feede)
My Sister Ariadne would, for thee have spunne the threede.
Therewith in crafty compast Maze to leade thee to and fro,
In ugly Laberynthus long returning from thy Fo.
Thee, thee O Sister deare whereso in all the Heaven thou are,
And shinest bright with blasing beames transform'de into a Starre,
I thee beseech come succour mee with like distresse now cloyde :
Alas us siely Sisters twaine one kinred hath destroyde.
The Sire thy smart, the sonne hath brewd the bane that me doth lees.
Beholde an Impe of royall race layde humbly at thy Knees,
Yet never staynde, and undefilde, an harmelesse innocent,
To thee alone of all the Worlde my crowching Knees are bent,
And for the nones my hawty heart, and Princely courage stout
I did abate, that humbly thee with teares entreate I mought.
HIP. O soveraygne Sire of Gods, dost thou abide so long to heare
This vile abhomination ? so long dost thou forbeare
To see this haynous villany ? if now the Skies be cleare,
Wilt thou henceforth at any time with furious raging hand
Dart out thy cracking thunder dint, and dreadfull lightnings brand ?
Now battred downe with bouncing bolts the rumbling Skies let fall
That foggy Cloudes with dusky drouping day may cover all,
And force the backward starting starres to slide a slope wythall
Thou starry crested crowne, and Titan prankt with beamy blase
Come out, with staring bush upon thy kindreds guilt to gase.
Dash out and drowne thy leaming lampe eclisde in glummy Skyes,
To shrink in shimmering shape: why doth thy right hand not aryse
O guide of Gods and men ? how haps the worlde yet doth not burne,
Enkindled with three forked brand ? on me thy thunder turne,

Dash out on mee thy bobbing bolt, and let thy fiery flake
Whirlde out with force, burnt Cinders of my wasted Carcasse make :
For guilty (Jove) I guilty am, deserved death I have,
My Stepdames Fancy I have fed : shall I most sinfull slave,
Be worthy thought to blot my Fathers honorable Bed ?
Canst thou for mischiefe such through mee alone be lightly sped ?
O Caitive thou of womankinde for guilt that beares the bell,
Whose enterprised hainous evill doth passingly excell,
Thy Monster breeding Mothers fault with whoredome shee alone
Defilde her selfe, when storming sighes with sorrow gan shee grone,
Through beastly lust of Bull, till it the Minotaurus sier
In act of generation, had quencht her foule desier :
And yet the time concealed long, the grim twishaped seede
At length bewrayd with Bullike browes, thy Mothers naughty deede,
The doubted Infant did disclose : that wicked wombe shee bare.
With thrise, yea, foure times blessed Fate of lyfe depriv'de yee are,
Whom swolne of waltring Seas have sonck, me cankred hate of breath
Dispoyled hath, and traytrous traynes have quelde by daunting death.
With Stepdames banes and sorcery O Father, Father myne,
I rue thy lot, not to be slayne of milder Stepdame thyne.
This mischiefe greater, greater farre the wickednesse doth passe
That by Medea despret Dame of Colchis practisde was.
Ph. And I doe know, what uncouth luck upon our stock hath light,
The thing that we should shun, we seeke, it is not in my might
To rule my selfe : through burning fire runne after thee I shall,
Through raging Seas, and craggy Rocks, through fleeting Ryvers all,
Which boyling waters ruffling rayse, what way so goe thou will,
I bedlem Wight with frantick fits will follow, follow still.
O stately Lorde before thy feete yet fall I once agayne.
Hip. Doe not with shamelesse fawning Pawes my spotlesse body staine.
What meaneth this ? with hawsing mee t' imbrace she doth begin :
Draw, draw my sword, with stripes deserv'de Ile pay her on the skin :

Her hayre about my left hand wound, her head I backward wrike,
No bloud Diana better spent thine Aulter yet hath dyde.
PH. Hippolytus, now dost thou graunt to mee mine owne desire,
Thou cooles my ramping rage, this is much more than I require,
That saving thus mine honesty I may be geven to death,
By bloudy stroake received of thy hand to loose my breath.
HIP. Avaunt, avaunt, preserve thy lyfe, at my hand nothing crave,
This filed Sword that thou hast toucht no longer will I have.
What bathing lukewarme Tanais may I defilde obtaine,
Whose clensing watry Channell pure may washe mee cleane againe ?
Or what Meotis muddy meare, with rough Barbarian wave
That boardes on Pontus roring Sea ? not Neptune graundsire grave
With all his Ocean foulding floud can purge and wash away
This dunghill foule of stane : O woode, O salvage beast I say :
NUT. Thy crime detected is : O soule, why droupes thou all agast ?
Let us appeach Hippolytus with fault upon him cast :
And let us lay unto his charge, how he by might unjust
Deflowre would his Fathers Wyfe with mischiefe, mischiefe must
Concealed bee : the best it is, thy foe first to invade,
Sith that the crime is yet unknowne who can be witnesse made,
That either first wee enterprisde, or suffred of him then ?
Come, come, in hast Athenians, O troupes of trusty men
Help, help, Hippolytus doth come, hee comes, that Villaine vile,
That Ravisher, and Lecher foule, perforce woulde us defile.
Hee threatens us denouncing death, and glittering Blade doth shake,
At her who chastly doth withstand, and doth for terrour quake :
Lo headlong hence for life and death hee tooke him to his flight,
And leaves his Sword in running rash, with gastly feare afright :
A token of his enterprise detestable wee keepe,
Sirs chearish her, that storming sighes with pensive breast doth weepe.
Her ruffled hayre, and shattred Locks still let them daggle downe,
This witnesse of his villany so beare into the Towne.
(O Lady mine be of good cheare. Plucke up your sprights againe,)
Why dost thou tearing thus thy selfe abhorre all peoples sight ?
Not blinde Mischaunce but fancy wont to make a shamelesse Wight.

HIPPOLYTUS

THE SECOND ACTE

CHORUS

Hippolytus even as the rageing storme away doth fly,
More swift than whirling Western wynde uptumbling cloudes in Sky,
More swift then flashing flames, that catch their course with sweeping sway,
When Stars ytost with whisking windes long fiery Drakes display.
Fame (wondring at of aldertime our Auncestours renowne)
Fare well with thee, and beare away olde worship from our Towne.
So much thy beauty brighter shines, as much more cleare and fayre,
The golden Moone with glorious Globe full furnisht in the Ayre
Doth shine, when as her fiery tips of wayning hornes doe close,
When lifting up her fulgent face in ambling Waine she goes,
Upon her nightwatch to attend, the Starres of lesser light
Their darckned Faces hide, as hee the Messenger of night
That watchword geves of th' evening tide and Hesperus hee hight,
That glading earst was bath'de in Seas, and hee the same agayne
When shades be shrunck, doth then the name of Lucifer obtayne.
Thou Bacchus blessed borne of Jove in warlicke India borne,
Thou Lad that evermore dost weare thy hayry bush unshorne,
Whose Javeling tuft with Ivy bunch, the Tygres makes adred,
And dost with labelde Myter use to pranck thy horny hed,
Hippolytus his staring Locks thou Bacchus shalt not stayne,
To woonder at thy loving lookes too much doe thou refrayne,
Whom (as the people doe report) the Ariadne bright,
For beauties name preferde before Bacchus that Bromius hight.
A brittle Jewell beauty is on mortall men employde,
Thou gift that for a season short of Mankinde arte enjoyde,
How soone alas with feathered foote hence dost thou fading slide?
The partching Sommers vapour hoate in Vers most pleasaunte pride
So withers not the Meadowes greene, (when as the scorching Sunne)
In Tropick ligue of burning Crab full hoate at Noone doth runne
And on her shorter clowdy Wheeles unhorseth soone the night.
With wanny Leaves downe hang the heads of withred Lillies whight,
The balmy bloomes and sprouting floure do leave the naked hed,
As beauty bright whose radiant beams in corauld Cheekes is spred,

Is dashed in the twincke of Eye : no day as yet did passe,
In which not of his beauty reft some pearles person was.
For Favour is a fleetyng thing : what wight of any wit
Wil unto frayle and fickle joy his confidence commit?
Take pleasure of it whyle thou mayst, for Tyme with stealing steps
Wil undermint, on howre past straygh in a worser leps :
Why flyest thou to the wildernes, to seeke thy succour there?
Thy beauty bydes not safer in the waylesse woods then here.
If Tytan hoyst his totteryng Cart on poynt of ful midday,
Thee shrowded close among the brakes the Naids wil assay,
A gadding troupe that beautyes Boyes do locke in fountaynes fayre,
To frame their seate then unto thee in senseles sleepe repayre,
Shal wanton Fayries, Nymphes of Frithes, that on the Hilles do walke,
Which Dryads mountayne Goblins haunt, that use on hilles to stalke :
Or when from high Starbearing poale Diana downe did looke
On thee that next old Arcades in heaven thy seate hast tooke,
Shee could not weilde her weltring wayne, and yet no foggy cloude
Eclipst her gleaming Globe, but we with tincking Pans aloude,
Can make a noyse, agrised at her dead and glowing light
We deemd hir charmd with Magicke verse of Thessant witches spright.
But thou didst cause hir busines, and madest her in a maze,
Whyse at thy pleasant lovely lookes the Goddesse stoode in gaze,
That rules the rayne of cloudy night she stopt her running race,
God graunt that seldome byting frost may pinch this comely face.
Let seldome scorching Sunny beams thy Cheekes with freckles die :
The Marble blue in quarry pittes of Parius that doth lie,
Beares not so brave a glimsyng glosse as pleasant seemes thy face
Whose browes with manly majesty support an awful grace.
And forehead fraught with gravity of Fathers countnaunce old :
His Ivory colourd necke although compare to Phœbe ye would,
His lockes (that never lacking knew) it selfe displaying wyde
On shoulder poyntes doth set them out, and also doth them hyde.
Thy curled forhead seemes thee well, and eake thy notted hayre,
That crumpled lies undight in thee a manly grace doth beare.
Thou Gods (though fierce and valiant) perforce dost chase, and farre
Dost overmatch in length of limmes, though yet but young thou arre,
Thou beares as big and boystrous brawnes as Hercules : thy breast,
Then Champion Mars more bourly bolstred out with broader chest :

On back of hornie hoofed Steedes if vawting thou do ryde,
With Bridle in thyne active hand more handsome canst thou guyde.
The trampling Cyllar horse of Spart, then Princely Castor could,
Thy Letherne loope amid thy dart with former fingers hould,
And drive thy launce with all thy pith, the active men of Creete,
That with their pitched dartes afarre do learne the marke to hit.
They shall not hurle a slender Reede, but after Parthian guyse
To shoote an arrow if they list into the open Skies.
Unsped without some Bird attaynt it shal not light on ground,
Unbath'd with lukewarme bloud of guttes in gory smoking wound,
And from amid the lofty Cloudes downe shalt thou fetch thy pray :
Few men (marke wel the tyme) have borne beauty unplagude away.
God send thee better lucke, and graunt thy noble personage
May passe unto the happy steps and stretch to dumpish age.
What mischief unattempt escapes a Womans witlesse rage?
Most haynous crymes shee meanes to lay to guiltles youngmans charge,
And thinkes to make her matter good with hayre thus rent at large,
She towseth eake the pranking of her head with watred plantes,
Her slye devyse no crafty kind of womans fetches wantes.
But who is this that in his face such princely port doth beare?
Whose lofty lookes with stately pace hie vauntst his head doth reare?
Lyke lusty young Pyrithous, he looketh in the face,
But that a faynting fallow pale his bleakish Cheekes disgrace,
And filthy baggage hangeth on his hash hayre raysde upright,
Lo Theseus, it is agayne restoard to earthly light:

THE THIRDE ACTE

THESEUS, NUTRIX

T length I scapt the glowinge glades of grim eternall Night,
And eake the underpropping poale, that each infernall Spright
Doth muffle in, shut up in shades loe how my dazelled eyes
Can scant abyde the long deffered light of Marble Skies.
Eleusis now fowre offringes of Triptolemus devydes,
And counterpaysed Day with Night now foure tymes Libra hydes.
I earnest in my Parlous toyle in doubt what lucke to have
Twixt dread of gastly Death, and hope my feeble life to save,
Some sparke of life stil in my breathles limmes abyding was,
When as embarkt on erkesome Stix Alcides downe did passe,
To succour me in dire distresse, who when the hellicke hound
From Tartares griesly gates in Chaynes he dragd above the ground,
And also me he caryed up into the World agayne
My tyred limmes doth sappy pith of former strength restrayne,
My feble faltring legges do quake, what lugging toyle it was
From bottom deepe of Phlegethon to world aloofe to passe ?
What dreary dole and mourning noyse is this that beates myne eares ?
Let some declare it unto mee : who blubbred so with teares
Lamenting loud and languishing within our gates appeares ?
This entertaynment fit is for a guest that comes from Hell.
Nu. A stubborne heart and obstinate in Phedras breast doth dwell,
With despret mind to slay her selfe our teares she doth despyse,
And giving up the gasping Ghoast, alas my Lady dyes.

TH. Why should she kill herselfe ? why die, hir spouse being come againe ?
NU. For this (my Lord) with hasty death she would her selfe have slaine.
TH. These troblous wordes some perlous thing I wot not what to tell.
Speake plain : what lumpe of glutting griefe her laded heart doth quel,
She doth complayne her case to none, but pensively and sad
She keepes it secrete to hir selfe, determind thus shee had,
To beare aboute with her the bane, wherewith she meanes to die.
Hie, hie thee fast, I pray thee now, now have wee neede to hye.
Our Pallace lockt with stately stoulpes set open by and by.

THESEUS, PHÆDRA

O MADAME Mate of Spousall bedde thus dost thou entertayne
The comming of thy loving Spouse ? and welcom home agayne
Thy long desyred Husbandes face ? why takes thou not away
My Sword out of my hand, and dost not cheare my Sprites (I saye)
Nor shewest me what doth the breath out of the body chase ?
PH. Alas my valiant Theseus even for thy royall mace,
Wherwith thy Kingdome thou dost weild, and by the noble raygne
Of thy belov'd posterity, and comming home agayne,
And for the worship that is due unto my fatall grave,
O let me die and suffer me, deserved death to have.
TH. What cause compelleth thee to die ? PH. If I the cause of death
Disclose, then shall I not obtayne the loosyng of my breath.
TH. No worldly wight (save I my selfe alone) the same shall heare,
Art thou affrayd to tel it in thy husbandes bashful eare ?
Speake out, thy secretes shrowd I shall within my faythful brest.
PH. What thou would other to conceale, kepe thou it first in rest.
TH. Thou shalt not suffred be to die. PH. From him that wisheth Death,
Death never can be seperate. TH. The crime that losse of breath

Ought to revenge, shew it to me. PH. Forsooth because I live.
TH. Alas do not my trilling teares thy stony stomacke grieve?
PH. It is the sweetest death, when one doth lothsome life forsake,
Bereft of such as should for him most woful weeping make.
TH. Stil standes she mum? the croked, old, ilfavord, hoblinge Trotte,
Hir Nurse for stripes and clogging bandes shall utter every jotte,
That shee forbid her hath to tell: in yron chaynes her bynd,
Let tawing whips wring out perforce the secrets of her mynd.
PH. Now I my selfe wil speak: stay yet. TH. Why dost thou turne aside
From me thy weeping Countenance? thy teares why dost thou hide
That gushing sodaine from thine eyes streame downe thy cheekes apace?
Why hidest thou thy flowing floudes with Coate before thy Face?
PH. Thee, thee, Creator of the Heavens to witnesse I doe call,
And thee O glittering fiery glede of Christall Sky with all,
And Phœbus thou from whom at first our royall Race hath roon.
With fawning face and flattring words in suite I was not woon.
For naked sword, and thundring threts, appauled was I not:
My brused bones abode the blowe, and stripes when sore he smote:
This blemish black of foule defame my bloud shall purge agayne.
TH. Declare what villaine is he that our honour so doth stayne?
PH. Whom least yee would mistrust. TH. To know who tis, ful sore I long.
PH. This Sword wil tel, which sore afright when people thick in throng
Resorted fast, the Leacher vile for hast did leave behinde,
Because the people preasing fast he dreeded in his minde.
TH. Ah out alas, O woe is mee, what villany see I?
Alas what uncouth Monster fowle of mischiefe I espy?
Beholde the royall Ivory engravde and purtred fine,
Emboast with golden studdes, upon th' enameld Haft doth shine,
(The Jewell of Actea lande) but whyther fled is hee?
PH. With light Heele running sore dismaide these servants did him see?

THE THIRD ACTE

Th. O sacred holinesse, O Jove betweene whose mighty hands
The Marble Poale with weltring sway in course directed stands,
And thou that second Scepter weilds in fomy fighting wave,
Why doth this cursed broode with such this wicked vengeance rave?
Hath he bene fostred up in Greece? or craggy Taurus wilde
Among hard rugged Rocks, and Caves, some savage Scythian Childe?
Or else in brutish Colchis Ile by Desart Phasis flood?
Cat after kinde hee is, and will th' unkindly Bastard blood
Returne unto his kinreds course, whence first his ligne hee clames.
This frantick fury up and downe comes of the warlicke Dames,
To hate the loyall leagues of love, and shunning long the use
Of Cupids campe, with tag, and rag, her body to abuse,
Become as good as ever twangd: O detestable kinde,
No better Soyle by any meanes can chaunge thy filthy minde.
The brutish beasts themselves doe loath th' abuse which Venus drawes,
And simple shamefastnesse it selfe observeth Natures lawes:
Where is the brag of Majesty, and fayned portly grace
Of manly minde, that hateth new, and olde things doth embrace?
O double dealing life, thou clokes deceiptful thoughts in brest,
And settest out a forhead fayre where frounced mynd doth rest:
The saucie Jacke with bashful brow doth malipiertnes hide:
The rashnes of the despret Dicke by stilnesse is unspide.
With show of right religion knaves villany mayntayne,
And guileful mealemouthd Gentlemen do hold with speaking playne:
The daynty wanton Carpet Knights of hardnes boast and prate,
That Woodraunger, that brainsicke beast who liv'd in chast estate
An undefyled Bachiler thou rude and homely clowne,
Thus dost thou watch thy tyme, to breede this blot in my renowne?
To make me Cuckold first of all did it delyght thy mynd,
First falling to thy spousall sport with mischiefe most unkind.
Now, now, to thee supernal Jove most hearty thankes I yeeld,
That with my first Antiope to dreary death I quelde,
That gone to dampish Stygian Dennes I left thee not behynd
Thy Mother: go, go Vagabond rawnge, rawnge, about to finde

Straunge forraine soyles, and outcast landes aloofe at world his end,
And Iles enclosd with th' Ocean floud to hell thy soule shall send :
Beneath among th' Antipodes thy selfe of harbring sped,
Though in the utmost lurking nooke, thou shroude thy miching heade,
Above the grisly Pallaces thou climbe of lofty Poale,
Or maist above the clottring Snow advaunce thy cursed Soule,
Beyond the brunt of Winter flawes and threatning rigour passe
And stormy wrath with rumbling rough of ysie Boreas,
With vengeance, vengeance violent fast hurling after thee,
With daunting plagues and pestilence thy sinnes shal scourged bee.
For life and death, about the world in every lurking hoale,
O fugitive I shal not cease stil to pursue thy soule.
But seeke and search for thee I shall in landes that lye a farre,
Al corners blynd and caves shut up, Dennes lockt with bolt and barre,
A thousand wayes unpassable no place shal me withstand.
My cursinges blacke shal light on thee there where revenging hande
With weapon can not worke the harme : thou knowest that Neptune great
My Syre who flotes on floudes, and waves, with forked Mace doth beat
Geve licence freely unto me three boones to chuse and crave,
Which willingly the God hath graunt, and sworne I shal it have
Protesting ugsome Stygian Lake, and hallowed hath his vow :
O breaker of the wrastling waves, avouch thy promise now.
Let never more Hippolitus behold th' eclipsed light,
And for the Fathers wrathful rage the cursed child downe smight,
To waile among the gastly sprites o Father bend thy might,
To give (alas) this lothsome ayde unto thy needy Sonne,
I of thy Majesty devyne exact not to be donne.
This chiefest bone, til puissant payse of ylles do us oppresse :
In bottom deepe of boylyng Tartar pit, and sore distresse,
In grisly Lymbo Jawes nigh garglefaced Ditis dimme,
Amid the crumpled threatning browes of Hellick Pluto grim,
To claime thy promise made to mee, as then I didde refrayne,
Now Syre thy fayth by promise due perfourme to me agayne.

Yet dost thou stay ? why rumble not the waltring waves yet husht, THE
Through foggy cloude in dusky skies with stormy blastes outrusht. THIRD
Unfold the mantel blacke of Night, and roll away the Skies, ACTE
Enforce the fighting floods brast out with mounting waves to ryse.
And conjure up the water hagges that in the Rockes do keepe,
The Ocean surges swellyng hie cast up from bottom deepe.

CHORUS

O Nature Grandame greate of Heavenly Sprites,
Eake Jove that guides Olimpus mighty sway,
That rakes the race of twinckling heavenly lightes
On spinning Spheare and order dost for aye
The stragling course of roaming planets hie,
And weildes about the whirling Axeltree
The weltring Poales, th' eternal course of Skie
To keepe in frame, what workes such care in thee
That earst the cold which hoary winter makes
Unclothes the naked wood, and now agayne
The shades returne unto the breary brakes.
Now doth the starre of Sommer Lion raygne,
Whose scalded necke with boyling heate doth frie,
Perbraking flames from fiery foming jawes :
With scorching heate the parched corne do drie :
Ech season so his kindly course in drawes.
But thou that weildes these thinges of massy might,
By whom the hugy world with egal payse
Even Ballanced doth keepe in compasse right,
Each Spheare by measurd weight that justly swaise,
Alas why dost thou beare a retchles breast
Toward mankind ? not casting any care
That wicked men with mischiefe be opprest,
And eake to see that good men wel do fare
Dame Fortune topsieturvy turnes at wil
The world, and deales her dole with blinded hand,
And fosters vice mayntayning mischiefe ill.
Fowle lust triumphes on good men brought in band

Deceipt in stately Court the sway doth weild,
In Lordinges lewde the vulgar sort delight,
With glee to such the Mace of might they yeeld,
Some magistrates they do both love and spight,
And pensive vertue brought to bitter bale,
Receyves reward that doth of right aryse,
The continent to Prison neede doth hale,
The Leacher raygnes enhaunced by his vice.
O fruitles shame, O counterfayted port.
But what newes may this messenger now bring,
Who with maine pace comes poasting in this sort,
And stayes with mourning countnance at the Kinge

HIPPOLYTUS

THE FOURTH ACTE

NUNTIUS, THESEUS

HEAVY happe and cruell chaunce of Servantes slavish state,
Why am I Poast to bring the newes of this il favord fate?
TH. Be not abasht the ruthful wracke with courage to declare:
My breast agaynst the brunt of broyles stil armed I prepare.
NUN. My foltring tongue doth speach unto my glutting griefe denye.
TH. Our stocke with sorrow shuken sore what cares do crush escrie.
NUN. Hippolytus (ay woe is me) is slayne by doleful death.
TH. Now Father do I know my Sonne bereaved of his breath,
For why the Leacher life is lost: shew in what sort he dide.
NUN. In all poast hast as fugitive to shunne the Towne he hyde
Once having caught his cutting course apace he scuddes away,
His prauncing Palfrayes straite he doth with Collers close araye
With curbed bittes their snaffled heads at wil he brydles in,
Then talking much unto himselfe to curse he doth beginne
His native soyle: alas deare Father, Father stil he cryes:
And angry lasheth with his whip, whyle loose his Bridle lies:
Then sodenly a hugy swolve gan swel amid the deepe,
And starteth up into the starres no pipling wind doth sweepe
Along the Seas in Heaven so lith no noyse at all there was:
The Seas ful calme even as their kindly Tyde doth drive them, passe.
Nor yet no boysterous Southerne wynd the Sycill sand turmoyles.
Nor yet with fomie ramping surge the raging gulph up boyles,
Heavde up by Westerne puffes: when as the rockes with flappyng flash
Do shake and drownd Lucates clive the hoary fome doth dash.

The tombling waves togeather tost on hils are heaped hie,
The swelling swolve with Monster much to land alofe doth flye,
Nor only shaken ships in Seas do suffer wracke hereby :
The land in hazard lyes of stormes a waltring wave is rold
In tottering wise a wallowing gulph with winding compas fold,
Drives downe I know not what withall : a flat uprisyng new
An head above the water brim doth rayse the Starres to vew.
In foggie cloud eclipsed is Apollos dusky gleede,
And Scyros Rocks whom Trumpe of Fame advaunst by dreary deede
Corynthus take whom double Sea on eyther side assayle :
While greatly we agriefd, these thinges do languishing bewayle,
The belking Seas yell out the grunting Rockes with all do rore :
The stabby Clive doth reke, from whence the water ebde before,
It frothes, and keping course by course it spewes the waters out,
As doth Physeter fish (that flittes the Ocean Coast about)
And gulping doth from yawning throat his flouds of water spoute.
The shaken surge did tottre strayte and brake it selfe in twayne :
With wracke (more violent then wee did feare) it rusht amayne
Agaynst the shore, beyond the bankes it breakes into the land :
And hideous Monster followes : these for feare did quaking stand.
TH. What shape that uncouth Monster had and body vast declare.
NU. A boasting Bull, his marble necke advaunced hye that bare,
Upraysd his lofty bristled Mayn on curled forhead greene
With shaggy eares prickt up his divers speckled hornes were seene.
(Whom Bacchus earst possessed had, who tames the Cattell wyld,
And eake the God that borne in flouds was bred a water Chyld)
Now puffing he perbraketh flames, and now as leaming light
With sparckling beams his goggle eyes do glare and glister bright.
His greasy larded necke (a marke for to be noted well)
With tough and knobby turnels hie out bumping big do swell.
His snorting Nostrilles wyde do grunt and yawning gulphes they sosse,
His breast and throtebag greenishly are dawbd with clammy mosse,
His side along begrymed is with Lactuse red of hue,
On snarling knots his wrinckled rumpe toward his face he drue,
His scaly haunch, and lagging tayle most ugly dragges hee up,
As Pristis in the deepe of Seas the swallowed Keele doth sup.

Or else perbraketh out agayne the undigested pup.
The earth did quake, the Cattel feard about the field do rampe,
The hunter starke with chilling feare beginnes to stare and stampe,
The heirdman had no mynd his scattrynge Heyfers to pursue,
The Deere amazed brake the pale and bad the Laundes adue.
But onely yet Hippolytus, devoyde of faynting feare
His neyng horses with the raynes of Bridles hard doth beare,
With wonted woordes he cheareth up his nymble Nagges afraide :
A steepe hie way at Argos lies with stony clives decaide,
That nodding overhangs the Sea which underfleetes that wayes :
That ugly Royle heere heates him selfe, and raging wrath doth rayse,
And kindling courage hoate, him force with burning breast assayes,
And chaufing efe himselfe before gan fret with angry hart.
Lo then into a scouring course on sodayne doth hee start,
With whirling pace he girding forth doth scarcely touch the ground,
Lighting a front the trimbling Cart with glaring Eyes hee glowmd.
Then also doth thy threatning Son with lowring browes upstart,
Nor chaungeth Countenaunce, but speakes with stout couragious hart.
This foolish feare doth not appaule my bold and hardned brest,
It comes to mee by kinde, that Bulls by mee should bee opprest.
His Steedes defying strait the Raynes plonge forward with the Cart,
As rage did prick them, sore afright beside the way they start.
This bias way among the Rocks they raunge, and wander wyde,
But as the Pylot (least the Barke should totter to one syde)
Doth beare it even in wrastling waves : so while his horses skip,
He ruleth them, now raines them hard, and now with winding whip
Free lashes on their buttocks layes : his Foe doth him pursue,
Now step by step, now meeting full agaynst his face hee flue.
Provoking terror every where. No further fly they might :
The horned beast with butting Browes gan run upon them right.
The trampling Gennets straught of wits doe straight way breake their ray,
The struggle striving hard to slip the Collar if they may.
And prauncing on their hinder Feete, the burden hurle on ground :
Thy Son flat falling on his Face, his body fast was bound,

Entangled in the winding ropes, the more he strives to loose
The slipping knots, he faster sticks within the sliding noose.
The Horses doe perceyve the broyle : and with the Waggon light
While none there is to rule the Raynes, with skittish feare afright
At randon out they ramping runne, (even as the Welkin hye
The Cart that mist his woonted waight, disdayning in the Skye
The dreery day that falsely was commit unto the Sun,
From off the fiery Marble Poale that downe askew doth run,
Flang Phaeton topsie torvey tost) his bloud begores the ground :
And dingd agaynst the rugged Rocks his head doth oft rebound :
The brambles rent his haled hayre : the edged flinty stones,
The beauty batter of his Face, and breake his crashing bones :
At Mouth his blaring tongue hangs out with squeased eyne out dasht,
His Jawes and Skull doe crack, abrode his spurting Braynes are pasht,
His cursed beauty thus defoylde with many wounds is spent :
The jotting Wheeles do grinde his guts, and drenched lims they rent.
At length a Stake with Trunchion burnt his ripped Paunch hath caught,
From rived Grine to th' Navell stead within his wombe it raught :
The Cart upon his Maister pawsde agaynst the ground ycrusht,
The Fellies stuck within the wounds, and out at length they rusht :
So both delay and Maisters limbs are broke by stresse of Wheeles :
His dragling guts then trayle about the wincing horses heeles.
They thumping with their horny Hooves agaynst his Belly kick,
From bursten Paunch on heapes his blouddy bowells jumble thick :
The scraiting Bryers on the Brakes with needle poynted pricks
His gory Carkas all to race with spelles of thorny sticks
And of his flesh ech ragged shrub a gub doth snatch and rent,
His men (a mourning troupe God knowes) with brackish teares besprent
Doe stray about the fielde, whereas Hippolytus was tore :
A piteous signe is to bee seene by tracing long of gore :
His howling Dogges their Maisters limmes with licking follow still :
The earnest toyle of woful Wights can not the coats up fill,

By gathering up the gobbets sparst and broken lumps of flesh.
Is this the flaunting bravery that comes of beauty fresh ?
Who in his Fathers Empyre earst did raigne as pryncely Peare
The Heyre apparant to the Crowne, and shone in honour cleare,
Lyke to the glorious Stars of Heaven, his Limmes in pieces small
Are gathred to his fatall Grave, and swept to funerall.
TH. O Nature that prevaylste too much, (alas) how dost thou binde
Whyth bonds of bloud the Parents breast ? how love we thee by kinde ?
Maugre our Teeth whom guilty eeke we would have reft of breath ?
And yet lamenting with my teares I doe bewayle thy death.
NUN. None can lament with honesty that which he wisht destroyde.
TH. The hugiest heape of woes by this I thinke to be enjoyde,
When flickering Fortunes cursed wheele doe cause us cry alas,
To rue the wrack of things which earst wee wished brought to passe.
NUN. If stil thou keepe thy grudge, why is thy Face with teares besprent ?
TH. Because I slue him, not because I lost him, I repent

CHORUS

What heape of happes do tumble upsyde downe
Th' estate of man ? lesse raging Fortune flies
On little things : lesse leaming lightes are throwne
By hand of Jove, on that which lower lies.
The homely couch safe merry hartes do keepe :
The Cotage base doth give the Golden sleepe.

The lofty Turrets top that cleaves the cloude
Withstandes the sturdy stormes of Southren wynde,
And Boreas boysterous blastes with threatning loud
Of blusteryng Corus shedding showres by kinde.
The reking Dales do seldome noiance take,
Byding the brunt of Lightninges flashing flake.

Th' advaunced crest of Caucasus the great
Did quake with bolt of lofty thundring Jove :
When he from cloudes his thunder dintes did beat,
Dame Cybels Phrygian fryth did trembling move :
King Jove in hawty heaven ful sore affright
The nighest thinges with weapons doth he smyght.

The ridges low of Vulgar peoples house
Striken with stormes do never greatly shake :
His Kingdomes coast Joves thundring thumpes do souse :
With wavering winges that houre his flight doth take
Nor flitting Fortune with her fickle wheele
Lets any wight assured joy to feele.

Who in the World beholds the Starres ful bright,
And chereful day forsaking gastly Death,
His sorrowfull returne with groning spright
He rewes, sith it deprivde his Sonne of breath
He seeth his lodging in his court agayne,
More doleful is then sharpe Avernus payne.

O Pallas unto whom all Athens land
Due homage oweth, because that Theseus thine
Among us worldly Wights againe doth stand,
And seeth the Heavens upon himselfe to shine,
And passed hath the parlous myrie Mud
Of stinking Stygian Fen, and filthy Flud.

Unto thy ravening Uncles dreery Gaile
O Lady chaste not one Ghost dost thou owe,
The Hellick Tyrant knowes his perfect tale,
Who from the Court this shriking shrill doth throwe?
What mischiefe comes in frantick Phædras brayne
With naked Sword thus running out amayne.

HIPPOLYTUS

THE FIFTE ACTE

THESEUS, PHÆDRA, CHORUS

HROUGH pierst with pangues of pensivenesse
what fury prickes thy brayne?
What meanes this bloudy blade? what meanes
this shriking out amayne?
And langishing upon the Corps which was thy
mallice made?
PH. O tamer of the wrastling waves mee, mee,
doe thou invade.
The Monstrous hags of Marble Seas to rampe on mee send out,
What ever Thetis low doth keepe with folding armes about,
Or what the Ocean Seas aloofe embrace with winding wave:
O Theseus that to thine alies dost still thy selfe behave
So Currishly, O thou that for thy loving Friends avayle
Dost never yet returne: thy Sonne and Father doe bewayle
Thy pasport brought by death, and bloud, thy stocke thou dost
destroy,
By love or hatred of thy wife thou workest still annoy:
O sweete Hippolytus thus I behold thy battred face,
And I it is, I wretch (alas) that brought thee to this case.
What Scinis forst thy lims so torne his snatching boughes to feele?
Or what Procrustes rackt and rent thee streacht on bed of Steele?
Or else what Minotaur of Crete that grim twishaped Bull
With horny head (that Dedalls dennes with lowing filleth full)
Hath thee in fitters torne? (aie me) where is thy beauty fled?
Where are our twinckling stars thine eyes? alas and art thou
ded?
Appeare a while, receive my words, for speake I shall none yll:
This hand shal strike the stroake, wherwith thy vengeance quite
I wil.

And sith that I, I Caitife, I, abridged have thy life,
Lo here I am content, to yeelde thee mine with bloudy knife.
If ghost may here be given for ghost, and breath may serve for breath,
Hippolytus take thou my soule, and come againe from death.
Behold my bowles yet are safe my lims in lusty plight,
Would God that as they serve for me, thy body serve they might,
Mine eies to render kindly light unto thy Carkasse ded,
Lo for thy use this hand of mine shall pluck them from my hed,
And set them in these empty cells and vacant holes of thine.
Thy weale of me a wicked Wight to win, do not repine.
And if a womans wofull heart in place of thine may rest,
My bosom straight breake up I shall, and teare it from my brest.
But courage stout of thine doth loth faint womans heart to have,
Thy Noble minde would rather go with manly heart to grave.
Alas be not so manly now, this manlinesse forbeare,
And rather choose to live a man with womans sprite and feare,
Then as no man with manly heart in darcknesse deepe to sit:
Have thou thy life, give me thy death that more deserveth it.
Can not my profer purchase place ? yet vengeance shal thou have,
Hell shall not hold me from thy syde nor death of dompish grave.
Sith fates wil not permit thee life, though I behest thee mine,
My selfe I shall in spite of fate my fatall twist untwine.
This blade shall rive my bloudy breast, my selfe I will dispoile
Of soule, and sinne at once: through floods and Tartar gulphes that boyle,
Through Styx and through the burning Lakes I wil come after thee:
Thus may we please the lowring shades, receive thou heere of mee
The parings of my Poll and Locks cut off from forehead torne,
Our hearts we could not joyne in one, yet wretches now forlorne
We shal togeather in one day our fatall hower close:
If thou be loyall to thy spouse, for him thy life then lose:
But if thou be uncestuous, dye for thy lovers sake.
Shall I unto my husbandes bed agayne my corps betake,
Polluted with so haynous crime ? O death the chiefest joy
Of wounding shame: Death onely ease of stinging Loves annoy:
We runne to thee: embrace our sowles within thy gladsome breast:
Harke Athens, harke unto my talke, and thou above the reste,

Thou Father worse unto thy Child than bloudy stepdame I.
False forged tales I told with shame, I fayning that did lye,
Which I of spite imagined, when raging breast did swarve :
Thou father falsly punisht hast him that did not deserve.
The youngman chast is cast away for myne uncestuous vice,
Both bashful he and guiltles was, now play thy wonted guyse.
My guilty breast with bloudy Launce of Sword deserv'd is riven.
The Dirge to th' dead to purge my spouse shal with my bloud be geven.
Thou father of the stepdame learne, what things thy Sonne should have
Of life deprived, as to lay his carkasse in a grave.
TH. O wanny Jawes of blacke Averne, eake Tartar dungeon grim,
O Lethes Lake of woful Soules the joy that therein swimme,
And eake ye glummy Gulphes destroy, destroy me wicked wight
And stil in pit of pangues let me be plunged day and night.
Now, now, come up ye Goblins grim from water creekes alow,
What ever Proteus hugie swolne aloofe doth overflow,
Come dowse me drownd in swallowes depe, that triumphe in my sinne :
And father thou that evermore ful ready prest hath binne
To wreake myne yre, adventring I a deede deserving death
With new found slaughter have bereft myne onely Sonne of breath.
His tattred lims I scatred have the bloudy field about,
Whyle th' innocent I punish doe, by chaunce I have found out
The truth of al this wickednes : heaven, starres, and sprites of hell
I pester with my treachery that me doth overquell.
No mischiefes hap remayneth more : iii. kingdomes know mee well :
We are returned to this World. For this did Hell unfold
His gates that burials twayne I might and double death beholde ?
Wherby I both a wyveles Wight and eakt a Sonles Sire,
May with one brand to wyfe and Sonne enflame the funeral fire.
O tamer of blackefaced light Alcides, now restore
Thy booty brought from Hel, redeeme to mee, to mee therfore
These Ghostes that now be gone, ah sinful wretch to death in vayne
I sue, most undiscrete by whom these wretched Wightes were slayne.

Imagining destruction sore aboute it wil I goe,
Now with thyne owne handes on thy selfe due vengeance do bestow :
A Pine tree bough downe straind perforce unto the ground alow,
Let slip into the open ayre shal cut my corpes in twayne.
From top of Scyrons Rockes I wil be tumbled downe amayne.
More grievous vengeance yet I have in Phlegethon River found,
Tormenting guilty Ghostes enclosd with fiery Channel round.
What pit and pangues shal plunge my soule already have I known,
That tyring toyle of Sisyphus that retchles rolling stone.
Let yeeld unto my guilty Ghost, and beyng layed on
These shoulders, these, these lifting handes of myne downe let it sway :
And let the fleeting floud aboute my lips deluded play.
Yea let the ravening grype come heare and Tytius paunch forsake.
For glutting foode with grasping Cleaze my liver let him take,
Encreasyng stil to feede the Foule, and for my tormentes sake.
And pause thou my Pyrothous Syre, and eke the snackle Wheele
That whirleth stil enforce my limmes thy swinging swift to feele.
Gape, gape, thou ground and swallow me thou cruell Chaos blynd,
This passage to thinfernall Sprightes is fit for me to find :
My Sonne I wil ensue, thou Prince of gastly ghostes in hell,
Dread not for chast wee come to thee : geve thou me leave to dwell
Among thy dreadful dennes for aye, and not to passe agayne.
Alas, my prayer at the Gods no favour can obtayne,
But if that mischiefe crave I should how ready would they bee ?
CH. O Theseus to thy plaint eternall tyme is graunted thee :
Provyde thy Sonne his Obit rytes, and shroude in dompish grave
His broken lims, which Monsters foule disperst and scattered have.
TH. The shreadings of this deare beloved carkasse bring to mee,
His mangled members hether bring on heapes that tombled be :
This is Hyppolytus, I do acknowledge myne offence,
For I it is, that have deprived thee of life and sense.
Least that but once, or onely I should be a guilty Wight,
I Sire attempting mischiefe have besought my Fathers might.
Lo I enjoy my fathers gift, O solitarinesse,
A grievous plague when feeble yeares have brought us to distresse,
Embrace these lims, and that which yet doth of thy sonne remayne,
O woeful wight in baleful breast preserve and entertayne.

These scattred scraps of body torne O Syre in order set,
The straying gobbetts bring agayne, here was his right hand set:
His left hand here instructed well to rule the raynes must be.
His left syde rybbs (ful wel I know to be bewayld of mee
With bitter teares) as yet alas are lost and wanting still,
O trembling handes behold this woful busines to fulfil,
And withered Cheekes forbid your streams of flowing tears to runne
Whyle that the father do accompt the members of his Sonne.
And eke patch up his body rent, that hath his fashion lost,
Disfigured foule with gorye woundes, and all about betost:
I doubt, if this of thee be peece, and peece it is of thee:
Here, lay it here, in th' empty place, here let it layed be,
Although perhap it lye not right: (aye me) is this thy face?
Whose beauty twinckled as a starre, and eake did purchase grace,
In sight of Foe procurd to ruth. Is this thy beauty lost?
O cruell will of Gods, O rage in sinne prevayling most.
Doth thus the Syre that great good turne perfourme unto his sonne?
Lo let thy fathers last farewel within thyne eares to runne,
My child whom oft I bid farewell: the whilst the fire shall burne
These bones, set ope his buriall bower, and let us fall to mourne
With loude lamenting Mopsus wise for both the coarses sake:
With Princely Pompe his funerall fire see that ye ready make,
And seeke ye up the broken parts in field dispersed round,
Stop hir up hurlde into a Pit, let heavy clodds of ground
Lie hard upon hir cursed hed.

FINIS

ŒDIPUS

THE FIFTH TRAGEDY OF SENECA

ENGLISHED THE YEAR OF OUR LORD

MDLX.

BY ALEXANDER NEVYLE

To the Right Honorable

MAISTER DOCTOR WOTTON

one of the Queenes Majesties privy Counsayle:

Alexander Nevyle wisheth Helth,

with encrease of Honor.

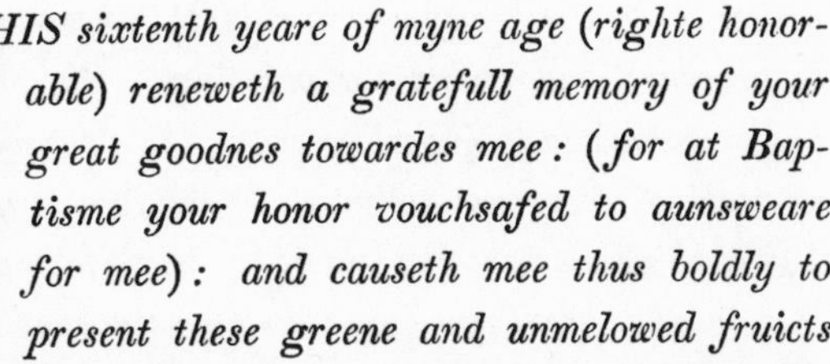

THIS sixtenth yeare of myne age (righte honorable) reneweth a gratefull memory of your great goodnes towardes mee: (for at Baptisme your honor vouchsafed to aunsweare for mee): and causeth mee thus boldly to present these greene and unmelowed fruicts of my first travailes unto you: as signes and testimonies of a well disposed minde unto your honor. Albeit when first I undertoke the translation of this present Tragœdy, I minded nothing lesse, than that at any tyme thus rudely transformed it shoulde come into the Printers hands. For I to none other ende removed him, from his naturall and lofty style, to our corrupt and base, or as some men (but untruly) affyrme it, most barbarous Language: but onely to satisfy the instant requests of a few my familiar frends, who thought to have put it to the very same use, that Seneca himselfe in his Invention pretended: Which was by the tragicall and Pompous showe upon Stage, to admonish all men of their fickle Estates, to declare the unconstant head of wavering

Fortune, her sodayne interchaunged and soone altered Face: and lyvely to expresse the just revenge, and fearefull punishments of horrible Crimes, wherewith the wretched worlde in these our myserable dayes pyteously swarmeth. This caused me not to be precise in following the Author, word for word: but sometymes by addition, somtimes by subtraction, to use the aptest Phrases in geving the Sense that I could invent. Whereat a great numbre (I know) will be more offended than Reason or Wysedome woulde they should bee. Thus as I framed it to one purpose: so have my frends (to whom I can not well deny any thyng that Frendshyps ryght may seeme justly to requyre) wrested it to another effect: and by this meanes blowen it abroade, by overrash and unadvised printing. By whych fond deede I know undoubtedly I shall receyve the poysoned infamies, of a number of venemous tonges. Wherefore (ryght honorable) as I geve these the first Fruicts of my travayle unto you: declaring therein the great goodwyll and duety that I owe unto your Honor, for the noble disposition of your vertuous mynde: so am I driven humbly to require your strong ayde, and assured defence agaynst the sclaunderous assaults of such malicious mouths, which obtayned: I shalbe the better encouraged agaynst an other time, to bestow my travaile in matters of farre greater weighte and importaunce. In the meane season (desiring your Honour to take these simple Attemptes of myne in good part:) I leave you to the tuition of the right high and mighty God: Who keepe you long in health, and graunt you many happy yeares: with encrease of Honor.

All your Honours to commaund.

Alexander Nevile.

ŒDIPUS

THE PREFACE TO THE READER

BEHOLD here before thy Face (good Reader) the most lamentable Tragedy of that most Infortunate Prince Œdipus, for thy profit rudely translated. Wonder not at the grosenesse of the Style : neyther yet accounte the Inventours Dylygence dysgraced by the Translators Neglygence : Who thoughe that he hath somtimes boldly presumed to erre from his Author, roving at randon where he list : adding and subtracting at pleasure : yet let not that engender disdaynefull suspition with in thy learned breast. Marke thou rather what is ment by the whole course of the History : and frame thy lyfe free from such mischiefes, wherewith the World at this present is universally overwhelmed, The wrathfull vengeaunce of God provoked, the Body plagued, the mynde and Conscience in midst of deepe devouring daungers most terribly assaulted, In such sort that I abhorre to write : and even at the thought thereof I tremble and quake for very inward griefe and feare of minde : assuredly perswading my selfe that the right high and immortall God, will never leave such horrible and detestable crimes unpunished. As in this present Tragœdy, and so forth in the processe of the whole hystory, thou maist right well perceyve. Wherein thou shalt see, a very expresse and lively Image of the inconstant chaunge of fickle Fortune in the person of a Prince of passing Fame and Renown, midst whole fluds of earthly blisse : by meare misfortune (nay rather by the deepe hidden secret Judgements of God) piteously plunged in most extreame miseries. The whole Realme for his sake in straungest guise grevously plagued : besides the apparaunt destruction of the Nobility : the generall death and spoyle of the Comminalty : the miserable transformed Face of the City, with an infinite number of mischiefes more, which I passe over unrehersed. Onely wish I all men by this Tragicall hystory (for to that entent was it written) to beware of Synne : the ende whereof is shamefull and miserable. As in the most infortunate fall of this unhappy Prince right playnely appeareth. Who by inward gripe of fearefull consuming Conscience wretchedly tormented : beholding the lamentable state of his vile infected Realmes, wasted by the burning rage of privy spoyling Pestilence, finds himselfe in tract of time, to be th' onely plague and misery of the almost quight destroied City. Whereupon calling together his Priests and Prophets, and asking counsaile of the Gods by them, for present remedy in those evils, wherewith the Realme was then universally overflowen : aunswere was made that the Plague should never ceasse, till king Laius death were throughly revenged : and the bloudy Murtherer driven into perpetuall exile. Which aunswere received, Œdipus, farre more curious in bowlting out the truth, than carefull of his own Estate : sodainly slides into an innumerable company of dredfull miseries. For as soone as he had once the perfect vewe of his own detestable deedes, and wicked misdemeanour cast before his eyes, together with the unnaturall killing of his Father Laius, the incestuous Mariage of his Mother Jocasta, the preposterous order of his ill misguyded lyfe, with a hundred moe like mischiefes, which chaste and undefiled eares abhorre to heare : fretting Fury common enemy and tormentor to corrupted consciences pricking him forward, all inflamed with Phrensie and boyling in inward heate of vile infected minde, hee rooteth out his wretched eyes unnaturally, bereaveth his Mother her life (though earnestly requested thereto) beastly, and in the ende in most basest kind of slavery, banisht, dieth miserably. Leaving behind him unto all posterities, a dreadfull Example of Gods horrible vengeaunce for sinne. Such like terrors as these requireth this our present Age, wherein Vice hath chiefest place, and Vertue put to flight, lies as an abject, languishing in great extremity. For the which cause, so much the rather have I suffred this my base translated Tragœdy to be published : from his Author in word and verse somewhat transformed, though in Sense litle altered : and yet oftentimes rudely encreased with mine owne simple invention : more rashly (I confesse) than wisely, wishing to please all : to offend none. But whereas no man lives so uprightly, whom slaundring tonges leave undiffamed, I referre my selfe to the Judgement of the wisest, litle esteeming the prejudiciall mouthes of such carping Marchaunts, whych suffer no mens doings almost to scape undefiled. In fine, I beseech all to gether (if so it might be) to beare with my rudenes, and consider the grosenes of our owne Countrey language, which can by no meanes aspire to the high lofty Latinists stile. Myne onely entent was to exhorte men to embrace Vertue and shun Vyce, according to that of the right famous and excellent Poet Virgil

Discite justiciam moniti, et non temnere divos.

This obtayned: I hold my selfe throughly contented: In the meane season I ende: wishing all men to shun Sin, the plaine (but most perilous) pathway to perfect infelicity.

A. Nevile.

THE SPEAKERS NAMES

Œdipus. Jocasta.
Chorus. Creon.
Tiresias. Manto.
Sanex. Phorbas.
[Nuntius].

SENECA HIS TENNE TRAGEDIES

THE FIRST ACTE

ŒDIPUS THE KING, JOCASTA THE QUEENE

HE Night is gon: and dredfull day begins at length t' appeere:
And Phœbus all bedim'de with Clowdes, himselfe aloft doth reere.
And glyding forth with deadly hue, a dolefull blase in Skies
Doth beare: Great terror and dismay to the beholders Eyes.
Now shall the houses voyde bee seene, with Plague devoured quight:
And slaughter that the night hath made, shall day bring forth to light.
Doth any man in Princely throne rejoyce? O brittle Joy,
How many ills? how fayre a Face? and yet how much annoy
In thee doth lurke, and hidden lies? what heapes of endles strife?
They judge amisse, that deeme the Prince to have the happy life.
For as the Mountaynes huge and hie, the blustring windes withstand,
And craggy Rocks, the belching fluds do bash, and drive from land:
Though that the Seas in quiet are, and calme on every side:
So kingdoms great all Windes and Waves of Fortune must abide.
How well shund I my Father deare Polybius Scepters late?
Exil'de, bereft of carefull feare, in Pilgrims happy state:
I call the Gods to witnes this, and Stars that glyde in Skyes.
A kingdome is befauln to mee, I feare least thereof ryse
A mischiefe, (mighty Jove,) to great I feare, alas I feare
Least these my handes have reft the life, of thee my Father deare.
Apollo byds mee this beware, and yet a mischiefe more
Foretels. Joc. Can any greater bee than that you tolde before?

Of Father slayne by sonnes own hand? ŒD. (O thrice unhappy state.)
With horror all dismaide I stand in dred of threatned fate.
I am ashamed my destnies fowle (O Queene) to thunder out,
And openly to blase my feare my trembling minde doth dout:
Yet out it goes. Phœbus me bids my Mothers Bed to fly,
As though that I her Sonne, with her incestuously should ly.
This feare, and onely this me causde my fathers kingdome great
For to forsake. I fled not thence when feare the minde doth beat.
The restlesse thought still dreds the thing, it knows can never chaunce.
Such fansies now torment my heart, my safety to advaunce,
And eke thyne ever sacred lawes (O Nature) for to keepe
A stately Scepter I forsooke, yet secret feare doth creepe
Within my breast: and frets it still with doubt and discontent,
And inward pangues which secretly my thoughts a sunder rent.
So though no cause of dred I see, yet feare and dred I all,
And scant in credit with my selfe, my thoughts my minde appall
That I cannot perswaded be though reason tell mee no,
But that the Web is weaving still of my decreed wo.
For what should I suppose the cause? a Plague that is so generall,
And Cadmus country wholy spoyles, and spreds it selfe through all?
Should mee, amongest so huge a heape of plagued Bodies spare?
And we alone amongst the rest reservde to mischiefes are?
O heavy hap. And bide I stil alone the spoyle to see?
Of Cities great, of men, of beasts, by plague that wasted bee?
And thou amongst so many ils, a happy lyfe to lead,
Couldst once perswade thy selfe (O wretch) without all feare or dread.
Of Phœbus secret Judgements to, and that in Kinges estate?
Thou, thou, infected hast the ayre, in such a filthy rate.
Thou art the onely cause of woe: by thee these evils rise,
By thee to grave on such a sorte, this wretched people plies.
The firy flaming frying heate, afflicted hearts that wasts,
Is not relievde as wont it was by cold and pleasaunt blasts.
The gentle western windes have left with healthful puffes to blow,
And now the fiery Dog with blase of boyling heate doth glow.

The Sunne in Leo burns so hoate, and so the earth doth broyle,
That fluds and hearbes are dryed up, and nought remaynes but soyle,
So throughly scorcht and stued with heate, that moisture all is gone,
And now amongst so many fluds, remaynes alas not one.
The places dry are onely seene the streames are drunken up.
And water that doth yet remayne : the soaking Earth doth sup.
The Moone with clowds quight over cast, all sadly forth she glides,
And dolefull darksom shades of night, the whole worlde overhides.
No Star on high at all doth shine, but black and hellike hue
Hath overshaded all the Skyes, whence deadly mists ensue.
The corne that wonted was to growe and fruitfully to spring,
Now to the voyded Barnes nought els, but empty stalkes doth bring.
No part of all our kingdome is free from destruction :
But all together run and rush, to utter confusion.
The old men with the yong (alas :) the Father with the chylde
The plague consumes. Both man and wife, all beasts both tame and wylde
Are spoyled by the Pestilence. No pompe at all remaynes,
That wonted was in Funeralles, to ease the mourners paynes.
Alas this spoile of people made, by plague hath dryde myne eyes :
And secretly within my breast, the griefe it boyling fryes.
And that, that wonted is to hap, in most extremest ills :
My teares are dry and glutting griefe my wretched breast it fills.
The crased father beares the sons, unto theyr dampish graves :
And after him with burden like, the Mother comes and raves :
And even lamenting as they stand, starck dead downe both they fall,
And mourners new in like estate, for them and theirs they call.
Who likewise in the midst of all their toyle and paynfull payne
Do drop into the grave they digd, and so the place doe gayne
That was prepar'de for others erst. A hell it were to heere
The horror, and the miseries that every where appeere.
A Tombe is made for noble men, fast on the people hie,
And in, their burdens fling. Great Pieres all unregarded lye
For lack of Graves, to Ashes cleane their bodyes some doe wast :
And some halfe burnt doe leave them there, and home away for hast

They run, and more they fetch, and then wood, fier, grave, and all
Doth want. And downe for very griefe the wretched mysers fall.
No prayers availe. No Arte can help this raging Plague t' appease :
For none almost is left alive each others woe to ease.
Before thine aulters heere O God my feeble hands I hold,
Requiring all my destinies, at once with courage bold.
And that by death I may prevent, my Countrey prest to fall.
For this, and only this (O God) upon thy name I call.
Let mee not be the last that dies : The last that goes to Grave.
Graunt this, and then (O mighty Jove) my full request I have.
O cruell Gods unkinde : O more than thrise unhappy Fates :
That onely mee denied is, that lyghtes on all Estates.
I meane a speedy death (alas) these evils to prevent,
And deadly woes that doe my heart with restlesse rage torment.
Leave of thy blubbering teares (O foole,) and fly these kingdomes foylde
With rotten plagues and Botches vile, and graves ech where dispoylde.
All which diseases thou unhappy guest didst bring with thee
Dispatch. Away. Goe hence. At least, unto thy parents flee.
Joc. What bootes it Sir these mischiefs great with piteous plaints to aggrevate.
Stoutly to beare adversity, is fitste for Kings estate.
When dred and daunger most assayle : when cruell Cares doe crush
Thy princely breast. Then oughtst thou most to beare and bide the push.
It is no poinct of courage stout to yeelde to fortunes frown.
Œd. Nay. Feare could never cause mee stoupe nor Fortune cast mee down.
My manly minde was never thraule to vaine and peavish feares,
But evermore in each assault, it pryncely courage beares.
No not a thousand glistering swords, nor Mars himselfe in fielde,
Can once dismay my Countenaunce, or cause my heart to yeelde.
The very Giaunts fierce and huge in fight withstand I dare.
That Monster Sphinx whose riddels through the world renowmed are,
Could not dismay my dredles heart, nor cause my courage slide
For all the terrors I beheld, I did that Fury byde.

I saw him belching Gubs of bloud, I viewde full well the fielde
That all to spatterd lay with bloud, and bones quight overheelde.
And when that he on Mountaynes top with mouth full huge to see,
Stoode gaping all with greedy Jawes to feede and pray on mee,
Oft fluttering with his fearefull wynges and shaking oft his tayle,
Began full like a Lyon fierce with threates mee to assayle.
Of whom straight way the Riddell I, it rusht into myne eares
With roring sound His winges he claps, the Rock for hast hee teares,
Desiring with my Bowels still his greedy Jawes to glut:
But I full soone assoyled had the question that he put.
And all the subtile poincts thereof, and twisted knots untwinde.
Joc. What makes you wish for death to late, and waste your wordes in wind.
You might have died than (you know) for Sphinx so noble slain.
This kingdom unto you, and yours for ever shall remain.
Œd. The ashes of that Monster vile, agaynst us doth rebell.
That vile mishapen lothsome Beast, that raging Feend of Hell,
Is cause of all the plague that doth this mournfull City smight.
Now only this remaynes alone, if Phœbus heavenly might,
Can any meanes invent for us, or way of mercy make:
Whereby these burning Plagues at length may haply chaunce to slake.

CHORUS

O more then thrise renowmed Stock of auncient Cadmus Race.
O mighty Thebes City great, O heavy ruthfull Case.
Loe now you lye all desolate, with Plague devoured quight.
Both you and all your Husbandmen. (O miserable sight.)
O fowle and fearefull Fate (alas) what causeth all this wo?
O God whence springs this Pestylence that us tormenteth so?
No age, no shape, no forme is sparde, but all confounded lye.
Thus happiest now the man I count, whose chaunce was first to dye.
For hee hath shund a thousand ills, which wretched Eyes have seene:
And mischiefes great that us doe presse from him are taken cleane.
O God withhold thy fury great, thy Plagues from us remove.
Ceasse of afflicted Soules to scourge, who thee both serve and love.

Powre downe on them diseases fowle, that them deserved have.
A Guerdon just for sinne (Oh God) this this of thee wee crave,
And onely this. We aske no more, the cause and all is thyne,
A thing not usde of Gods it is, from pity to declyne.
My heart doth pant, and trembling cold through all my lims doth run,
As oft as I remembring, count the noble Stockes undun,
By death and dolfull destenies that overwhelmed lye,
And yet alas the people stil to Grave doe faster hye.
In long Aray all in a rancke by thousandes on a roe,
On every side, in every streate to buriall fast they goe.
The seven broade wyde open Gates, are not enough for way,
But throngd the people pestred stand still in a fearefull stay,
And in the mydst of all theyr toyle with corses on their backes,
The number that before doth poast the hinder number slackes.
The corses in the streates doe lye and Grave on Grave is made,
But all in vayne. For nought it boots, the plague cannot be stayde.
The sacrifices don to Gods have to to ill successe,
And such straunge sights and signes doe rise that nought els I can gesse,
But that at hand with gastly pawes, is utter destruction,
With thousand ills accompayned and extreme confusion.
The sheepe of rot by heapes as thick, as dogges doe fall and dye,
And belching out their wasted lunges, on grounde doe sprawling lye.
And I my selfe of late did see: (a sight unseene before,)
As our high priest stoode sacrifising at the Temple dore,
And strake with grievous bloudy wound the golden horned Bull
When downe with liveles lump he drops and members made full dull.
And all the wounde wide bleeding gapes and black goard bloud out spues.
And yet the blade unsprinckled was. The bloud it boyling stues
And bubbles on the ground. Alas what do these things portend?
Oh mighty Jove at length vouchsafe some good and happy end,
At length withhold thy hand (O God) and health unto us send.
Nothing (alas) remaynes at all, in wonted old estate,
But all are turned topset downe, quight voyd and desolate
The faynting horse for sodayne paine from back his burden lats,
And after on his maisters brest his liveles lyms he squats:
Who cries for help: but all in vain the beastes in field that bide
Unkept: unknowen wayes and paths do raunge and overstride.

The Bull for lacke of foode and meate in field all faintyng lyes,
And all his flocke dispersed quight, the sely Shephard dyes.
The herdman eke amongst his beasts his fatal breath expiers
And to the heavens with piteous cries, commends his last desiers.
The Harts without all feare of wolves do lyve in wretched peace.
The rage, and wrathful roring sounds of ramping Lions cease.
The vengeaunce wyld outragious Beares are now as tame as sheepe
The ugly Serpent that was wont, the Rocky Dennes to keepe.
Oft quaffing poisoned Venom sups in inward heat shee boyles.
And all inflamed and schorcht, in vayne for lenger lyfe she toyles.
The woods are not adourned now, with fresh and lyvely hue,
The wonted shades are gon. All things are quight out of their Que :
No greenish grasse on ground doth grow, the earth no moisture soupes,
The Vine withouten any sap, his drowsy head down drowpes.
What shal I say ? all things (alas) are writhen out of course,
And as they seeme to me, are lyke, to fare still worse and worse.
O mighty God above ? when ende these everduryng yls ?
When cease these plages ? that giltles bloud thus fierce and raging spils ?
I thinck but we almost alyve, there do no men remayne :
Whom dolful Darts of Destenies, on earth have left unslayne
I thinke the darcksome shades of hell where filthy fluds do flow,
Where plages and vile diseases too, where dredfull horrors grow,
And all the furies brasten loose do mischiefes on us throw,
With Botch and blane of sundry kindes which sothern blasts do blow,
And wrekful vexed hagges of hell do breath and on us bringe :
The angry fendes of hell I thinke their vengeanuce on us flinge
And out their mortall poyson spue which they agaynst us beare,
Lo see how greedy death on us with scowling eyes doth leare.
See, see. Oh Jove how fast hee throwes his Dartes. Not one he spares
But all confounds. His thretning force, withstand no Creature dares.
No doubt the lothsom Feryman the sinfull soules that traynes
Through stincking fluds, his labour loths that he for us sustaynes.
Such presse by plumps to him is made which still renews his paynes.
But harke yet monsters more then these, the Fame abroade doth fly
That hellishe Dogges with bawling sound were heard to howle and cry,
And that the ground with trembling shooke, and under feete did move.
And dreadfull blasing Comets bright were seene in Skies above.

And gastly shapes of men besides, to wander on the ground.
And wood, and trees on every syde, did fearefully resound.
Besides all this straung Ghosts were seene in places where they stoode
And Ryvers more then one or two, that ran all blacke goord bloode.
O cruell plague, O vile disease, farre worse then speedy death.
O wee unhappy thrise and more, who doe prolonge our breath
In these accursed dayes and tymes. But harke to mee a while.
When first this lothsome plague begins these Mysers to defile,
It takes them thus. A feareful Cold through al their bones doth run,
And Cold and Heate togeather mixt, their sences all venome.
Than litle lothsome markes appeare, and all their bodies spot.
And all their members flaming glow, and burning fast doe rot.
The Lights, the Lungs, the heart, the Guts, and all that inwarde lies,
And all the secret partes iscorcht, with deadly fier fries.
The bloud all clotterd in their Cheekes, in cluster lies by lumps,
And it and heate together makes, great, straung, and ruddy bumps.
And bloud and flesh congeled stands, in Face as stiffe as stake.
And Eyes in' head fast fixed set, and often trickling make.
And downe apace whole fluds they steame, and clots and drops doe trill,
And all the skin from of their Face, by flakes and scales doth pill.
A thousand fearefull sounds at once, into their eares doe rush.
And lothsome bloud out of their Nose, by stilling streames doth gush.
The very anguish of their heart doth cause them for to shake.
And what with payne and heate, and feare, their woried lims doe quake.
Then some the running Ryvers haunt, and some on ground doe wallow,
And some agayne their thirst to slake, cold water gulping swallow.
Thus all our country tost with plague in Griefe it waltering lies.
And still desiring for to dye, a thousand deathes it dyes.
But God to heare them then is prest : and death to none denyes.
Besydes al this, the church some do frequent : but not to pray,
But onely for to glut the Gods, with that that they do say.
But who is this that comes to Court in hast with poasting pace ?
What ? ist Creon that noble Prince (for deedes and stately race ?)
Or doth my mynd opprest with care thinges false for true contrive ?
Creon it is long looked for, his sight doth me revyve.

THE SECONDE ACTE

THE FIRST SCENE

ŒDIPUS, CREON

OR feare my body chilles, alas, and trembling all I stand
In quakinge dread. I seke and toyle, these mischiefes to withstand.
But al in vayne I spend my thoughtes it wil not be, I see,
As long as all my sences thus by cares distracted bee.
My mynd desyrous stil (Oh God,) the truth for to unfold,
With doubtful Dread is daunted so, that it can scant upholde
It selfe. O Brother deare, if way or meane of health thou know,
Declare it out and sticke not all the truth to me to show.
CRE. The Oracle (most noble king) ys darke, and hidden lies.
ŒD. Who doubtful health to sicke men brings, all health to them denies.
CRE. Apolloes use yt is the troth in darkesome dens to hold.
ŒD. And Œdipus of Gods it hath thinges hidden to unfold:
Speake out, tell all, and spare not man: all doubtes I can discus.
CRE. Apollo then (most noble King) himselfe commaundeth thus.
By exile purge the Princes seat, and plague with vengeance due
That haples wretch, whose bloudy handes of late King Laius slue:
Before that this perfourmed bee, no hope of milder ayer:
Wherfore do this (O King) or else All hope of helpe dispayre.
ŒD. Durst any man on earth attempte, that noble Prince to slaye?
Shew me the man that I may him dispatch out of the way.
CRE. God graunt I may it safely tel: the hearyng was to terrible,
My senses all amased are: it is a thing so horrible,

That I abhorre to utter it (oh God) for feare I quake
And even at the very thought my lims beginne to shake.
Assoone as I Appollos Church, had entred in affrayd,
Uppon my face flat downe I fell, and thus to him I prayd.
Oh God if ever thou didst rue, on wretched misers state,
If ever men opprest thou easd, or didst their cares abate,
If ever thou in present neede didst present helpe declare,
If ever thou afflicted Hartes with cares consumd didst spare :
Shew now thy wonted clemency and pitty knowne of yore.
Scant had I sayd : Resounding all the mountaynes thondring rore :
And filthy feendes spout out their flames out of their darksome caves.
And woods do quake, and hilles do move, and up the surging waves
Do mount unto the skies aloft, and I amased stand,
Still looking for an aunsweare at Apollos sacred hand.
When out with ruffled hayre disguisd the Prophet comes at last :
And when that shee had felt the heate of mighty Phœbus blast,
All puffyng out she swelles in rage, and pattring still she raves,
And scant she entred had into Apollos shyning caves,
When out a thundring voyce doth brust that 's farre above mans reach.
So dreadful seemed then to me the mighty Phœbus speach.
Than thus he spake and thus at length into myne eares he rusht
Whyle sprawling stil the Prophet lay before the doores in dust.
The Thebane City never shal be free from plagues (quoth he,)
Except from thense the Kingkiller forthwith expulsed bee :
Unto Apollo knowen he was, or ever he was borne
Do this : or else no hope of health, to this the gods have sworn.
And as for thee, thou shalt not long in quiet state indure,
But with thy self wage war thou shalt and war thou shalt procure
Unto thy children deare : and crepe agayn thou shalt into thy mothers wombe.
ŒD. Loke what the Gods commaunded have accomplished shalbe.
Nor never shal these eyes of myne abyde the day to see,
A King of kingdome spoyld by force, by guyle or craft supprest.
A kinge to kinges the prop ought be, and chiefest cause of rest :

No man regardes his death at all whom living he doth feare.

CR. Great cause makes mee my Princes death conceale and closly beare.

ŒD. Ought any cause of feare or griefe, thy duty for to let ?

CRE. The threatning of the prophesyes, do stil my breast beset.

ŒD. Let us (sith God commaunds) forthwith some good attonement make

If any way, or meanes there be their wrathful rage to slake.
Thou God that sits on seate on high, and al the world dost guide,
And thou by whose commaundement the Starres in Skies do glide :
Thou, thou that onely ruler art of Seas, of Floods, and all,
On thee and on thy Godhead great, for these requestes I call.
Who so hath slayne king Laius, oh Jove I do thee pray,
Let thousand ils upon him fall, before his dying day.
Let him no health ne comfort have, but al to crusht with cares,
Consume his wretched yeares in griefe, and though that death him spares
Awhyle. Yet mischiefes all, at length uppon him light.
With all the evils under Sun, that ugly monster smight.
In exile let him live a Slave, the rated course of life.
In shame, in care, in penury, in daunger and in strife.
Let no man on him pity take, let all men him revyle.
Let him his Mothers sacred Bed incestuously defyle.
Let him his father kill. And yet let him do mischiefes more.
What thing more haynous can I wish then that I wisht before ?
Let him do all those illes I say, that I have shund and past.
All those and more (if more may be) oh God upon him cast.
Let him no hope of pardon have : but sue and all in vayne.
All hellish Furies on him light, for to encrease his payne.
O Jove powre downe thy fury greate, thy thundring thumpes out throw
Let Boreas boysterous blastes and stormy plagues upon him blow.
Consume him quight. Fret out his guttes with pockes and botches vile
Let all diseases on him light that wretched bodyes fyle.
Let these and more (if more may be) uppon that Monster fall.
Let Harpies pawes and greedy paunche devoure his members all.

Let no man him regard : or seeke his limmes in grave to lay :
But let him dye ten thousand deathes before his dying day.
By this my Kingdome I do sweare, and Kingdome that I left,
By al my Countrey Gods that bene in Temples closely kept,
I sweare, I vow, I do protest, and thereto witnes take :
The Starres, the Seas, the Earth and all that ere thy hand did make.
Except that I my selfe forthwith this bloudy monster find,
To wreake the wrath of God some way with solempne oth I bynde.
And so my father, Polybius his happy dayes outlyve.
And so my mother Merope, no mariage new contrive :
As he shall dye that did this deede, and none shal him excuse.
Whoso he be here I protest for that he shortly rues :
But where this wicked deede was don Creon now tell me playne :
Both by what meanes ? and where : and how King Laius was slayne.

CREON. Passing through Castalia woods and mountayns heapt with snoe
Where groves and scrubs, and bushes thicke and brambles sharp do groe,
A threepathd crooked way there is that diversly doth goe.
One unto Bacchus citty bends that Phoce doth hight,
The other to Olenius, forth stretcheth out aright :
The third that reacheth through the vales and by the rivers lyes
Tends downe unto the Bancks wherby Eleia water plyes.
There unawares (O piteous chaunce) a troup of theves entraps
The noble prince, and murders him, hence spring these great mishaps
Which heape you realms with hideous woes and plagues on every side,
By just decree of heavenly powers which can no murder bide.
But see Tiresias where he coms with old and trembling pace.
I thincke Apolloes heavenly might have brought him to this place.
See where he comes : and Manto too, his steps directing stayes
Tis he who for your grace (O king) and for your countrie prayes.

THE SECOND SCENE

ŒDIPUS, TYRESIAS, MANTO

Come holy priest (to Phœbus next) these doubtfull aunswers lose :
And whom that destines will to dye, straightwayes to me disclose.
Ty. Renowmed Prince, though still I stand in silence dumme dismayde :
And though by inwarde feare of mynde my lingring tonge is stayde :
Yet pardon me (O noble Prince,) and geve me leave a while.
From lack of sight springs Ignoraunce which powre hath to exile
Unspotted Truth from doubtfull breasts. This thing ful well you knoe,
But whither God and Countrey calles, with willing minde I goe.
Let deadly fatall destenies, be boulted out at length.
O King if I of greener yeares had now my wonted strength :
This matter soone discust should be, and I would take in hande,
My selfe in presence of the Gods, in temple for to stande.
A mighty Oxe all coulourd white, up on the Aulters reare,
Which never yet on weried necke, the croked yoake did beare.
And Manto thou, O daughter mine, mine onely prop and stay :
The secret hidden misteries, and sacred signes out say.
Ma. The beast before the Aulter stands. Ty. To Gods a prayer make,
And on the holy Aulters eke, some pleasaunt odors shake.
Ma. Tis done. And all the fiers fierce, with incence bright doe flame.
Ty. O Manto now what signes seest thou ? how doe thy matters frame ?
What ? doth the fire the Sacrifice encompas rounde about ?
Ma. Not so. But first it mounts aloft, and streight it flasheth out.
Ty. Well Yet, how doth the sacred flame all shining bright and cleare
It selfe on high unto the Skies, with sparkeling flakes upreare ?
Or doeth it oft rebounding backe, it selfe from Skyes unfould ?
Or all with rumbling roring noyse, about the place ist rould ?

Or dim'd with smoke, ist tost from place to place, now heere, now theare?
MA. Not one. But diverse colours mixt the flame doth with it beare,
Much like unto the Rainbow, which with sundry paynted hues
Foreshewes unto the husbandmen the weather that ensues.
What colour it wants, or what it hath, to me is like uncertayne.
Now is it black, now blue, now red, and even now agayne
Quight out it is. Yet once agayn, all fierce it flashing flames:
But lo, yet mischiefs more then this, unluckely it frames.
The fier quight a sunder parts, and flame with flame doth fight.
O father I abhorre to see this ugly lothsome sight.
The Wyne to blud is turned quight, and all the Prynces hed
With thicke black clouds encompast is, with smoke all overspred.
O father tell what this portends? TY. What should I tell alas?
My mynde for feare astonied stands, and trembling cold doth pas
Through all my lims. What shall I say? or where shall I begin?
O cruell Plagues, O wrekfull Gods, O vengeaunce due for sin.
Some dyre and blouddy deed (Alas) these hydeous signes declare.
Whats that the Gods would have revealde, and yet doe bid beware
To utter it? By certaine signes their wrath is oft descride:
Such signes appeere, and yet they seeme their fury great to hide.
They are ashamde: I wot nere what. Come hither, quickly bring
Some salt with thee, and it upon the sacrifice goe fling.
What? are their lookes pleasant and milde, and doe they gently bide
The touching of thy sacred hands? MA. What may this thing betide?
The Bull (a wonder great to see) his head on hie he lifts
And turned still unto the East, from thence it alway shifts,
Still lothing as hee seemes to me, of heaven to see the light,
Oft scouling with his blearing eyes with gastely ruthfull sight.
TY. But doth one blow them drive to ground, or more then one they have?
MA. The Heifer as it seemde, enflamd with courage stoute and brave
Upon the mortall Blade did rush, and there hirselfe destries:
When out the bloud it foming spoutes, and mounts unto the Skies.

The brawny Bull twise stroke or thrise, with groveling groning tyres,
And toyling up and down he moyles. And still to live desires.
And yet at length with much ado, his brutish breath expiers.
TY. What ? doth the wounde wide open gape, or is it closed up ?
Or doth the deepnes of the hole, the bloud in soking sup ?
MA. Out of the wounded Heifers breast Black bluish waters rush.
As for the Bull, but litle bloud out of his wounds doth gush.
It back rebounds, and from his Mouth and Eyes by streames doth flow.
But what these dreadfull signes portend the Gods aloone doe know.
TY. By this unhappy Sacrifice, great feares within mee rise.
But tell mee now : In the inner parts, what secret hidden lies ?
MA. O Father what meanes this (alas) that more then wonted guise
The Inwards stir ? and shake my hands, and heaving oft arise,
The bloud by streames out of the vaynes, full straungly skips aloft.
The heart all schorcht and hidden lies, and strykes are seene full oft,
Of Colour very wan and pale : The chiefest parts doe want.
The Lyver blackish gall out spurts, and somwhat rysing pants.
And that, that myschiefes great, to kingdoms doth foreshow :
Two heads are seene, and yet both heads one skin doth overgrow
And overheales them quight. But yet the skin, it is so thin
That easely one may discerne what lieth hid therein.
And that which horror doth encrease, a man may plainly see
How both the heart, the Lights, and Lungs, and all disturbed bee.
The fearefull noyse and sound you heere is not of beasts, but fier
That roaring on the Alters makes, presaging wrekefull yre
Of angry Gods who doe foretell some purpose that they have,
For to revenge some foule misdeede that vengeance just doth crave.
No part his proper place observes, nor keepes his order due :
But altogether quight disguisde, with an unwonted hue.
Mishapen, out of frame, transformde, displaced quight (alas)
What thing is that the Gods entend ere long to bring to pas ?
ŒD. Why then declare from whence, and why these deadly signes arise,
With courage stout I will it heare, it shall not once aggrise
My valiaunt mynd. Extremest ils have power to banish feare.
TY. You will wishe that unhard which you so much desyre to heare.

ŒD. Yet sence the Gods wil have him known tell me (I say) his name
That slue your King. Ty. Nor wing, nor womb of Bird or beast the same
Can tell (O king) new sacrifice, new meanes we must invent.
From dredfull darke infernall damps some Fury must be sent
These mischiefes great for to unfolde. Or els King Ditis hee,
That Empyre keepes on griesly Ghosts, entreated needes must bee
These things forthwith for to disclose. Tell who shall have the charge,
A King thou art, than maist not thou go through those kingdoms large.
ŒD. Than noble Creon thou shalt goe, this payne is first for thee :
Who must this crown and kingdome great enjoy after mee.

THE THIRDE ACTE

THE FIRSTE SCENE

ŒDIPUS, CREON

HOUGH that thy Face where sadnes sits in heavy mourning guise,
Nought els portend, but dedly griefes, and mischiefes stil to ryse :
Yet tel some meanes wherby at length the Gods we may appease,
And purchase to our Kingdomes wast, some hope of health and ease.

CRE. Alas you byd me that disclose which feare doth byd me hyde.
ŒD. If that the Thebane Citties great, by doleful plagues destryde
Perce not thy hart : yet oughtest thou, these Kingdomes for to rue
Which were unto thy brothers house, of auncient title due.
CRE. You wish the thing to know, which you wil wish unknown at length.
ŒD. Why so ? a simple remedy of litle force and strength
Is ignoraunce of our estate when daungers us betyde.
But what ? wilt thou so great a good for common safety hide ?
CRE. Irkesome Medcines and perilous in sicknes I abhorre.
ŒD. And I likewyse at Subjects hands disdayne to take a dorre,
Speake out with speed, or else by proofe of torment thou shalt find
How daungerous a case it is to gawle a Princes mynd.
CRE. Kinges often use to wish untolde, which they had tel before.
ŒD. Go to, dispatch and cease in time to vexe me any more.
Except that thou forthwith to me this heinous deede disclose :
The gods I do protest, to death for al thou onely goes.
CRE. O pardon me most noble king. O let me hold my pes,
Of al the gracis Princes graunt, what favour may be lesse ?

ŒD. As though the silence hurts not more both king and countries weale:
Then spech oft tymes: which subjects thoughts to Princes doth reveale?
Dispatch at once, stir me no more, thou knowst my guise of olde.
CRE. Silence denied, what priviledge may silly Subject holde?
ŒD. A traytor he is, who silence keepes, when king commaunds to speake.
CRE. Then pardon my constrayned speach, sith silence for to breake
You me compell. A dolefull tale (O king) my tongue must tell,
And which I feare your majesty will not interpret well.
ŒD. Was ever man rebukt for that, that he was bid to say?
CRE. Well than since needes I must: I am contented to obay.
A wood there is from City farre, enhaunst with stately trees:
Where many a plant and herbe doth grow, which Phœbus never sees:
With everduring bushes greene, the Cypresse there doth ryse,
And puts his olde and loffty head within the cloudy Skyes.
The auncient Time-eaten Oke with crooked bended lims,
The Teyl tree fine: The Alder which in Neptunes kingdoms swims,
The Bayes with bitter beries eke the Elmes deere friends to Vynes,
And many a noble tree besides, as Mirtels, Firres, and Pynes.
Amidst them all, one tree there is with large out stretched armes,
Whose roring sound, and craking noyse the lesser woods Icharmes,
And overshades them all: a Tree of monstrous huge estate,
Beset with fearefull woods: there is that dyre and dreadfull gate
That leades to lothsome Lymbo Lake, and pyts that ever flowe.
Where choked miry mud doth streame with slimy course full slowe.
Here when the priest was entred in, with comely aged pace,
He stayed not: No neede there was, for night was still in place.
Than all the ground wyde open gapes, and smouthering vapours ryse,
And fyre and smoke, and styfling stink, mounts up unto the Skyes.
The Priest with wayling weede iclad, his fatall rod out tooke:
And entring in, in blacke Aray, full often times it shooke.
With heavy cheere and dolful pace: his hoary haire was twynde
With bowes of mortall Ewe. A tree wherewith the mourners winde

Theyr mourning heads, and Garlands make. In this guise all arayde,
The sacred Priest doth enter in, with trembling lims dismayde :
Than in the Sheepe, and Oxen blacke, by backwarde course are drown.
And odoures sweete, and Frankencence, on flaming fyres are thrown.
The beasts on burning Altars cast, do quake with schorched lims :
And bloudy streames with fyre mixt, about the Aultars swims.
Than on the darke infernall Gods, and him that rules them all :
With deadly shriking voyce aloude, the Prophet gins to call.
And rouls the Magick verse in mouth, and hidden Artes doth prove :
Which eyther power have to appease or els the Gods to move.
Than bloudy streaming Lycours black, with broyling heate doe boyle :
And all the Beasts consume and burn. The Prophet than to toyle
Begins. And mixed wyne and Mylke upon the Aultars throwes.
And all the Dongeon darke, and wyde with streaming bloud it flowes.
Than out with thundring voyce agayne the Prophet calles and cryes,
And straight as much with mumbling mouth he champs in secret wyse.
The trees do turne. The Rivers stand. The ground with roring shakes.
And all the world as seemes to mee, with fearefull trembling quakes.
I am heard, I am heard, than out aloude the Priest began to cry :
Whan all the dampned soules by heapes abrode outrushing fly.
Then woods with rumbling noyse, doe oft resounding make.
And Heaven, and Earth together goe. And bowes and trees do crake.
And Thunders roore. And Lightnings flash. And waves aloft doe fly.
And ground retyres : and Dogs doe bawl : and Beastes are heard to cry.
And whyther long of Acheron, that lothsom Flud that flowes
All stinking streames : or of the earth, that out her Bowels throwes,

Free place to Sprights to geve : or of that fierce infernall Hound,
That at such times doth bustling make with chayns, and ratling sound.
The Earth al wide it open gapes. And I did see on ground,
The Gods with colour pale and wan, that those dark kingdoms keepe.
And very night I saw in deede, and thousand shapes to creepe,
From out those filthy stinking Lakes, and lothsom pits of Hell.
Where all the evils under Son, in darksom shades doe dwell.
So quaking all for feare I stoode with minde right sore apalde,
Whilst on those Gods with trembling mouth the Priest full often calde.
Who all at once, out of theyr dens did skip with griesly Face.
And Monsters grim, and stinging Snakes seemd wander in that place.
And all the fowlest Feendes of Hell, and Furies all were theare.
And all transformed Ghosts and sprights, that ever Hell did beare.
With Cares, and all Diseases vyle, that mortall mynds doe crush,
All those, and more I sawe out of those Dongeons deepe to rush.
And Age I sawe, with riveled Face, and Neede, and Feare, and Death,
And Fyre, and flames, and thousand ills out from those Pits to breath.
Then I was gon : and quight amazd The wenche in worser case.
And yet of olde, acquaynted with her Fathers Artes she was.
The Priest himselfe unmooved stoode, and boldly cited owt :
Whole Armies of king Ditis men, who clustring in a Rowt :
All flittring thin like Cloudes, disperst abrode in Ayre doe fly.
And bearing sundry shapes and formes doe scud about in Sky,
A thousand woods I thinke have not so many leaves on trees.
Ten thousand medowes fresh have not so many flowers for bees.
Ten hundred thousand rivers not so many Foule can show :
Nor all the drops and streams, and gulphes that in the Seas do flow,
If that they might be wayed, can sure so great a number make
As could those shapes and formes that flew from out of Limbo lake:
Both Tantalus and Zetus too, and pale Amphions Ghost :
And Agave, and after her ten thousand Sprightes do post.

Than Pentheus, and more and more, in like estate ensue :
Til out at length comes Laius with foule and grisly hue :
Uncomly drest in wretched plight with fylth all overgrowne :
All perst with wounds, (I loth to speake) with bloud quight overflown.
A Miser ryght as seemd to me, and most of Misers all :
Thus in this case, at length he spake, and thus began to call.
O Cadmus cruel Citty vyle, that stil delightste in bloud,
O Cadmus thou, which kinsmens death, accountst as chiefest good.
Teare out the blooudy Bowels of your Children, learne of me,
Do that, and rather more, then you would byde the day to see
Like ills as late on mee are light. Loe mothers love (alas)
Hath causd the greatest misery that ere in Theba was.
The Countrey with the wrath of Gods at this tyme is not tost,
Nor yearth nor ayre infect is not the cause that all bene lost.
No No. A bloudy King is cause of all these mischiefes great :
A bloudy wretch : A wretched child that sits in Fathers Seate :
And Mothers bed defyles (O wretch) and entreth in agayne,
In places whence he came from once and doubleth so her payne,
Whilst that hee fils the haples wombe wherin himselfe did lie
With graceles seede and causeth her twise childbirthes pangues to try :
Unhappy Sonne, but Father worse and most unhappy hee,
By whom the lawes of sacred shame so sore confounded bee.
For that that very bestes (almost) do all abhorre to do,
Even of his mothers body he hath brothers gotten two.
O mischiefe great : O dredful deede, then Sphinx, O monster more :
Example unto ages all of Gods foretold before.
But I thee, thee, that Scepter holdst, thy Father wil pursue,
And wreacke my selfe on thee and thyne with plagues and vengeance due.
All restles rage of spite and paine I will uppon thee blow,
And all the furies foule of hell uppon thee I will throw.
I wil subvert thy Houses cleane, for this thy lothsome lust :
I wil do this thou wretch : And thee, and thyne consume to dust.

Wherfore dispatch at once (I say) into exile drive your King.
That ground that first of all he leaves, with fresh grene grasse shall spring,
And sweete, and pleasaunt Ayre, and healthfull blasts shall ryse,
And all the evills under Sun, that mortall men surprise :
The Pocks, the Piles, the Botch, the blaine, and death with him shall fly,
And with him mischiefs all shall passe, and Monsters under Sky.
And as for him I know hee would depart with willing mynde :
But I will clog his Feete, and hands, his way he shall not finde.
But groping with his aged staffe, shall passe from place to place.
This shall he doe. And none shall rue upon his ruthfull case.
Rid you the Monster from the Earth, for Heaven let mee alone.
No sooner sayd, but straight away, his dreadfull Ghost was gone,
And fast by thousands after him, th' other Sprights in hyde :
Than Cold and trembling feare began through all my bones to glyde.
ŒD. The thing I alwayes fearde, I see upon mee now is layde :
But slender props they are (God wot) whereby your Treason is stayde.
Meropa my Mother deare, shall mee from this defend :
Polybius eke shall purge mee quight, from Actions all, that tend
To murder, or to incest vile, they both shall mee excuse.
In such a case no meanes at all of tryall I refuse.
Lay what you can unto my charge. No fault in mee remayns.
The Thebanes long or I came heere, of Laius death complayns.
My Mother yet alyve, my Father still in like estate.
No, no, this is some doltishe drift, of yon false Prophets pate.
Or else some mighty God above, doth beare me no good will,
And seekes by Plagues on mee to wreke his wrathfull vengeaunce stil.
Ah Sir I am glad at length I smell your drifts and fetches fyne.
I know the whole confederacy, your sleights I can untwyne.
That beastly Priest, that bleareyed wretch beelyes the Gods and mee :
And thee thou Traytour in my place hath promist king to bee.
CRE. Alas would I my Sister of her lawfull kingdome spoyle ?
Thinke you such treason may have place in brothers breast to boyle ?

Yf that myne Oth could me not keepe content with my degree :
But that contemning meane estate, I would clime aloft to bee.
Yet should ill Fortune mee deter, from such attempts I trowe :
Whose guise it is on Princes heads, huge heapes of Cares to throwe.
I would advise your grace betimes this charge from you to cast :
Least lingring long all unawares, you be opprest at last.
Assure your selfe, in baser state, more safer you may live :
And shun a thousand Cares, and Griefs : which Princes hearts doe rive.
ŒD. And dost thou me exhort thou slave my kingdome for to leave ?
O faythlesse head, O shamelesse heart, that could such treasons weave ?
Darst thou attempt thou villayne vile this thing, to me to breake ?
And fearst thou not in such a cause so boldly for to speake.
CRE. I would perswade them so (O King) who freely might possesse
Their Realmes such piteous cares I see, do Prynces hearts oppresse :
But as for you of force you must your Fortunes chainge abyde.
ŒD The surest way for them that gape for kingdoms large and wyde,
Is first things meane, and rest, and peace, and base estate to prayse :
And yet with Tooth and Nayle, to toyle to mount aloft alwayes.
So often times, most restlesse beastes doe chiefly rest commend.
CRE. Shall not my service long suffice my truth for to defend ?
ŒD. Time is the onely meanes for such as thou to worke theyr will.
CRE. It is so syr, but as for mee, of goods I have my fill.
A great resort. A pleasaunt life : from Princely cares exempt.
All these might (surely) mee disswade from such a foule attempt.
There is no day almost (O King) the whole yeare thorow out,
Where in some royall gyfts are not from countreys round about
Unto mee sent, both Golde, and pearles, and things of greater cost,
Which I let passe, least I should seeme but vainly for to bost.
Besides the life of many a man hath bin preservde by mee.
In such a blisfull state (O King) what can there wanting bee ?
(ŒD. Good Fortune can no meane observe, but stil she preaseth higher.)
CRE. Shall I than guilelesse die (alas,) my cause and all untryde ?
ŒD. Were unto you at any time my life, my deedes discride ?

Did any man defend mee yet ? or els my causes pleade ?
And guiltlesse yet I am condemn'de to this you doe mee leade,
And mee expresse example give, which I entend to take.
What measure you doe meat to mee, lyke measure must I make
CRE. The minde which causelesse dred appawls, true cause of feare bewraies
That conscience is not guiltles sure, which every blast dismaies.
ŒD. Hee that in midst of perilles deepe, and daungers hath bene cast,
Doth seeke all meanes to shun like ills as hee hath overpast.
CRE. So hatreds ryse. ŒD. Hee that to much doth use ill will to feare,
Unskilfull is : and knowes not how, hee ought him selfe to beare
In kings estate. For feare alone doth Kingdomes chiefly keepe.
Than hee that thus doth arme himselfe from feare all free may sleepe.
CRE. Who so the cruell tyrant playes, and guiltlesse men doth smight,
Hee dreadeth them that him doe dread, so feare doth chiefly light
On causers chiefe. A just revenge for bloudy mindes at last.
ŒD. Come take this traytor vile away, In dongeon deepe him fast
Enclose. There for his due deserts, let him abide such payne
And scourge of minde (as meete it is) false traytors to sustayne.

CHORUS

See, see, the myserable State of Prynces carefull lyfe.
What raging storms ? what bloudy broyles ? what toyle ? what endlesse stryfe
Doe they endure ? (O God) what plagues ? what griefe do they sustayne ?
A Princely lyfe : No. No. (No doubt) an ever duringe payne.
A state ene fit for men on whom Fortune woulde wreke her will.
A place for Cares to couch them in. A doore wyde open still
For griefes and daungers all that ben to enter when they list.
A king these Mates must ever have, it bootes not to resist.
Whole fluds of privy pinching feare, great anguishe of the minde :
Apparent plagues, and dayly griefes. These playfayres Princes finde.

And other none, with whom they spend, and passe theyr wretched dayes.
Thus hee that Princes lives, and base Estate together wayes,
Shall finde the one a very hell, a perfect infelicity :
The other eke a heaven right, exempted quight from mysery.
Let Œdipus example bee of this unto you all,
A Mirrour meete, A Patern playne, of Princes carefull thrall.
Who late in perfect Joy as seem'de, and everlasting blis,
Triumphantly his life out led, a Myser now hee is,
And most of wretched Misers all, even at this present tyme,
With doubtfull waves of feare Itost, subject to such a Cryme
Whereat my tongue amased stayes, God graunt that at the last,
It fall not out as Creon tolde. Not yet the worst is past,
(I feare.)

ŒDIPUS

THE FOURTH ACTE

THE FIRSTE SCENE

ŒDIPUS, JOCASTA

Y mynde with doubtfull waves of dread, is tossed to and fro,
I wot not what to say (Alas) I am tormented so.
For all the Gods on me doe cry, for paynes and vengeaunce due.
They say that these my guiltlesse hands, king Laius lately slue.
But this my conscience voyde of crime and mynde from mischiefe free :
To Gods untried, to mee well known denies it so to bee :
Full well I doe remember once, by chaunce I did dispatch
A man who sought by force with mee presumptuously to match.
His purpose was (a fond attempt) my Chariot for to stay,
This I remember well enough, the strife was in the way.
And he a man well steept in yeares, and I a lusty bloud,
And yet of meere disdayne and pride in vayne hee mee withstood.
But this from Thebes farre was done, a croked three pathd way,
That was the place in which we fought : it hard by Phocis lay.
Deare Wyfe resolve my doubts at once, and mee expresly tell,
How old was Laius the King whan this mischaunce befell ?
Was he of fresh and lusty yeares ? or stricken well in age
When he was kilde ? O ease my thoughts of this tormenting rage.
Joc. Betwixt an old man an a yong : but nearer to an olde.
Œd. Were there great Bands of men with him his Person to upholde ?
Joc. Some by the way deceived were, and some deterd by payne :
A fewe by toyle and labour long, did with their Prince remayne.

ŒD. Were any slayne in his defence? Joc. Of one report is rife,
Who constant in his princes cause full stoutly lost his lyfe.
ŒD. It is enough, I knowe the man that hath this mischiefe done.
The number and the place agrees. The time untried alone
Remaynes: Than tell what time hee died, and when that he was slaine.
Joc. Tis ten yeares since: you now revive my chiefest cares againe.

THE SECOND SCENE

SENEX, ŒDIPUS

The Corinth people all (O King) in Fathers place to rayn
Doe call your Grace: Polybius doth eternall rest obtayn.
ŒD. O God what Fortune vyle doth mee oppresse on every side?
How doe my sorrowes still encrease? Tell how my Father dide.
SEN. No sicknesse (sir) but very age did of his life him reave.
ŒD. And is hee dead? in deede? not slayne? what joy may I conceave?
How may I now triumph? the Gods to witnesse I doe call,
To whom are known my hidden thoughts and secret workings al:
Now may I lift to skyes my hands, my hands from mischiefe free.
But yet the chiefest cause of feare remayneth still to mee.
SEN. Your Fathers kingdom ought al dred out of your mind to drive.
ŒD. That I confesse. But secret thoughts my trembling heart do rive
With inward doubt of deepe distresse, my Mother I do feare.
This grudge is that continually my heart doth rent and teare.
SEN. Do you your Mother feare? on your return that onely stayes.
ŒD. I feare not her: but from her sight, a godly zeale mee frayes.
SEN. What will you her a Wydow leave? ŒD. Now, now, thou woundst my heart.
This, this, and onely this (alas,) is cause of all my smart.
SEN. Tell me (O king) what doubtfull feare doth presse thy princely brest:
Kings councels I can well conceale that ben with Cares opprest.
ŒD. Least as Apollo hath foretolde, I should a Mariage make
With myne owne Mother: only this fowle feare doth make me quake.

SEN. Such vayne and pevysh feares, at length from out your breast exyle.
Meropa your Mother is not in deede, you do your selfe beguile.
ŒD. What vauntage should it be to her adopted Sonnes to have ?
SEN. A kingdom she shall gayne thereby. Her Husband layde in grave,
The chiefest prop to stay her Realmes from present confusion,
Is children for to have : and hope of lawfull succession.
ŒD. What are the meanes whereby thou dost these secrets understand.
SEN. My selfe (your grace) an Infant gave into your fathers hand.
ŒD. Didst thou me to my Father geve ? Who than gave me to thee ?
SEN. A Sheparde sir, that wonted on Cytheron Hills to bee.
ŒD. What made thee in those woods to raunge ? what hadst thou there to do ?
SEN. Upon those Hils my Beasts I kept, somtime a Sheepeherde to.
ŒD. What nots, what privy marks hast thou, wherby thou dost me know ?
SEN. The holes that through your feete are borde from whence your name did gro.
ŒD. Declare forthwith what was his name that gave me unto thee.
SEN. The kings chief Shephard than that was, delivered you to mee.
ŒD. What was his name ? SEN. O king old mens remembrance soone doth fayle :
Oblivion for the chiefest part, doth hoary heads assayle,
And drowns their former memory of things long out of mynde.
ŒD. What ? canst thou know the man by sight ? SEN. Perhaps I should him finde,
And know by Face. Things overwhelmd by time, and quight opprest,
A small marke oft to mynde revokes, and fresh renues in brest.
ŒD. Sirs bid the Herdmen forthwith drive theyr Beasts to Aulters all.
Away with speede, make hast, the Master Sheepherds to mee call.
SEN. Sith that your destny this doth hyde, and Fortune it detayne
And closely keepe, let it be so, from opening that refrayne
That long conceald hath hidden lyen, that seeke not to disclose :
Such things outsercht and found oftimes agaynst the sercher goes

ŒD. Can any mischiefe greater be ? than this that now I feare.
SEN. Advise you wel remembre fyrst what weight this thing doth beare :
That thus you goe about to search, and sift with Tooth and Nayle,
Observe the golden meane : beware beare still an equall sayle.
Your Countreys wealth (O King) your lyfe, and all upon this lyes.
Though you stir not, bee sure at length your Fortune you escryes.
A happy state for to disturbe doth nought at all behove.
ŒD. When things be at the worst, of them a man may safely move.
SEN. Can you have ought more excellent ? than is a Prynces state ?
Beware least of your Parents found it you repent to late.
ŒD. No (father) no I warrant that : repent not I (I trow.)
I seeke it not to that entent. I have decreed to know
The matter at the full. Wherefore I will it now pursue.
Lo Phorbas : where hee trembling coms, with comely aged hue,
To whom of all the kinges flock then, the care and charge was due.
Dost thou his name, his speach, his Face, or yet his person know ?
SEN. Me thinks I should have seene his Face, and yet I cannot show
The places where I have him seene, small time brings such a chainge,
As well acquaynted Faces oft, to us appeare full strainge.
This looke is neyther throughly known, nor yet unknown to mee.
I cannot tell : I doubt it much, and yet it may be hee.
In Laius tyme long since when hee these Kingdomes great did keepe :
Wast thou not on Citheron hils chiefe Shepard to his sheepe ?

THE THIRDE SCENE

PHORBAS, SENEX, ŒDIPUS

SOMETIME a charge of sheepe I had, unworthy though I weer,
And did upon those hills chiefe rule on other Shepards beare.
SEN. Knowst thou not me. PH. I cannot tell. ŒD. Didst thou once give this man
A Childe. Speake out, why dost thou stay ? if so, declare it than.
Why dost thou blush and doubting stand, troth seeketh no delay ?
PH. Things out of minde you call agayne, almost quight worne away.

ŒD. Confesse thou slave, or els I sweare, thou shal constrayned bee.
PH. In deede I doe remembre once, an Infant yong by mee
Delyvered was unto this Man: but well I wot in vayne
I know he could not long endure, nor yet alyve remayne.
Long since he is dead (I know it well) hee lives not at this day.
SEN. No? God forbid, he lives no doubt, and long may live I pray.
ŒD. Why dost thou say the child is dead, that thou this man didst give?
PH. With Irons sharp his feete were board, I know he could not live,
For of the sore a swelling rose, I saw the bloud to gush
From out of both the wounds: and down by powring streames to flush.
SEN. Now stay (O king) no farther now, you know almost the troth.
ŒD. Whose child was it? tell me forthwith. PH. I dare not for mine Othe.
ŒD. Thine Oth thou slave? Some fyre here. Ile charme thine Othe and thee,
With fyre and flames: except forthwith thou tell the troth to mee.
PH. O pardon me, though rude I seeme, I seeke not to withstand
Your graces minde: (most noble king.) My life is in your hand.
ŒD. Tell me the troth, what child, and whose, What was his Mothers name?
PH. Born of your wyfe. ŒD. O gaping earth devour my body quight:
Or else thou God that ruler art of houses voyde of light,
To Hell my Soule with thunder boltes to Hell my Soule down dryve,
Where griesly Ghosts in darknesse weepe, and endlesse payne do lyve.
For thee alone, these Plagues doe rage. For thee these mischiefes ryse.
For thee the Earth lyes desolate. For thee thou wretch the Skies
Infected are. For thee, for thee, and for thy filthy lust,
A hundred thousand guiltlesse men, consumed are to dust.
O people throw: cast heapes of stones upon this hatefull Hed:
Bath all your swords within my brest: you furies overshed
My restlesse thoughts with raging woes: and plungde in seas of pain,
Let mee those horrors still endure, which damned soules sustain.

You citizens of Stately Thebes vex me with torments due.
Let Father, Son, and Wyfe, and all with vengeance me pursue.
Let those that for my sake alone with plagues tormented bee
Throw darts, cast stones, fling fier and flames, and tortures all on mee.
O shame : O slaunder of the World : O hate of Gods above :
Confounder O of Nature thou to lawes of sacred love,
Even from thy birth an open Foe. Thou didst deserve to dye
As soone as thou wast born. Go, go, unto the Court thee hye,
There with thy Mother (slave) triumph rejoyce as thou maist do,
Who hast thy house encreased with unhappy children so.
Make haste with speede, away, some thing thy mischiefs worthy finde,
And on thy selfe wrecke all the spight of thy revenging minde.

CHORUS

Fortune the guide of humaine lyfe doth al things chaunge at will.
And stirring stil, with restles thoughts our wretched minds doth fill.
In vayn men strive their stars to kepe when hideous tempests rise :
And blustring windes of daungers deepe sets death before their eyes.
Who saith he doth her fauning feele ? and chaungeth not his minde,
When fickle fight of Fortunes wheele doth turne by course of kinde.
These grevous plagues from privat house to princely Thrones do flow,
And oft their minds with cares they souse and thick upon them strow.
Whole heapes of griefe and dyre debate, a wofull thing to see :
A princely lyfe to mysers state, converted for to bee.
O Œdipus thy fatall fall, thy dreadfull mischiefs ryght,
Thy dolfull state, thy mysery, thy thrise unhappy plight :
These things shall blase through all the world : what heart may then rejoyce
At thy distresse ? I can no more : my teares doe stop my voyce.
But what is he that yonder stamps ? and raging puffs and blowes,
And often shakes his vexed head, some mischiefe great hee knowes.
Good sir your countnaunce doth import some great and fearefull thing,
Tell us therefore (if that you may) what newes from Court you bring.

ŒDIPUS

THE FIFTE ACTE

NUNTIUS

HEN Œdipus accursed wretch, his fatall fals had spied,
To hell he damnd his wretched soule and on the Gods he cryed
For vengeaunce due. And posting fast with franticke moode and griesly hue,
Unto his dolefull Court hee went, his thoughts for to pursue.
Much like a Lion ramping wylde, his furious head that shakes,
And roares with thundring mouth alowd, and often gnashing makes,
None otherwise this miser farde. A lothsome sight to see.
Besides himselfe for very rage, he still desires to dye.
And rowling round his wretched Eyes with vysage pale and wan :
Ten thousand Curses out he powres. Himselfe the unhappiest man
Of all that live, he doth account : as justly he may doe.
A wretch, a slave, a caitife vyle. The cause of all our woe.
And in this case enflamd with spight he cries, he stamps, he raves,
And boyling in his secret thoughts, he still desyres to have
All torments under sun that may his Cares conceivde encrease.
O wretched wyght, what should hee doe ? What man may him release ?
Thus foming all for rage at mouth, with sighes, and sobs, and grones,
His damned head ten thousand times, as oft his weryed bones
He beats. And often puffing makes, and roares, and swels, and sweats,
And on the Gods for death hee calles, for Death hee still entreats.
Three times he did begin to speake : and thryse his tong did stay,
At length he cried out alowd : O wretch. Away, away.

Away thou monstrous Beast (he sayd :) wilt thou prolong thy lyfe ?
Nay rather some man strike this breast with strooke of bloudy knyfe.
Or all you Gods above on mee your flaming fiers outcast :
And dints of Thunderbolts down throw. This is my prayer last.
What greedy vile devouring Gripe, upon my guts will gnaw ?
That Tigre fierce my hatefull limmes will quight a sunder draw ?
Loe, here I am you Gods : Loe, heere, wreke now on me your will :
Now, now you fyry Feendes of Hell, of vengeaunce take your fill.
Send out some wilde outragious beast, send Dogs mee to devoure,
Or els all ils you can devise, at once upon me powre.
O wofull soule. O sinfull wretch. Why dost thou feare to dye ?
Death only rids from woes thou knowst. Than stoutly Death defie.
With that his bloudy fatall Blade, from out his sheath he drawes,
And lowd he rores, with thundring voice, Thou beast why dost thou pawse ?
Thy Father cursed caitife thou, thy Father thou hast slayne
And in thy Mothers bed hast left an everduring stayne.
And Brothers thou hast got : nay Sons thou liest : thy Brothers all
They are. Thus for thy monstrous lust thy Countrey down doth fall.
And thinkst thou than for all these ils enough so short a payne ?
Thynkst thou the Gods will be apeasde, if thou forthwith be slayne ?
So many mischiefes don : and ist enough one stroke to byde ?
Account'ste thou it sufficient paynes, that once thy sword should glide
Quight through thy guilty breast for all ? why than dispatch and dye.
So maist thou recompence thy Fathers death sufficiently.
Let it be so : what mends unto thy Mother wilt thou make ?
Unto thy children what ? these plagues (O wretch) how wilt thou slake ?
That thus for thee thy countrey wastes ? One push shall ende them all.
A proper fetch. A fine devise. For thee a worthy fall.
Invent thou monstrous beast forthwith : a fall even worthy for
Thy selfe invent : whom all men hate and loth, and doe abhor.
And as dame Natures lawfull course is broke (O wretch) by thee,
So let to such a mischiefe great, thy Death agreeing bee.

O that I might a thousand times, my wretched lyfe renewe,
O that I might revyve and dye by course in order dewe
Ten hundred thousand times and more : than should I vengeance take
Upon this wretched head. Than I perhaps in part should make
A meete amends in deede, for this my fowle and lothsom Sin.
Than should the proofe of payne reprove the life that I live in.
The choyse is in thy hand thou wretch, than use thine owne discretion,
And finde a meanes, whereby thou maist come to extreame confusion.
And that, that oft thou maist not doe, let it prolonged bee.
Thus, thus, maist thou procure at length an endlesse death to thee.
Serch out a death whereby thou mayst perpetuall shame obtayne :
And yet not dye. But still to live in everlasting payne.
Why stayst thou man ? Go to I say : what meane these blubbring teares ?
Why weepst thou thus ? Alas to late. Leave of thy foolysh feares.
And ist enough to weepe thinkst thou ? shall teares and wayling serve ?
No wretch it shall not be. Thou dost ten thousand deaths deserve.
Myne eyes doe dally with mee I see, and teares doe still out powre.
Shall teares suffice ? No, no, not so I shall them better scowre.
Out with thine Eyes (he sayd :) and then with fury fierce enflam'de,
Like to a bloudy raging Feend and monstrous beast untam'de,
With fiery flaming spotted Cheekes his breast he often beats,
And scratch, and teare his Face hee doth and Skin a sunder treats,
That scarse his eyes in head could stand so sore he them besets.
With furious fierce outrageous minde hee stamps and cries alowd :
And roares and ralyes, with ramping rage. Thus in this case he stood,
Perplext, and vexed sore in minde, with deadly sighs and teares.
When sodenly all franticklike himselfe from ground hee teares,
And rooteth out his wretched Eyes, and sight a sunder teares.
Then gnasheth hee his bloudy Teeth, and bites, and gnawes, and champs,
His Eyes all bathd and brude in bloud, for fury fierce he stamps.

And raging more than needes (alas,) his Eyes quight rooted out:
The very holes in vayne hee scrapes so sore the wretch doth dout:
Least sight should chaunce for to remayne he rents and mangels quight
His Face, his Nose, his Mouth, and all whereon his hands do light
Hee rygs and ryves. Thus fowly rayd (alas) in piteous plight,
At length his head aloft he lifts, and therewith geves a shright.
And when he sees that all is gone, both light, and sight, and all,
Than schriching out: he thus begins upon the Gods to call.
Now spare you Gods, now spare at length my countrey prest to fall.
I have done that you did commaund: Your wraths revenged bee.
This wretched looke, this mangled face, is fittest now for mee.
Thus speaking, down the blackish bloud by streams doth gushing flow
Into his mouth. And clottred lumps of flesh the place doth strow
Wherein hee standes.
Beware betimes, by him beware, I speake unto you all:
Learne Justice, truth, and feare of God by his unhappy fall.

CHORUS

Mans lyfe with tumbling fatal course of fortunes wheele is rowld,
To it give place, for it doth run all swiftly uncontrowld.
And Cares and teares are spent in vayn, for it cannot be stayed,
Syth hie decree of heavenly powers perforce must be obayed.
What mankind bydes or does on earth it cometh from above,
Then wayling grones powrd out in griefe do nought at all behove
Our life must have her pointed course, (alas) what shall I say:
As fates decree, so things do run, no man can make them stay.
For at our byrth to Gods is known our latter dying day.
No Prayer, no Arte, not God himselfe may fatall fates resist.
But fastned all in fixed course, unchaunged they persist.
Such ende them still ensues as they appointed were to have,
Than fly all feare of Fortunes chaung, seeke not to lyve a slave
Enthrald in bondage vyle to feare. For feare doth often bring
Destnies that dreaded ben and mischiefs feard upon us fling.

Yea many a man hath come unto his fatall ende by feare.
Wherefore set pevish feare aside, and worthy courage beare.
And thou that subject art to death. Regard thy latter day,
Thinke no man blest before his ende. Advise thee well and stay.
Be sure his lyfe, and death, and all, be quight exempt from mysery
Ere thou do once presume to say: this man is blest and happy.
But thou alas, see where he coms: a wretch withouten Guide,
Bereft of sight. Halfe spoyld of lyfe: without all Pomp, and Pride
(That unto Kings Estate belongs.)

THE SECOND SCENE

ŒDIPUS, CHORUS, JOCASTA

Well, well, tis done: more yet? No, no, no mischiefs more remaynes.
My Fathers Rytes performed are. What God on Mysers paynes
That rues within this Cloud hath rolde, and wrapt my wretched Pate.
Ah sir: this is a life alone. This is a happy State.
This is a case ene fit for thee, for thee thou wretch, for thee.
From whose accursed sight the Sun, the Stars and all doe flee.
Yet mischiefs more, who gives to doe? The dreadfull day I have
Escapt. Thou filthy Paracide: thou vile mischievous Slave.
Unto thy right hand nought thou owst, all things performed bee
O woe is mee that ever I liv'de this lucklesse day to see.
Where am I now? Alas, alas, the light and all doth mee
Abhor: O wretched Œdipus this looke is first for thee.
Chor. See, see, where Jocasta coms, with fierce and furious moode,
Quight past her selfe. For very rage shee frets and waxeth woode.
Much like to Cadmus daughter mad, who late hir Sonne did kill.
Fayne would she speake her mynde: for feare (alas) she dares not: still
Shee stayes, and yet from out her breast these ills have quight exilde
All shamefastnes. See how shee lookes, with count'naunce fierce and wilde.

Joc. Fayne would I speake, I am afraide. For what should I thee call
My Son? doubt not. Thou art my Son. My Son thou art for all
These mischiefs great: alas, alas I shame my Son to see.
O cruell Son. Where dost thou turn thy Face? Why dost thou flee
From me. From me thy Mother deare? Why dost thou shun my sight?
And leave me thus in misery, with Cares consumed quight.
Œd. Who troubles me? Let me alone. I thought not to be founde:
Who now restores myne Eyes to mee, Mother? or Mothers sounde?
Our labour all is spent in vayne, now may wee meete no more,
The Seas devide those meetings vile that wee have had before.
The gaping earth devide us both, th' one from th' other quight.
Still let our feete repugnant bee. So shall I shun the light
That most of all me grieves. So shall I space obtaine to wayle
These bleeding woes on every side, that doe my thoughtes assayle.
Joc. The Destenies are in fault. Blame them. Alas, alas, not wee.
Œd. Spare now. Leave of to speake in vayne, spare now O Mother mee,
By these Reliques of my dismembred body I thee pray.
By myne unhappy Children pledges left. What shall I say?
By all the Gods I thee beseech. By all that in my name
Is good or bad, let mee alone. Alas you are to blame
To trouble mee. You see what hell my haplesse heart doth payne.
You see that in my Conscience ten thousand horrors raine.
Joc. O dying heart: O sindrownd soule. Why dost thou faint alas?
Why dost thou seeke and toyle in vayne these ills to overpas?
What meane these sighes, and scalding teares? why dost thou death refuse?
Thou mate of all his mischiefs thou, by whose meanes onely rues
The law of nature all: by whom, Ah, Ah, confounded lies,
Both God, and man, and beast, and all that eyther lives or dies.
Die thou, dispatch at once thrust through thy vile incestuous brest:
Thou hast none other meanes (alas) to set thine heart at rest.

Not thou, if God him selfe, if he his flaming fiers should throw
On thee, or mischiefs all by heapes upon thy body strow,
Couldst once for thy deserved ills due paines or vengeaunce pay :
Some meanes therefore to wreak Gods wrath upon thy selfe assay.
Death, death now best contenteth mee, then seeke a way to dye.
So maist thou yet at length finde end for all thy misery.
O Son lend mee thy hand : sith that thou art a Paracyde,
This labour last of all remaynes, this labour thee doth byde.
Dispatch rid mee thy mother deare from all my deadly woe :
It will not be : no prayers availe. Thy selfe this deede must doe.
Take up this sword. Goe to, with this thy husbande late was slayne.
Husband ? thou term'st him false : hee was thy syer : O deadly payne.
Shal I quight through my brest it drive ? or through my throte it thrust ?
Canst thou not choose thy wound ? away : die, die, (alas) thou must.
This hateful womb then wound (O wretch) this, this with thine own hand
Strike, strike it hard : (O spare it not) sith both a husband, and (The same a Son it bare.)
CHOR. Alas, alas, shee is slaine, she is slayne, dispatched with a push :
Who ever sawe the like to this : see how the bloud doth gush.
O heavy doulfull case : who can this dyrefull sight enduer
Which for the hideousnesse thereof might teares of stones procuer :
ŒD. Thou God, thou teller out of Fates. On thee, on thee, I call
My Father onely I did owe, unto the Destinies all.
Now twise a Paracide, and worse than I did feare to bee :
My Mother I have slayne, (Alas) the fault is all in mee.
O Œdipus accursed wretch, lament thine owne Calamity,
Lament thy state, thy griefe lament, thou Caitife borne to misery.
Where wilt thou now become (alas ?) thy Face where wilt thou hyde ?
O myserable Slave, canst thou such shamefull tormentes byde ?
Canst thou which hast thy Parents slain ? Canst thou prolong thy life ?
Wilt thou not dye ? deserving Death : thou cause of all the griefe,

And Plagues, and dreadfull mischiefs all that Thebane City prease.
Why dost thou seeke by longer life, thy sorrowes to encrease ?
Why dost thou toyle and labour thus in vayne ? It will not bee.
Both God, and man, and beast, and all abhorre thy Face to see.
O Earth why gapst thou not for me ? why doe you not unfolde
You gates of hell mee to receave ? why doe you hence withholde
The fierce Infernall Feends from me, from me so wretched wight ?
Why breake not all the Furyes lose this hatefull head to smight
With Plagues ? which them deserved hath (alas) I am left alone,
Both light, and sight, and comfort all from mee (O wretch) is gone.
O cursed head : O wicked wight, whom all men deadly hate.
O Beast, what meanst thou still to live in this unhappy state ?
The Skies doe blush and are ashamed, at these thy mischiefes great :
The Earth laments, the Heavens weepe, the Seas for rage doe freat,
And blustring rise, and stormes doe stir, and all thou wretch for thee,
By whose incest, and bloudy deedes all things disturbed bee.
Quight out of course, displaced quight, O cursed fatall day,
O mischiefes great, O dreadfull times, O wretch, away, away.
Exile thy selfe from all mens sight, thy life halfe spent in misery,
Goe end consume it now outright in thrise as great calamity.
O lying Phœbe thine Oracles my sin and shame surmount :
My Mothers death amongst my deedes, thou never didst recount.
A meete Exploict for me that am to Nature deadly Foe.
With trembling fearefull pace goe forth, thou wretched monster goe,
Grope out thy wayes on knees in darke thou miserable Slave.
So maist thou yet in tract of time due paynes and vengeaunce have
For thy mischevous lyfe. Thus, thus, the Gods themselves decree.
Thus, thus, thy Fates : thus the skyes appoint it for to bee.
Then headlong hence, with a mischiefe hence, thou caitife vyle away.
Away, away, thou monstrous Beast. Goe, Run. Stand, stay,
Least on thy Mother thou doe fall.

All you that wearyed bodies have, with sickenesse overprest,
Loe, now I fly : I fly away, the cause of your unrest.
Lift up your heads : a better state of Ayre shall strayght ensewe
Whan I am gone : for whom alone, these dreadfull myschiefs grewe.

And you that now, halfe dead yet live in wretched misers case,
Help those whom present torments presse forth, hye you on apace.
For loe, with me I cary hence all mischiefes under Skyes,
All cruell Fates, Diseases all that for my sake did ryse,
With mee they goe: with me both griefe, Plague, Pocks, Botch, and all
The ills that eyther now you presse, or ever after shall.
With me they goe, with me: these Mates bin meetst of all for mee,
Who am the most unhappiest wretch that ever Sun did see.

FINIS

Volume Two

THE SIXTE TRAGEDIE OF THE MOST GRAVE AND PRUDENT AUTHOR LUCIUS ANNÆUS SENECA

ENTITULED TROAS

WITH DIVERS AND SUNDRYE ADDITIONS TO THE SAME, BY JASPER HEYWOOD

TO THE READER

LTHOUGH (Gentle Reader) thou mayst perhaps thinke mee arrogant, for that I onely among so many fine wittes and towardly youth (with which England this day florisheth) have enterprised to set forth in english this present piece of the flowre of all writers, Seneca, as who say, not fearing what graver heads might judge of me, in attempting so hard a thing, yet upon well pondering what next ensueth, I trust both thy selfe shalt cleare thine owne suspicion, and thy chaunged opinion shal judge of me more rightfull sentence. For neither have I taken this worke first in hand, as once entending it should come to light (of well doynge wherof I utterly dispayred) and beynge done but for myne owne private exercise, I am in myne opinion herein blameles, thoughe I have (to prove my selfe) privately taken the part which pleased me best of so excellent an author, for better is tyme spent in the best then other, and at first to attempt the hardest writers, shall make a man more prompt to translate the easier with more facility. But now since by request, and frendship of those, to whom I could denye nothinge, this worke agaynst my will extorted is out of my hands, I needes must crave thy pacience in reading, and facility of judgement: when thou shalt apparently se my witles lacke of learning, prayng thee to consider how hard a thing it is for mee to touch at ful in all poynts the authors mynd, (beyng in many places verye harde and doubtfull,

and the worke much corrupt by the default of evil printed Bookes) and also how farre above my power to keepe that Grace and majestye of stile, that Seneca doth, when both so excellent a writer hath past the reach of all imitation, and also this our English toung (as many thinke, and I here fynd) is farre unable to compare with the Latten : but thou (good Reader) if I in any place have swerved from the true sence, or not kept the roialty of speach, meete for a Tragedie, impute the one to my youth and lacke of iudgement : the other to my lacke of Eloquence. Now as concerninge sondrye places augmented and some altered in this my translation. First forasmuch as this worke seemed unto mee in some places unperfite, whether left so of the Author, or parte of it loste, as tyme devoureth all thinges, I wot not, I have (where I thought good) with addition of myne owne Penne supplied the wante of some thynges, as the firste Chorus, after the first acte begynninge thus, O ye to whom etc. Also in the seconde Acte I have added the speache of Achilles Spright, rysyng from Hell to require the Sacrifyce of Polyxena begynning in this wyse, Forsakinge now, etc. Agayne the three laste staves of the Chorus after the same Acte : and as for the thyrde Chorus which in Seneca beginneth thus, Que vocat sedes ? For as much as nothing is therein but a heaped number of farre and straunge Countries, considerynge with my selfe, that the names of so manye unknowen Countreyes, Mountaynes, Desertes, and Woodes, shoulde have no grace in the Englishe tounge, but bee a straunge and unpleasant thinge to the Readers (excepte I should expound the Historyes of each one, which would be farre to tedious,) I have in the place therof made another, beginninge in this manner, O Jove that leadst, etc. Which alteration may be borne withall, seynge that Chorus is no part of the substaunce of the matter. In the rest I have for my slender learninge endevored to keepe touch with the Latten, not worde for woorde or verse for verse, as to expounde it, but neglectynge the placinge of the wordes, observed their sence. Take Gentle Reader this in good woorth with all his faultes, favour my first beginninges, and amende rather with good will such things as herein are amisse, then to deprave or discommende my labour and paynes, for the faultes, seyng that I have herein, but onelye made waye to other that canne farre better doe this or like, desiryng them that as they can, so they would. Farewel gentle Reader and accept my good will

THE ARGUMENT

THE ten yeares siege of Troy, who list to heare,
And of thaffayres that there befell in fight:
Reade ye the workes that long since written were,
Of all Thassaultes, and of that latest night,
When Turrets toppes in Troy they blased bright.
Good Clerkes they were that have it written well,
As for this worke, no word therof doth tell.

But Dares Phrygian, well can all report,
With Dictis eke of Crete in Greekish toung
And Homer telles, to Troye the Greekes resort
In scanned verse, and Maro hath it song
Ech one in writ hath pend a stoary long,
Who doubtes of ought, and casteth care to knowe
These antique Authors, shal the story showe,

The ruines twayne of Troy, the cause of each,
The glittering helmes, in fieldes the Banners spread,
Achilles yres, and Hectors fightes they teach.
There may the jestes of many a Knight be read:
Patroclus, Pyrrhus, Ajax, Diomed,
With Troylus, Parys, many other more,
That day by day, there fought in field full sore.

And how the Grekes at end an engine made:
A hugie horse where many a warlike Knight
Enclosed was: the Trojans to invade
With Sinons craft, when Greekes had fayned flight,
While close they lay at Tenedos from sight,
Or how Eneas els as other say,
And false Antenor did the towne betray.

TROAS

THE ARGUMENT

But as for me I naught therof endight,
Myne Author hath not all that story pend :
My pen his wordes in English must resight,
Of latest woes that fell on Troy at end,
What finall fates the cruell God could send.
And how the Greekes when Troy was burnt gan wreake
Their ire on Trojans, therof shall I speake.

Not I with spere who pearced was in fielde,
Whose throate there cutte, or head ycorved was
Ne bloudshed blowes, that rent both targe and shield
Shal I resight, all that I overpasse.
The worke I wryght more woeful is alas,
For I the mothers teares must here complayne,
And bloud of babes, that giltles have bene slayne

And such as yet could never weapon wreast,
But on the lap are wont to dandled bee,
Ne yet forgotten had the mothers breast,
How Greekes them slew (alas) here shall ye see
To make report therof ay woe is mee,
My song is mischiefe, murder, misery,
And hereof speakes this doleful tragedy.

Thou fury fel that from the deepest den
Couldst cause this wrath of hell on Troy to light,
That worckest woe guyde thou my hand and pen,
In weeping verse of sobbes and sighes to wryght,
As doth myne author them bewayle aright :
Helpe woefull muse for mee besemeth wel
Of others teares, with weeping eye to tell.

When battered were to ground the towres of Troy
In writ as auncient authors do resight,
And Greekes agayne repayrde to Seas with joy,
Up riseth here from hel Achilles Spright,
Vengeance he craves with bloud his death to quight.
Whom Paris had in Phœbus temple slayne,
With guile betrapt for love of Polyxeine.

THE ARGUMENT

And wrath of hel there is none other pryce
That may asswage : but bloud of her alone
Polyxena he craves for sacrifyce,
With threatninges on the Grecians many one
Except they shed her bloud before they gone.
The Sprightes the hell, and depest pittes beneath,
O Virgin dere, (alas) do thrust thy death.

And Hectors sonne, Astyanax (alas)
Pore seely foole his Mothers onely joy,
Is judged to die by sentence of Calchas
Alas the whyle, to death is led the boy,
And tumbled downe from Turrets tops in Troy.
What ruthful teares may serve to wayle the woe
Of Hectors wyfe that doth her child forgoe.

Her pinching pange of hart who may expresse,
But such as of like woes, have borne a part ?
Or who bewayle her ruthful heavines
That never yet hath felt therof the smart ?
Ful well they wot the woes of heavy hart.
What is to leese a babe from mothers breast,
They know that are in such a case distrest.

First how the Queene lamentes the fall of Troy,
As hath mine author done, I shall it wryght :
Next how from Hectors wyfe they led the boy
To die, and her complayntes I shall resight,
The maydens death then I must last endight.
Now who that liste the Queenes complaint to here,
In following verse it shall forthwith appeare.

THE SPEAKERS NAMES

HECUBA Queene of Troy.
A company of women.
TALTHYBIUS a Grecian.
AGAMEMNON King of Greeks.
ASTYANAX.
NUNCIUS.
CALCHAS.
PYRRHUS.
CHORUS.
ANDROMACHA.
An old man TROJAN.
ULYSSES.
HELENA.
The Spright of Achilles.

TROAS

THE FIRST ACTE

HECUBA

HO so in pompe of prowde estate, or kingdome sets delight:
Or who that joyes in Princes courte to beare the sway of might.
Ne dreads the fates which from above the wavering Gods downe flinges:
But fast affiance fixed hath, in frayle and fickle thinges:
Let him in me both se the Face, of Fortunes flattering joy:
And eke respect the ruthful end of thee (O ruinous Troy)
For never gave shee playner proofe, then this ye present see:
How frayle and britle is the state of pride and high degree,
The flowre of flowring Asia, loe whose fame the heavens resound,
The Worthy worke of Gods above, is batered downe to ground.
And whose assaultes they sought afar, from West with Banners spred
Where Tanais cold her braunches seven, abroad the world doth shed.
With hugie host and from the East, where springes the newest dea,
Where Lukewarme Tygris channell runnes, and meetes the ruddy sea.
And which from wandring land of Scythe, the band of widowes sought:
With fire and sworde thus battered be her Turrets downe to nought.
The walles but late of high renowne lo here their ruinous fall:
The buildinges burne, and flashing flame, swepes through the pallas al.
Thus every house ful hie it smoakes, of old Assarackes lande:
Ne yet the flames withholdes from spoyle, the greedy Victors hand,
The surging smoake, the asure skye, and light hath hid away:
And (as with cloude beset) Troyes Ashes staynes the dusky day.

Through pearst with ire and greedy of hart, the victor from a farre
Doth view the long assaulted Troy, the gaine of ten yeares warre,
And eke the miseryes therof abhorres to looke uppon,
And though he se it yet scant himselfe, believes might be wonne,
The spoyles thereof with greedy hand they snatch and beare awaye :
A thousand shippes would not receive aboorde so huge a pray.
The yreful might I do protest of Gods adverse to mee,
My countryes dust, and Troyan King I call to witnes thee,
Whom Troy now hydes, and underneath the stones art overtrode :
With al the Gods that guides the Ghost, and Troy that lately stoode.
And you also you flocking Ghostes of al my children dere :
Ye lesser Sprightes what ever ill, hath hapned to us here.
What ever Phœbus watrish face, in fury hath foresayde :
At raging rise from seas when earst, the monsters had him frayde.
In childbed bandes I saw it yore, and wist it should be so :
And I in vayne before Cassandra told it long agoe.
Not false Ulysses kindled hath these fires, nor none of his :
Nor yet decepytful Sinons craft, that hath bene cause of this.
My fyre it is wherwith ye burne, and Parys is the brand
That smoaketh in thy towres (O Troy) the flowre of Phrygian land.
But ay (alas) unhappy age, why dost thou yet so sore
Bewayle thy Countries fatall fall, thou knewest it long before :
Behold thy last calamityes, and them bewayle with teares :
Account as old Troys overturne, and past by many yeares,
I saw the slaughter of the King, and how he lost his life :
By Th' aulter side (more mischiefe was) with stroake of Pyrrhus knife
When in his hand he wound his lockes, and drew the King to ground,
And hid to hiltes his wicked sword, in deepe and deadly wound.
Which when the gored King had tooke, as willing to bee slayne,
Out of the old mans throate he drew his bloudy blade agayne.
Not pitty of his yeares (alas) in mans extreamest age :
From slaughter might his hand withhold, ne yet his yre asswage :
The Gods are witnes of the same, and eake the sacrifyes,
That in his kingdome holden was, that flat on ground now lies.
The father of so many Kings Pryam of auncient name,
Untombed lieth and wants in blase of Troy his funerall flame.

Ne yet the Gods are wreakt, but loe his Sonnes and daughters all,
Such Lordes they serve as doth by chance of lot to them befall.
Whom shall I follow now for pray ? or where shall I be led ?
There is perhaps amonge the Greekes that Hectors wyfe wil wed.
Some man desyres Helenus spouse, some would Antenors have,
And in the Greekes their wantes not some that would Cassandra crave :
But I (alas) most woeful wight whom no man seekes to chuse,
I am the only refuge left, and me they cleane refuse.
Ye careful captive company, why stints your woful crye ?
Beate on your breastes and piteously complayne with voyce so hye,
As meete may be for Troyes estate, let your complayntes rebound
In toppes of Trees : and cause the hills to ring with terible sounde.

THE SECOND SCENE

THE WOMAN. HECUBA

Not folke unapt, nor new to weepe (O Queene)
Thou wilst to wayle by practise are wee taught,
For all these yeares in such case have we bene,
Since first the Troyan guest, Amiclas soughte
And saild the Seas, that led him on his way
With sacred ship, to Cibell dedicate
From whence he brought his unrepyning pray,
The cause (alas) of all this dire debate,
Ten tymes now hydde the hilles of Idey bee,
With snowe of Sylver hew all over layd.
And bared is, for Troyan rages each tree,
Ten tymes in field, the harvest man afrayde,
The spikes of Corne hath reapt, since never day
His wayling wantes new cause renewes our woe.
Lift up thy hand, (O Queene) crie well away :
We follow thee, we are wel taught thereto.
Hec. Ye faythful fellowes of your casualty,
Untie thattyre, that on your heads ye weare,
And as behoveth state of misery,
Let fall aboute your woeful neckes your hayre.

In dust of Troy rub all your armes about,
In slacker weede and let your breastes be tyed
Downe to your bellies, let your limmes lye out,
For what wedlocke should you your bosomes hyde ?
Your garmentes loose, and have in readines
Your furious handes uppon your breast to knocke.
This habite well beseemeth our distresse,
It pleaseth me. I know the Troyan flocke :
Renew agayne your longe accustomde cryes,
And more then earst lament your miseryes.
We bewayle Hector.
Wo Our hayre we have untide, now every chone,
All rent for sorrow of our cursed cace,
Our lockes out spreads, the knottes we have undone
And in these ashes stayned is our face.
Hec. Fill up your handes and make therof no spare,
For this yet lawful is from Troy to take :
Let downe your garmentes from your shoulders bare,
And suffer not your clamour so to slake.
Your naked breastes wayte for your handes to smight,
Now dolor deepe now sorrow shew thy might :
Make all the coastes that compas Troy about
Witnes the sounde of all your careful crye,
Cause from the Caves the eccho to cast out :
Rebounding voyce of all your misery :
Not as she wontes, the latter word to sound
But all your woe from farre let it rebound :
Let al the Seas it heare, and eke the land,
Spare not your breastes with heavy stroake to strike,
Beate ye your selves, ech one with cruell hand
For yet your wonted crie doth me not like.
We bewayle Hector.
Wo. Our naked armes, thus here we rent for thee,
And bloudy shoulders, (Hector) thus we teare :
Thus with our fistes, our heades lo beaten bee
And all for thee, behold we hale our heare,
Our dugges alas, with mothers hands be torne,
And where the flesh is wounded round about

Which for thy sake, we rent thy death to morne
The flowing streames of bloud, they spring thereout.
Thy countres shore, and destinies delay.
And thou to wearied Trojans wast an ayde,
A wall thou wast, and on thy shoulders Troy
Ten yeres it stode, on thee alone it staide,
With thee it fell: and fatall day alas
Of Hector both, and Troy but one there was.
HEC. Enough hath Hector: turne your plaint and mone
And shed your teares for Pryame every chone.
WO. Receive our plaintes, O lord of Phrigian land
And old twise captive king, receive our feare,
While thou wert king Troy hurtles then could stand
Though shaken twise, with Grecian sword it weare,
And twise did shot of Hercles quiver beare,
At latter losse of Hecubes sonnes all
And roges for kings, that high on piles we reare:
Thou father shutst our latest funerall.
And beaten downe, to Jove for sacrifies.
Like liveles blocke, in Troy thy carkas lies.
HEC. Yet turne ye once your teares another way,
My pryams death should not lamented be.
O Troyans all, ful happy is Pryame say,
For free from bondage, downe descended hee,
To the lowest Ghoste: and never shall sustayne
His Captive necke with Greekes to yoked bee.
Hee never shal behold the Atrids twayne
Nor false Ulisses ever shall he see,
Not hee a pray for Greekes to triumph at.
His necke shall subject to their conquestes beare
Ne geve his handes to tye behynde his backe,
That to the rule of Scepters wonted weare,
Nor following Agamemnons chare, in bande
Shall he bee pompe, to proude Mycenas land.
WO. Ful happy Pryame is, each one wee say
That toke with him his Kingdome then that stoode
Now safe in shade, he seekes the wandring way,
And treads the pathes of all Elizius wood,

And in the blessed Sprightes, ful happy hee,
Agayne there seekes to meete with Hectors Ghost.
Happy Pryam, happy who so may see,
His Kingdome all, at once with him be lost.

CHORUS ADDED TO THE TRAGEDY BY THE TRANSLATOR

O ye to whom the Lord of Lande and Seas,
Of Life and Death, hath graunted here the powre,
Lay downe your lofty lookes, your pride appeas,
The crowned King fleeth not his fatall howre.
Who so thou be that leadst thy land alone,
Thy life was limite from thy mothers wombe,
Not purple robe, not Glorious glittering throne,
Ne crowne of Gold redeemes thee from the tombe :
A King he was that wayting for the vayle,
Of him that slew the Minotaure in fight :
Begilde with blacknes of the wonted saile
In seas him sonke, and of his name they hight.
So he that wild, to win the golden spoyle
And first with ship, by seas to seeke renowne,
In lesser wave, at length to death gan boyle,
And thus the daughters, brought their father downe :
Whose songes, the woodes hath drawen, and rivers held,
And birdes to heare his notes, did theirs forsake,
In peece meale throwne, amid the Thracian field,
Without returne hath sought the Stigian lake.
They sit above, that holde our life in line,
And what we suffer downe they fling from hie,
No carke, no care, that ever may untwine
The thrids, that woven are above the skie,
As witnes he that sometyme King of Greece,
Had Jason thought in drenching seas to drowne,
Who scapt both death and gaind the Golden fleece,
Whom fates advaunce, there may no powre plucke downe
The highest God sometyme that Saturne hight
His fall him taught to credite their decrees

The rule of heavens : he lost it by their might,
And Jove his sonne now turnes the rolling Skies.
Who weneth here to win eternall welth,
Let him behold this present perfite proofe.
And learne the secrete stoppe of chaunces stelth,
Most nere alas, when most it seemes aloofe.
In slipper joy let no man put his trust :
Let none dispayre that heavy haps hath past :
The swete with sowre she mingleth as she lust
Whose doubtful web pretendeth nought to last.
Frailtie is the thride, that Clothoes rocke hath sponne,
Now from the Distaffe drawne now knapt in twaine
With all the world at length his end he wonne,
Whose works have wrought, his name should great remaine
And he whose travels twelve, his name display,
That feared nought the force of worldly hurt,
In fine (alas) hath found his fatall daye,
And died with smart of Dianyraes shurt.
If prowes might eternity procure,
Then Priam yet should live in lyking lust,
Ay portly pompe of pryde thou art unsure,
Lo learne by him, O Kinges yee are but dust.
And Hecuba that wayleth now in care,
That was so late of high estate a Queene,
A mirrour is to teach you what you are
Your wavering wealth, O Princes here is seene.
Whom dawne of day hath seene in high estate
Before Sunnes set, (alas) hath had his fall :
The Cradels rocke, appoyntes the life his date
From setled joy, to sodayne funerall.

THE SECOND ACTE

The Spright of Achilles added to the Tragedy by the Translator

THE FIRST SCENE

ORSAKING now the place tenebrouse,
And deepe dennes of thinfernall region
From all the shadowes of illusious
That wander there the pathes ful many one
Lo, here am I returned al alone,
The same Achil whose fierce and heavy hande
Of al the world no wight might yet withstand.

What man so stout of al the Grecians host,
That hath not sometyme crav'd Achilles aide,
And in the Troyans, who of prowes most
That hath not feard to see my Banner splaide ?
Achilles lo, hath made them all affrayde.
And in the Greekes hath bene a piller post,
That sturdy stode agaynst their Troyan host.

Where I have lackt the Grecians went to wracke,
Troy proved hath what Achills sword could doe,
Where I have come the Troyans fled a backe,
Retyring fast from field their walles unto :
No man that might Achilles stroke fordoe
I dealt such stripes amid the Trojan route,
That with their bloud I staynd the fields aboute.

Mighty Memnon that with his Persian band,
Would Pryams part with all might mayntayne,

THE SECOND ACTE

Lo now he lyeth and knoweth Achilles hand,
Amid the field is Troylus also slayne.
Ye Hector great, whom Troy accompted playne
The flowre of chivalry that might be found,
All of Achilles had theyr mortall wound.

But Paris lo, such was his false deceipt,
Pretending maryage of Polixeine,
Behynd the aulter lay for me in wayte
Where I unwares have falne into the trayne
And in Appolloes church he hath me slayne,
Wherof the Hel will now just vengeance have,
And here agayne, I come my right to crave.

The deepe Averne my rage may not sustayne,
Nor beare the angers of Achilles spright.
From Acheront I rent the spoyle in twayne,
And though the ground I grate agayne to sight:
Hell could not hide Achilles from the light,
Vengeance and bloud doth Orcus pit require,
To quench the furies of Achilles yre.

The hatefull land, that worse then Tartare is
And burning thrust excedes of Tantalus,
I here beholde againe, and Troy is this
O, travell worse, then stone of Sisyphus
And paines that passe the panges of Tityus
To light more lothsome furie hath me sent
Then hooked wheele, that Ixions flesh doth rent.

Remembred is alowe where sprites do dwell
The wicked slaughter wrought by wyly way.
Not yet revenged hath the deepest hell,
Achilles bloud on them that did him slay
But now of vengeance come the yrefull day
And darkest dennes of Tartare from beneath
Conspire the fautes, of them that wrought my death.

Now mischiefe, murder, wrath of hell draweth nere,
And dyre Phlegethon floud doth bloud require :
Achilles death shall be revenged here
With slaughter such as Stygian lakes desyre :
Her daughters bloud shall slake the spirites yre,
Whose sonne we slew, whereof doth yet remayne,
The wrath beneath, and hell shalbe their payne.

From burning lakes the furies wrath I threate,
And fire that nought but streames of bloud may slake
The rage of winde and seas their shippes shall beate,
And Ditis deepe on you shall vengeance take,
The sprites crie out, the earth and seas do quake,
The poole of Styx ungratefull Greekes it seath,
With slaughtred bloud revenge Achilles death.

The soyle doth shake to beare my heavy foote
And fearth agayne the sceptors of my hand,
The pooles with stroake of thunderclap ring out,
The doubtful starres amid their course do stand,
And fearfull Phœbus hides his blasing brande
The trembling lakes agaynst their course do flite,
For dread and terrour of Achilles spright.

Great is the raunsome ought of due to mee,
Wherwith ye must the sprightes and hell appease,
Polyxena shal sacrifysed be,
Upon my tombe, their yreful wrath to please,
And with her bloud ye shall asswage the seas,
Your ships may not returne to Greece agayne
Til on my tombe Polyxena be slayne.

And for that she should then have bene my wyfe,
I wil that Pyrrhus render her to mee,
And in such solemne sort bereave her life,
As ye are wont the weddings for to see,
So shal the wrath of Hel appeased bee,
Nought els but this may satisfy our yre,
Her wil I have and her I you require.

THE SECOND SCENE

TALTHIBIUS. CHORUS

ALAS how long the lingring Greekes in haven do make delay,
When eyther warre by seas they seeke or home to passe theyr way.
CH. Why, shew what cause doth hold your ships ? and Grecian navy stayes,
Declare if any of the Gods have stopt your homeward wayes.
TAL. My mynd is mas'd, my trembling sinewes quake and are affeard,
For straunger newes of truth then these I thinke were never heard.
Lo I my selfe have playnly seene in dawning of the day,
When Phœbus first gan to approch and drive the starres away,
The earth all shaken sodaynly and from the hollow grownde
My thought I hard with roaryng crye a deepe and dreadful sound:
That shoke the woods, and al the trees rong out with thunder stroke,
From Ida hils downe fel the stones, the mountayne toppes were broke.
And not the earth hath onely quakt, but all the Sea likewyse.
Achilles presence felt and knew, and high the surges ryse,
The cloven ground Erebus pittes then shewd and deepest dennes,
That downe to Gods that guyde beneath, the way appeard from hence,
Then shoke the tombe from whence anone in flame of fiery light,
Appeareth from the hollow caves Achilles noble spright.
As wonted he his Thracian armes and banners to disploy
And weild his weighty weapons wel agaynst thassaultes of Troy,
The same Achilles seemde he than that he was wont to bee
Amid the hostes and easly could I know that this was hee.
With carkasse slayne in furious fight, that stopt and fild each floude,
And who with slaughter of his hand made Xanthus runne with bloud
As when in Chariot high he sate with lofty stomacke stoute,
Whyle Hector both and Troy at once he drew the walles aboute.
Alowd he cride, and every coast rang with Achilles sound,
And thus with hollow voyce he spake, from bottom of the ground.

The Greekes shal not with litle pryce redeeme Achilles yre,
A princely raunsome must they geve, for so the fates require :
Unto my ashes Polyxene spoused shal here be slayne
By Pyrrhus hand, and al my tombe her bloud shal overstayne.
This sayd, he strayght sanke downe agayne to Plutoes deepe region,
The earth then cloasd, the hollow caves were vanished and gon,
Therwith the wether waxed clere, the raging wyndes did slake,
The tombling seas began to rest and al the tempest brake.

THE THIRD SCENE

PYRRHUS. AGAMEMNON. CALCHAS

WHAT tyme our sayles we should have spread, uppon Sygeon Seas,
With swift returne from long delay, to seeke our homeward wayes.
Achilles rose whose onely hand, hath geven Greekes the spoyle
Of Troia sore annoyde by him, and leveld with the soyle,
With speede requiting his abode and former long delay,
At Scyros yle, and Lesbos both amid the Ægæon sea.
Til he came here in doubt it stoode of fall or sure estate,
Then though ye hast to graunt his wil ye shall it geve to late.
Now have the other captaynes all the pryce of their manhood,
What els reward for his prowesse then her al onely blood ?
Are his desertes think you but light, that when he might have fled,
And passing Pelyus yeares in peace, a quiet life have led,
Detected yet his mothers craftes, forsooke his womans weede,
And with his weapons prov'd himselfe a manly man indeede :
The King of Mysya, Telephos that woulde the Greekes withstand,
Comming to Troy, forbidding us the passage of his land :
To late repenting to have felt Achilles heavy stroke,
Was glad to crave his health agayne where he his hurt had tooke :
For when his sore might not be salv'd as told Apollo playne,
Except the speare that gave the hurte, restoared help agayne.
Achilles plasters cur'd his cuttes, and sav'd the King alive :
His hand both might and mercy knew to slay and then revyve.
When Thebes fel : Eetion saw it and might it not withstand,
The captive King could nought redresse the ruin of his land.

Lyrnesus litle likewyse felt his hand and downe it fill,
With ruine overturned like from top of haughty hil.
And taken Bryseys land it is and prisoner is she caught
The cause of strife betweene the Kinges is Chryses come to naught.
Tenedos yle wel knowne by fame and fertile soyle he tooke
That fostreth fat the Thracian flockes and sacred Cilla shooke.
What bootes to blase the brute of him whom trumpe of fame doth show,
Through all the coastes where Caicus floud with swelling stream doth flow ?
The ruthful ruine of these realmes so many townes bet downe,
Another man would glory count and worthy great renowne.
But thus my father made his way and these his journeys are,
And battayles many one he fought whyle warre he doth prepare.
As wisht I may his merits more shall yet not this remayne.
Wel knowne and counted prayse enough that he hath Hector slayne
Duryng whose life the Grecians al might never take the towne,
My father onely vanquist Troy, and you have pluct it downe.
Rejoyce I may your parentes prayse and brute abroade his actes,
It seemeth the sonne to follow well his noble fathers facts,
In sight of Priam Hector slayne, and Memnon both they lay,
With heavy cheere his parentes wayld to mourne his dying day.
Himselfe abhord his handy worke in sight that had them slayne,
The Sonnes of Goddes Achilles knew were borne to die agayne.
The woman queene of Amazons that grev'd the Greekes ful sore
Is turnd to flight then ceast our feare wee dread their bowes no more.
If ye wel waigh his worthynes Achilles ought to have
Though he from Argos or Mycenas would a Virgin crave,
Doubt ye herein ? allow ye not that straight his wil be done.
And count ye cruel Pryams bloud to geve to Peleus sonne ?
For Helen sake your owne childes bloud appeasd Dianas yre
A wonted thing and done ere this it is that I require.
AG. The onely fault of youth it is not to refraine his rage
The Fathers bloud already sturres in Pryams wanton age :
Somtime Achilles grievous checkes I bare with pacient hart,
The more thou mayst, the more thou oughtst to suffer in good part
Wherto would yee with slaughtred bloud a noble spirit stayne ?
Thinke what is meete the Greekes to do, and Troyans to sustayne.

The proude estate of tyranny may never long endure.
The King that rules with modest meane of safety may be sure.
The higher step of princely state that fortune hath us signd
The more behov'th a happy man humility of mynd
And dread the chaunge that chaunce may bring, whose gifts so sone be lost
And chiefly then to feare the Gods, whyle they the favour most.
In beating downe that warre hath wonne, by proofe I have ben taught,
What pompe and pride in twinke of eye, may fall and come to naught.
Troy made me fierce and proude of mynde, Troy makes me frayd withal:
The Grekes now stand wher Troy late fel, ech thing may have his fal.
Sometyme I graunt I did my selfe, and Sceptors proudly beare,
The thing that might advaunce my hart makes me the more to feare
Thou Priam perfit proofe presentst thou art to mee eftsones:
A cause of pride, a glasse of feare a mirrour for the nones,
Should I accoumpt the sceptors ought but glorious vanity
Much like the borowed brayded hayre, the face to beautify.
One sodayne chaunce may turne to naught, and mayme the might of men
With fewer then a thousand shippes, and yeares in lesse then ten.
Not she that guydes the slipper wheele of fate, doth so delay:
That she to al possession grauntes, of ten yeares setled stay.
With leave of Greece I wil confesse, I would have wonne the towne
But not with ruine thus extreme to see it beaten downe.
But loe the battel made by night and rage of fervent mynd,
Could not abyde the brydling bitte that reason had assignd.
The happy sword once staind with blood unsatiable is,
And in the darke the fervent rage doth strike thee more amis.
Now are we wreakt on Troy so much let all that may remayne.
A Virgin borne of Princes bloud for offring to be slayne
And geven be to stayne the tombe and ashes of the ded,
And under name of wedlocke see the guiltles bloud be shed,
I wil not graunt for myne should bee thereof both fault and blame,
Who when he may, forbiddeth not offence: doth wil the same.

PYR. And shall his sprights have no reward their angers to appeyse ?
AGA. Yes very great, for all the world shall celebrate his prayse,
And landes unknowen that never saw the man so praysd by fame,
Shall heare and kepe for many yeares the glory of his name.
If bloudshed vayle his ashes ought strike of an Oxes hed,
And let no bloud that may be cause of mothers teares, be shed.
What furious fransy may this be that doth your will so leade,
This earnest carefull suite to make in travayle for the dead ?
Let not such envy towarde your father in your heart remayne,
That for his sacrifice yee would procure an others payne.
PYR. Proude tirant, while prosperity thy stomacke doth advaunce,
And cowardly wretch that shrinks for feare in case of fearefull chaunce.
Is yet agayne thy breast enflamde, with brand of Venus might ?
Wilt thou alone so oft deprive Achilles of his right ?
This hand shall give the sacrifice, the which if thou withstand
A greater slaughter shall I make, and worthy Pyrrhus hand.
And now to long from Princes slaughter doth my hand abide,
And meete it were that Polyxene were layde by Priams side.
AGA. I not deny, but Pyrrhus chiefe renowne in warre is this,
That Pryam slaine with cruell sworde, to your father humbled is.
PYR. My fathers foes we have them known, submit themselves humbly,
And Pryam presently yee wot, was glad to crave mercy.
But thou for feare not stout to rule, liest close from foes up shit :
While thou to Ajax, and Ulysses, dost thy will commit.
AGA. But needes I must, and will confesse, your father did not feare :
When burnt our fleete with Hectors brands, and Greeks they slaughtred weare.
While loytring then a loofe he lay, unmindfull of the fight,
In steede of armes with scratch of quill. his sounding harp to smight.
PYR. Great Hector then despising thee, Achilles songes did feare :
And Thessale ships in greatest dread, in quiet peace yet weare.
AGA. For why aloofe the Thessale fleete, they lay from Troyans handes,
And well your father might have rest, he felt not Hectors brandes.

PYR. Well seemes a noble king to give an other king reliefe.
AGA. Why hast thou then a worthy king berieved of his life ?
PYR. A poinct of mercy sometime is, what lives in care to kill.
AGA. But now your mercy mooveth you a virgins death to will.
PYR. Account yee cruell now her death whose sacrifice I crave.
Your own deere daughter once yee knowe, your selfe to th'aulters gave.
AGA. Naught els could save the Greekes from seas, but th' only bloud of her :
A king before his children ought, his countrey to prefer.
PYR. The law doth spare no captives bloud nor wil'th their death to stay.
AGA. That which the law doth not forbid, yet shame doth oft say nay.
PYR. The conquerour what thing he list, may lawfully fulfill.
AGA. So much the lesse he ought to list, that may do what he will.
PYR. Thus boast ye these as though in all ye onely bare the stroke :
When Pyrrhus loosed hath the greekes, from bond of ten yeres yoke.
AGA. Hath Seyros yle such stomaks bred ? PYR. No bretherns wrath it knoes.
AGA. Beset about it is with wave. PYR. The seas it do enclose.
Thyestes noble stocke I know and Atreus eke full well,
And of the bretherns dire debate, perpetuall fame doth tell.
AGA. And thou a bastard of a mayde, defloured prively.
Whom (then a boy) Achilles gat, in filthy lechery.
PYR. The same Achill that doth possesse, the raigne of Gods above,
With Thetys seas : with Æacus sprights, the starred heaven with Jove.
AGA. The same Achilles that was slaine, by stroke of Paris hande.
PYR. The same Achilles, whom no god, durst ever yet withstand.
AGA. The stoutest man I rather would his checkes he should refraine
I could them tame, but all your bragges, I can full well sustaine.
For even the captives spares my sword : let Calchas called be.
If destynies require her bloud, I will thereto agree.
Calchas whose counsel rulde our ships, and navy hither brought,
Unlookst the poale and hast by arte the secretes thereof sought,
To whome the bowelles of the beast, to whom the thunder clap,
And blasyng starre with flaming traine, betokeneth what shall hap.

Whose words with dearest price I bought, now tell us by what meane
The will of Gods agreeth that we returne to Greece againe.
CAL. The fates apoint the Greekes to buy their waies with wonted price.
And with what cost ye came to Troy, ye shal repayre to Greece.
With bloud ye came, with bloud ye must from hence returne againe,
And where Achilles ashes lieth, the virgin shal be slaine,
In seemely sort of habite, such as maydens wont ye see,
Of Thessalie, or Mycenas els, what time they wedded be.
With Pyrrhus hand she shal be slaine, of right it shalbe so
And meete it is that he the sonne, his fathers right should do.
But not this onely stayeth our shippes, our sayles may not be spred,
Before a worthier bloud then thine, (Polixena) be shed,
Which thirst the fates, for Priames nephew, Hectors litle boy :
The Grekes shal tumble hedlonge down, from highest towre in Troy.
Let him there die, this onely way ye shal the gods appeas,
Then spread your thousand sayles with joy ye neede not feare the seas.

CHORUS

May this be true, or doth the Fable fayne,
When corps is deade the Sprite to live as yet?
When Death our eies with heavy hand doth strain,
And fatall day our leames of light hath shet,
And in the Tombe our ashes once be set,
Hath not the soule likewyse his funerall,
But still (alas) do wretches live in thrall?

Or els doth all at once togeather die?
And may no part his fatal howre delay.
But with the breath the soule from hence doth flie?
And eke the Cloudes to vanish quite awaye,
As danky shade fleeth from the poale by day?
And may no jote escape from desteny,
When once the brand hath burned the body?

THE SIXTH TRAGEDY

What ever then the ryse of Sunne may see,
And what the West that sets the Sunne doth know.
In all Neptunus raygne what ever bee,
That restless Seas do wash and overflow,
With purple waves stil tombling to and fro.
Age shal consume : each thing that livth shal die,
With swifter race then Pegasus doth flie.

And with what whirle, the twyse sixe signes do flie,
With course as swift as rector of the Spheares,
Doth guide those glistering Globes eternally.
And Hecate her chaunged hornes repeares,
So drauth on death, and life of each thing weares,
And never may the man returne to sight
That once hath felt the stroke of Parcas might.

For as the fume that from the fyre doth passe,
With tourne of hand doth vanish out of sight
And swifter then the Northren Boreas
With whirling blaste and storme of raging might,
Drivth farre away and puttes the cloudes to flight,
So fleeth the sprighte that rules our life away,
And nothing taryeth after dying day.

Swift is the race we ronne, at hand the marke
Lay downe your hope, that wayte here ought to win,
And who dreads ought, cast of thy carefull carke :
Wilt thou it wot what state thou shalt be in,
When dead thou art as thou hadst never bin.
For greedy tyme it doth devoure us all,
The world it swayes to Chaos heape to fall.

Death hurtes the Corpes and spareth not the spright,
And as for all the dennes of Tœnare deepe,
With Cerberus kingdome darke that knowes no light,
And streightest gates, that he there sittes to keepe,
They Fancies are that follow folke by sleepe
Such rumors vayne, but fayned lies they are,
And fables like the dreames in heavy care.

These Three Staves following are added by the Translatour

O dreadful day, alas, the sory time.
Is come of all the mothers ruthful woe,
Astianax (alas) thy fatal line
Of life is worne, to death strayght shalt thou goe,
The sisters have decreed it should be so,
There may no force (alas) escape there hand,
There mighty Jove their will may not withstand.

To se the mother, her tender child forsake,
What gentle hart that may from teares refrayne
Or who so fierce that would no pity take,
To see (alas) this guiltles infant slayne,
For sory hart the teares myne eyes do stayne
To thinke what sorrow shall her hart oppresse,
Her litle child to leese remedilesse.

The double cares of Hectors wife to wayle,
Good Ladies have your teares in readines,
And you with whom should pity most prevayle,
Rue on her griefe : bewayle her heavines.
With sobbing hart, lament her deepe distresse,
When she with teares shall take leave of her son,
And now (good Ladies) heare what shall be done.

THE THIRD ACTE

ANDROMACHA. SENEX. ULISSES

LAS ye careful company, why hale ye thus your hayres ?
Why beate you so your boyling breasts and stayne your eyes with tears ?
The fall of Troy is new to you but unto me not so,
I have foreseene this careful case ere this tyme long agoe
When fierce Achilles Hector slew and drew the Corpes aboute
Then then me thought I wist it well, that Troy should come to naught
In sorrowes sonke I senceles am and wrapt (alas) in woe,
But sone except this babe me held, to Hector would I goe :
This seely foole my stomacke tames amid my misery,
And in the howre of heaviest happes permittes me not to die,
This onely cause constraynes me yet the gods for him to pray
With tract of tyme prolonges my payne, delayes my dying day :
He takes from me the lacke of feare the onely fruit of ill.
For while he lives yet have I left wherof to feare me still.
No place is left for better chaunce with worst wee are opprest
To feare (alas) and see no hope is worst of all the rest.
SEN. What sodayne feare thus moves your mynd, and vexeth you so sore ?
AND. Stil stil (alas) of one mishap there ryseth more and more,
Nor yet the doleful destenies of Troy be come to end.
SEN. And what more grievous chaunces yet prepare the Gods to send ?
AND. The caves and dennes of hel be rent for Troyans greater feare,
And from the bottoms of their tombes the hidden sprightes appeare.

May none but Greekes alone from hel returne to life agayne ?
Would God the fates would finish soone the sorrowes I sustayne.
Death thankful were, a common care the Troyans all oppresse,
But me (alas) amaseth most the feareful heavines.
That all astonied am for dreade, and horrour of the sight :
That in my sleepe appeard to mee by dreame this latter night.
SEN. Declare what sightes your dream hath shewd, and tell what doth you feare.
AND. Two parts of al the silent night almost then passed were,
And then the cleare seven clustered beams of starres were fallen to rest,
And first the sleepe so long unknowne my wearyed eyes opprest.
If this be sleepe the astonied mase of mynd in heavy moode,
When sodaynly before myne eyes the spright of Hector stoode.
Not like as he the Greekes was wont to battail to require :
Or when amid the Grecians shippes, he threw the brandes of fyre.
Nor such as raging on the Trees, with slaughtring stroake had slayne
And bare indeede the spoyles of him that did Achilles fayne.
His countenaunce not now so bright, nor of so lively cheere,
But sad and heavy like to owres and clad with ugly hayre
It did me good to see him though when shaking then his head :
Shake of thy sleepe in hast he sayd, and quickly leave thy bed :
Convay into some secrete place our sonne (O faythful wife)
This onely hope there is to helpe find meane to save his life.
Leave of thy piteous tears he sayd, dost thou yet wayle for Troy ?
Would God it lay on Ground ful flat so ye might save the boy.
Up stirre he sayd thy selfe in hast convay him privily.
Save if ye may the tender bloud of Hectors progeny
Then strayght in trembling feare I wake and rold myne eyes aboute
Forgettyng long my child pore wretch, and after Hector sought.
But strayght (alas) I wist not how the Spright away did passe,
And mee forsooke before I could my husband once embrasse.
O childe, O noble fathers broode and Trojans only joy,
O worthy seede of thauncient bloud, and beaten house of Troy.
O ymage of thy father loe, thou lively bearst his face,
This countnaunce lo my Hector had, and even such was his pace.

The pitch of all his body such, his handes thus would he beare.
His shoulders high, his threatning browes, even such as thine they were
O sonne : begot to late for Troy, but borne to soone for mee,
Shal ever tyme yet come agayne, and happy daye may be,
That thou mayst once revenge and build agayne the towres of Troy,
And to the towne and Troyans both restore their name with joy ?
But why do I (forgetting state of present destenye),
So great thinges wish ? enough for captives is to live only :
Alas what privy place is left my litle childe to hide ?
What seate so secret may be found where thou maist safely bide ?
The towre that with the walles of gods so valiaunt was of might,
Through all the world so notable, so flourishing to sight,
Is turnde to dust : and fire hath al consumd'e that was in Troy,
Of all the towne not so much now is left to hide the boy.
What place were best to choose for guile, the holy tombe is heere,
That thenmies sword will spare to spoile wher lythe my husband deere.
Which costly worke his father built, king Pryame liberall :
And it up raisde with charges great, for Hectors funerall.
Herein the bones and ashes both of Hector (loe) they lie,
Best is that I commit the sonne to his fathers custodie.
A colde and fearefull sweat doth runne, through out my members all,
Alas I carefull wretch do feare, what chaunce may thee befall.
SEN. Hide him away : this onely way hath saved many more,
To make the enmies to beleve, that they were dead before.
He wil be sought : scant any hope remaineth of safenes,
The paise of his nobility doth him so sore oppres :
AND. What way wer best to worke : that none our doings might bewray ?
SEN. Let none beare witnes what ye do, remove them all away.
AND. What if the enmies aske me : where Astianax doth remaine ?
SEN. Then shall ye boldelie answere make that he in Troy was slaine.
AND. What shal it helpe to have him hid ? at length they will him finde.
SEN. At first the enmies rage is fierce, delay doth slake his minde.

AND. But what prevailes, since free from feare we may him never hide ?
SEN. Let yet the wretch take his defence, me carelesse there to bide.
AND. What land unknowne out of the way, what unfrequented place
May keepe thee safe ? who ayds our feare ? who shall defend our case ?
Hector, Hector that evermore thy friendes didst wel defend
Now chiefly ayde thy wyfe and child and us some succour send.
Take charge to keepe and cover close the treasures of thy wyfe,
And in thy Ashes hyde thy sonne, preserve in tombe his life.
Draw neare my Childe unto the Tombe, why fliest thou backward so ?
Thou takst great scorne to lurke in dens, thy noble hart I know.
I see thou art asham'd to feare shake of thy princely mynd,
And beare thy breast as thee behoves as chaunce hath thee assynd.
Behold our case : and se what flocke remayneth now of Troy
The tombe : I woeful captive wretch and thou a seely boy,
But yeeld we must to sory fates thy chaunce must breake thy breast,
Go to, creepe underneath thy fathers holy seats to rest.
If ought the fates may wretches helpe thou hast thy savegard there.
If not : already then pore foole thou hast thy sepulchere.
SEN. The tombe him closely hides : but least your feare should him betray
Let him here lie and farre from hence goe ye some other way.
AND. The lesse he feares that feares at hand, and yet if neede be so,
If ye thinke meete a little hence for safety let us goe.
SEN. A litle whyle keepe silence now, refrayne your plaint and crie,
His cursed foote now hether moves the Lord of Cephalie.
AND. Now open earth, and thou my spouse from Stix rend up the ground,
Deepe in thy bosome hyde thy sonne that he may not be found.
Ulysses comes with doubtful pace and chaunged countenaunce,
He knittes in hart deceiptful craft for some more grievous chaunce.
UL. Though I be made the messenger of heavy newes to you,
This one thing first I shal desyre that ye take this for true,
That though the wordes come from my mouth, and I my messuage tell
Of truth yet are they none of myne ye may beleve me wel.

It is the word of al the Greekes, and they the authors be,
Whom Hectors bloud doth yet forbid their countries for to see.
Our careful trust of peace unsure doth stil the Greekes detayne,
And evermore our doubtful feare yet drawth us backe agayne.
And suffreth not our wearyed handes our weapons to forsake,
In child yet of Andromacha, while Troyans comfort take.
AND. And sayth your Augure Calchas so? UL. Though Calchas nothing sayde
Yet Hector telles it us himselfe, of whose seede are we frayde.
The worthy bloud of noble men oft tymes we se it playne,
Doth after in their heires succede and quickly springes agayne.
For so the hornles youngling yet, of high and sturdy beste,
With lofty necke and braunched brow, doth shortly rule the rest.
The tender twig that of the lopped stocke doth yet remayne,
To match the tree that bare the bough, in time startes up again
With equall top to former wood the roume it doth supply,
And spreads on soyle alow the shade, to heaven his braunches hye.
Thus of one sparke by chaunce yet left it hapneth so ful oft.
The fyre hath quickly caught his force and flamth agayn aloft.
So feare we yet least Hectors bloud might rise er it be long,
Feare castes in all thextremity and oft interprets wrong.
If ye respect our case ye may not blame these old soldiars
Though after years and monthes twice five, they feare again the wars.
And other travails dreadyng Troy, not yet to be wel wonne,
A great thing doth the Grecyans move, the feare of Hectors son.
Rid us of feare, this stayeth our fleete, and pluckes us back agayne,
And in the haven our navy stickes, til Hectors bloud be slayne.
Count me not feerce for that by fates I Hectors sonne require,
For I as wel if chaunce it would Orestes should desyre.
But since that needes it must be so, beare it with pacient hart:
And Suffer that which Agamemnon suffred in good part.
AND. Alas my child would God thou wert yet in thy mothers hand.
And that I knew what destenies thee held or in what land.
For never should the mothers fayth her tender child forsake:
Though through my breast the enmies al, their cruell weapons strake.

Nor though the Greekes with pinching bondes of yron my handes had bound,
Or els in fervent flame of fyre beset my body rounde.
But now my litle Child (pore wretch alas) where might he bee ?
Alas, what cruel desteny what chaunce hath hapt to thee ?
Art thou yet ranging in the fieldes and wandrest ther abroad ?
Or smothred else in dusty smoake of Troy : or overtroad ?
Or have the Greekes thee slayne (alas) and laught to see thy bloud ?
Or torne art thou with jawes of beastes ? or cast to foules for foode ?
Ul. Dissemble not, hard is for thee Ulisses to deceave,
I can ful wel the mothers craftes and subtilty perceave.
The pollecy of Goddesses Ulisses hath undone,
Set al these fayned wordes assyde, tel mee where is thy sonne ?
An. Wher is Hector ? where al the rest that had with Troy their fall ?
Where Priamus ? you aske for one but I require of all.
Ul. Thou shalt constrayned be to tell the thing thou dost deny.
And. A happy chaunce were Death to her that doth desyre to dye.
Uli. Who most desires to die, would faynest live when death drawth on,
These noble wordes with present feare of death woulde soone be gone
And. Ulisses if ye wil constrayne Andromacha with feare,
Threaten my life for now to dye my cheefe desyre it were.
Ul. With stripes with fyre tormenting death we wil the truth out wrest
And dolour shal thee force to tel the secrets of thy brest.
And what thy hart hath depest hid for payne thou shalt expresse,
Oft tymes thextremity prevayles much more then gentlenesse.
And. Set me in midst of burning flame, with woundes my body rent,
Use al the meanes of cruelty that ye may al invent.
Prove me with thirst and hunger both, and every torment trye,
Pearce through my sides with burning yrons, in prison let me lie.
Spare not the worst ye can devyse (if ought be worse then this)
Yet never get ye more of me. I wot not where he is.
Uli. It is but vayne to hyde the thinge that strayght ye wil deteckt,
No feares may move the mothers hart, she doth them al neglect.
This tender love ye beare your child, wherin ye stand so stoute,
So much more circumspectly warnth the Greekes to looke about.

Least after ten yeares tract of tyme and battell borne so farre,
Some one should live that on our children might renew the warre,
As for my selfe, what Calchas sayth, I would not feare at all
But on Telemachus I dread, the smart of warres would fall.
AND. Now will I make Ulisses glad and all the Greekes also,
Needes must thou woeful wretch confesse declare thy hidden woe.
Rejoyce ye sonnes of Atreus there is no cause of dread.
Be glad Ulisses tell the Greekes that Hectors sonne is dead.
UL. By what assurance proves thou that? how shal we credite thee?
AND. What ever thing the enmies hand may threaten hap to me
Let speedy fates me slay forthwith, and earth me hyde at ones
And after death from tombe agayne, remove yet Hectors bones,
Except my sonne already now, do rest among the dead.
And that except Astianax into his tomb be led.
ULISS. Then fully are the fates fulfild with Hectors childes disceace,
Now shal I beare the Grecians word, of sure and certayne peace.
Ulisses why what dost thou now? the Greekes wil every chone,
Beleeve thy wordes, whom creditst thou? the mothers tale alone.
Thinkst thou for savegard of her child the mother wil not lye?
And dread the more the worse mischaunce to geve her sonne to die?
Her fayth she byndes with bond of oth, the truth to verify,
What thing is more of weight to feare, then so to sweare and lye?
Now call thy craftes togeather al, bestirre thy wittes and mynd,
And shew thy selfe Ulisses now, the truth herein to find.
Search wel thy mothers mynd: behold shee weepes and wayleth out,
And here and ther with doubtful pace, she raungeth al aboute,
Her careful ears she doth apply to harken what I say,
More frayd shee seemes then sorrowful. Now worke some wily way.
For now most neede of wit there is and crafty pollecy,
Yet once agayne by other meanes I wil the mother trye.
Thou wretched woman maist rejoyce, that dead he is: (alas)
More doleful death by destenie for him decreed ther was.
From Turrets top to have bene cast and cruelly bene slayne.
Which onely towre of all the rest doth yet in Troy remayne.
AND. My spright failth me, my limmes do quake, fear doth my wits confounde.
And as the Ise congeals with frost, my bloud with could is bound.

UL. She trembleth loe: this way, this way I wil the truth out wreaste,
The mothers fear detecteth all the secrets of her breast:
I wil renew her feare goe sirs bestir ye spedely
To seeke this enmye of the Greekes where ever that he lie.
Wel done he wil be found at length, goe to stil seke him out,
Now shal he dye, what dost thou feare, why dost thou looke about?
AND. Would God that any cause there were yet left that might me fray,
My hart at last now all is lost hath layd all feare away.
ULISS. Sins that your child now hath ye say already suffred death,
And with his bloud we may not purge the hostes as Calchas sayth.
Our fleete passe not (as wel inspired doth Calchas prophecy)
Till Hectors ashes cast abroad the waves may pacify.
And tombe be rent now sins the boy hath skapt his desteny.
Needes must we breake this holy tombe wher Hectors ashes lie.
AN. What shal I do? my mynd distracted is with double feare,
On thone my sonne, on thother syde my husbandes ashes deare.
Alas which part should move me most, the cruel Goddes I call
To witnes with me in the truth, and Ghostes that guide thee all
Hector that nothing in my sonne is else that pleaseth me.
But thou alone God graunt him life he might resemble thee:
Shal Hectors ashes drowned bee? hide I such cruelty,
To see his bones cast in the Seas? yet let Astyanax die,
And canst thou wretched mother bide thyne owne childes death to see?
And suffer from the hie towres top that headlong throwne he be?
I can and wil take in good part, his death and cruel payne,
So that my Hector after death be not remov'd agayne.
The boy that life and sences hath may feele his payne and dye,
But Hector lo his death hath plast at rest in tombe to lie.
What dost thou stay? determine which thou wilt preserve of twayne.
Art thou in doubt? save this: loe here thy Hector doth remayne,
Both Hectors be, thone quicke of spright and drawing toward his strength
And one that may perhaps revenge his fathers death at length.

Alas I cannot save them both : I thinke that best it were,
That of the twayne I saved him that doth the Grecians feare.
UL. It shalbe done that Calchas words to us doth prophecye,
And now shall all the sumptuous worke be throwne downe utterly.
AN. That once ye sold ? UL. I wil it all from toppe to bottome rend.
AN. The fayth of Goddes I call uppon Achilles us defend,
And Pyrrhus ayd thy fathers right. UL. This tombe abroad shall lye :
AN. O mischiefe, never durst the Greekes show yet such cruelty.
Ye straine the temples and the Gods that most have favourd you,
The dead ye spare not, on their tombes your fury rageth now.
I wil their weapons all resist my selfe with naked hand,
The yre of hart shal geve me strength their armour to withstand.
As fierce as did the Amazones beate down the Greekes in fight,
And Menas once enspierd with God, in sacrifyce doth smyght,
With speare in hand, and while with furyous pace she treads the ground
And wood as one in rage she strykes, and feeleth not the wound
So wil I runne on midst of them and on theyr weapons dye,
And in defence of Hectors tombe among his ashes lie.
UL. Cease ye : doth rage and fury vayne of women move ye ought ?
Dispatch with speede what I commaund, and plucke downe al to naught.
AN. O slay me rather here with sword rid me out the way,
Breake up the deepe Avern, and rid my destenies delay.
Rise Hector and beset thy foes, breake thou Ulisses yre,
A spright art good enough for him, behold he casteth fire,
And weapon shakes with mighty hand do ye not Greekes him see ?
Or els doth Hectors spright appear but onely unto me ?
UL. Downe quight withal. AN. What wilt thou suffer both thy sonnes be slayne,
And after death thy husbandes bones to be remov'd agayne ?
Perhaps thou mayst with prayer yet appease the Grecians all.
Els downe to ground the holy tombe of Hector streight shall fal.
Let rather die the childe pore wretch and let the Greekes him kil,
Then father and the sonne should cause the tone the others yll.

Ulisses, at thy knees I fal, and humbly aske mercie,
These handes that no mans feete els knew, first at thy feete they lye.
Take pitty on the mothers case and sorrowes of my breast,
Vouchsafe my prayers to receive and graunt me my request.
And by how much the more the Goddes have thee advaunced hie
More easely stryke the pore estate of wretched misery.
God graunt the chast bed of thy godly wyfe Penelope,
May thee receive, and so agayne Laerta may thee see,
And that thy sonne Telemachus may meete thee joyfully,
His graundsires yeares, and fathers witte, to passe ful happely.
Take pity on the mothers teares, her litle child to save,
He is my onely comfort left, and th' onely joy I have.
UL. Bryng forth thy sonne and aske.

THE SECOND SCENE

ANDROMACHA

COME hither child out of the dennes to mee,
Thy wretched mothers lamentable store,
This Babe Ulisses (loe) this Babe is hee,
That stayeth your ships and feareth you so sore.
Submit thy selfe my sonne with humble hand,
And worship flat on ground thy maysters feete,
Thinke it no shame as now the case doth stand :
The thing that Fortune wilth a wretche is meete,
Forget thy worthy stocke of Kingly kynd,
Thinke not on Priams great nobility,
And put thy father Hector from thy mynde,
Such as thy Fortune let thy stomacke bee,
Behave thy selfe as captive bend thy Knee,
And though thy grief pearce not thy tender yeares,
Yet learne to wayle thy wretched state by mee,
And take ensample at thy mothers teares.
Once Troy hath seene the weeping of a child,
When litle Priam turnde Alcides threats,
And he to whom all beastes in strength did yelde,
That made his way from hel, and brake their gates,

His litle enmies teares yet overcame.
Priam he sayd receive thy liberty,
In seat of honor kepe thy Kingly name,
But yet thy Sceptors rule more faythfully.
Lo such the conquest was of Hercules.
Of him yet learne your hartes to mollify,
Do onely Hercles cruel weapons please,
And may no end be of your cruelty ?
No lesse then Pryam, kneeles to thee this boy,
That lieth and asketh onely life of thee.
As for the rule and governaunce of Troy
Where ever Fortune wil ther let it bee.
Take mercy on the mothers ruthful teares
That with their streames my cheekes do overflow,
And spare this guiltles infantes tender yeares
That humbly falleth at thy feete so lowe.

THE THIRD SCENE

ULISSES. ANDROMACHA. ASTIANAX

Of truth the mothers greate sorow, both move my hart full sore.
But yet the mothers of the Greekes of neede must move me more,
To whom this boy may cause in time a great calamitie.
Andr. May ever he the burnt ruines of Troy reeviste ?
And shall these handes in time to come, ereckt the towne againe ?
If this be thonely helpe we have, there doth no hope remain
For Troy, we stand not now in case to cause your feare of mynde,
Doth ought avayle his fathers force, or stocke of noble kinde ?
His fathers heart abated was, he drawen the walles abought.
Thus evil haps, the haughtiest heart at length they bring to nought,
If ye wil needes oppresse a wretch what thing more grievous were
Then on his noble neck he should the yoke of bondage bere ?
To serve in life doth any man this to a King denye ?
Ul. Nor Ulisses with his death, but Calchas prophecy.
An. O false inventor of deceipt and hainous cruelty,
By manhode of whose hand in warre no man did ever dye

But by disceipt and crafty trayne of mynd that mischiefe seekes,
Before this time ful many one dead is, yea of the Greekes,
The Prophets wordes and guiltles Gods saist thou my sonne require,
Nay : mischiefe of thy breast it is, thou dost his death desyre.
Thou night souldier, and stout of hart a little child to slay.
This enterprise thou takste alone and that by open day.
UL. Ulisses manhood wel to Greekes to much to you is knowne,
I may not spend the tyme in wordes, our Navy wil be gone.
AND. A little stay, while I my last farewel geve to my child,
And have with oft embracing him my greedy sorrowes fild.
ULI. Thy grievous sorrowes to redresse, would God it lay in mee,
But at thy wil to take delay of tyme I graunt it thee.
Now take thy last leave of thy Sonne, and fil thy selfe with teares,
Oft tymes the weeping of the eyes, the inward griefe out weares.
AN. O deere, O sweete, thy mothers pledge, farewel my onely joy,
Farewel the flowre of honor left of beaten howse of Troy.
O Troyans last calamity and feare to Grecians part
Farewel thy mothers onely hope, and vayne comfort of hart.
Oft wisht I thee thy fathers strength and halfe thy graundsires yeares
But all for naught the Gods have all dispoynted our desires.
Thou never shalt in regal court thy sceptors take in hand,
Nor to thy people geve decrees nor leade with law thy land.
Nor yet thine enmies overcome by might of handy stroke,
Nor sende the conquerde nations all under thy servile yoke.
Thou never shalt beat downe in fight, and Greekes with sword pursew.
Nor at thy Charyot Pyrrhus plucke, as Achill Hector drew
And never shal these tender handes thy weapons weild and wrest,
Thou never shalt in woods pursue the wyld and mighty beast.
Nor as accustom'd is by guyse and sacrifice in Troy,
With measure swift : betweene the aulters shalt thou daunce with joy.
O grievous kind of cruel death that doth remayne for thee,
More woeful thinges then Hectors death the walles of Troy shall see.
ULISS. Now breake of al thy mothers tears, I may no more tyme spende,
The grievous sorrowes of thy hart wil never make an end.

AN. Ulisses spare as yet my teares and graunt awhyle delay,
To close his eyes yet with my handes er he depart away.
Thou diest but young: yet feard thou art thy Troy doth wayte for thee,
Goe noble hart thou shalt agayne the noble Troyans see.
ASTI. Helpe me mother? AN. Alas my child why tak'st thou holde by me?
In vayne thou calst where helpe none is I can not succour thee.
As when the litle tender beast that heares the Lyon crye,
Straight for defence he seekes his damme, and crouching downe doth lye,
The cruel beast when once removed is the damme away,
In greedy jaw with ravening bit doth snatch the tender pray:
So straight the enmies wil thee take, and from my side thee beare
Receive my kisse and teares pore childe, receive my rented hayre,
Depart thou hence now ful of mee, and to thy father goe,
Salute my Hector in my name and tel him of my woe:
Complayne thy mothers griefe to him if former cares may move
The sprightes: and that in funerall flame thy leese not all their love.
O cruel Hector suffrest thou thy wyfe to be opprest?
With bond of Grecians heavy yoke, and liest thou still at rest?
Achilles rose: take here agayne my teares and rented heare,
And (al that I have left to send) this kisse thy father beare.
Thy coat yet for my comfort leave, the tomb hath touched it
If of his ashes ought here lye Ile seeke it every whit.
UL. There is no measure of thy teares, I may no longer stay,
Deferre no further our returne, breake of our shippes delay.

CHORUS ALTERED BY THE TRANSLATOUR

O Jove that leadst the lampes of fire, and deckst with flaming starres the skye,
Why is it ever thy desire to care their course so orderly?
That nowe the frost the leaves hath worne, and now the spring doth close the tree.
Now fiery Leo rypes the corne, and stil the soyle should chaunged be?

But why art thou that all dost guide, betweene whose hands the poale doth sway,
And at whose wil the Orbs do slyde, careles of mans estate alway?
Regarding not the goodmans case, not caryng how to hurt the yll.
Chaunce beareth rule in every place and turneth mans estate at will.
She geves the wronge the upper hand, the better part she doth oppresse,
She makes the highest low to stand, her Kingdome all is orderlesse.
O parfite profe of her frailty, the princely towres of Troy beat downe,
The flowre of Asia here ye see with turne of hand quight overthrowne.
The ruthful ende of Hectors son, whom to his death the Greekes have led,
His fatall howre is come and gone, and by this tyme the Child is ded:
Yet still (alas) more cares encrease, O Troyans doleful destenie,
Fast doth approach the maydes decease, and now Polixena shall die.

THE FOURTH ACTE

HELENA. ANDROMACHA. HECUBA

HAT ever woeful wedding yet, were cause of funerall,
Of wayling, teares, bloud, slaughter els or other mischiefes all,
A worthy match for Helena, and meete for me it ware,
My wedding torch hath bene the cause of al The Troyans care.
I am constraynd to hurt them yet, after their overthrow,
The false and fayned mariages of Pyrrhus must I showe.
And geve the mayde the Greekes attyre and by my pollecy :
Shal Paris sister be betrayd and by disceypt shal die.
But let her be beguiled thus, the lesse should be her payne
If that unware without the feare of death she might be slayne.
What ceasest thou the wil of Greekes, and messuage to fulfill ?
Of hurt constraynd the fault returnth to th' auter of the ill.
O noble Virgin of the famous house and stocke of Troy,
To thee the Grecians have me sent, I bring thee newes of joy,
The Gods rue on thy afflicted state, more merciful they bee,
A greate and happy maryage loe they have prepard for thee.
Thou never should if Troy had stoode, so nobly wedded be,
Nor Priam never could prefer thee to so hie degree.
Whom flowre of all the Grecians name the prince of honour hie,
That beares the Scepters over all the lande of Thessaly
Doth in the law of wedlocke chose, and for his wyfe require.
To sacred rightes of lawful bed, doth Pyrrhus thee desyre :
Loe Thetis great with al the rest, of Gods that guide by sea.
Each one shall thee accompt as theirs and joy by wedding day

And Peleus shal thee daughter call when thou art Pirrhus wyfe,
And Nereus shall accompt thee his the space of all thy life.
Put of thy mourning garment now, this regall vesture weare,
Forget henceforth thy captive state and seemly broyd thy hayre.
Thy fall hath lift thee higher up, and doth thee more advaunce,
Oft to be taken in the warre doth bring the better chaunce.
AN. This ill the Troyans never knew in all their griefs and payne,
Before this tyme ye never made us to rejoyce in vayne.
Troy towres geve light, O seemely tyme for mariage to be made,
Who would refuse the wedding day that Helayne doth perswade ?
The plague and ruine of each parte behold dost thou not see,
These tombes of noble men, and how their bones here scattered bee ?
Thy brydebed hath bene cause of this, for thee all these be ded,
For thee the bloud of Asia both and Europe hath bene shed.
When thou in joy and pleasure both the fighting folke from farre,
Hast viewde : in doubt to whom to wish the glory of the warre.
Goe to, prepare the mariages, what neede the Torches light ?
Behold the Towres of Troy do shine with brands that blase ful bright.
O Troyans all set to your handes, this wedlocke celebrate :
Lament this day with woeful cry and teares in seemly rate.
HEL. Though care do cause the want of wit, and reasons rule denye,
And heavy hap doth ofttymes hate his mates in misery,
Yet I before most hateful judge dare wel defend my part,
That I of all your grevous cares sustayne the greatest smart.
Andromacha for Hector weepes, for Priam Hecuba,
For onely Paris privily bewayleth Helena.
A hard and grievous thing it is captivity to beare,
In Troy that yoke I suffred long a prisoner whole ten yeare.
Turnd are the fates, Troy beaten downe, to Greece I must repeare,
The native countrey to have lost is ill, but worse to feare.
For dread therof you neede not care your evilles all be past,
On me both partes wil vengeance take al lightes to me at last.
Whom each man prisoner takes God wot shee standes in slipper stay,
And me not captive made by lot yet Paris led away,
I have bene cause of all these wars, and then your woes were wrought,
When first your shippes the Spartayn Seas and land of Grecia sought.

But if the Goddesse wild it so that I their pray should be,
And for reward to her beautyes judge shee had appoynted me,
Then pardon Paris : thinke this thing in wrathful judge doth lie,
The sentence Menelaus geves, and he this case shall trye.
Now turne thy playntes Andromacha, and weepe for Polyxeyne
Mine eyes for sorrowes of my hart theyr teares may not refrayne.
AN. Alas, what care makes Heleyn weepe ? what griefe doth she lament ?
Declare what craftes Ulisses castes, what mischiefe hath he sent ?
Shall shee from height of Idey hil be hedlong tombled downe ?
Or else out of the turrets toppe in Troy shal she be throwne ?
Or wil they cast her from the clieves into Sygeon seas ?
In bottom of the surging waves to end her ruthful days ?
Show what thy countnaunce hides and tell the secrets of thy breast :
Some woes in Pyrhus wedding are farre worse then all the rest.
Go to, geve sentence on the mayd, pronounce her desteny :
Delude no longer our mishappes, we are prepard to die.
HEL. Would God the'xpounder of the Gods would geve his dome so right
That I also on poynt of sword might leese the lothsome light,
Or at Achilles tombe with stroake of Pyrrhus hand be slayne :
And beare a part of al thy fates O wretched Polixeyne
Whom yet Achilles woeth to wed, and where his ashes lie,
Requireth that thy bloud be shed, and at his tombe to die.
AN. Behold loe how her noble mynd of Death doth gladly heare,
She deckes her selfe : her regal weede in seemely wyse to weare,
And to her head she settes her hand the broyded hayre to lay,
To wed she thought it Death, to die she thinkes a wedding day.
But helpe (alas) my mother sounds to heare her daughters death,
Aryse plucke up your heart and take agayne the panting breath.
Alacke good mother how slender stay, that doth thy life sustayne ?
A little thinge shall happy thee thou art almost past payne.
Her breath returnes : she doth revyve, her lims their life do take.
So see when wretches fayne would die, how death doth them forsake.
HEC. Doth yet Achilles live (alas) to work the Troyans spight ?
Doth he rebell agaynst us yet ? O hand of Paris light.
The very tombe and ashes loe, yet thirsteth for our bloud,
A happy heape of children late on every syde mee stoode.

It wearied me to deale the mothers kisse among them al,
The rest are lost, and this alone now doth me mother call.
Thou onely child of Hecuba, a comfort left to me,
A stayer of my sory state and shall I now leese thee ?
Depart O wretched soule, and from this carefull carcas flie,
And ease me of such ruthfull fates, to see my daughter die.
My weepyng wets (alas) my eyes, and staines them over al,
And downe my cheekes the sodeine streames and showres of teares do fal.
But thou deare daughter maist be glad, Cassandra would rejoyse,
Or Hectors wife thus wed to be if they might have their choyse.
AND. We are the wretches Hecuba in cursed case we stande,
Whom straight the shippe shal tosse by seas into a forraine land.
But as for Heleyns grieves be gone and turned to the best,
She shal againe her natyve countrey se and live at rest.
HELE. Ye would the more envy my state if ye might know your owne.
ANDR. And grouth there yet more griefe to me that erst I have not known ?
HELE. Such masters must ye serve as doth by chaunce of lots befal.
ANDR. Whose servaunt am I then become, whom shall I maister call ?
HELE. By lot ye fall to Pyrhus hands, you are his prisoner.
ANDR. Cassandra is happy, fury saves perhaps and Phœbus her.
HELE. Chiefe kinge of Greekes Cassandra keepes and his captive is shee.
HEC. Is any one amonge them all that prysoner would have me ?
HELE. You chaunsed to Ulysses are his pray ye are become.
HEC. Alas what cruell, dyre and yrefull dealer of the dome.
What god unjust doth so devide the captives to their lordes ?
What grievous arbiter is he ? that to such choyce accordes,
What cruel hand to wretched folke, so evil fates hath caste ?
Who hath amonge Achilles armour, Hectors mothers plaste ?
Now am I captive, and beset with all calamitie.
My bondage grieves me not, but him to serve it shameth mee.
He that Achilles spoyles hath won, shall Hectors also have :
Shall barraine lande enclosde with seas receive my boanes in grave ?
Leade me Ulysses where thou wylt, leade me I make no stay,
My master I, and me my fates, shall follow every way.

Let never calme come to the seas, but let them rage with winde,
Come fire and sword, mine owne mischaunce and Priams let me finde.
In meane time haps this deepe distres my cares can know no calme :
I ran the race with Priamus, but he hath won the Palme,
But Pyrrhus comes with swiftned pace and thretning browes doth wrest.
What stayste thou Pyrrhus ? strike thy sword now through this woful brest.
And both at ones the parents of thy fathers wife now slay,
Murderer of age, likes thee her bloud ? he draw my daughter away
Defile the gods and staine the sprights, of hel with slaughtred bloud,
To aske your mercy what avayles ? our prayers do no good.
The vengeance aske I on your ships, that it the gods may pleas,
According to this sacrifice, to guide you on the seas.
This wishe I to your thousand sayles, Gods wrath light on them all,
Even to the ship that beareth me, what ever may befall.

CHORUS

A Comfort is to mans calamity
A dolefull flocke of felowes in distres.
And sweete to him that mournes in miserie
To here them wayle whom sorowes like oppres
In deepest care his griefe him bites the les,
That his estate bewayles not all alone,
But seeth with him the teares of many one.

For still it is the chiefe delight in woe,
And joy of them that sonke in sorrowes are,
To see like fates by fall to many moe,
That may take part of all their wofull fare,
And not alone to be opprest with care.
There is no wight of woe that doth complayne,
When all the rest do like mischaunce sustayne.

In all this world if happy man were none,
None (though he were) would thinke himselfe awretch,
Let once the ritch with heapes of Gold be gone,
Whose hundred head his pastours overretch,
Then would the poore mans hart begin to stretch.
There is no wretch whose life him doth displease,
But in respect of those that live at ease.

Sweete is to him that standes in deepe distresse,
To see no man in joyful plight to bee,
Whose onely vessel wind and wave oppresse,
Ful sore his chaunce bewayles and weepeth hee,
That with his owne none others wracke doth see
When he alone makes shipwracke one the sand,
And naked falles to long desyred land.

A thousande sayle who seeth to drench in Seas,
With better will the storme hath overpast
His heavy hap doth him the lesse displease
When broaken boardes abroade be many cast,
And shipwrackt shippes to shore they flit ful fast,
With doubled waves when stopped is the floud,
With heaps of them that there have lost theyr good.

Ful sore did Pirrhus Helens losse complayne,
What time the leader of his flocke of shepe,
Uppon his backe alone he bare them twayne,
And wet his Golden lockes amid the deepe,
In piteous playnt (alas) he gan to weepe.
The death of her it did him deepe displease,
That shipwracke made amid the drenching seas.

And piteous was the playnt and heavy moode
Of woful Pyrrha and eke Deucalion
That nought beheld aboute them but the floud,
When they of all mankynd were left alone
Amid the seas ful sore they made their mone
To see themselves thus left alive in woe
When neyther land they saw, nor fellowes moe.

Anone these playnts and Troyans teares shall quaile,
And here and there the ship them tosse by seas :
When trompets sound shal warne to hoyse up sayle,
And through the waves with wind to seeke their waies
Then shall these captives goe to ende their dayes
In land unknowne : when once with hasty ore
The drenching deepe they take and shunne the shore.

What state of mynd shal then in wretches bee ?
When shore shall sinke from sight and seas aryse ?
When Idey hill to lurke aloofe they see ?
Then poynt with hand from farre wher Troia lies,
Shall child and mother : talking in this wyse :
Loe yonder Troy, where smoke it fumeth hie,
By this the Troyans shal their countrey spie.

TROAS

THE FIFTH ACTE

NUNCIUS. ANDROMACHA. HECUBA

DYRE, fierce, wretched, horrible, O cruell fates accurste,
Of Mars his ten yeares bloudshed blows the wofulst and the worst.
Alas which should I first bewayle? thy cares Andromacha?
Or els lament the wretched age of woful Hecuba?

HEC. What ever mans calamityes ye wayle for myne it is.
I beare the smart of al their woes, each other feeles but his
Who ever he, I am the wretch all happes to me at last.

NUN. Slayne is the mayd, and from the walles of Troy the child is cast.
But both (as them became) they toke their death with stomacke stout.

AND. Declare the double slaughters then, and tell the whole throughout.

NUN. One towre of all the rest ye know doth yet in Troy remayne,
Where Pryam wonted was to sit, and view the armies twayne.
His litle Nephew eke with him to lead, and from a farre,
His fathers fightes with fire and sword, to show on feats of war.
This towre, sometyme wel knowne by fame, and Troyans honor most,
Is now with captaynes of the Greekes, beset on every coast.
With swift recourse and from the shippes, in clustred heaps anone,
Both tagge and ragge they runne to gase what thing should ther be done.
Some clime the hilles to seeke a place where they might see it best,
Some one the rockes a tiptoe stande to overloke the rest.

Some on their temples weare the pine, some beech, some crownes of bay,
For garlandes torne is every tree, that standeth in theyr way:
Some from the highest mountaynes top aloofe beholdeth all,
Some scale the buildinges halfe burnt, and some the ruinous wall.
Yea some there were (O mischief loe) that for the more despyghts,
The tombe of Hector sits uppon beholders of the sight.
With princely pace Ulisses then past through the preased band
Of Greekes, King Priams litle nephew leading by the hand.
The Child with unrepyning gate past through his enmies handes,
Up toward the walles, and as anone in turrets top he standes,
From thence adowne his lofty lookes he cast on every part,
The neerer death more free from care he seemd and feare of hart.
Amid his foes his stomacke swelles, and fierce he was to sight,
Like Tygers whelpe, that the rats in vayne with tothles chap to bight.
Alas, for pitty then each one, rew on his tender yeares,
And al the route that present were, for him they shed their teares.
Yea not Ulisses them restraynd, but trickling downe they fal,
And onely he, wept not (poore foole) whom they bewayled al.
But whyle on Gods Ulisses cald, and Calchas wordes expound,
In midst of Pryams land (alas) the child leapt downe to ground.
AND. What cruel Calchas could or scith such slaughter take in hand?
Or by the shore of Caspyan Sea, what barbarous lawles land.
Busyridis to th'aulters yet no infantes bloud hath shed,
Nor never yet were children slayne for feast of Diomed.
Who shal alas in tombe thee lay, or hyde thy limmes agayne?
NU. What limmes from such a headlong fall could in a child remayne?
His bodies payse throwne downe to ground, hath batred al his bones.
His face, his noble fathers markes are spoyld agaynst the stones.
His necke unjoynted is, his head so dasht with flint stoane stroake
That scattered is the brayne about, the scul is al to broake.
Thus lieth he now dismembred corpes, deformd and all to rent.
AND. Loe herein doth he yet likewyse, his father represent.
NUN. What time the Child hath headlong falne thus from the walls of Troy,
And al the Greekes themselves bewaild the slaughter of the Boy,

Yet strayght returne they backe, and at Achilles tombe agayne
The second mischiefe goe to worke, the death of Polixeine.
This tombe the waves of surging seas, beset the utter side,
The other part the fields encloase aboute, and pastors wyde.
In vale envyroned with hils, that round aboute do ryse,
A sloape on height erected are the bankes in Theatre wyse.
By al the shore then swarme the Greekes, and thicke on heaps they
prease
Some hope that by her death they shall theyr shippes delay release.
Some other joy their enmies stocke thus beaten downe to bee :
A greate part of the people, both the slaughter hate, and see.
The Troyans eke no lesse frequent their owne calamityes
And all affrayd, beheld the last of all their miseryes.
When first proceeded torches bright as guise of wedlocke is.
And author therof led the way the Lady Pindaris.
Such wedlocke pray the Troyans then, God send Hermiona
And would God to her husband so, restoard were Helena.
Feare masd each part, but Polixeine her bashful looke downe cast :
And more then earst her glittering eyes and beauty shyn'd at last.
As sweetest seems then Phœbus light, when downe his beams do
sway,
When starres agayne with night at hand opprest the doubtful day.
Astonnied much the people were, and all they her commende,
And now much more then ever earst, they prays'd her at her end.
Some with her beauty moved were, some with her tender yeares :
Some to behold the turnes of chaunce, and how each thing thus
wears.
But most them moves her valiant minde, and lofty stomacke hie,
So strong, so stout, so ready of hart and wel prepard to dye.
Thus passe they forth and bold before King Pirrhus goeth the mayde,
They pitty her, they marvel her, their hartes were all affrayde.
As sone as then the hard hil top (where die she should) they trode,
And hie uppon his fathers tombe the youthful Pyrrhus stoode.
The manly mayd she never shronke one foote, nor backward drew,
But boldely turnes to meete the stroke, with stoute unchanged hew,
Her corage moves eche one, and loe a strange thing monstrous like,
That Pyrhus even himselfe stoode stil for dread, and durst not
strike.

But as he had, his glittring sword in her to hilts up doon,
The purple bloud, at mortall wound, then gushing out it spoon.
Ne yet her corage her forsooke, when dieng in that stounde,
She fell as the'rth should her revenge with ireful rage to ground.
Each people wept, the Troyans first with privy fearful crye,
The Grecians eake, each one bewayld her death apparantly.
This order had the sacrifyce, her bloud the tombe up dronke,
No drop remaynth above the ground, but downe forthwith it sonke.
HEC. Now go, now goe ye Greekes, and now repayre ye safely home.
With careles shippes and hoised sailes now cut the salt sea fome.
The Child and Virgin both be slaine, your battels finisht are.
Alas where shal I end my age ? or whether beare my care ?
Shal I my daughter, or my nephew, or my husband mone ?
My countrey els, or all at once ? or else my selfe alone ?
My wish is death that children both and virgins fiercely takes
Where ever cruel death doth hast to strike, it me forsakes,
Amid the enmies weapons all, amid both sword and fyre,
All night sought for, thou fleest from me, that do thee most desyre.
Not flame of fyre, not fall of towre, not cruel enmies hand
Hath rid my life, how neere (alas) could death to Priam stand ?
NUN. Now captives all with swift recourse repayre ye to the saies,
Now spread the ships their sayls abroad, and forth they seeke theyr
waies.

FINIS

THE SEVENTH TRAGEDYE OF L. ANNAEUS SENECA

ENTITULED MEDEA

TRANSLATED OUT OF LATIN INTO ENGLISHE

BY JOHN STUDLEY

THE ARGUMENT TO THE TRAGEDY,

BY THE TRANSLATOR

CARE sore did grype Medeas heart to see
Her Jason, whom shee tendred as her lyfe,
And rescued had from plunge of perills free,
Renouncing her, to take another wyfe.
Love spent in vayne breedes hate and malice rife,
Enkindling coales whose heate and greedy flame
(Save streames of bloud,) nought els can quench the same.

Medea mad in troubled mynde doth muse,
On vengeaunce fell, to quit her grievous wrong.
Rough plagues at length entendeth shee to use :
Yll venemous thinges shee charmes with charming song,
Seekes out a Bane made of their poyson strong,
In Trayterous gifts a Robe, and chayne of Golde,
Nycely shee doth the hidden poyson folde.

Sent are the Gyfts to Creuse and her Syre,
They taking them that brought their dole to passe,
Unware are burnt by meanes of charmed fyre.
Due vengeaunce yet for Jason greater was,
Lyfe first on chylde by Mothers hande (alas)
Expired hath, which though it him aggryse,
Yet his other chylde shee slayes before his eyes.

THE SPEAKERS NAMES

MEDEA.
CHORUS.
NUTRIX.
CREON.
JASON.
NUNTIUS.

MEDEA

THE FIRST ACTE

MEDEA

GODS whose grace doth guide their ghostes that joy in wedlocke pure,
O Juno thou Lucina hight, on whom the chary cure
Alotted is of those that grone in paynfull chyld-bed bandes,
O Pallas by whose heavenly arte, Sir Typhis cunning handes
Have learnde to bridle with his helme his newly framed boate,
Wherewith the force of fighting fluds hee breaking rides a floate.
O God whose forked Mace doth stormes in rigour rough appeas,
And cause the ruffling surges couch amid the rampinge Seas :
O Titan who upon the swift and werling Hemisphær
Devides the chearefull day and night by egall turnes t'appere,
O threefolde shapen Hecate that sendest forth thy light,
Unto thy silent Sacrifice that offered is by night,
By whom my Jason sware to mee O heavenly powers all,
And yee on whom Medea may with safer conscience call,
O Dungeon darke, most dreadfull den of everlasting night,
O dampned Ghosts : O kingdome set against the Gods aright :
O Lord of sad and lowring lakes, O Lady dyre of Hell,
(Whom though that Pluto stale by force yet did his troth excell
The ficle fayth of Jasons love, that hee to mee doth beare,)
With cursed throate I conjure you, O grisly Ghostes appeare.
Come out, come out, yee hellish hagges, revenge this deede so dyre,
Bring in your scratting pawes a burning brand of deadly fyre.
Rise up yee hiddeous divelish Feendes, as dreadfull as yee weare,
When unto me in wedlocke state yee did sometime appeare.
Worke yee, worke yee, the dolefull death of this new wedded Wyfe,
And martir yee this Father in lawe : depryve of breath and lyfe

King Creons ruthfull family : in plunge of passing payne
Torment yee mee, that on my spouse doe wishe this woe to raygne :
Preserve my Jasons life, but yet let him be bayted out
A myching, raging, runnagate, in forren townes about.
To passe from dore to dore, with care to begge his needy bread,
Not knowing in what harbring place to couch his curssed head :
A banisht wretch, disdaynde of all, and still in feare of lyfe,
Then let him wish ten thousand times for me agayne his Wyfe :
This famous gest whom every man will entertayne and have,
Let him be driven at straungers gates the table crummes to crave.
And that my bytter bannings may with mischiefe most abounde,
God graunt in gulph of like distresse his chyldren may be drounde,
To synke in sorrowes stormes, that doe their mother overflowe :
Now, now, I have, I have the full reveng of all my woe,
I have dispatcht : my pyteous playnt and wordes in vayne I lose :
What shall not I with vyolence get up agaynst my foes ?
And wring out of theyr wrested hands the wedding torch so bryght ?
Shall I not force the firmament to lose his shrinking lyght ?
What doth my Graundsirs Phœbus face this heavy hap beholde ?
And standing gasyng at this geare yet westwarde is he rolde,
On glystring chariot hoysted hyghe, and keepes his beaten Race,
Amid the christall colourde skye, why turnes hee not his Face,
Retyring fast into the East backe up the day to twyne ?
O Father Phœbe to me, to me, thy Chariot reynes resigne,
That I advaunced up, about the marble skyes may ryde,
Bequeath thy brydle unto mee, and give me grace to guide
Thy yoked prauncing teame, with yerking lasshe of burning whip,
That with thy fervent fyry beames on purple poale doe skip.
Let Corynth countrey burnt to dust by force of flame and fyre
Gyve place, that both the tumbled seas may joyne : whom to retyre
It doth compell, and dassheth of from banke on eyther syde,
Least meete in one their chanels might, whose streames hee doth devide
No way to worke theyr deadly woe I have but this at hande,
That to the wedding I should beare a ruthfull brydall brande,
Anoying Creons carelesse Court : when finished I have
Such solemne service, as that ryght of sacrafice doth crave.

Then at the Aulters of the Gods my chyldren shalbe slayne,
With crimsen colourde bloud of Babes their Aulters will I stayne,
Through Lyvers, Lungs, the Lights and Heart, through every gut and gal
For vengeaunce breake away perforce, and spare no bloude at all :
If any lusty lyfe as yet within thy soule doe rest,
If ought of auncient corage still doe dwell within my brest,
Exile all foolysh Female feare, and pity from thy mynde,
And as th' untamed Tygers use to rage and rave unkynde,
That haunt the croking combrous Caves, and clumpred frosen clives,
And craggy Rockes of Caucasus, whose bitter colde depryves
The soyle of all Inhabitours, permit to lodge and rest,
Such salvage brutish tyranny within thy brasen brest.
What ever hurly burly wrought doth Phasis understand,
What mighty monstrous bloudy feate I wrought by Sea or Land,
The like in Corynth shalbe seene in most outragious guise,
Most hyddious, hatefull, horrible, to heare, or see wyth eyes,
Most divelish, desperate, dreadfull deede, yet never knowne before,
Whose rage shall force heaven, earth, and hell to quake and tremble sore.
My burning breast that rowles in wrath, and doth in rancour boyle,
Sore thrysteth after bloud, and wounds with slaughter, death, and spoyle,
By renting racked lyms from lyms to drive them downe to grave :
Tush, these be but as Fleabytings, that mentioned I have :
As weyghty things as these I did in greener girlishe age,
Now sorrowes smart doth rub the gall and frets with sharper rage,
But sith my wombe hath yeelded fruict, it doth mee well behove,
The strength and parlous puissaunce of weightier illes to prove.
Be ready wrath, with all thy might that fury kindle may,
Thy foes to their destruction bee ready to assay :
Of thy devorsement let the Pryce to match, and counterpayse
The proude and precious pryncely pomp of these new wedding dayes.
How wilt thou from thy spouse depart ? as him thou followed hast
In bloud to bath thy bloudy handes and traytrous lyves to wast.
Breake of in time these long delayes, abanden now agayne,
This lewd alliaunce, got by guilt, with greater guilt refrayne.

CHORUS ALTERED BY THE TRANSLATOUR

Who hath not wist that windy words be vayne,
And that in talke of trust is not the grounde,
Heere in a mirrour may hee see it playne,
Medea so by proofe the same hath founde.
Who being blind by blinded Venus Boy,
Her bleared Eyes could not beholde her blisse :
Nor spy the present poyson of her Joy,
While in the grasse the Serpent lurked is,
The shaft that flew from Cupids golden bowe,
With feathers so hath dimd her daseld Eyes,
That cannot see to shun the way of woe :
The ranckling head in dented heart that lyes,
So dulles the same, that can not understand
The cause that brought false Jason out of Greece,
To come unto her fathers fertile Land,
Is not her love, but love of golden Fleece.
Yet was his speache so pleasaunt and so milde,
His tongue so filde, his promises so fayre,
Sweete was the fowlers Song that hath beguilde
The seely byrd, brought to the limed snare.
Faith in his Face, trust shined in his Eyes,
The blushing brow playne meaning seemde to showe,
In double hearte blacke treason hydden lies,
Dissembling thoughts that weave the webbe of woe.
The honyed Lyppes, the tongue in suger dept
Doe sweete the poyson rancke within the breast,
In subtle shew of paynted sheath is kept,
The rusty knife of treason deemed least :
Lyfe seemes the bayte to sight that lyeth brim,
Death is the hooke that underlies the same,
The Candell blase delights with burning trim
The Fly, till shee bee burned in the flame.
Who in such showes least deemed any ills.
The hungry fyshe feares not the bayte to Brooke,
Till up the lyne doe pluck him by the gylls,
And fast in throate hee feeles the deadly hooke.
Woe Jason, woe to thee most wretched man,
Or rather wretch Medea woe to thee,

Woe to the one that thus dissemble can,
Woe to the other that trayned so might bee.
Thoughtst thou Medea his eyes to bee the glasse,
Wherein thou might the Face of thoughts beholde?
That in his breast with wordes so covered was,
As cancred brasse with glosse of yealow golde?
Did thou suppose that nature (more then kinde)
Had placde his heart his lying lyppes betweene,
His lookes to be the mirrour of his minde?
Fayth in fayre Face hath sildome yet ben seene.
Who listneth to the flatering Maremaides note
Must needes commit his tyred eyes to sleepe,
Yeelding to her the taking of his boate,
That meanes unware to drowne him in the deepe.
What booteth thee Medea to betray
The golden Fleece to fawning Jasons hande,
From Dragons teeth him safely to convay,
And fyry Bulles the warders of the lande?
Why for his sake from father hast thou fled,
And thrust thy selfe out from thy native soyle?
Thy brothers bloud what ayled thee to shed,
With Jason thus to travell and to toyle?
Beholde the meede of this thy good desarte,
The recompence that hee to thee doth gyve.
For pleasure, payne, for joy, most eger smarte,
With clogging cares in banishment to live.
Thou, and thy Babes, are like to begge and starve
In Nation straunge, (O myserable lyfe)
Whyle Jason from his promyses doe swarve,
And takes delight in his new wedded Wyfe.
O Ground ungrate, that when the husband man
Hath tilled it, to recompence his toyle
No Corne, but Weedes, and Thystles render can,
To stinge his handes, that Fruict seekes of his Soyle.
Such venome growes of pleasaunt coloured flower:
Loe, Prynces loe, what deadly poyson sup
Of Bane, erst sweete, now turned into sower,
Medea dranke out of a goulden Cup.

THE SECOND ACTE

MEDEA. NUTRIX

YE mee, (alas) I am undone, For at the Brydall cheare,
The warble note of wedding songs resounded in mine eare.
Yet for all this scant I my selfe, yet scant beleve I can,
That Jason would play such a prancke, as most unthanckfull man,
Both of my Countrey, and my Syre, and kingdome me to spoyle,
And yet forsake mee wretch forlorne, to stray in forrein soyle.
O hath he such a stony heart, that doth no more esteeme,
The great good turnes, and benefits that I imployde on him ?
Who knowes, that I have lewdly used enchauntments for his sake,
The rigour rough, and stormy rage, of swelling Seas to slake.
The grunting firy foming Bulles, whose smoking guts were stuft
With smoltring fumes, that from theyr Jawes, and nosthrils out they puft.
I stopt their gnashing mounching mouths, I quencht their burning breath,
And vapors hot of stewing paunch, that els had wrought his death,
Or feedes hee thus his fansy fond, to thinke my skill of charme
Abated is, and that I have no power to doe him harme ?
Bestract of wits, with wavering minde perplext on every part,
I tossed, and turmoyled am, wyth wayward crasy hart.
Now this, now that, and neyhter now, but now another way,
By divers meanes I toyle, that so my wrong reveng I may.
I would the wretch a brother had : but what ? he hath a Wyfe.
Goe cut her throate, with gastly wounds bereve her of her lyfe.
On her ile worke my deadly spight : her, her alone I crave,
To quit such bitter sowsing stormes, as I sustayned have.

If any graund notorious guilt in all Pelasga Land
Be put in practise, yet unknowne unto thy harming hand,
Thereof to get experience the time doth now begin :
Thy former feates doe byd thee take good hope to thryve herein :
Let all thy guilts with thronging thick assemble thee to ayde,
The golden Fleece (the chiefe Novell) of Colchis Ile betrayde.
My tender Brother eke, that with my Syer did mee pursue,
Whom with his secret partes cut of, I wicked Virgin slewe,
Whose shreaded and dismembred corps, with sword in gobbits hewd,
(A wofull Coarse to th' Fathers heart) on Pontus ground I strewd.
How hory headded Pelias his wythred age to shyft
To greener yeares, for longer lyfe : his daughters by my dryft
His members all and mangled flesh with licour scalding hot
Ysodden, and perboyled have, in seething brasen pot.
How oft in haynous bloud have these my cruell handes bene dyed ?
And never any guilt as yet by wrath inflamde I tryed.
But now the parlous poysning wound of Cupids percing dart,
Doth boyle and rage within my breast, it ranckles at my hart.
But how could Jason it redresse, whom fortunes froward wyll
Hath yeelde unto anothers hande, at lust to save or spill ?
O rage of rusty cancred minde, this sclaundrous talke amende,
If Fortunes grace will graunt it thus, let him unto his ende
Lyve still my Jason as he was : but if not Jason myne,
Yet caytife suffer Jason live, though Jason none of thyne :
Who being mindefull still of us some favour let him showe,
For these good turnes that our good will could earst on him bestowe :
King Creon is in all the fault, and onely worthy blame,
Who puffed up with Scepter proude, unable for to frame
His fickle minde to modesty, made breach twixt us agayne,
Whom Hymens bands, and link of love had made but one of twayne,
By whom eke from her tender brats the mother (wretch) is drawne,
Hee breakes the vowe, that gaged is with such a precious pawne.
Seeke after such a villaynes bloud, in daunting pangs of smart,
Let him alone bee surely dowst, such is his due desart,
A dungell hept of Cinders burnt his Pallayce make I shall,
That Malea where in winding strights, the lingring ships doe crall,
Shall gase on smolthring turrets tops turmoylde in crackling flame.
Nu. For godsake (Madame) I you pray your tongue to silence frame.

Eke hyde your privy languishing and greefe in secret vayne :
Who with a modest minde abides the Spurs of pricking payne,
And suffereth sorrowes paciently, may it repay agayne.
Who beares a privy grudge in breast, and keepes his malyce close,
When least suspection is thereof, may most annoy his Foes.
He leeseth oportunity who vengeaunce doth requyre,
That shewes by open sparkes the flame the heate of kindled fyre.
ME. Small is the grype of griefe that can to reasons lore obay,
And sneking downe with stealing steps can slyly slip away.
But they that throughly sowsed are with showers of greater payne,
Can not digest such corsyes sharpe, but cast it up agayne :
Fayne would I give them trouncing girds. NU. Good daughter deare asswage
Th'unbrydled sway and boyling heate of this thy gyddy rage :
Scant maist thou purchase quietnesse, although thou held thy tongue.
ME. The valiaunt heart dame Fortune yet durst never harme with wrong,
But dreading dastards downe she drives. NU. If any corage dure,
And harbred be in noble breast, now put the same in ure.
ME. The show of sturdy valiant heart, at any time doth shyne.
NU. No hope doth in adversity thy way to scape assygne.
ME. Hee that hath none affiaunce left, nor any hope at all,
Yet let him not mystrust the luck of ought that may befall.
NU. Thy Countrey cleane hath cast thee of, to let thee sinke or swim,
As for thy husband Jason hee, there is no trust in him :
Of all the wealth and worldly mucke wherewith thou didst abounde
No porcion remaynes at all, whereby some helpe is founde.
ME. Medea yet is left, (to much) and here thou mayst espy
The Seas to succour us in flyght, and landes aloofe that ly :
Yea yron tooles, with burning brands we have to worke them woe,
And Gods that with the thunder dint shall overquell our foe :
NU. Who weares the goldencrested crowne him dred with awe yee should.
ME. My Father was a King, yet I betrayed his Fleece of gould.
NU. Can not the deadly vyolence of weapons make thee feare ?
ME. No, though such grisly Lads they were, as whilom did appeare,

That bred of gargell Dragons teeth in holow gaping grounde,
When mutually in bloudy fight eche other did confounde.
NU. Then wilt thou cast thy self to death. ME. Would God that I were dead.
NU. Fly, fly to save thy life. ME. Woe worth the time that once I fled.
NU. What O Medea. ME. Why shall I fly? NU. A mother deere art thou,
Fly therefore for thy childrens sake. ME. Yee see by whom, and how,
A wretched Mother I am made. NU. Thy lyfe by flight to save
Dost thou mistrust? ME. Nay, fly I will, but vengeaunce first ile have.
NU. Then some shall thee at heeles pursue, to wrecke the same agayne.
ME. Perhap ile make his comming short. NU. Be still, and now refrayne
O despret dame thy thundring threates, and slake your raging ire.
Apply, and frame thy froward will as time and tides requyre.
ME. Full well may fortunes welting wheele to begging bring my state,
As for my worthy corage, that shee never shall abate.
Who bowncing at the Gates, doth cause the creaking dores to Jar?
It is the wretch (Creon his selfe,) whom princely power far
Hath lift aloft, with lordly looke, puft up with pouncing pryde,
That hee may Corinth countrey, with the sway of Scepter guide.

CREON. MEDEA

MEDEA that ungracious Imp, King Ætas wicked chylde,
Yet hath not from our careful realme her lingring foote exilde.
Som naughty drift she goes about, her knacks of old we kno,
Her jugling arts, her harming hands are known wel long ago.
From whom will shee withhold her harme? whom will this cruel beast
Permit to live, from perrill free, in quietnesse and rest?
Cleane to cut of this parlous plague it was our purpose bent,
But Jason by entreting hard, did cause us to relent.

At his request we graunted have, her life she shall enjoy,
Let her acquit our countrey free from feare of all annoy :
Yea saufely let her pack her hence, in eger giddy fit,
With lumpish lowring looke shee comes in talke with me to knit :
Sirs keepe her of and set her hence, least us she touch perhap,
And drive her backe from comming nigh, commaunde her keepe her clap.
And let her learne at length, how that her selfe submit she may,
The puissaunt payse and majesty of Princes to obay.
Run, hie thee quickly, trudge apace, have hence out of my sight
This horrible, most odious quean, this monstrous wicked wight.
ME. My soveraygne liege, what greater crime have I or lesse offence
Commit against thy majesty, to be exiled hence ?
CR. Alas, the guiltlesse woman doth demaunde a reason why :
ME. If thou be Judge indifferent, ordaynde my cause to try,
Consider then my doubtfull case, and wey the ground of it :
If thou be king, commaund a Judge for such a matter fit.
CR. The princes powre thou shalt obey, b' it eyther right or wrong.
ME. The prosperous pryde of wronging crownes cannot endeuer long.
CR. Avaunt, and yell out thy complaynts at Colchis, get thee hence.
ME. Full gladly will I get mee home, if he that brought me thence,
Vouchsafe to beare me backe agayne. CR. Alas, to late aryse
Entreating wordes, when as decree is taken otherwise.
ME. He that not hearing eyther part, pronounceth his decree,
Unrighteous man accoumpted is, though ryght his sentence bee.
CR. Whyle Pelias trusted to thy talke, from lyfe to death hee fell.
Go to, begyn, we gyve you leave your goodly tale to tell.
ME. That type of Regall majesty, that erst by Fortunes hand,
Advaunced to I dyd attayne, hath taught mee understand,
How hard a thing it is of wrath the rygour to asswage,
When burning heate of boyling breast in flames begins to rage.
Eke for th' advauncement of their power more to display in sight
Theyr kingly corage bolstred out with majesty of might.
They deeme it doth import asway, and hath a greater grace,
Whome stately scepter causde to climbe aloft to prouder place.
To persever with fansye fonde, in that to reasons spyght,
Whose greedy choyce attaynted fyrst his minde with vayne delight.

For though in piteous plyght I lye, throwne downe to great decay,
With beauty hap, and ruthfull chaunce, to myserable stay,
Thus hunted out from place to place, forsoke and left alone,
A wyddow while my husband live, with cause to wayle and mone,
Perplext in maze of misery, wyth cloying cares so ryfe,
Yet whylom I in golden trone have led in happy lyfe.
By high and noble parentage my bryght renowne doth shyne.
From Phœbus eake my Graundsire great deryved is my ligne.
Whear sylver streamed Phasis flood his wasshing waves doth shed,
Or with contrary croking wayes his bathing channell spred,
What ever wandring coast stretcht out is left aloofe behynde,
From whence the roaming Scithyan Sea his channell forth doth fynde,
Where as Mæotis fenny plashe with pure fresh water sprynges,
Doth season sweete the briny Sea, that tyde in thyther brynges.
Eke all the coastes envyroned and kept within the bankes
Of Thermodon, where warlike troupes, and armed wyddowes ranckes,
With paynted bucklers on their armes holde all the land in feare,
With rigour rough of threatning sword, with force of denting speare.
So farre to all these wandring coastes and countreyes round about,
My Fathers ample regiment at large is stretched out.
I being thus of noble Race, and in an happy plight,
With glorious glosse of pryncely pomp in honour shining bright,
Then pearelesse Peares my Spousall bed did seeke and sue to have,
But those to be theyr loving Feeres, now other Ladyes crave :
Rashe, ficle, pevish, undiscreete, and wavering Fortunes wheele,
Hath cast me out, the crusshing cares of banishment to feele.
In Scepter proude and hauty Crowne fix thine affyaunce fast.
Sith upsidowne with welkin wheele, whole mounts of wealth is cast.
This Prynces doe possesse, that should theyr royalty display,
Whose fame shall never razed be, with storme of lowring day,
To succour those whom misery in pit of paynes doth souse,
To shield and harber suppliaunts in roofe of loyall house.
This onely brought I from my Realme, the precious golden Fleece,
That Jewell chiefe, and eke the flower of Chyvalry in Greece,
The sturdy prop, the Rampter strong the bulwarke of your wealth,
And Hercules the boystrous Imp of Jove I kept in health.

It was by meanes of my good will that Orpheus did escape,
Whose harmony the livelesse Rocks with such delight did rape,
That forced even the clottred lumpes with hobling prickt to praunce,
And eke the jocond nodding woods with footing fine to daunce.
And that those heavenly twins Castor, and Pollux did not dy,
My dew desart is doubled twise, sith them preserved I.
Of Boreas blustring out with puffed Cheekes, his blasing Breath,
His wynged Sons I kept alive both Calais, and Zeath.
And Linceus that with pearcing beames, and sharper sight of Eye,
Could Navies on the farther banke of Sicill shore espy.
And all the Mynians that did come the golden Fleece to win.
As for the Prince of Princes all, I will not bring him in.
With silence Jason will I passe, for whom though him I save,
Yet is not Greece in debt to mee, no recompence I crave.
To no man him I doe impute, the rest I brought agayne
For your avayle, that you thereby some profit might attayne.
But onely on my Jason deare, him for my owne loves sake
I kept in store, that hee of mee his wedded Wyfe should make.
None other fault (God wot) yee have to charge mee with but this
That Argo Ship by meanes of mee returned saufely is.
If I a shamefast mayde had not with Cupids bayte bene caught,
If more my Fathers health to have then Jasons I had sought,
Pelasga land had bene undone, and falne to great decay,
The lusty valiaunt Capitaynes, had cleane bene cast away :
And joly Jason fyrst of all this now thy sonne in lawe,
The Buls had rent his swalowed lims in fiery chomping jawe.
Let Fortune fight agaynst my case as list her elvish will,
Yet never shall it grieve my heart, repent my deede I nill,
That I should for so many kings their reling honour save,
The guerden due that I for this my crime commit must have,
It lyeth Creon in thy hande, if thus it lyketh thee,
Condemne my guilty ghost to death, but render fyrst to mee
My fault that forced me offend, then Creon graunt I this,
Receaving Jason (cause of cryme) I guilty did amisse.
Thou knowst that I was such an one when couring low I lay,
Before thy feete in humble wise and did entreating pray,
Thy gracious goodnes mee to graunt some succour at thy hande.
For me a wreatch and wreatched Babes I aske within this lande

Some cotage base, in outcast hole, some couching corner vile,
If from the towne thou drive us out to wander in exile,
Then some by place aloofe within this realme let us obtayne.
Cr. How I am none that tyrant like with churlish Scepter raygne,
Nor proudly or disdaynfully, with hawty corage hie,
With vaunting foote doe stamp them downe that undertroden lye,
And daunted are in carefull vale, thys playnly doth disclose,
In that to mee of late I such a sonne in lawe have chose,
Who was a wandring pilgrim poore, with sore afflictions fraight,
Dismayde with terrour of his foe, that lay for him in wayght.
Because Acastus having got the crowne of Thessail lande,
Requyreth in thy guilty bloude to bath his wreackfull hande.
He doth bewayle that good olde man his feeble father slayne,
Whom waight of yeres with bowing back to stoupe alow constrayne
The godly mynded systers, all yblinde with misty vale
And cloking colour of thy craft durst ventrusly assayle.
That mount of myschiefe marveylous, to mangle, heaw, and cut,
Theyr Fathers dere unjoynted limmes in boyling Caldron put.
But for thy open guiltinesse if thou can purge the same,
Strayght Jason can discharge him selfe from blot of guilty blame:
His gentle handes were never staynde with goare of any bloude.
Aloofe from your conspyracie refrayning farre hee stoode.
His harmelesse handes put not in ure with goary tooles to mell.
But thou that setst on fyre fyrst these mighty mischiefes fell,
Whom shamelesse womans wily braine and manly stomack stout
Doe set a Gog, for to attempt to bring all ils about.
And no regarde at all thou hast, how sounding trumpe of fame
With ringing blast of good or ill doe blowe abrode thy name:
Get out and clense my fyled realme, away together beare
Thyne hearbes unmilde of sorcery, my Lyeges ryd fro feare.
Transporte thee to some other lande, whereas thou may at ease
With odious noyse of divelish charme, the troubled Gods disease.
Me. If needes thou wylt have mee avoyde, my shyp to mee restore,
Or els my mate with whom I fyrst aryved on this shore:
Why dost thou bid that by my selfe I onely should be gone?
I came not heather at fyrst wythout my company alone.
If this do thee aggryese, that brunt of warres thou shalt sustayne,
Commaund us both the cause thereof to shun thy realme agayne:

Sith both are guilty of one art, why dost thou part us twayne?
For Jasons sake, not for myne owne, poore Pelias was slayne.
Annex unto my traytrous flight the conquerde booty brave,
My hoary headded naturall sier, whom I forsaken have,
With brothers bloudy flesh that mangled was with carving knife,
Or ought of Jasons forged lies he gabbes unto his wyfe.
These dreary deedes are none of myne, so oft as I offend,
Not for myne owne commodity, to come thereby in thende.
CR. Time is expierd, by which thou ought to have bene gone away,
Wyth keeping such a chat, why dost thou make so long delay?
ME. Yet of thy bounty ere I goe, this one boone will I crave.
Although the mother banished, so sore offended have,
Let not the vengeaunce of my fault through wrathfull deadly hate,
Myne innocent and guiltlesse Babes torment in wreached state.
CR. Away: with loving friendly grype thy children I embrace,
And as a father naturall take pity on theyr case.
ME. Even for the prosperous good encreace of fertill spousall bed,
Of Glauce bright thy Daughter deare, whom Jason late hath wed,
And by the hope of fruictfull seede, whose flowre in time shall bloome;
By th' onour of thy glystring crowne, ythralde to fortunes doome,
Whych shee so full of chop and chaunge, with ficle turning wheele
Whirls up and downe, in staggring state makes to and fro to reele,
I thee beseech, sith to exile I am departing now
O Creon but a litle pawse for mercy mee alow,
Whyle of my mourning brats with kysse, my last farewell I take,
Whyle gaspe of fayling breath perhap my shyvering lyms forsake.
CR. With craft entending some deceipt thou cravest this delay.
ME. What falshode for so litle time be cause of terrour may?
CR. No jot of time is short ynough displeasure to prevent.
ME. Can not one jot to weeping Eyes, and trylling teares be lent?
CR. Although agaynst thy ernest suite unlucky dread do stryve,
One day to settle thee away, content I am to gyve.
ME. This is to much, and of the same somwhat abrydge yee may.
CR. Make speede apace if from our land thou get thee not away,
Ere Phœbus horse with golden gleede theyr streaming beames doe shed,
Of dawning lampe, thou art condemde to leese thy wretched hed.

The holy day, and brydall both doe call me hence away :
And wils mee at the sacred aare of Hymeneus to pray.

CHORUS

Lavish of life and dreadlesse was the wyght,
Attempting fyrst in slender tottring Barge
Wyth sliving Ore the slyced wave to smyte,
And durst commit the dainty tender charge
Of hazered life to inconstant course of wynde,
That turnes with chaunge of chaunces evermore,
To vew the land forsooke aloofe behynde,
And shooving forthe the Ship fro safer shore,
And glauncing through the fomy Channell deepe
On sunder cut with slender Stemme the wave,
Twixt hope of lyfe, and dread of death to sweepe,
In narrow gut him selfe to spill or save :
Experience yet of Planets no man had,
They needed not the wandring course to knowe
Of Starres, (wherewith the paynted sky is clad,)
Nor Pleiads, (which returne of sayling show)
Nor Hyads (that with showrs the Seas doe beate)
No nor the sterne Amaltheas horned head
(Who gave the lyppes of sucking Jove the Teate)
Were wont to put the blundering ships in dread.
They feared not the northerne Isy wayne,
Whych lazy olde bootes wieldes behinde,
And twynes about, no name yet could they fayne
For Boreas rough, nor smother western wynde.
Yet Typhys bould on open seas durst show
His hoysted sayles, and for the wyndes decree
New lawes : as now full gale aloofe to blow,
Now tackle turnde to take syde wynde alee,
Now up to farle the crossayle on the mast,
There safe to hang, the topsayle now to spred,
Now missel sayle, and drabler out to cast,
When dagling hanges his shottring tackle red

Whyle stearsman stur, and busye never blin,
With pyth to pull all sayles eke to display,
With tooth and nayle all force of wynde to wyn,
To sheare the seas and quick to scud awaye.
The golden worlde our fathers have possest,
Where banysht fraude durst never come in place,
All were content to live at home in rest,
With horye head, gray beard, and furrowed face
Whych tract of time within his countrey brought.
Riche having lytle, for more they did not toyle,
No vente for wares, nor Traficque far they sought,
No wealth that sprange beyond theyr native soyle,
The Thessail shyp together now hath set,
The Worlde that well with Seas dissevered lay,
It biddes the flouds with Oares to be bet,
And streames unknowen with shipwrack us to fray
That wicked Keele was lost by ruthfull wrack
Ytossed through such perylles passing great,
Where Cyanes Rocks gan rore as thunder crack,
Whose bouncing boult the shaken soyle doth beat.
The sowsing Surges dasshed every starre,
The pesterd seas the cloudes aloft berayde,
This scuffling did bould Typhis minde detarre,
Hys helme did slip from trembling hande dismayde.
Then Orpheus with his drowping Harp was mum,
Dead in her dumpes the flaunting Argos glee,
All husht in rest with silence wexed dum,
What hardy heart astound heere would not bee?
To see at once eche yawning mouth to gape,
Of Syllas gulph compact in wallowing paunch,
Of dogges, who doth not loth her mongrell shape,
Her visage, breast, and hyddeous ugly haunch :
Whom erketh not the scoulde with barking still?
To here the Mermaydes dyre who doth not quayle,
That lure the Eares with pleasaunt singing shrill
Of such as on Ausonius Sea doe sayle :
When Orpheus on his twanckling Harpe did play,
That earst the Muse Calliop gave to him.

Almost those Nymphes that wonted was to stay
The shyps, he causd fast following him to swim.
How deerely was that wicked journey bought?
Medea accurst, and eke the golden Fleece,
That greater harme then storme of seas hath wrought
Rewarded well that voyage first of Greece.
Now seas controulde doe suffer passage free,
The Argo proude erected by the hand
Of Pallas first, doth not complayne that shee
Conveyde hath back the kynges unto theyr land.
Eche whirry boate now scuddes aboute the deepe,
All stynts and warres are taken cleane away,
The Cities frame new walles themselves to keepe,
The open worlde lettes nought rest where it lay:
The Hoyes of Ind Arexis lukewarme leake,
The Perseans stout in Rhene and Albis streame
Doth bath their Barkes, time shall in fine out breake
When Ocean wave shall open every Realme.
The wandring World at will shall open lye.
And Typhis will some newe founde Land survay,
Some travelers shall the Countreys farre escrye,
Beyonde small Thule, knowen furthest at this day.

THE THIRD ACTE

NUTRIX. MEDEA

HY trotst thou fisking in and out so rash from place to place ?
Stand styll, and of thyne eger wrath suppresse the ruthfull race,
The rigour rough of ramping rage from burning breast out cast,
As Bacchus bedlem priestes that of his spryte have felt the blast,
Run franticke, hoyting up and downe with scitish wayward wits,
Not knowing any place of rest, so prickt with frowarde fits,
On cloudy top of Pindus Mounte all hyd with Snow so chyll :
Or els upon the lofty riddge of braunched Nisa hyll :
Thus starting still with frounced mynde she walters to and froe,
The signes pronouncing proofe of pangues her frensy Face doth show
With glowing cheekes and bloud red Face, with short and gasping breath,
Shee fetcheth deepe ascending sighes from sobbing heart beneath,
Now blyth she smiles, ech tumbled thought in pondring braine she beats,
Now stands she in a mammering, now myschiefe sore she threats.
With chafing fume she burnes in wrath, and nowe she doth complayne,
With blubbering teares a fresh bylive shee weepes and wayles agayne.
Where will this lumpish loade of cares with headlong sway allight ?
On whom entendeth shee to worke the threates of her despight ?
Where will this huge tempestious surge slake downe it selfe agayne ?
Enkindled fury new in breast begins to boyle a mayne.

Shee secretly entendes no mischiefe small nor meane of sise
To passe her selfe in wickednes her busy braynes devise.
The token olde of pinching ire full well ere this know I :
Some haynous, huge, outragious, great, and dredfull storme is nye :
Her firy, scowling, steaming Eyes, her hanging Groyne I see,
Her powting, puffed, frowning Face, that signes of freating bee.
O myghty Jove beguile my feare. Me. O wretch if thou desire,
What measure ought to payse thy wrath then learne by Cupids fire
To hate as sore as thou didst love, shall I not them anoy
That doe unite in spousall bed, theyr wanton lust t'enjoy ?
Shall Phœbus fiery footed horse goe lodge in western wave
The drowping day, that late I did with humble crowching crave,
And with such ernest busie suite so hardly graunted was ?
Shall it depart ere I can bring my devylish dryft to passe ?
Whyle hovering heaven doth counterpaysed hang with egall space,
Amid the marble Hemispheares, whyle rounde with stinted race,
The gorgeous Sky above the Earth doth spinning roll about,
Whyles that the number of the sandes, lyes hid unserched out,
While dawning day doth keepe his course with Phœbus blase so bright,
While twinkling starres in golden traynes doe garde the slumbry nyght,
While Isie under propping poale with whyrling swyng so swift,
The shyning Beares unbathde about the frosen Sky doe lift,
While flushing floudes the frothy streames to rustling Seas doe send,
To gird them gript with plonging pangues my rage shall never end.
With greater heate it shall reboyle, lyke as the brutishe beast,
Whose tyranny most horrible, exceedeth all the rest,
What greedy gaping whyrle poole wide what parlous gulph unmilde,
What Sylla coucht in roring Rockes, or what Charybdes wylde,
(That Sicill, and Ionium Sea by frothy waves doth sup)
What Ætna bolking stifling flames, and dusky vapours up,
(Whose heavy payse with stewing heate hath smoldring crush beneath
Encelades, that fiery flakes from choked throte doth breath)
Can with such dreadfull menaces in sweeting fury fry ?
No ryver swift no troubled surge of stormy Sea so hye,

Nor sturdy seas (whom ruffling winds with raging force to rore)
Nor puissaunt flash of fyre, whose might by bosytrous blast is more,
May byde my angers violence : my fury shall it foyle :
His court Ile over hourle, and lay it leavell with the soyle.
My Jasons heart did quake for feare of Creon cruell king,
And least the king of Thessaly would warre upon him bring.
But loyall Jove that hardens hearts makes no man be afright.
But beete, that he convict hath yeelde himselfe to Creons might.
Yet once hee might have visited, and come to me his wyfe,
To talke, and take his last farewell, if daunger of his life
In doing this (hard harted wretch most cruell) he should feare,
He being Creons sonne in law, for him it lefull were,
To have proroged somwhat yet my heavy banishment,
To take my leave of chyldren twayne one onely day is lent :
Yet doe I not complayne, as though the time to short I thought.
As proofe shall playne pronounce, to day, to day, it shall bee wrought,
The memory whereof no tract of time shall wype away.
With malice bent agaynst the Gods my wrath shall them assay :
And rifling every thing, both good, and bad, I will turmoyle.
Nu. Madame thy minde that troubled is, and tost with such a broyle
Of swarming ills, thy vexed breast now set at rest agayne,
The pevish fond affections all of troubled mynde refrayne.
Me. Then onely can I be at rest, when every thing I see
Throwne headlong topsie turvey downe to ruthfull ende with mee.
With mee let all things cleane decay : thy selfe if thou doe spill,
Thou maist drive to destruction what els with thee thou will :
Nu. If in this folly stiffe thou stand, beholde what after clappes
Are to bee fearde, none dare contrive for Prynces trayning trappes.

JASON. MEDEA

O LUCKLESSE lot of frowarde Fates, O cruell Fortunes hap,
Both when she list to smite, or spare, in woe she doth us wrap
A like, the salve that God hath geven so oft to cure our griefe
More noyeth then the sore it selfe, and sendeth lesse reliefe :
If for her good deserts to me, amendment I should make,
I hazard should my ventrous lyfe to leese it for her sake.

If I will shun my dismall day, and will not for her dy,
Then want the love of loyalty, O wretched man must I.
No dastards dread my stomacke stout can cause to droupe and shrynke,
But meere remorse appaulleth me, when on my babes I thynke.
For why ? when carefull parents are once reft of lyfe and breath,
Sone after them their wretched seede are drawne to dolefull death.
O Sacred righteousnesse (if thou enjoye thy worthy place
In perfect blisse of happy heaven) I call upon thy grace,
And thee for witnesse here alledge, how for my childrens part
With pity prickt I have commit these things agaynst my hart.
And so I thinke Medea her selfe the Mother rather had,
(Though franticklу as now she fares with rage of heart so mad
And doth abhor with paynfull yoke of combrous cares to toyle)
Her spousall bed, then that her seede should take the plunging foyle.
I did determine in my minde, to goe her to entreate
With gentle wordes, and pray her cease in fervent wrath to freate.
And loe, on me when once she caste the beames of glauncing Eye,
Full blythe she leapes, she jumpes for joy, in fits she ginnes to fry.
Deepe deadly blackish hate she seemes in outwarde brow to beare,
And wholly in her frowning face doth glutting griefe appeare.
ME. I packing, packing, Jason, am : this still to chop, and chaunge
The fleeting soyle of my abode, to mee it is not straunge.
The cause of my departure yet (to me is straung) and new.
I wonted was in followinge thee all places to eschew :
I will depart, and get me hence, to whom for helping hande
Entendest thou to sende us forth, whom hence to fly the land
Thou dost compell with thine alies ? shall I repayre agayne
To Phasis flood, to Colchis Isle, or to my fathers raygne ?
Or goary sweeting fieldes, that with my brothers blood do reeke ?
What harbring lands aloofe dost thou commaund us out to seeke ?
What seas appoint yee me to passe ? shall I my journey dryve,
Uppon the parlous hatefull jawes of Pontus to arrive,
By which I did saufe conduct home kings valiaunt armies great,
Where roaring rocks with thundring noise the flapping waves do beate,
Or on the narrow wrackfull shore of Simplegades twayne ?
Or els to small Hiolcos towne can I retourne agayne ?
Or toyle, the gladsome pleasaunt lands of Tempes to attayne ?

All places that I opened have unto thy passage free,
I shut them up agaynst my selfe, now whether sendste thou mee ?
A banisht wretch to banishment thou wouldest have encline,
Yet to the place of her exyle, thou canst not her assygne.
Yet for all that without delay I must depart and go :
And why ? forsoth the king his sonne in law commaundeth so.
Well : nothing will I stand against, with grypes of passing payne
Let me be scourgde, of my desarts such is the gotten gayne.
Let Creon in his pryncely ruffe lay to his heavy handes,
To whyp an whore in torments sharp, with iron gives and bandes
Let her be chaynd, in hydeous hole of night for aye her locke :
Let her be cloyed with pestring payse of restlesse rowling rocke.
Yet lesse than I deserved have, in all this shall I finde :
O thou uncurteous Gentleman, consider in thy mynde
The flamy puffes, and firy gaspes of gastly gaping bull,
And Ætas catell rych with Fleece of gorgeous golden wooll,
That went to graze amid so great and mighty feares in fielde,
Of uncontrouled Nation, whose soyle doth armies yeelde.
Revoke to minde the deadly dartes of sodayne starting foe,
When gastly warriour (Tellus broode) to ground agayne did goe,
Through slaughter red of mutuall launce, to this yet further passe,
The lurched Fleece of Phrixes Ramme, that all thine errand was.
And ugsome Argos slumberlesse, whom fast I causde to keepe
His wery watching winking eyes with unaquaynted sleepe.
My brother eke, whose fatall twist of feeble lyfe I shred,
And guilt that wrought so many guiltes when as with thee I fled.
The daughters whom I set on worke entrapt in wily trayne,
To stay theyr fire, that shall not ryse to quickned lyfe agayne.
And how to travell other realmes, I set myne owne at nought.
By that good hope which of thy seede conceaved is in thought,
Eake by thy stable Mansion place, and mighty monsters, that
Downe beaten for thy health, I causde before thy feete to squat,
And by these drudging hands of myne unspared for thy sake,
For dread of daungers over past that caused thee to quake,
By heavens above, and seas belowe, that witnesse bearers bee,
To knitting of our maryage up, thy mercy vayle to mee.
Of all the heapes of treasure great so farre of being fet,
Which Ætas savage Scythians dyd travell for to get

From Ind, where Phœbus scorching blase doth dye the people blacke.
Of all this golde which in our bowers wee coulde not well compacke,
But tricke and trym wee garnished our groves with golde so gay,
I banisht wretch of all this stuffe gat nought with mee away,
Except my brothers slaughterd flesh, yet I employed the same
On thee: the cares of countreyes health, my honesty and shame.
My Father, and my brother both hath yeelded place to thee,
This is the dowry that thou had my wedded spouse to bee.
To her whom thou dost abrogate restore her goods agayne.
JA. When Creon in malicious moode had thought thee to have slayne,
Entreated with my teares, exyle and life he gave to thee.
ME. I tooke it for a punishment, but surely as I see
This banishment is now become a friendly good rewarde.
JA. While thou hast time to goe, be gone, for most severe and harde
The kings displeasure ever is. ME. Thus wouldst thou dodge mee out?
Thy hated trull cast of thou dost, that please Creuse thou mought.
JA. Dost thou Medea upbrayde mee with the breach unkynde of love?
ME. And slaughter vyle, with trechery, whereto thou didst mee move.
JA. When all is done what canst thou lay my guiltines to stayne?
ME. Even whatsoever I have done. JA. Yet more this doth remayne:
That thy ungracious wickednes of harme should mee accuse.
ME. Thine, thine they are, they are all thine what ever I did use
Who that of lewdnesse reapes the fruict, is grafter of the same
Let every one with infamy thy wretched Spouse defame,
Yet doe thou onely take her part, her onely doe thou call
A just and undefiled wight, without offence at all.
If any man shall for thy sake polute his hand with ill,
To thee let him an innocent yet be accompted still.
JA. The life is lothsome that doth worke his shame who hath it chose.
ME. The life whose choyse doth worke thy shame thou ought againe to lose.
JA. Let reason rule thy eger mynde so vext with crabbed ire,
And for thy tender childrens case to bee at rest requyre.

ME. I doe defy it, wholy I detest it, I forsweare
That bretheren bred unto my barnes Creusas wombe shall beare
JA. It will be trim, when as a Queene of majesty and myght
Hath issue, kinne unto the seede of thee a banisht wight.
ME. So cursed day shall never on my wretched children shine,
To mingle base borne basterdes with the bloud of noble Lygne.
Shall Phœbus stocke (that beares the lamp of heaven in starry throne)
Be macht with drudging Sisiphus that roules in hell the stone ?
JA. What meanest thou wretch, both thee and mee in banishment to yoke ?
I pray then hence. ME. When humbly I my mynde to Creon broke,
Hee gave an eare unto my suite. JA. What lyeth in my myght
To doe for thee ? ME. If no good turne, then doe thy worst dispyght.
JA. On this side with his swerd in hand king Creon doth mee scarre:
On other part with armed hoast Acast doth mee detarre.
ME. Medea eke to coape with these, that more apaull us may :
Go to, to skyrmishe let us fall, let Jason be the pray :
JA. I yeelde whom sore adversities have tyerd with heavy sway.
Learne thou to dred thy lucklesse lot that ofte doth thee assay.
ME. I evermore have rulde the swinge of fortunes wavering will.
JA. Achastus is at hand, and nygh is Creon thee to spyll :
ME. Take thou thy heeles to scape them both, I doe not thee advise
That thou agaynst thy father in lawe in traytrous armes should ryse.
Nor in Achast thy cosens bloud thy wounding handes to gore,
The vowes unto Medea made, doe trouble thee so sore.
Whyle yet thou hast not spilt there bloud, yet fly with mee away.
JA. When armies twayne their banners of defiance shall display,
And marching forth in fielde to fyght seeke battayle at my hande,
Who then for us encounter shall their puissaunce to withstand ?
ME. If Creon and Achastus king encampe together shall,
Admit that these in one with them should joyne their powers all
My Countreymen of Colchis Ile, and Ætas lusty kyng,
Suppose the Scythians joyne with Greekes, to ground I wil them bring,

Cleane put to foile. JA. The puissaunt power of hawty mace I feare.
ME. Take heede, least more thou do affect the same, then for to cleare
Thy selfe of Creons servile yoke. JA. Least some suspicion grow,
Of this our tatling long here let us make an ende and goe.
ME. Now Jove hurle out thy flames and force thy thundring bolts to fly,
With fiery drakes bright brandishing disparst in burning sky :
Strayne forth thy dreadfull threatning arme, dispose in due aray
The tossing dint of lightning flashe, that wrecke our quarrell may.
With rumbling cracke of renting cloud cause all the world to quake,
And levell not thy hovering hand to stryke with firy flake
Uppon my pasht and crushed corpes, or Jasons Carcasse slayne :
For whether of us thou smight to death his due rewarde shall gayne,
Thy thumps of thwacking boltes on us amisse they cannot light.
JA. Fy, let thy mynde on matters runne that seeme a modest wight,
And use to have more cheerefull talke : if any thing thou crave,
Within my fathers house to ease thy flyght, thou shalt it have.
ME. Thou knowst my minde both can, and eke is wont, to doe no lesse,
Then to contemne the brittell wealth that Prynces doe possesse.
This, this shalbe the onely boone that at thy hande I crave,
As mates with me in banishment, my children let mee have,
That resting on theyr sighing breastes my carefull mourning hed,
I may my chrystall teary streames into theyr bosomes shed.
But as for thee, new gotten sonnes of wife new wed doe stay.
JA. I graunt that unto thy request I wishe I might obey :
But nature mee with pity pryckes, that needes I must deny.
For though both Creon and Achast, in torments force mee lye,
I could not yeelde unto theyr willes : on this my lyfe doth rest :
In times of teares this is the joy of dull afflicted brest,
For better farre I can abyde the wante of vitall breath,
And succour of my lymmes, or loose the light of worlde by death.
ME. What love unto his seely Babes is deeply graft in him ?
This worketh well I have him tript, loe now there lyeth brim.
An open place whereby receave a venny soone hee may.
Let mee or I departe, unto my seely children say.

These lessons of my last adewe, and graunt to mee the space,
With tender grype of colling last theyr loving limmes t' embrace :
This wilbe comforte to my heart : yet at the latter woorde
I aske no more but onely that you shoulde mee this affoorde.
If eger anguish cause my tongue to cast out woords unkinde,
Let all thing fly, let nothing be engraved in your minde,
But let remembraunce otherwhyle of mee to touch your thought,
Let other thinges be wypte away that byle of wrath hath wrought.
JA. I have forgotten every whit, God graunt thou may of shake
These surging qualmes of frounced minde and milder mayste it make :
For quietnesse doth worke theyr ease that dented are with woe.
ME. What is he slily slipt and gon ? falles out the matter so ?
O Jason dost thou sneake away, not having minde of mee,
Nor of those former great good turnes that I have done for thee ?
With thee now am I cleane forgot : but I will bryng about
That from thy carefull sighing minde shall not bee banisht out :
Apply to bring this to effect, call home thy wits agayne,
And all thy wyly fetches farre, eache artificiall trayne.
This is the perfect fruict that may to thee of mischiefe spryng,
To presuppose that mischiefe is not graft in any thing.
Scant have I opportunity for my pretensed guile,
Because wee are mistrusted sore : but try I will the whyle
To set upon them in such sort, as none can deeme my sleyght :
March forth, now venture on, fall to, both what lyeth in thy myght,
And also what doth passe thy power. O faythfull nourse and mate
Of all my heavy heart breaking, and dyvers cursed fate.
Come help our simple meane device. Remayning yet I have
A robe of Pall the present that our heavenly Graundsire gave,
Chiefe monument of Colchis Ile, which Phœbus did bestow
On Ætas for a pledge, that him his father he might know.
A precious fulgent gorget eake, that bravely glytters bryght,
And with a seemely shyning seame of golden thryds is dight,
Through wrought betwene the row of pirles doe stand in borders round,
Wherewith my golden crispen Locks is wonted to be cround.
My lytle children they shall beare these presents to the Bryde,
That first with slibber slabbar sosse of chauntments shalbe tryde.

Request the ayde of Hecate in redinesse prepare
The lamentable sacrifice upon the bloudy Aare
Enforce the fiers catching holde upon the rafters hye
With crackling noyse of flamy sparkes rebound in azur sky.

CHORUS

No fiers force, nor rumbling rage of boistrus blustring winde,
No dart shot whirling in the skies, such terrour to the minde
Can drive, as when the ireful wife doth boile in burning hate
Deprived of her spousall bed, and comfort of her mate,
Nor where the stormy southerne winde with dankish dabby face,
Of hoary winter sendeth out the gusshing showres apace.
Where veighment Isters waumbling streame comes waltring downe amayne,
Forbidding both the banks to meete, and cannot oft contayne
Him selfe within his channels scoupe, but further breakes his way,
Nor Rodanus whose russhing streame doth launch into the sea,
Or when amid the floured spring with hotter burning sunne,
The winters snowes disolvde with heate downe to the ryvers runne :
The clottred top of Haemus hill to water thin doth turne,
Such desperate gogin flame is wrath that inwardly doth burne,
And modest rule regardeth not, nor brydels can abyde,
Nor dreading death, doth wish on dinte of naked blade to slyde.
O Gods be gratious unto us, for pardon we do crave,
That him who tamde the scuffling waves, vouchsafe yee would to save.
But Neptune yet the Lord of Seas with frowning face will lower,
That over his second Scepter men to tryumph have the power.
The boy that rashly durst attempt that great unweldy charge
Of Phœbus everlasting Carte, and roving out at large,
Not bearing in his recklesse breast his fathers warnings wyse,
Was burned with the flames which he did scatter in the Skyes.
None knew the costly glimsing glades, where straggling Phaëton rode,
Passe not the path, where people safe in former tyme have trode.
O fondling, wilfull, wanton boy, doe not dissolve the frame
Of heaven, sith Jove with sacred hand hath halowed the same.
Who rowde with valiaunt Oares tough, that were for Argo made,
Hath powled naked Pelion mounte of thycke compacted shade.

Who entred hath the fleeting rockes and serched out the toyle
And tyring travels of the seas, and hath on salvage soyle
Knit fast his stretched Cable rope, and going forth to land,
To cloyne away the forren golde with greedy snatching hand.
Unto the seas (because that hee transgrest theyr lawes devin)
By this unlucky ende of his, he payes his forfeyte fine.
The troubled seas of theyr unrest for vengeaunce howle and weepe,
Syr Typhis who did conquer fyrst the daunger of the deepe,
Hath yeelded up the cunning rule of his unweldy sterne,
To such a guide, as for that use hath neede as yet to learne.
Who giving up his Ghost aloofe from of his native lande,
In forreyn more lyes buryed vile with durty soddes in sande.
He sits among the flittring soules that straungers to him weare.
And Aulis Isle that in her minde her masters losse doth beare,
Held in the Ships, to stand and wayle in croking narrow nooke :
That Orpheus Calliops sonne who stayde the running Brooke,
Whyle he recordes on heavenly Harpe with twanckling finger fine,
The wynde layde downe his pipling blastes : his harmony divine
Procurde the woods to styr them selves, and trees in traynes along
Came forth with byrds that held their layes and listned to his song.
With lims on sunder rent in fielde of Thrace he lyeth dead.
Up to the top of Heber floude, eke haled was his head.
Gone downe he is to Stygian dampes, which seene hee had before,
And Tartar boyling pits, from whence returne hee shall no more.
Alcydes banging bat did bringe the Northern laddes to grounde.
To Achelo of sundry shapes he gave his mortall wounde.
Yet after he could purchase peace both unto sea and land,
And after Ditis dungeon blacke rent open by his hand,
He lyving spred himselfe along on burning Oetas hill :
His members in his proper flame the wretche did thrust to spill :
His bloud he brewd with Nestors bloud, and lost his lothsome lyfe
By traytrous gyft that poysoned shyrt receaved of his wyfe.
With tuske of bristled groyning Bore Anceus lyms were torne.
O Meleagar (wicked wight) to grave by thee were borne
Thy mothers brethren twayne, and shee, for it with ruthfull hand,
Hath wrought thy dolefull desteny, to burne thy fatall brand.
The rash attempting Argonantes deserved all the death
That Hylas whom Alcides lost bereft of fading breath.

That springall which in sowsing waves of waters drowned was :
Goe now yee lusty bloudes, the Seas with doubtfull lot to passe,
Though Idmon had the calking skyll of destenies before,
The serpent made him leave his lyfe in tombe of Liby shore.
And Mopsus that to other men could well theyr fates escry,
Yet onely did deceyve him selfe uncertayne where to dy,
And he that could the secret hap of things to come unfoulde,
Yet dyde not in his countrey Thebes. Dame Thetis husband oulde
Did wander like an outlawde man. Our Palimedes syre
Did headlong whelm him selfe in seas. Who at the Greekes retyre
From Troy, to rushe on rockes did them alure with wily light,
Stout Ajax Oleus did sustayne the dint of thunder bright,
And cruell storme of surging seas, to quite the haynous guilt,
That by his countrey was commit, in seas he lyeth spilt.
Alceste to redeeme her husbands Phereus lyfe from death,
The godly Wyfe upon her spouse bestowed her panting breath.
Proude Pelias that wretch him selfe who had them first assay
The golden Fleece that booty brave by ship to fetch away,
Perboylde in glowing cauldron hoate with fervent heate hee fryes,
And fleeting peecemeale up and downe in water thin he lyes.
Inough, inough, revenged are O Gods the wronges of seas,
Be good to Jason, doing that hee did, his Eame to please.

THE FOURTH ACTE

NUTRIX

Y shivering minde amazed is, agast, and sore dismayde :
My chillish lims with quaking colde do tremble all afrayde :
Such plagues and vengeance is at hand, in what exceeding wise
Do sharp assaults of greedy griefe still more and more arise,
And of it selfe in smothering breast enkindlesse greater heate ?
Oft have I seene how ramping rage hath forced her to freate,
With franticke fits, mad, bedlem wise, against the Gods to rayle,
And eke bewitched ghosts of heaven in plunging plagues to trayle :
But now Medea beates her busie brayne to bring to passe
A myschiefe greater, greater farre, then ever any was.
Erewhile when hence she tript away astonished so sore,
And of her poyson closset close shee entred had the dore :
Shee powreth out her Jewels all, abrode to light shee brings
That which she dreading lothed long, most irksome ugly things :
She mumbling conjures up by names of ills the rable rout,
In hugger mugger cowched long, kept close, unserched out :
All pestlent plagues she calles upon, what ever Libie lande,
In frothy boyling stream doth worke, or muddy belching sande :
What tearing torments Taurus breedes, with snowes unthawed still
Where winter flawes, and hory frost knit hard the craggy hill,
She layes her crossing hands upon each monstrous conjurde thing,
And over it her magicke verse with charming doth she sing :
A mowsie, rowsie, rusty route with cancred Scales Iclad
From musty, fusty, dusty dens where lurked long they had,
Doe craull : a wallowing serpent huge, his combrous Corps out drags
In fiery foming blaring mouth his forked tongue hee wags.

He stares about with sparkling eyes, if some he might espy,
Whom snapping at with stinging spit he might constrayne to dy :
But hearing once the magycke verse he husht as all a gast,
His body boalne big, wrapt in lumps on twining knots hee cast.
And wambling to and fro his tayle in linkes he rowles it round.
Not sharp enough (quoth she) the plagues and tooles that hollow ground
Engenders for my purpose are, to heaven up will I call,
To reach me stronger poyson down, to frame my feate with all.
Now is it at the very poynt, Medea thou assay,
To bring about some farther fetch then common Witches may.
Let downe, let downe, that sprawling Snake that doth his body spred,
As doth a running brooke abroade his myghty channell shed.
Whose swelling knobs of wondrous sise and boystrous bobbing bumpes
Doth thumpe the great and lesser beare that feele his heavy lumpes.
The bygger beare with golden gleede the greekish fleete doth guyde,
But by the lesse the Sidon ships their passage have espide.
He that with pinch of griping fist doth bruse the adders twayne,
His strening hard and clasping hande, let him unknit agayne.
And crushe their squeased venome out, come further thou our charme
O slymy serpent Python, whom Dame Juno sent to harme
Diana, and Apollo both, (those heavenly spyrites twayne)
With whom Latona traveling did grone with pynching payne.
O Hydra whom in Lerna poole Alcides gave the foyle,
And all the noysome vermen vyle that Hercules did spoyle.
Which when on sunder they were cut with slysing deadly knyfe,
Can knit agayne their sodred partes, and so recover lyfe.
Help wakefull Dragon Argos, whom first magicke wordes of myne
Made Morpheus locke thy sleepy liddes, and shut thy slugring eyne.
Then having brought above the ground of Serpents all the rout,
Of filthy weedes the ranckest bane shee pyckes, and gathers out,
That spryng on knotty Eryx hill where passage none is founde,
Among the ragged Rockes, or what on Caucasus his grounde
Doth grow that still is clad in Coate of hoary moary frost.
That evermore unmelt abydes, whose spattred fylde is softe

With gubbs of bloud, that spowteth from Prometheus gaping maw,
Whose guts with twitching talent out the gastly gripe doth draw.
Or any other venemous herbe amonge the Medes that growes,
That with their sheafe of arowes sharp in field do scare their foes.
Or what the light held Parthian to serve her turne can sende,
Or els the rych Arabians, that dyp theyr arrowes ende
In poyson strong : the juyce of all Medea out doth wrynge,
That underneath the frosen poale in Swevia land doth sprynge.
Whose noble state Hircinus woode doth high enhaunce and reare.
Or what the pleasaunte soyle doth yeelde in pryme of smiling veare,
When nature byddes the byrd begin her shrowding nest to builde,
Or when the churlyshe Boreas blast sharpe winter hath exilde,
The trym aray of braunche and bough to cloth the naked tree,
And every thinge with bitter coulde of Snowe congealed bee.
In any pestilent flower on stalke of any hearbe doth growe,
Or noysome juyce doth lye in rotten wrythen rootes alowe,
Hath any force in breading bane, those takes shee in her hande.
Some plaugy hearbes did Athos yeelde that mount of Thessayle lande.
And other Pindus roches hye and some uppon the top
Of Pingeus, but tender twigges the cruell Sythe did lop :
These Tigris ryver norisht up, that choakes his whyrlpoale deepe
With stronger streame. Danubius those in fostring wave did keepe.
Those did Hidaspus mynister, who by the parching zone
With lukewarme silver channell runnes, so rych with precious stone.
And Bethis sonne, who gave the name unto his countrey great,
And with his shallowe foarde agaynst the Spanyshe seas doth beat.
This hearbe aboade the edge of knyfe in dawning of the day
Ere Phœbus Face gan peepe, bedect with glittring goulden spray
His slender stalke was snepped of in deepe of silent nyght,
His corne was cropt, whyle she with charme her poysned nayles did dight.
Shee chops the deadly hearbes, and wrings the squesed clottered bloud
Of Serpentes out, and filthy byrdes of irkesome miry mud
She tempers with the same, and eake she brayes the heart of Owle
Foreshewing death with glaring Eyes, and moaping Vysage foule,

Of shryke Owle hoarce alyve she takes the durty stinking guts,
All these the framer of this feate in dyvers percels puts.
This hath in it devouring force of greedy spoyling flame,
The frosen ysle dulling coulde engenders by the same.
Shee chauntes on those the magicke verse, that workes no lesser harme,
With bustling frantickely shee stampes, and ceaseth not to charme.

MEDEA

O FLITTRING Flockes of grisly ghostes that sit in silent seat
O ougsome Bugges, O Gobblins grym of Hell I you intreat :
O lowryng Chaos dungeon blynde, and dreadfull darkned pit,
Where Ditis muffled up in Clowdes of blackest shades doth sit,
O wretched wofull wawling soules your ayde I doe implore,
That linked lye with gingling Chaynes on wayling Limbo shore,
O mossy Den where death doth couche his gastly carrayne Face :
Relesse your pangues, O spryghts, and to this wedding hye apace.
Cause yee the snaggy wheele to pawse that rentes the Carkas bound,
Permit Ixions racked Lymmes to rest upon the ground :
Let hungry bytten Tantalus wyth gawnt and pyned panche
Soupe up Pirenes gulped streame his swelling thyrst to staunche.
Let burning Creon byde the brunt and gyrdes of greater payne,
Let payse of slyppery slyding stone type over backe agayne
His moylyng Father Sisyphus, amonges the craggy Rockes.
Yee daughters dyre of Danaus whom perced Pychers mockes
So oft with labour lost in vayne this day doth long for you
That in your lyfe with bloudy blade at once your husband slewe.
And thou whose aares I honored have, O torch and lampe of night,
Approche O Lady myne with most deformed vysage dight :
O threefolde shapen Dame that knitst more threatning browes then one,
According to the countrey guise with dagling locks undone
And naked foote, the secrete grove about I halowed have,
From dusky dry unmoysty cloudes the showers of rayne I crave.
Through me the chinked gaping ground the soked seas hath drunk,
And mayner streame of th' ocian floud beneath the earth is sunk,

That swelteth out through hollow gulph with stronger gushing rage.
Then were his suddy wambling waves whose power it doth asswage
The heavens with wrong disturbed course and out of order quight,
The darkned sonne, and glimmering stars at once hath shewed theyr light,
And drenched Charles his stragling wayne hath ducte in dasshing wave,
The framed course of roaming time racte out of frame I have.
So my enchauntments have it wrought, that when the flaming sunne
In sommer bakes the parched soyle then hath the twigges begunne,
With sprowting blossom fresh to blome, and hasty winter corne
Hath out of harvest seene the fruite to barnes on suddein borne.
Into a shallowe foorde his sture distreame hath Phasis wast,
And Isters channell being in so many braunches cast,
Abated hath his wrackfull waves, on every silent shore
He lyeth calme : The tumbled flouds with thundring noyse did rore,
When couched close the windes were not moving pippling soft,
With working wave the prauncing seas have swolne and leapt aloft,
Whereas the wood in alder time with thicke and braunched bowe
Did spread his shade on gladsome soyle no shade remayneth now.
I rolling up the magicke verse at noone time Phœbus stay,
Amyd the darkned Sky, when fled was light of drowsy day.
Eke at my charme the watry flockes of Heyæds went to glade.
Time is it Phœba to respect the service to thee made :
To thee with cruell bloudy hands these garlands greene were twynde
Which with his folding circles nyne the serpent rough did bynde.
Have here Tiphoias fleshe, that doth in Ætnas Fornace grone,
That shoke with battery violent king Joves assaulted trone.
This is the Centaures paysoned bloud which Nessus villayne vyle
Who made a rape of Dianire entending her to fyle,
Bequethed her when newly wounde he gasping lay for breath,
While Hercles shaft stack in his Ribs, whose launce did worke his death :
Beholde the Funerall cinders heere which up the poyson dryed
Of Hercules who in his fyre on Oeta mountayne dyed :
Loe heere the fatall brand, which late the fatall sisters three
Conspyred at Meleagers byrth, such should his destny bee,

To save alyve his brethyng corpes, while that might whole remayne,
Which saufe his mother Althe kept, till he his uncles twayne,
(That from Atlanta would have had the head of conquered Bore,)
Had reft of lyfe whose spightfull death Althea tooke so sore,
That both she shewed her ferventnesse in systers godly love,
When to revenge her brothers death meere nature did her move,
But yet as mother most unkynde, of nature most unmylde,
To hasten the untymely grave of her beloved chylde,
Whyle Meleagers fatall brande she wasted in the flame,
Whose swelting guts and bowels moult consumed as the same,
These plumes the Harpyes ravening fowles for hast did leave behinde
In hidden hole whose cloase accesse no mortall wight can fynd.
When fast from Zethes chasing them with speedy flight they fled.
Put unto those the fethers which the Stymphal byrde did shed,
Whom duskyng Phœbus dymned lyght syr Hercules did stynge,
And galled with the shafte, that he in Hydraes hyde did flynge.
You Aares have yeelde a clattring noyse I knowe, I knowe of olde,
How unto mee my Oracles are wonted to bee toulde,
That when the trembling flowre doth shake then hath my Goddes great,
Vouchsafe to graunt mee my request as I did her intreate,
I see Dianas waggon swife, not that whereon shee glydes,
When all the night in darkned Sky with Face full ope shee rydes :
With countnaunce bright and blandishing but when with heavy cheare,
With dusky shimmering wanny globe, her lampe doth pale appeare.
Or when shee trots about the heavens wyth horseheade rayned strayte,
When Thessayle Witches with the threats of charming her doe bayte.
So with thy dumpish dulled blase, thy cloudy faynting lyght,
Sende out, amid the lowring sky, the heart of people smyght
Wyth agonies of suddeyne dread, in straung and fearefull wyse,
Compell the pretious brasen pannes with jarring noyse to ryse
Through Corinth countrey every where, to shielde thee from this harme,
Least headlong drawne thou be from heaven to earth by force of charme.

An holy solempne sacryfice to worship thee wee make,
Imbrewed with a bloudy turphe the kindled Torche doth take
Thy sacred burning night fyre at the dampishe mory grave.
Sore charged with thy troubled ghost my head I shaken have,
And ducking downe my Necke alowe with shryking lowde have shrig,
And groveling flat on floore in traunce have lyen in deadmans plight.
My ruffled Lockes about myne eares downe dagling have ben bownd,
Tuckt up about my temples twayne with gladsome garland crownde
A drery braunche is offred thee from filthy Stigis flood.
As is the guise of Bacchus priestes the Coribanthes wood,
With naked breast and dugges layde out Ile pricke with sacred blade
Myne arme, that for the bubling bloude an issue may bee made,
With trilling streames my purple bloude let drop on Th'aulter stones.
My tender Childrens crusshed fleshe, and broken broosed bones
Lerne how to brooke with hardned heart : in practise put the trade
To florishe fearce, and keepe a coyle, with naked glittring blade :
I sprinkled holy water have, the launce once being made,
If tyred thou complaynest that my cryes thee overlade,
Give pardon to my ernest suite, O Perseus sister deare,
Still Jason is the onely cause that urgeth mee to reare
With squeking voyce thy noysome beames, that sting like shot of bo
So season thou those sawced robes to worke Creusas woe,
Wherewith when shee shall pranke her selfe the poyson by and by
To rot her inward mary out, within her bones may fry,
The secret fyer bleares their eyes with glosse of yeallow golde,
The which Prometheus gave to mee that fyer fylcher bolde.
On whom for robbery that he did in heavens above commit,
With massy payse great Caucasus th'unweldy hill doth sit,
Where under with unwasted wombe he lyes, and payes his payne,
To feede the cramming foule with gubs of guts that growes agayne.
He taught mee with a prety sleyght of conning, how to hyde
The strength of fyer close kept in, that may not be espyde,
This lyvely tinder Mulciber hath forged for my sake,
That tempred is with brymstone quick at fyrst touch and take.
Eke of my Cosen Phaëton a wyldefyer flake I have
His flames the monstrous staghard rough Chimera to mee gave,

In head and breast a Lyon grim, and from the Rump behynde
He sweepes the flower with lagging Tayle of Serpent fearce by kynde
In Rybbes, and Loynes along his paunche yshaped lyke a Goate.
These Fumes that out the Bull perbrakte from fyry spewinge throat
I gotten have and brayde it with Medusas bitter gall
Commaunding it in secret sorte to duske and cover all :
Breath on these venoms Hecate, with deadly myght inspyre,
Preserve the touching poulder of my secret covert fyre,
O graunt that these my cloked craftes so may bewitch theyr Eyes,
That lykelyhoode of treason none they may heerein surmyse :
So worke that they in handling it may feele no kynde of heate :
Her stewing breast, her seathing vaynes, let fervent fyer freate
And force her rosted pyning lymmes to drop and melt away,
Let smoke her rotten broyling bones : enflame this bryde to day
To cast a lyght with greater gleede on fryseled blasing heare
Then is the shyning flame that doth the wedding torches beare.
My suite is harde, thryse Hecate a dreadfull barking gave
From dolefull cloude a sacred flash of flamy sparkes shee drave.
Eche poysons pryde fulfilled is : call forth my chyldren deare,
By whom unto the cursed Bryde these presentes you may beare :
Goe forth, goe forth my lytle Babes, your mothers cursed fruite,
Goe, goe, employ your paynes with brybe and earnest humble suite
To purchase grace, and eke to earne you favour in her sight.
That both a mother is to you, and rules with Ladies might.
Goe on, apply your charge apace, and hye you home agayne,
That with embracing you I may my last farewell attayne.

CHORUS

What sharpe assaultes of cruell Cupids flame
Wyth gyddie heade thus tosseth to and froe
This bedlem Wyght, and divelysh despret dame
What roving rage her pricks to worke this woe?
Rough rancours vile congeales her frosen face,
Her hawty breast bumbasted is wyth pryde,
Shee shakes her heade, shee stalkes wyth stately pace,
Shee threates our king more then doth her betyde.

Who would her deeme to bee a banisht wyght,
Whose skarlet Cheekes doe glowe with rosy red?
In faynting Face, with pale and wanny whyght
The sanguyne hewe exyled thence is fled.
Her chaunging lookes no colour longe can holde,
Her shifting feete still travasse to and froe.
Even as the fearce and ravening Tyger olde
That doth unware his sucking whelpes forgoe,
Doth rampe, and rage, most eger ferce and wood,
Among the shrubs and bushess that doe growe
On Ganges stronde that golden sanded flood,
Whose silver streame through India doth flowe.
Even so Medea sometime wantes her wits
To rule the rage of her unbrydeled ire,
Nowe Venus Sonne, wyth busie froward fits,
Nowe Wrath, and Love enkyndle both the fire.
What shall shee doe? when will this heynous wyght
With forwarde foote bee packing hence away
From Greece? to ease our Realme of terrour quight,
And prynces twayne whom she so sore doth fray:
Nowe Phœbus lodge thy Charyot in the West,
Let neyther Raynes, nor Brydle stay thy Race,
Let groveling light with Dulceat nyght opprest
In cloking Cloudes wrapt up his muffled Face,
Let Hesperus the loadesman of the nyght,
In Western floode drench deepe the day so bryght.

MEDEA

THE FIFTH ACTE

NUNTIUS. CHORUS. NUTRIX. MEDEA. JASON

LL things are topsy turvy turnde, and wasted cleane to nought.
To passing great calamity our Kingdome State is brought.
The Syre and Daughter burnt to dust in blendred Cynders lye.
CH. What trayne hath them entrapt? NU. Such as are made for Kinges to dye,
False traitrous gifts. CH. What privy guile could wrapped be in those?
NU. And I doe mervayle at this thing and skant I can suppose
That such a mischiefe might be wrought by any such device.
CH. Report how this destruction and ruine should aryse.
NU. The fyzzing flame most egerly doth scoure with sweeping sway
Eache corner of the Prynces court, as though it should obay,
Commaunded thereunto so flat on flowre the Pallace falles:
Wee are in dread least further it will take the townishe walles.
CH. Cast quenching water on it then to slake the greedy flame.
NU. And this that seemeth very straunge doe happen in the same,
The water feedes the fier fast, the more that wee doe toyle
It to suppresse, with hotter rage the heate begins to boyle:
Those thinges that wee have gotten for our help it doth enjoy.
NUT. Medea thou that doest so sore king Pelops lande anoy,
Twine hence in hast thy forwarde foote, at all assayes depart
To any other kinde of coaste. ME. Can I finde in my hart
To shun this lande? if hence I had first falne away by flight,
I would have traveled backe agayne, to gase at such a sight.
To stande and see this wedding new, why stayst thou doting mynde?
Apply, apply, thy sore attempt, that good successe doth finde.
What great exployt is this, that thou of vengeaunce dost injoy?
Still art thou blynded witlesse wench with vale of Venus boy?

Is this suffisaunce for the griefe ? is roote of rancour ded,
If Jason leade a single lyfe in solitary bed ?
Some netling, thorny, stinging plagues unpractised devise :
Prepare thy selfe in redines and fall to on this wyse :
Let all bee fishe that commes to Net, have no respect of ryghte,
From mynde on mischiefe fixed fast let shame be banisht quyte :
The vengeaunce they receaved at my lytle chyldrens hand,
Is nothing worth : in earnest ire ententive must thou stand.
When heate of wrath begins to coole, cheere up thy selfe agayne :
Rayse up those touches olde that wonted were in thee to raygne,
That buried deepe in breast doe lye : and as for all the same
That yet is wrought : Of godlinesse let it usurpe the name :
Doe this, and I shall teach them learne, what tryfling cast it was,
And common practisde flimflam trick that erst I brought to passe.
By this my raging malady a preamble hath made,
To shew what howgier heapes of harmes shall shortly them invade
What durst my rude unskilfull hand assay that was of wayght ?
What could the mallice of a Gyrle invent her foes to bayte ?
Still conversaunt with wicked feates Medea am I made.
My blunt and dulled braynes hath so ben beate about this trade.
O so I joy, I joy, that I smote of my brothers head,
And slasht his members of : eake that from parents had I fled :
And filched have the privy fleece, loe Mars that sacred was.
It glads my heart that I to bring olde Pelias death to passe :
Have set his daughters all on worke : O griefe picke out a way
Not any guilt thou shalt with unacquainted hand assay
Against whom wrath entendest thou to bend thyne Irefull might ?
Or with what weapon dost thou meane thy trayterous foes to smight?
I know not what my wrathfull minde consulted hath within,
And to bewray it to himselfe, I dare not yet begin.
O rash and unadvised foole, I make to hasty speede :
O that my Foe had gotten of his Harlots body Seede :
But what so ever thou by him enjoyest, suppose the same
To bee Creusas Babes, of them let her enjoy the name.
This vengeaunce, this doth like mee well good reason is there, why,
The last attempt of ils, thou must with stomacke stout apply.
Alas yee litle seely fooles that erst my children were,
The plaguing price of Fathers fault submit your selves to beare.

O, horrour huge with sodayne stroke my heart doth overcom :
With ycie dulling colde congealde my Members all benum.
My shivering lims appauled sore for gastly feare doe quake,
And banisht rage of malice hoate begins it selfe to slake :
The hatefull heart of wife agaynst her Spouse hath yeelded place,
And pitious mothers mercy milde restoreth natures face.
O shall I shed their guiltlesse bloude ? shall I the frame unfoulde
Of that which loving natures hande hath wrought in me her moulde ?
O doting fury chaunge thy minde, conceive a better thought,
Let not this haynous savage deede by meanes of mee be wrought.
What cryme have they (poore fooles) commit, for which they should abye ?
Upon theyr Father Jason right all blot of blame should lye.
Medea yet theyr Mother I am worser farre then hee.
Tush let them frankly goe to wracke, no kith nor kin to mee
They are : dispatch them out of hand : holde, holde, my babes they be
God wot, most harmelesse lambes they are, no crime nor fault have they :
Alas they bee mere innocents, I doe not this denay :
So was my brother whom I slew : O false revolting mynde,
Why dost thou staggring to and fro such chaunge of fancies fynde ?
Why is my Face be sprent with teares, what makes mee falter so,
That wrath and love with striving thoughts doe leade me to and fro ?
Such fighting fancies bickringe stormes my swarving minde detarre,
As when betweene the wrestling windes is raysed wrangling warre,
Echewhere the tumbling wallowing waves, are hoyst and reared hye
Amid the justling swolves of seas, that hot in fury frye :
Even so my hart with strugling thoughts now sinks, now swells amaine,
Wrath sometyme chaseth vertue out, and vertue wrath agayne.
O yeelde thee, yeelde, a grising griefe, to vertue yeelde thy place :
Thou onely comforte of our stocke in this afflicted case,
Come heather, come deere loved Impe, with colling mee imbrace,
Whyle that by me your mother deere sweete Boyes yee are enjoyed,
So long God graunt your Father may you kepe from harme uncloyed,
Exile and flight approach on mee, and they shall by and by
Be pulde perforce out of myne armes, with vapourde weeping Eye,

Sore languishing with mourning heart, yet let them goe to grave
Before their fathers Face, as they before their mothers have :
Now rancorus griefe, with firy fits begins to boyle agayne,
The quenched coales of deadly hate do fressher force attayne.
The rusty rancour harbred long within my cancred brest
Starts up, and stirres my hand anew in mischiefe to bee prest.
O that the rablement of brats which swarmde aboute the syde
Of Niobe that scornefull Dame, who perisht by her pryde
Had taken lyfe out of his lymmes, O that the fates of heaven
A fruictfull mother had me made of chyldren seven and seven.
My barreyne wombe for my revenge hath yeelded litle store :
Yet for my sire and brother, twayne I have, there needes no more :
Whom seeke this rufflyng rowt of Feendes with gargell Visage dight?
Where will they deale theyr stripes, or whom with whips of fier smight ?
Or whom with cruell scorching brande and Stygian faggot fell,
With mischief great to cloy, entendes this army black of hell ?
A chopping Adder gan to hisse with wrethings wrapped rounde,
As soone as did the lasshing whyp flerte out with yerking sounde.
Whom bumping with thy rapping post Megæra wilt thou crush ?
Whose ghost doth heere mishapt from hell with scatered members
rush ?
My slaughtred brothers ghost it is that vengeaunce coms to crave :
According to his dyre request due vengeaunce shall hee have.
But flap thou fearce the fierbrandes full dasshed in myne Eyes,
Dig, rent, scrape, burne, and squeas them out, loe ope my breast it lyes,
To fighting furies bobbing strokes, O brother, brother bid
These royles, that preasse to worrey mee, them selves away to rid.
Downe to the silent soules alowe not taking any care :
Let mee be left heare by my selfe alone, and doe not spare
To bast and capperclaw these armes that drewe the bloudy blade :
To quench the furies of thy sprite, that thus doe mee invade,
With this right hand the sacrifice on thaulter shalbe made.
What meanes this sudden trampling noyse ? a band of men in Armes
Come bustling towarde us, that mee will cloy with deadly harmes.
To ende this slaughter set upon I will my selfe convay
Up to the garrets of our house, come Nurce with me away,
Bestow thy body hence with mee from daunger of our foes.
Now thus my mynde on mischiefe set thou must thy selfe dispose,

Let not the flickering fame and prayse in darkenesse bee exilde
Of stomack stout, that you did use in murthering of thy childe.
Proclaime in peoples eares the prayse of cruell bloudy hand.
JA. If any faythfull man here bee, whom ruine of his land,
And slaughter of his Prynce doe cause in pensive heart to bleede,
Step forth that yee may take the wretch that wrought this deadly deede.
Heere, heere, yee joly champions lay loade with weapons heere,
Have now, hoyst up this house, from low Foundacion up it reare.
ME. Now, now my Scepter guilt I have recovered once agayne :
My Fathers wronges revenged are, and eke my brother slayne :
The goulden cattels Fleece returnde is to my native land,
Possession of my realme I have reclaymed to my hand :
Come home is my virginity, that whilom went astray.
O Gods as good as I coulde wisshe, O joyfull wedding day,
Goe shrowde thy selfe in darknesse dim, dispatcht I have this feate:
Yet vengeaunce is not done inough, to coole our thristy heate.
O soule why dost thou make delay? Why dost thou doubting stande?
Goe foreward with it yet thou mayst, whyle doing is thy hande :
The wrath that might should mynister doth qualefy his flame :
The pryckes of sorrow twitch my heart attayne with blusshing shame:
Through rygour of thy heynous gore, O wretch, what hast thou done?
Though I repent a caityfe vile I am, to slea my sonne :
Alas I have committed it, importunate delight,
Still egged on my frowarde mynde that did against it fight :
And loe the vayne conject of this delight increaseth still,
This onely is the thing that wants unto my wicked will,
That Jasons eyes shoulde see this sight as yet I doe suppose,
Nothing it is that I have done, my travell all I lose,
That I employde in dyry deedes, unlesse hee see the same.
JA. Loe heere shee looketh out, and leanes upon the houses frame,
That pitchlong hanges with falling sway : here heape your fiers fast,
Whereby the flames that shee her selfe enkindled, may her wast.
ME. Goe Jason, goe the obit rights the windinge sheete and grave
Make ready for thy sonne, as last behoveth him to have,
Thy spouse and eke thy father in lawe that are entomde by mee
Received have the dutyes that to deade mens ghostes agree.
This childe hath felt the deadly stroke and launch of fatall knife,
And this with wailesome murther like shall lose her tender life.

JA. By all the sacred ghostes of heaven, and by thy oft exile,
And spousall bed, which breach of love in mee did not defile,
Now spare, and save the life of him my childe and also thyne:
What ever cryme committed is, I graunt it to be myne:
Make mee a bloudy sacrifice to dew deserved death,
Take from my sinfull guilty head the use of vitall breath.
ME. Nay sith thou wilt not have it so as greeves thy pynched minde,
Heere way to wreck my vengeaunce fell, my burning blade shall finde.
Avaunt, now hence thou pesaunt prowd employ thy busy payne,
To reape the fruites of virgins bed, and cast them of agayne
When mothers they are made. JA. Let one for dew revenge suffice.
ME. If greedy thyrst of hungry handes that stil for vengeaunce cries,
Myght quenched bee with bloude of one, then aske I none at all,
And yet to staunche my hungry griefe the number is to small,
If onely twayne I slea, if pleadge of love lye secrete made,
My bowels Ile unbreast, and search my wombe with poking Blade.
JA. Now finish out thy deadly deede, that enterprised is,
No more entreataunce will I use, yet onely graunt mee this,
Delay awhyle his dolefull death, that I may take my flyght,
Least that myne eyes with bleeding hearte should vew that heavy sight.
ME. Yet linger eger anguishe yet to slea this chylde of thyne.
Ronne not to rashe with hasty speede, this dolefull day is myne:
The time that wee obtayned have of Creon wee enjoy.
JA. O vile malitious mynded wretch my lothsome life destroy.
ME. In craving this thou speakst, that I should shew thee some releefe,
Well goodinough, all this is done: O ruthfull giddy greefe,
This is the onely sacrifice that I can thee provide,
Unthankfull Jason hether cast thy coyesh lookes asyde.
Loe heare dost thou beholde thy wyfe? thus ever wonted I,
When murther I had made, to scape, my way doth open lye
That I may spring into the skyes: the flying serpents twayne
Submitted have theyr scaly Neckes to yoake of ratling wayne,
Thon Father have thy sonnes agayne, I in the wandring Skye
In nymble wheeled Waggon swyfte, will ryde advaunced hye.
JA. Goe through the ample spaces wyde, infect the poysoned Ayre,
Beare witnesse, grace of God is none in place of thy repayre.

FINIS

THE EIGHTH TRAGEDYE OF L. ANNAEUS SENECA

ENTITULED AGAMEMNON

TRANSLATED OUT OF LATIN INTO ENGLISHE

BY JOHN STUDLEY

THE ARGUMENT

Agamemnon, Generall of that Noble Army of the Greekes, which, after tenne yeares siege wanne Troy, committed the entyer Government of his Countrey and Kingdome (duringe his absence) to his Wyfe Clytemnestra. Who forgetting all Wyvely loyalty, and Womanly chastity, fell in lawelesse love and used adulterus company with Ægysthus, sonne to Thyestes, whom aforetime Atreus being his owne naturall Brother, and Father to this Agamemnon, in reveng of a former adultry had, caused to eate hys owne two Children.

At length, understandinge by Eurybates, that Troy was wonne, and that her husband Agamemnon was comming homewarde with a yonge Lady named Cassandra, daughter to king Priamus : partly enraged with jealousy, and disdaine thereof, and partly loath to loose the company of Ægysthus her Coadulterer, practyzed with him how to murther her husbande. Which accordingly they brought to passe : and not resting so contented, they also put Cassandra to deth, imprisoned Electra Daughter to Agamemnon, and soughte to have slayne his Sonne Orestes. Which Orestes fleeing for savegard of his lyfe to on Strophilus, hys dead Fathers deare friend : was by him secretly kept a longe time, till at length, comming prively into Mycene, and by his Systers meanes conducted where his Mother Clytemnestra and Ægysthus were, in revenge of his Fathers death, killed them both.

THE SPEAKERS NAMES

Thyestes.
Chorus.
Clytemnestra.
Nutrix.
Ægisthus.
Eurybates.
A Company of Greekes.
Cassandra.
Agamemnon.
Electra.
Strophilus.

AGAMEMNON

THE FIRST ACTE

THYESTES

EPARTINGE from the darkned dens which Ditis low doth keepe,
Loe heere I am sent out agayne from Tartar Dungeon deepe,
Thyestes I, that wheather coast to shun doe stande in doubt,
Th' infernall fiendes I fly, the foalke of earth I chase about.
My conscience lo abhors, that I should heather passage make,
Appauled sore with feare and dread my trembling sinewes shake :
My fathers house, or rather yet my brothers I espy,
This is the olde and antique porche of Pelops progeny.
Here first the Greekes on prynces heads doe place the royall crowne,
And heere in throne aloft they lye, that jetteth up and downe,
With stately Scepter in theyr hand, eake heere theyr courts doe ly,
This is theyr place of banquetting, returne therefore will I.
Nay : better were it not to haunt the lothsome Limbo lakes,
Where as the Stygion porter doth advaunce with lusty crakes
His tryple gorge be hong with Mane shag hairy, rusty, blacke :
Where Ixions Carkasse linked fast, the whirling wheele doth racke,
And rowleth still upon him selfe : where as full oft in vayne
Much toyle is lost (the tottring stone down tumbling backe agayne)
Where growing guts the greedy gripe do gnaw with ravening bits.
Where parched up with burning thirst amid the waves he sits,
And gapes to catch the fleeting flood with hungry chaps beguilde,
That payes his paynefull punishment, whose feast the Gods defilde :
Yet that olde man so stept in yeares at length by tract of time,
How great a part belonges to mee and portion of his crime ?

Account wee all the grisly ghostes, whom guilty sounde of ill,
The Gnosian Judge in Plutoes pyts doth tosse in torments still :
Thyestes I in driery deedes will farre surmount the rest,
Yet to my Brother yelde I, (though I gorgde my bloudy brest)
And stuffed have my pampred paunche even with my chyldren three,
That crammed lye within my Rybs and have theyr Toumbe in mee,
The bowels of my swallowed Babes, devowred up I have,
Nor fickle Fortune mee alone the Father doth deprave,
But enterprysing greater guilte then that is put in ure,
To file my Daughters bawdy Bed, my lust shee doth alure.
To speake these words I doe not spare, I wrought the haynous deede,
That therefore I through all my stocke, might parent still proceede.
My Daughter driven by force of Fates and destenyes devyne,
Doth breede younge bones, and lades her wombe, with sinfull seede of myne.
Loe, nature chaunged upside downe, and out of order tornde
This myngle mangle hath shee made, (O fact to be forlornde)
A Father and a Grandsyre loe, confusedly I am,
My daughters husband both become, and Father to the same.
Those babes that should my Nephewes bee, when nature rightly runnes,
She being tumbled doth confounde, and mingle with my sonnes.
The chrystall clearenesse of the day, and Phœbus beames so bryght,
Are myxed with the foggy cloudes, and darkenesse dim of nyght.
When wickednes had wearied us, to late truce taken was,
Even when our detestable deedes were done and brought to passe.
But valiaunt Agamemnon hee graund captayne of the Hoste,
Who bare the sway among the Kinges, and ruled all the roste,
Whose flaunting Flag, and Banner brave, displayde in royall sorte,
A thousand sayle of sowsing ships did garde to Phrygian porte,
And with their swelling shatling sayles the surging seas did hide,
That beateth on the bankes of Troy, and floweth by her side :
When Phœbus Carte the Zodiack ten times had over runne,
And waste the battred Walles doe lye of Troy destroyde and woonne,
Returnde he is to yeelde his throate unto his traytresse Wyfe.
That shall with force of bloudy blade bereve him of his lyfe.

AGAMEMNON

The glytering Swerd, the hewing Axe, and wounding weapons moe, THE
With bloud for bloud new set abroche shall make the floore to flow. FIRST
With sturdy stroke, and boystrous blow, of pithy Pollaxe geven ACTE
His beaten braynes are pasht abroade, his cracked Skull is reven.
Now myschiefe marcheth on a pace, now falshoode doth appeare,
Now Butchers slaughter doth approche, and murther draweth neare.
In honour of thy natyve day Ægisthus they prepare
The sollemne feast with juncketing, and daynty tothsome fare.
Fy, what doth shame abashe thee so, and cause thy courage quayle ?
Why doubts thy righthand what to doe ? to smite why doth it fayle?
What he forecasting might suspect, why shouldst thou take advyse ?
Why frettest thou, demaunding if thou may it enterpryse ?
Nay : if a mother it beseeme, thou rather mayst surmyse.
What now ? how hapneth it that thus the smiling sommers night,
When Phœbus from Th' antipodes shoulde render soone the lyght,
On sudden chaung their turnes with nights that last and lynger longe,
When wynters Boreas bitter blastes, doth puffe the trees amonge ?
Or what doth cause the glyding starres to stay still in the sky ?
Wee wayght for Phœbus : to the Worlde bryng day now by and by.

CHORUS

O Fortune, that dost fayle the great estate of kinges,
On slippery sliding seat thou placest lofty thinges
And setst on tottring sort, where perils do abound
Yet never kingdome calme, nor quiet could be found :
No day to Scepters sure doth shine, that they might say,
To morrow shall wee rule, as wee have done to day.
One clod of croked care another bryngeth in,
One hurly burly done, another doth begin :
Not so the raging Sea doth boyle upon the Sande,
Where as the southern winde that blowes in Afryck Lande,
One Wave upon another doth heape wyth sturdy blast :
Not so doth Euxine Sea, his swelling waves up cast :
Nor so his belching streame from shallow bottom roll,
That borders hard upon the ysy frosen poall :

Where as Bootes bryght doth twyne his Wayne about,
And of the marble seas doth nothing stande in doubt.
O how doth Fortune tosse and tomble in her wheele
The staggring states of Kynges, that readdy bee to reele?
Fayne woulde they dreaded bee, and yet not setled so
When as they feared are, they feare, and lyve in woe.
The silent Lady nyght so sweete to man and beast,
Can not bestow on them her safe and quiet rest:
Sleepe that doth overcome and breake the bonds of griefe,
It cannot ease theyr heartes, nor mynister reliefe:
What castell strongly buylt, what bulwarke, tower, or towne,
Is not by mischyefes meanes, brought topsy turvye downe?
What ramperd walles are not made weake by wicked warre?
From stately courtes of Kings doth justice fly afarre:
In pryncely Pallaces, of honesty the lore,
And wedlocke vowe devout, is let by lytle store.
The bloudy Bellon those doth haunt with gory hand,
Whose light and vaine conceipt in paynted pomp doth stand.
And those Erinnys wood turmoyles with frensyes fits,
That ever more in proud and hauty houses sits,
Which ficle Fortunes hand in twinkling of an eye,
From high and proude degre drives downe in dust to lye.
Although that skyrmishe cease, no banners be displayed
And though no wyles be wroughte, and pollecy be stayed,
Downe paysed with theyr waight the massy things do sinke,
And from her burden doth unstable Fortune shrynke.
The swelling Sayles puft up with gale of westren wynde,
Doe yet mystrust thereof a tempest in theyr mynde:
The threatning tops (that touch the cloudes) of lofty towres
Bee sonest payde, and bet with south wynde rainy showres:
The darksome woode doth see his tough and sturdy Oke,
Well waynde in yeares to be cleane overthrown and broke:
The lyghtnings flashing flame out breaking in the Sky,
First lyghteth on the mounts, and hilles that are most hy.
The bodies corpulent and of the largest syse
Are ryfest styll to catch diseases when they ryse.
When as the flocke to grase, in pasture fat is put,
Whose Necke is larded best, his throate shall first be cut:

What Fortune doth advaunce and hoysteth up on hye,
Shee sets it up to fall agayne more greevously.
The thinges of midle sort, and of a meane degree,
Endure above the rest and longest dayes do see :
The man of meane estate most happy is of all,
Who pleased with the lot that doth to him befall,
Doth sayle on silent shore with calme and quiet tide,
And dreads with bruised barge on swelling Seas to ryde :
Nor launcing to the depe where bottom none is found,
May with his rudder search, and reach the shallow ground.

THE SECOND ACTE

CLYTEMNESTRA. NUTRIX

DROWSIE dreaming doting soule, what commeth in thy brayne
To seeke about for thy defence what way thou mayst attayne ?
What ayels thy skittish waiward wits, to waver up and downe ?
The fittest shift prevented is, the best path overgrowne
Thou mightest once mayntayned have thy wedlocke chamber chast,
And eake have ruld with majesty, by fath conjoyned fast :
Now nurtures lore neglected is, all ryght doth clean decay,
Religion and dignity with faith are worne away.
And ruddy shame with blushing cheekes so farre god wot is past,
That when it would it cannot now come home againe at last.
O let me now at randon runne with bridle at my will :
The safest path to mischiefe is by mischiefe open still.
Now put in practise, seeke aboute, search out and learne to find
The wylie traynes, and crafty guyles of wicked womankind :
What any divelish trayterous dame durst do in working woe,
Or any wounded in her wits by shot of Cupids bowe.
What ever rigorous stepdame could commit with desperat hand,
Or as the wench who flaming fast by Venus poysoning brand,
Was driven by leud incestuous love in ship of Thessail land,
To flit away from Colchos yle, where Phasis channel deepe,
With silver streame downe from the hylles of Armenie doth sweepe.
Get weapons good, get bylbowblades or temper poyson strong,
Or with some yonker trudge from Grece by theft the seas along :
Why dost thou faynt to talke of theft, exile or privie flight ?
These came by hap, thou therfore must on greatter mischiefe light.

THE SECOND ACTE

NUT. O worthy Queene amonge the Greekes that beares the swinging sway,
And borne of Ledas royall bloud, what muttring dost thou say?
What fury fel inforceth thee, bereaved of thy wits,
To rage and rave with bedlam braynes, to fret with franticke fittes?
Though madam thou do counsayle keepe, and not complayne thy case,
Thyne anguish playn appeareth in thy pale and wanny face.
Reveale therfore what is thy griefe, take leasure good and stay,
What reason could not remedy, oft cured hath delay.
CLIT. So grievous is my careful case which plungeth me so sore,
That deale I cannot with delay, nor linger any more.
The flashing flames and furious force of fiery fervent heate,
Outraging in my boyling brest, my burning bones doth beate:
It suckes the sappy marow out the juice it doth convay,
It frets, it teares, it rents, it gnaws, my guttes and gall away.
Now feble feare stil egges mee on (with dolor beyng prest)
And cankred hate with thwacking thumpes doth bounce upon my brest.
The blynded boy that lovers hartes doth reave with deadly stroake,
Entangled hath my linked mynd with leawd and wanton yoke:
Refusing stil to take a foyle, or cleane to be confound:
Among these broyles, and agonies my mynd beseging round,
Loe feble, weary, batred downe, and under troden shame,
That wrestleth, striveth, strugleth hard, and fighteth with the same.
Thus am I driven to divers shores and beat from banke to banke,
And tossed in the fomy floods that strives with corage cranke.
As when here wynd, and their the streame when both their force wil try,
From sandes alow doth hoyst and reare the seas with surges hye.
The waltring wave doth staggeryng stand not weting what to do,
But (hoveryng) doubtes, whose furious force he best may yeld him to
My kingdome therfore I cast of, my sceptor I forsake,
As anger, sorrow, hope, me leade, that way I meane to take.
At all adventure to the seas I yeld my beaten Barge,
At randon careles wil I runne, now wil I rove at large
Whereas my mynde to fancy fond dath gad and runne astray,
It is the best to chuse that chaunce, and follow on that way.

NU. This desprat dotage doth declare, and rashnes rude and blynde,
To chuse out chaunce to be the guyde and ruler of thy mynd.
CLI. He that is driven to utter pinch and furthest shift of all,
What neede he doubt his doubtful lot or how his lucke befall ?
NUT. In silent shore thou saylest yet thy trespas we may hyde,
If thou thy selfe detect it not, nor cause it be descryde.
CL. Alas it is more blasd abroade, and further it is blowen,
Then any cryme that ever in this princely court was sowen.
NU. Thy former falt with pensive hart and sorrow thou dost rew.
And fondly yet thou goest about, to set abroch a newe.
CL. It is a very folishnes to kepe a meane therein.
NU. The thing he feares he doth augment who heapeth sinne to sinne.
CLI. But fire and swoard to cure the same the place of salve supply.
NU. There is no man who at the first extremity wil trye.
CL. In working mischiefe men do take the rediest way they fynde.
NU. The sacred name of wedlocke once revoke and have in mynd.
CLI. Ten yeares have I bene desolate, and led a widowes life,
Yet shall I entertayne a new my husband as his wyfe ?
NU. Consider yet thy sonne and heire whom he of thee begot.
CLY. And eake my daughters wedding blase as yet forget I not.
Achilles eke my sonne in law to mynd I do not spare,
How wel he kept his vow that he to me his mother sware.
NU. When as our navy might not passe by wynd nor yet by streame,
Thy daughters bloud in sacrifyce their passage did redeme :
Shee sturd and brake the sluggish seas, whose water stil did stand,
Whose feble force might not hoyse up the vessels from the land.
CL. I am ashamed herewithal, it maketh me repyne,
That Tyndaris (who from the Gods doth fetch her noble ligne)
Should geve the ghost t' asswage the wrath of Gods and them appease,
Wherby the Grekish navy might have passage free by seas.
My grudging mynd stil harpes uppon my daughters wedding day,
Whom he hath made for Pelops stock the bloudy raunsome pay.
When as with cruel countenaunce embrewd with gory bloud,
As at a wedding alter syde th' unpitiful parent stoode,
It erked Calchas woful hart, who did abhorre the same,
His Oracle he rewd, and eke the backe reflicting flame :

O wicked and ungracious stocke that winnest il with yll,
Tryumphing in thy filthy feats encreasyng leaudnes still.
By bloud we win the waveryng windes, by death wee purchase warre.
NU. But by this meanes a thousand ships at once released are :
CLY. With lucky fate attempt the seas did not the losed rout ?
For Aulis Ile, th' ungracious fleete from port did tumble out :
As with a lewde unlucky hand the warre he did beginne,
So Fortune favored his successe to thrive no more therin.
Her love as captive holdeth him whom captive he did take,
Not moved with the earnest suite that could Achilles make,
Of Phœbus prelat Sminthicall he did retayne the spoyle :
When for the sacred virgins love his furious breast doth boyle :
Achilles rough and thundring threats could not him qualify.
Nor he that doth direct the fates above the starry skye.
To us he is an Augur juste, and keepes his promise due,
But while he threats his captive truls of word he is not true.
The savage people fierce in wrath once might not move his spright,
Who did purloyne the kindled tentes with fyer blasing bryght :
When slaughter great on Greekes was made in most extreamest fyght
Without a foe he conquered, with leanes pines awaye,
In lewd and wanton chamber trickes he spends the idle day,
And freshly still he fedes his lust, least that some other while
His chamber chast should want a stewes, that might the same defile.
On Lady Brises love againe his fancy fonde doth stand,
Whom he hath got, that wrested was out of Achilles hand.
And carnal copulation to have he doth not shame,
Though from her husbands bosome he hath snacht the wicked dame.
Tushe, he that doth at Paris grudge, with wound but newly stroke
Eflamd with Phrygian Prophets love, his boyling brest doth smoke.
Now after Troyan boties brave, and Troy orewhelm'd he saw,
Retourned he is a prysoners spouse, and Pryams sonne in law.
Now heart be bold, take corage good, of stomacke now be stowt,
A field that easely is not fought, to pitch thou goest about.
In practise mischiefe thou must put, why hopst thou for a day,
While Priams daughter come from Troy in Grece do beare the swaye ?
But as for the poore sely wreth, a wayteth at thy place
Thy wyddow, virgyns, and Orest his fatherlyke in face,

Consyder theyr calamityes to come, and eake their cares,
Whom all the peril of the broyle doth threat in thy affayres.
O cursed captive, woful wretch, why dost thou loyter so ?
Thy little brats a stepdame have whose wrath wil worke their woe.
With gashing sword (and if thou can none other way provide)
Nor thrust it through anothers ribbes then launch thy gory syde,
So murther twayne with brewed bloud, let bloud immixed be,
And by destroying of thy selfe destroy thy spouse with thee.
Death is not sawst with soppes of Sorrow if some man els I have,
Whose breathlesse corse I wish to passe with me to deadly grave.
NU. Queene, brydle thyne affections, and wysely rule thy rage,
Thy swelling moode now mittigate, thy choller eake asswage.
Way wel the wayghty enterpryse that thou dost take in hand,
Tryumphant victor he returnes of mighty Asia land :
Avenging Europes injury with him he bringes away
The spoyles of sacked Pargamy a huge and mighty pray.
In bondage eake he leades the foalke of long assaulted Troy,
Yet darest thou by pollecie attempt him to annoy ?
Whom with the dynt of glittring sword Achilles durst not harme,
Although his rash and desperat dickes the froward Knight did arme :
Nor Ajax yet more hardy man up yelding vitall breath,
Whom frantike fury fell enforst to wound himselfe to death :
Nor Hector he whose onely life procurde the Greekes delay,
And long in warre for victory enforced them to stay :
Nor Paris shaft, whose conning hand with shot so sure did ayme :
Nor mighty Memnon swart and blacke, had power to hurt the same :
Nor Xanthus flood, where to and fro deade carkasses did swimme,
With armour hewd and therewithall some maymed broken limme :
Nor Symois, that purple wawmes with slaughter died doth steare.
Nor Cygnus lilly whyte, the Sonne of fenny God so deare :
Nor yet the musteryng Thrasian host : nor warlike Rhesus kinge :
Nor Amazons, who to the warres did paynted Quivers bring,
And bare theyr hatches in their handes with Target and with shield,
Yet had no powre with ghastly wound to foyle him in the field.
Syth he such scouringes hath escapt and plungde of perilles past,
Entendest thou to murther him returning home at last ?
And sacred alters to prophane with slaughters so unpure ?
Shal Greec thadvenger let this wronge long unrevengde endure

The grym and fearce coragious horse, the battayles, shoutes, and cryes,
The swelling seas which bruised barkes do dread when stormes aryse,
Behold the fieldes with streames of bloud oreflowne and depely dround,
And al the chevalry of Troy in servile bandage bounde,
Which Greekes have writ in registers. Thy stubborne stomacke bynd,
Subdue thy fond affections, and pacify thy mynde.

THE SECOND SCENE

ÆGYSTHUS. CLYTEMNESTRA

THE cursed tyme that evermore my mynd did most detest,
The dayes that I abhorred have and hated in my breast,
Are come, are come, that myne estate wil bring to utter wracke :
Alas my hart why dost thou fayle, and faynting flyest backe ?
What dost thou meane at first assalte from armour thus to flye,
Trust this, the cruel Gods entend my doleful destenie,
To wrap thee in with perils round and catch thee in a band ?
Endever drudge with all thy power their plagues for to withstand :
With stomacke stoute rebellious to fyre and sword appeale.
CLI. It is no plague, if such a death thy native destnies deale.
ÆG. (O partner of my perils all begot of Leda thou)
Direct thy doynges after myne, and unto thee I vow,
This drosel sluggish ringleader, this stout strong harted sire,
Sal pay thee so much bloud agayne as shed he hath in fyre.
How haps it that his trembling cheekes to be so pale and whight,
Lying agast as in a traunce with faynting face upright.
CL. His conscience wedlocke vow doth pricke and bringes him home again,
Let us returne the selfe same trade a new for to retayne,
To which at first we should have stucke and ought not to forsake,
To covenaunt continent a new let us our selves betake :
To take the trade of honesty at no tyme is to late :
He purged is from punishment whose hart the cryme doth hate.

THE EIGHTH TRAGEDY

Æg. Why whither wilt thou gad (o rash and unadvysed dame ?)
What dost thou earnestly beleeve, and firmly trust the same,
That Agamemnons spousall bed wil loyall be to thee ?
That nought doth underprop thy mynd which might thy terrour bee?
His proud successe puft up to high with lucky blast of wynde,
Might make so cranke, and set aloft his hawty swelling mynd :
Among his peares he stately was ere Troyan turrets torne,
How thinke ye then his stomacke stoute, by nature geven to scorne,
In haughtines augmented is more in himselfe to joy,
Throughe this triumphant victory and conquest got of Troy ?
Before his voyage Miceane King most mildly did he raygne,
But now a Tyrant truculent returnd he is agayne.
Good lucke and proude prosperity do make his hart so ryse.
With what great preparation prepared solemne wyse,
A rabblement of strumpets come that clong about him al ?
But yet the Prophetesse of Thebe (whom God of truth we call)
Appeares above the rest : she keepes the King, shee doth him guyde :
Wilt thou in wedlocke have a mate and not for it provyde ?
So would not shee, the greattest greefe this is unto a wyfe,
Her husbandes minion in her house to leade an open life.
A Queenes estate cannot abyde her peere with her to raygne,
In jelous wedlocke wil not her companion sustayne.
Cl. Ægist in desprat moode agayn why setst thou mee a flote ?
Why kindlest thou the sparkes of yre in imbers covered hot
If that the victors owne free will release his captives care,
Why may not I his Lady spouse have hope as wel to fare ?
One law doth rule in royal throne, and pompous princelye Towres,
Among the vulgar sorte, another in private simple bowers.
What though my grudging fancy force that at my husbandes hand,
Sharpe execution of the law I stubbernly withstande ?
Recording this that haynously offended him I have :
He gently wil me pardon graunt who neede the same to crave ?
Æg. Even so on this condition thou mayst with him compound,
To pardon him if he agayne to pardon the be bounde.
The subtil science of the law, the statutes of our land,
(That long agoe decreed were) thou dost not understand.
The Judges be malicious men, they spyght and envye us,
But he shal have them partiall his causes to discus.

This is the chiefest priviledge that doth to Kinges belong.
What lawes forbiddeth other men, they doe, and doe no wronge.
CLY. He pardned Helen, she is wed to Menela agayne
Which Europe all with Asia did plunge alike in payne.
ÆG. No Ladies Lust hath ravisht yet Atrides in his life,
Nor privily purloyned his hart betrothed to his wyfe.
To picke a quarrel he beginnes and matter thee to blame,
Suppose thou nothing hast commit that worthy is of shame ?
What boteth him whom Princes hate an honest life to frame ?
He never doth complayne his wrong, but ever beares the blame.
Wilt thou repayre to Spart and to thy countrey trudge aryght ?
Wilt thou become a ronnagate from such a worthy wight ?
Devorcement made from Kinges wil not so let the matter scape,
Thou easest feare by fickle hope, that falsly thou dost shape :
CLI. My trespas is disclosd to none, but to a trusty wight :
ÆG. At princes gates fidelity yet never enter might.
CL. I wil corrupt and feede him so with silver and with gold,
That I by bribing bynd him shall no secrets to unfold :
ÆG. The trust that hyred is and bought by brybes and moneis fee,
Thy counsell to bewray agayne with brybes entyste will be.
CL. The remnaunt left of shamefastnes of those ungracious trickes,
Wherin of late I did delyght, my conscience freshly prickes.
Why kep'st thou such a busie sturre and with thy flatring speach
Enstructing me with lewd advyse dost wicked counsell preach ?
Shall I forsooth of royall bloud with al the speede I can
Refuse the King of Kinges, and wed an outcast banisht man ?
ÆG. Why should you thinke in that Thiest was father unto mee.
And Agamemnon Atreus sonne he should my better be ?
CLY. If that be but a tryfle small, and nephew to the same.
ÆG. I am of Phœbus linage borne, wherof I do not shame.
CL. Why makste thou Phœbus author of thy wicked pedagrew,
Whom out of heaven ye forst to flye when bridle backe he drew,
When Lady Night with mantel blacke did spread her sodin shade,
Why makest thou the Gods in such reproachfulnes to wade ?
Whose father hath thee conning made by sleight and subtil guyle
To make thy kinsman Cockold whyle his wyfe thou do defyle.
What man is he whom we do know to be thy fathers mate,
Abusing lust of Lechery in such unlawful rate ?

Avaunt, go packe thee hence in hast, dispatch out of my sight
This infamy, whose blemish staynes this bloud of worthy wyght.
ÆG. This is no new exile to me that wickednes do haunt,
But if that thou (O worthy Queene) commaund me to avaunt,
I wil not only strayght avoyde the house, the towne, and field,
My life on sword at thy request I ready am to yeeld.
CLI. This heynous dede permit shall I (most churlish cruell drab)
Agaynst my wil though I offend, the fault I should not blabbe :
Nay, rather come apart with mee, and let us joyne our wittes
To wrap our selves out of this woe and parlous threatning fits.

CHORUS

How chaunt it lusty laddes, Apollos prayse subborne,
To thee the frolicke flocke their crowned heads adorne.
To thee King Inachs stocke of wedlocke chamber voyde,
Brayd out their virgins lockes and theron have employd
Theyr savory garlandes greene Itwist of laurell bow.
Draw neare with us, O Thebes, our dauncing follow thou.
Come also ye that drinck of Ismen bubling flood,
Wheras the Laurell tree ful thicke on bankes doth bood.
Eake ye whom Mando mild, the Prophetesse divine,
(Foreseyng fate) and borne of high Tiresias lygne,
Hath stird to celebrate with sacred use and right.
Appollo and Dian borne of Latona bright.
O Victor Phæbe unbend thy noked bow agayne,
Syth quietnes and peace anew we do retayne.
And let thy twanckling harpe make melody so shril,
Whyle that thy nimble hand stryke quavers with thy quill.
No curious descant I nor lusty musick crave,
No jolly rumbling note, nor trouling tune to have.
Bur on thy treble Lute (according to thy use)
Stryke up a playnsong note as when thy learned muse
Thy lessons do record, though yet on baser string
It lyketh thee to play the song that thon did singe :
As when from fyery heaven the dint of lightning flue,
Sent downe by wrath of Gods the Titans overthrew,

Or else when mountaynes were on mountaynes heaped hie
That rayse for Giauntes fell theyr steppes into the skye,
The mountayne Osla stoode on top of Pelion layd,
Olymp (wheron the Pynes theyr budding braunches braide)
Downe paised both : drawe nere O Juno noble dame,
Both spouse of mighty Jove and sister to the same.
Thou that dost rule with him made joynter of his mace,
Thy people we of Grece geve honor to thy grace :
Thou onely dost protect from perilles Argos land,
That ever careful was to have thyne honour stand,
Most supplient thereunto thou also with thy might
Dost order joyful peace and battails fearce of fyght
Accept O conquering Queene these braunches of the bayes
That Agamemnon here doth yeld unto thy prayse :
The hollow boxen pype (that doth with holes abound)
In synging unto the doth geve a solemne sound :
To thee the Damsels eake that play uppon the stringes,
With conning harmony melodious musicke singes.
The matrons eke of Greece by ryper years more grave,
To these the Taper pay that vowed oft they have,
The Heyferd young and whyte companion of the Bull.
Unskilful yet by proofe the paynful plow to pull.
Whose neck was never worne nor gald with print of yoke,
Is in thy temple slaine receiving deadly stroke.
O Lady Pallas thou of most renoumed hap
Bred of the brayne of Jove that smites with thunder clap,
Thou lofty Troian towres of craggy knotty flint
Hast bet with battring blade, and stroke with javeling dint :
The elder matrones with the dames that yonger be
Together in myngled heapes do honour due to thee,
When thou approching nighe thy comming is espyde,
The priest unbarres the gate, and opes the Temple wide :
By clustring thronges the flocks thine altars haunt apace,
Bedeckte with twisted crownes so trim with comely grace.
The olde and auncient men well stept and grown in yeares,
Whose feeble trembling age procureth hory hayres,
Obtayning their request crav'de of thy grace devine,
Do offer up to thee their sacrifysed wyne,

O bright Dian whose blase sheds light three sondry waies
We myndful are of thee, and render thankefull prayse,
Delon thy native soyle thou diddest fyrmely bynde,
That to and fro was wont to wander with the wynde :
Which with foundation sure mayn ground forbyds to passe
For Navies (after which to swim it wonted was)
It is become a road defying force of wynd,
The mothers funeralles of Tantalus his kinde.
The daughters seven by death thou victresse dost accompt
Whose mother Niobe abydes on Sipil mount
A lamentable rocke and yet unto this howre
Her teares new gushing out the marble old doth powre.
The Godhead of the Twins in sumpteous solemne wyse,
Both man and wyfe adore with savory sacrifyce.
But thee above the rest O father great and guide,
Whose mighty force is by the burning lightning tryde :
Who when thou gavest a becke and didst thy head but shake
At once thextremest poales of heaven and earth did quake,
O Jupiter the roote that of our lynage arte,
Accept these offered gifts and take them in good parte :
And thou O graundsire great to thy posteritie
Have some remorse, that do not swarve in chyvalrie.
But yonder lo with stiving steps the souldier comes amayne
In all post hast, with token that good newes declareth plaine,
A Lawrell braunch, that hangeth on his speare head he doth bringe
Eurybates is come, who hath ben trusty to the kynge.

AGAMEMNON

THE THIRD ACTE

EURIBATES. CLYTEMNESTRA

ORE tyred after many yeares with travayle and wyth toyle,
Scant credityng my selfe, the Gods of thys my natyve soyle,
The temple, and the alters of the saincts that rule the skye,
In humble sort wyth reverence devoutly worship I.
Now pay your vowes unto the Gods : returned is agayne
Unto his countrey court, where wont he was to rule, and reigne,
Prynce Agamemnon, victor he, of Grece the great renoume.
CLY. The tydings of a message good unto mine eares is blowne.
Where stayes my spouse whom longing for ten yeres I have out scand ?
What doth he yet sayle on the seas, or he is come a land ?
Yet hath he fyxt and set his foote back stepping home agayne
Uppon the sandy shore, that longe he wished to attayne ?
And doth he styll enjoy his health enhauncte in glory great,
And painted out in pompe of prayes whose fame the sky doth beate ?
EU. Blesse we with burning sacrifice at length this lucky day.
CLI. And eke the Gods though gracious, yet dealing long delay :
Declare if that my brothers wyfe enjoy the vytall ayre,
And tel me to what kind of Coast my sister doth repayre.
EURI. God graunt, and geve us better newes then this that thou dost crave,
The heavy hap of fyghting flouds forbiddes the truth to have :
Our scattred fleete the swelling seas attemptes in such a plight,
That ship from ship was taken cleane out of each others sight.
Atrides in the waters wyde tormoyld and straying farre
More vyolence by seas sustaynd then by the bloudy warre,

And as it were a conquerd man escaping home al weete
Now bringeth in his company of such a mighty fleete,
A sort of brused broken barkes, beshaken, torne, and rent.
CLI. Shew what unlucky chaunce it is that hath our navy spent,
What storme of seas dipersed hath our Captaynes hear and there.
EURY. Thou willest me to make report of heavy woful geare.
Thou biddest me most greevous newes with tydinges good to part
For uttring of this woeful hap my feeble mynd doth start,
And horribly appauled is with this so monstruous ill.
CLY. Speake out and utter it : himselfe with terrour he doth fill
Whose hart his owne calamity and carke doth loath to know :
The hart whom doubted domage dulles with greater griefe doth glow.
EU. When Troyan buildings blasing bright did burne away and broyle,
Enkindled first by Grekish brand, they fall to part the spoyle :
Repayring fast unto the seas agayne we come aboord,
And now the souldiers weary loynes were eased of his sword,
Their bucklers cast aside, uppon the hatches lie above.
Their warlike handes in practise put, and Oers learne to move :
Ech little hindraunce seemes to much to them in hasty plight,
When of recourse the Admirall gave watchword by his light,
And trumpet blast beganne to cal our army from delay,
The paynted Pup with gilded snowt did first guyde on the way
And cut the course, which following on a thousand shippes did ryve,
Then first a wynd with pipling puffes our launcing ships did dryve,
Which glyded downe upon our sayles the water beyng calme
With breath of westerne wynd so myld scant moved any walme.
The shyning seas bespred about with shippes doth glister bright,
And also coverd with the same lay hid from Phœbus lyght :
It doth us good to gase uppon the naked shore of Troy :
The desart Phrygian plots so bare to vew wee hop for joye :
The yeuth each one besturres themselves, and striking altogeather,
They tough their oers and with their toyle they helpe the wynd and weather :
They tug and chearely row by course, the spirting seas up dash,
Agaynst the ratling ribs of ships the flapping floods do flash,
The hory froth of wrestling waves which ores aloft doth rayse,
Do draw and trace a furrow through the marblefaced seas.

When stronger blast with belly swolne our hoysted sayles did fil,
They row no more, but let the Pup to goe with wynd at wil,
Their sheryng oers layd assyde our Pilot doth espye,
How farre from any land aloofe our sayles reculing flye.
Or bloudy battels doth display the threats of Hector stout,
Or of his ratling waggings tels, wherein he rode about.
Or how his gashed carkas slayne and traynd about the field
To funeral flames and obit rightes for coyne agayne was yeld.
How Jupiter embathed was al in his royall bloud.
The frolicke fish disposed was to mirth in Tyrren floud,
And fetching friskes both in and out playes on the waters brim,
And on his broade and fynny backe about the seas doth swim,
With gambals quicke in ringes around and side to side enclynd,
Erwhyle he sportes afront the pup, and whips agayne behynd,
Now sidling on the snout before the dalying wanton route
With jocundary joly tryckes doth skip the fleete about.
Sometyme he standeth gasing on and eyes the vessels bright,
Now every shore is covered cleane, and land is out of sight,
The parlous poynt of Ida rocke in sight doth open lye,
And that alone espie we could with fyrmly fixed eye,
A duskye clowde of stifling smoake from Troy did smolter blacke,
When Titan from the weary neckes the heavy yokes did slacke.
The fading light did groveling bend, and downe the day did shrowd,
Agaynst the Starres amounting up a litle misty clowde
Came belching out in yrksome lompe, and Phœbus galland beams
He spewd uppon, bestayning them duct downe in Westerne streams.
The Sunne set swarving in such sort with divers chaunge of face,
Did geve us cause to have mistrust of Neptunes doubted grace,
The evening first did burnish bright, and paynt with starres the sky,
The wyndes were layed, and cleane forsooke our sayles that quiet lie,
When cracking, ratling, rumbling noyse, rusht down with thundring sway
From top of hills, which greatter sturre doth threaten and bewraye.
With bellowinges, and yellinges lowde, the shores do grunt and grone,
The craggy clyves and roaring rocks do howle in hollow stone.
The bubling waters swelles upreard before the wrastling wynd,
When sodaynly the lowring light of Mone is hid and blynd.

The glymsing starres do goe to glade, the surging seas are tost
Even to the skyes among the clowdes the light of heaven is lost
More nightes in one compacted are with shadow dim and blacke,
One shadow upon another doth more darknes heape and packe,
And every sparke of light consum'd the waves and skyes do meete,
The ruffling windes range on the seas, through every coast they flit.
They heave it up with violence, oreturnde from bottom low,
The westerne wynd flat in the face of Easterne wynd doth blow.
With hurley burley Boreas set ope his blasting mouth,
And girdeth out his boysteous breth agaynst the stormy south,
Each wynd with al his might doth blow and worketh daungers deepe,
They shake the floods, a sturdy blast along the seas do sweepe,
That rolles and tumbles wave on wave, a northern tempest stronge,
Aboundance great of flacky snow doth hurle our shippes amonge.
The southwynd out of Libia, doth rage uppon a shold,
And with the puissant force therof the quicksandes up be rold,
Nor bydeth in the south which doth with tempest lumpe and lower,
And force the flowing floods to rise by powring out a shower.
The stubberne Eurus, Earthquakes made, and shoke the countries East,
And Eos cost where Phœbus first aryseth from his rest.
How violent Corus stretcht and tare his yawning breast ful wyde ?
A man would sure have thought the world did from his center slyde,
And that the frames of Heaven broke up the Gods adowne would fall
And Chaos darke confused heape would shade and cover all.
The streame strave with the wynd, the wynd dyd beare it downe againe.
The springing sea within his bankes can not it selfe contayne,
The raging showre his trilling droppes doth mingle with the seas,
And yet in all this misery the fynd not so much ease
To see and know what ill it is that worketh theyr decay.
The darknes dim oppresseth still and keepes the light away :
The blackfacst night with Hellicke hue was clad of Stygian lake,
And yet ful oft with glimsing beames the sparkling fyre out brake,
The clowde doth cracke, and beyng rent the lightning leapeth out,
The wretches like the same so well it shyning them about,
That stil they wish such light to have (although God wot but yll)
The navy swaying downe it selfe doth cast away, and spill.

One side with other side is crackt, and helme is rent with helme,
The ship it selfe the gulping seas do headlong overwhelme.
Erwhyle a greedy gaping gulph doth sup it up amayne,
Then by and by tost up aloft it spewes it out againe,
She with her swagging full of sea to bottome lowe doth sinke,
And drencheth deepe asyde in floods her totring broken brinke
That underneath a dosen waves lay drowned out of sight,
Her broken plankes swim up and downe, spoyld is her tackle quight,
Both sayle and Oers cleane are lost, the mayne mast eke is gone
That wonted was to beare upright the sayle yard thereuppon,
The timber and the broken bordes lye on the waters brim,
When cold and shivering feare in us doth strike through every lim,
The wysest wits entocksicate dare nothing enterprise,
And cunning practise naught avayles when feareful stormes aryse,
The mareners letting duty slip stand staring all agast,
Their scoping ores sodaynly out of their handes are wrast.
To prayer then apace we fall, when other hope is none,
The Greekes and Troyans to the Gods alyke do make their mone.
Alacke what succour of the fates may wee poore wretches fynd ?
Agaynst his father Pyrrhus beares a spyteful cankred mynd,
At Ajax grudge Ulisses doth, king Menela doth hate
Great Hector : Agamemnon is with Priam at debate.
O happy man is he that doth lye slayne in Troyan ground,
And hath deservde by handy stroake to take his fatall wound,
Whom fame preserveth, taking up his tombe in conquerd land
Those momes whose melting cowardes hart durst never take in hand
Or enterprise no noble acte, those force of floods shall drowne
But fate forbearing long, wil take stoute Brutes of high renoume,
Ful wel we may ashamed be, in such a sort to dye,
If any man his spyteful mynd yet can not satisfye,
With these outragious plunging plagues that downe from Gods are sent,
Appease at length thy wrathful God agayne and eake relent.
Even Troy for pity would have wept to see our woefull case,
But if that in thy boyling breast black rancour still have place,
And that the Greekes to ruin run, it bee thy purpose bent,
Why doe these Troyans goe to wrack? for whom thus are wee spent?

Asswage the rygour of the sea that threatning hilles up reares :
This drenched Fleete the Troyan folke and Greekes together beares.
Then from theyr prayers are they put, theyr foultring tonges doe stay,
The roring seas doth drowne their voyce and caryes their cries away.
Then mighty Pallas armed with the lepping lightning fyre,
That teasty Jove doth use to hurle provokt to swelling yre,
With threatning Javeling in her hand, her prowesse meanes to try,
And eke her force whose boyling breast with Gorgon fits doth fry,
Or what with Target she can doe, and with her Fathers fyre.
Then from the Skyes another storme begins abroade to spyre,
But Ajax nothing yet dismaide all force withstandeth stout,
Whom when hee spred his swelling sayles with Cable stretched out,
The lightning downe did wryng him hard, and wrapt him in her flame,
And flang another flasshing dint of lightning on the same,
With all her force and violence her hand brought back agayne,
She tost him out, as late that feate her father tought her playne
Both over Ajax and his Pup she flyeth overthwart,
And renting man and shyp, of both shee beares away a part,
His corage nought abated yet hee all to singde doth seeme,
Even like a stubberne ragged Rocke amid the striving streame,
Hee traynes along the roaring seas and eke the waltring wave
By shoving on his bourly breast in sunder quite he drave,
The Barke with hand he caught, and on it selfe did rype it over,
Yet Ajax shyneth in the floud which darknesse blinde doth cover.
At length attayning to a rocke his thundring crakes were these,
I conquered have the force of fyre and rage of fighting seas,
It doth mee good, to mayster thus the anger of the skye,
With Pallas wrath, the lightning flames and floods tumultyng hye.
The terrour of the warlyck god once could not make me flye,
The force of Mars and Hector both at once sustaynd have I.
Nor Phœbus dartes could me constrayne from him one foote to shoon,
All these beside the Phrygians subdued we have, and woon.
When other Mecocks flinges his darts shall I not them withstand ?
Yea, what if Phœbus came himselfe, to pytch them with his hand ?
When in hys melancholy moode he boasted without meane,
Then father Neptune lyft his heat above the waters cleane.

The beaten rocke with forked mace he undermyning pluckte
From bottom loose, and suncke it downe, when downe himself he duckt.
There Ajax lay, by land, by fyre, and storme of seas destroid,
But we by suffering shypwrack, are with greater plagues anoyd.
A subtyle shallow floud there is flowne on a stony shold,
Where crafty Caphar out of syght the lurking rocks doth hold,
Uppon whose sharpe and ragged tops the swelling tide doth flow,
The boyling waves do beat thereon still sweaing to and fro.
A turret nodding over it doth hange with fallyng sway,
From whence on either side from height prospect espy wee may
Two seas: and on this hand the coast where Pelops once did raygne,
And Isthmus floud in narrow creeke, reculing back agayne,
Doth stop Ionian sea, least into Hellespont it run,
On th' other part is Lemnon floud that fame by bloudshed woon
On th' other side Calcedon towne doth stand agaynst this forte,
And Aulis Ile that stayde our ships that thyther did resorte.
This Castell heere inhabyte doth our Palimedes sier,
Whose cursed hand helde in the top a brand of flaming fier
That did alure our fleete, to turne on lurking rockes a ryght,
Entysing them with wily blaze to come unto the lyght.
All into fitters shaken are the vessels on the sholde,
But other some doe swym, and some upon the rockes are roulde.
And other slipping backe agayne so to eschew the Rocks,
His brused Rybs and ratling sides agaynst eche other knocks,
Whereby the other hee doth breake, and broken is himselfe.
Then woulde they launce into the deepe, for now they dread the shelfe,
This peck of troubles chaunct to hap in dawning of the day.
But when the Gods (besought of us) began the rage to stay,
And Phœbus golden beames began a freshe to render lyght,
The dolefull day discried all the domage done by nyght.
CLY. O whether may I now lament, and weepe with wayling sad?
Or shall I els in that my Spouse returned is bee glad?
I doe rejoyce, and yet I am compelled to bewayle
My countreyes great calamity that doth the same assayle.
O Father great whose majesty doth thundring Scepters shake,
The lowring Gods unto the Greekes now favourable make,

With garlands greene let every head rejoysing now be crounde,
To thee the pype in sacryfice melodiously doth sounde,
And on thyne aulter lyeth slayne an Heyferd lilly whight,
Before the same doe present stand with hanging lockes undight,
A carefull Troyan company in heavy wofull plight,
On whom from high the Lawrell tree with spredding braunch doth
shyne,
Whose vertue hath inspyred them with Phœbus grace divine.

CHORUS. CASSANDRA

Alas the cruell sting of love how sweetely doth it taste,
A misery to mortall man annext whyle lyfe doth last?
The pathe of mischiefe for to flye, now sith there is a gap,
And wretched soules be franckly calde from every wofull hap,
By death, a pleasaunt port, for aye in rest them selves to shroude,
Where dreadfull tumultes never dwell nor stormes of Fortune
proude:
Nor yet the burning firy flakes of Jove the same doth doubt,
When wrongfully with thwacking thumpes he raps his thunder out:
Heere Lady Peace th' inhabitours doth never put in flight,
Nor yet the victors threatning wrath approching nygh to sight,
No whyrling western wynde doth urge the ramping seas to praunce,
No dusty cloude that raysed is by savage Dimilaunce,
On horseback riding rancke by rancke, no fearce and cruell host,
No people slaughtred, with their townes cleane topsie turvey tost:
Whyle that the foe with flaming fyre doth spoyle and waste the wall,
Untamed and unbridled Mars destroyes and batters all:
That man alone who forceth not the fickle fates a strawe,
The vysage grim of Acheront whose eyes yet never sawe,
Who never vewd with heavy cheare the ugsome Limbo lake,
And putting lyfe in hasarde, dare to death him selfe betake.
That person is a Prynces peare, and lyke the Gods in myght,
Who knoweth not what death doth meane is in a pitious plight.
The ruthfull ruin of our natyve countrey wee behelde
That wofull nyght, in which the roofes of houses overquelde,
In Dardans City blasing bryght with flasshing fiery flames,
When as the Greekes with burning brandes enkindle did the frames,

That Troy whom war and deedes of armes might not subdue and take.
As once did mighty Hercules, whose Quyver causde it quake,
Which neither he that Peleus sonne, and sonne to Thetis was,
Nor whom Achilles loved so wel, could ever brynge to passe,
When glytering bright in field he ware false armour on his back,
And counterfayting fearse Achill the Troyans drave to wrack.
Nor when Achilles he hym selfe his minde from sorow wrast,
And Troyan women to the walles did scuddyng leape in hast.
In myserie she lost her proud estate, and last renoume,
By being stoutly overcome, and hardly pulled downe.
Yeares fyve and fyve did Troy resiste, that yet hereafter must,
In one nyghts space by destenie be layed in the dust.
Theyr fained giftes well have we tried that huge and fatall gin.
We lyght of credit, with our owne ryght hand have haled in,
That fatall gyft of Greekes : what tyme at entry of the gap
The huge hors did shyveryng stand, where in them selves did wrap
The captaynes close, in holow vautes with bloudy war yfreight,
When lawfully we might have tryde, and serched their deceit :
So by theyr owne contryved snares the grekes had bin confound :
The brasen bucklers being shooke did gyve a clattring sound.
A privy whyspering often tymes came tyckling in our ear,
And Pyrrhus (in a murreynes name so ready for to heare,
The crafty councell picked out of false Ulisses brayne,)
Did jangle in the holow Vautes, that range thereof agayne.
But fearing and suspecting nought the headdy youth of Troy
Layde handes upon the sacred ropes, to hale and pull with joy.
On this syde younge Astyanax came garded with his trayne,
On th' other part Pollixena disponsed to bee slayne
Upon Achilles tombe, she coms with maydes, and hee with men,
A joly flocke with equall yeares as younge as they were then.
Theyr vowd oblations to the gods in holy day attyre,
The matrons bryng and so to church repayreth every syre.
And all the city did alyke, yea Hecuba our queene
(That synce the woful Hectors death or now was never sene)
She mery is : O griefe accurst, of all thy sorowes depe
For whych that first or last befell entendest thou to wepe ?

Our battred walles which heavenly hands erected have and framde ?
Or els the burning temples which upon their Idols flamde ?
Lamenting these calamyties wee have not time and space,
O mighty parent Pryam we poore Troyans wayle thy case.
The olde mans thratling throate I sawe, (alas) I saw yborde
With cruell Pryrhus blade, that scante with any bloud was gorde.
CAS. Refraine your teares that down your cheekes should tricle evermore,
With woefull waylings piteously your pryvate friendes deplore :
My myseries refuse a mate, so much accurst as I,
To rewe my carefull case, refrayne your lamentable cry.
As for myne owne distresse to moorne, I shall suffice alone.
CHO. To mingle teares with other teares it doth us good to mone :
In those the burning teary streames more ardently doe boyle,
Whom secret thoughts of lurking cares in privy breast turmoyle :
Though that thou were a Gossop stout, that brooke much sorrow may,
I warraunt thee, thou myghtest well lament this sore decay.
Not sad and solemne Aedon that in the woodes doth singe
Her sugred Ditties finely tunde on sweete and pleasaunt stringe :
Recording Itys woefull hap in divers kynde of note,
Whom Progne though he were her chylde and of her wombe begot,
For to reveng his fathers fault, she did not spare to kill :
And gave his flesh and bloude for foode the fathers Maw to fill.
Nor Progne who in Swallowes shape upon the rydges hye
Of houses sits in Biston towne bewayling piteously,
With chattering throate, of Tereus her spouse the cruell act,
(Who did by strength and force of armes a shamefull brutishe fact.
Defile the syster of his wyfe, fayre Philomel by name,
And eke cut out her tonge, least shee should blab it to his shame)
Though Progne this her husbandes rape lamenting very sore
Doe wayle, and weepe with piteous plaint, yet can shee not deplore
Sufficiently, though that shee woulde, our countreyes piteous plight,
Though he himselfe among the Swans syr Cygnus lilly whight,
Who dwelles in streame of Ister floud, and Tanais channell coulde,
His weeping voyce most ernestly though utter out hee woulde :
Although the morninge Halcyons with dolefull sighes doe wayle,
At such time as the fighting floudes their Cyex did assayle,

Or rashly wexing boulde attempt the Seas now layde at rest,
Or being very fearefull feede their broode in tottring nest,
Although as squemishe hearted men those priestes in bedlem rage,
Whom mother Cyble being borne on high in lofty stage,
Doth moove, to play on shaimes, Arys the Phrygian to lament,
Yet can not they this lot bewayle, though brawn from armes they rent.
Cassandra, in our teares there is no measure to refrayne,
Those miseryes all measure passe, that plunged us in payne.
The sacred fillets from thy heads, why dost thou hate and pull ?
They chiefly ought to worship God, whose hearts with griefe be dull.
CAS. My feare by this affliction is cleane abated all,
Nor praying to the heavenly Ghostes for mercy will I call.
Although they were disposde to chase and fret in fustien fumes,
They nothing have me to displease, Fortune her force consumes.
Her spyte is worne unto the stumpes, what countrey have I left ?
Where is my Syre ? am I of all my systers quite bereft.
The sacred tombes and alter stones our bloud have drunke and swylde,
Where are my brethren blessed knot ? destroyed in the fylde.
All widdow Wyves of Priams sonnes may easly now beholde,
The Pallace voyde and cast of court of silly Priam olde.
And by so many marriages so many Wyddowes are,
But onely Hellen comming from the coast of Lacon farre.
That Hecuba the mother of so many a pryncely wyght,
Whose fruitfull Wombe did breede the brand of fyer blasing bryght :
Who also bare the swinge in Troy, by practise now doth learne,
New lawes and guise of desteny in bondage to discerne.
On her shee taketh heart of grace with lookes so sterne and wylde,
And barketh as a bedlem bitch about her strangled chylde,
Deare Polidor, the remnaunt left, and onely hope of Troy,
Hector and Priam to revenge, and to restore her joy.
CHO. The sacred Phœbus Prophet is with sodayne silence husht :
A quaking trembling shivering feare throughout her lims hath rusht :
Her Face as pale as Ashes is, her Fillits stande upryght,
The soft and gentle goldilockes starte up of her affright.

Her panting breathing breast stuft up within doth grunt and grone,
Her glaring bryght and steaming Eyes are hether and thyther throwne.
Now glauncing up and downe they roll: now standing stiff: they stare.
She stretcheth up her head more streyght then commonly she bare,
Boult up she goes, her wrastling Jawes that fast together clinge,
She doth attempt by divers meanes, on sunder how to wringe.
Her mumbling words in gabling mouth shut up she doth asswage,
As Menas mad that Bacchus aares doth serve in furious rage.
CAS. How doth it hap (O sacred tops of high Parnassus hill)
That me berapt of sence, with prickes of fury fresh yee fill?
Why doe you me with ghost inspyre, that am besyde my wits?
O Phœbus none of thyne I am, releasse me from the fits:
Infixed in my burning breastes the flames extinguish out,
Who forceth me with fury fell to gad and trot about?
Or for whose sake inspyrde with spryte mad mumbling make must I?
Why play I now the Prophet colde, sith Troy in dust doth ly?
The day doth shrynke for dread of warre, the night doth dim mine eyes,
With mantell blacke of darknesse deepe cleane coverd is the skyes:
But loe two shining Sunnes at once in heaven appeareth bryght,
Two Grecian houses muster doe their armies twayne to fight.
Amonge the mighty Goddesis in Ida woodes I see,
The fatall sheepherd in his throne as umpier plast to bee:
I doe advise you to beware, beware (I say) of kynges,
(A kindred in whose cancred heartes olde privy grudges springes)
That countrey clowne Ægisthus he this stocke shall overthrowe,
What doth this foolish despret dame her naked weapons showe?
Whose crowne entendeth shee to cracke in weede of Lacon lande,
With Hatchet (by the Amazons invented first) in hand?
What face of mighty majesty bewitched hath myne eyes?
The conquerour of salvage beastes Marmarick Lyon lyes,
Whose noble necke is wurried with currish fange and tooth,
The churlish snaps of eger Lyonesse abyde hee dooth.
Alacke yee ghostes of all my friendes why should yee say that I,
Among the rest am onely safe, from perils farre to ly?

Fayne father follow thee I would, Troy being layde in dust.
O brother terrour of the Greekes, O Troyans ayde and trust.
Our auncient pomp I doe not see, nor yet thy warmed handes,
(That fearce on Greekish flaming fleete did fling the fyry brandes)
But mangled members, schorched corps, and eake thy valiaunt armes,
Hard piniond and bounde in bands sustayning greevous harmes :
O Troyolus, a match unfit encountering with Achill
(That myghty man of armes) to soone come unto thee I will.
I doe delight to sayle with them on stinking Stygian flood,
To vew the churlishe mastife cur of hell, it doth mee good.
And gaping mouthed Kingdome darke of greedy Ditis raygne.
The Barge of filthy Phlegethon this day shall entertayne,
Mee conquering, and conquered, and Prynces soules with all.
You flitering shades I you beseeche, and eake on thee I call,
O Stygian poole (whereon the Gods theyr solemne othes doe take)
Unbolt a whyle the Brasen bars of darksome Lymbo lake,
Whereby the Phrygian folke in hell may Micean state beholde.
Looke up yee silly wretched soules, the fates are backward roulde.
The sqally sisters doe approch, and deale their bloudy strokes,
Their smultring faggots in their handes halfe brunte to ashes smokes.
Their vysages so pale doe burne, with fyry flaming eyes :
A garment blacke theyr gnawed guts doth gyrde in mourning guyse.
Dire dread of night begins to howle, the bones of body vast
With lying long doe rot corrupt in miry pudle cast.
Beholde, the wery aged man his burning thyrst forgot,
The waters dalying at his lippes to catch endevors not :
But mourneth for the funerall, that shall ensue anon.
The Troyan Prynce his royall robes tryumphant putteth on.
Cho. The furious rage cleane overpast begins it selfe to slake,
And slyps away, even as a Bull that deadly wounde doth take
On gasshed neck afront the aares : come let us ease at last
Her lymbes, that of the spryte of God hath felt the mighty blast.
Returning home agayne at length and crounde with Lawrell bow
(A signe of worthy victory) is Agamemnon now.
The Wyfe to meete her Husband, doth her speedy passage ply,
Returning hand in hand, and foote by foote most lovingly.

THE FOURTH ACTE

AGAMEMNON. CASSANDRA

T length I doe arryve agayne uppon my native soyle :
God save thee O deare loved Lande, to thee so huge a spoyle
So many barbarous people yeelde : the flowre of Asia, Troy :
To beare thy yoake submits her selfe, that longe did live in joy.
Why doth this Prophet (on the grounde her sprawling body layde)
Thus reele and stagger on her necke, all trembling and dismayde ?
Sirs, take her up, with Lycour warme let her bee chearished.
Now peepes she up agayne, with drouping eyes sonke in her head :
Plucke up thy spryte, heere is the porte wisht for in misery :
This day is festivall. Cas. At Troy so was it wont to bee.
Ag. Let us to Th'alters worship gyve. Cas. At Th'alters died my sire :
Ag. Pray we to Jove. Cas. To Jove whose grace divine doth me inspire ?
Ag. Dost thou suppose that Troy thou seest ? Cas. And Priam eke I see.
Ag. Troy is not heere. Cas. Where Helen is there take I Troy to bee.
Ag. Feare not as maide to serve thy dame. Cas. Nay fredome draweth ny.
Ag. Take thou no thought how thou shalt live. Cas. All cares for to defy,
Death gives a courage unto mee. Ag. Yet say I once agayne
There is no daunger left, whereby thou mightest hurt sustayne.

CAS. But yet much troublous daunger doth hang over thy head I wot.

AG. What mischiefe may a victor dread? CAS. Even that he dreadeth not.

AG. Yee trusty many of my men come cary her away,
Till of the spryte shee ryd her selfe, least fury force her say
That may be prejudiciall, her tongue she cannot frame.
To thee O Father flinging forth the lightnings flasshing flame,
That dost disperse the cloudes, and rule the course of every starre,
And guyde the Globe of Earth, to whom the booties woon by warre
With triumphe victors dedicate: to thee O Juno hight
The syster deare of doughty Jove, (thy husband full of might)
Both I and Greece with flesh and bloude, and eke our vowed beast,
And gorgious gyftes of Arabie, give worship to thy hest.

CHORUS

O Greece by noble Gentlemen in honour shyning cleare,
O Greece to wrathfull Juno thou that art the darling deare,
Some jolly worthy lusty bloude thou fosters evermore,
Thou hast made even the Gods, that were a number odde before.
That puissaunt mighty Hercules a noble Impe of thyne
Deserved by his travels twelve, rapt up in heaven to shyne.
For whom the heavens did alter course, and Jupiter withall
Did iterate the howers of nyght, when dampishe dewe doth fall.
And charged Phœbus chariot swyfte to trot with slower pace,
And leasurely bright lady Moone thy homeward Wayne to trace,
Bryght Lucifer that yeare by yeare his name a newe doth chaunge,
Came backe agayne, to whom the name of Hesper seemed straunge.
Aurora to her common course her reared head addrest,
And couching backward downe agayne the same shee did arest
Upon the shoulder of her spouse, whose yeares with age are worne
The east did feele, so felt the west, that Hercules was borne.
Dame nature coulde not cleane dispatch, to utter in one night,
That boystous lad: the whyrling worlde did wayght for such a wight.
O babe whose shoulders underprop the ample spacious sky,
In clasped armes thy prowesse did the crusshed Lyon try.

Who from his fyry yawning throate spewes out his broyling brande,
The nimble hynde in Menall mount hath knowne thy heavy hande :
The Bore hath felt thy fyst, which did Arcadia destroy.
The monstrous conquerde Bull hath rorde that Creta did anoy.
The Dragon dyre that breeding beast in Lerna poole he slewe,
And chopping of one head forbad thereof to ryse anewe,
With clubbed brusing battring batte he crankly did subdew.
(The brethren twins that tewde on Teate) whereof three monsters grew.
Of tryple formed Gerion the spoyle into the east,
A drove of Cattell Hercules did fetch out of the weast.
Away from tyraunt Diomede the Thracian horse he led,
Which neyther with the grasse that grew by Styrmon floud he fed,
Nor yet on Heber bankes, but them the villayne did refresh
His greedy mounching cramming jades with aliaunts bloud and flesh.
Their rawfed Jawes imbrewde were with the carmans bloud at last,
The spoyles and shaftes Hipolyte saw from her bosome wrast
As sone as he with clattring shaft the dusky cloude did smite,
The Stymphall byrde that shadowed the sunne, did take her flight.
The fertill tree that apples beares of golde, did feare him sore,
Which never yet acquayntaunce had with Tasters tooth before.
But whipping up with lively twigges into the ayre she flyes,
And whyle the chinking plate doth sound then Argos full of eyes,
The watchman shrinking close for colde that sleepe yet never knew,
Doth heare the noyse whyle Hercules with mettall of yellow hew
Well loden packs away, and left the grove befilched cleane.
The hound of hell did holde his tongue drawne up in tryple cheane,
Nor barke with any boughinge throate, nor coulde abyde the hewe
Or colour of the heavenly lyght, whose beames he never knewe.
When thou wert captayne Generall, and didst conduct our Hoste,
(They that) of Dardans Lygne, to come theyr Stocke doe falsly boste,
Were vanquished by force of armes and since they felt agayne
Thy Gray goose winge, whose bitternesse to feare might them constrayne.

AGAMEMNON

THE FIFTE ACTE

CASSANDRA

WITHIN a revell rexe is kept, as sore as ever was,
Even at the ten yeares siege of Troy: What thing is this? (alas)
Get up my soule, and of the rage avengement worthy crave:
Though Phrygians wee bee vanquished, the victory we have.
The matter well is brought aboute: up Troy thou rysest now,
Thou flat on floore hast pulde down Greece, to ly as low as thou.
Thy Conquerour doth turne his Face: my prophesying spright
Did never yet disclose to mee so notable a sight:
I see the same, and am thereat, and busied in the broyle,
No vision fond fantasticall my senses doth beguile:
Such fare as Prygians feasted with on last unhappy night
At Agamemnons royall courte full daintily they dight:
With purple hangings all adornde the brodred Beds doe shyne,
In olde Assaracks goblets gylt they swincke and swill the wyne.
The King in gorgyous royall robes on chayre of State doth sit,
And pranckt with pryde of Pryams pomp of whom he conquerd it.
Put of this hostile weede, to him, (the Queene, his Wyfe gan say,)
And of thy loving Lady wrought weare rather thys aray.
This garment knit. It makes mee loth, that shivering heere I stande.
O shall a King be murthered, by a banisht wretches hande?
Out, shall Th'adulterer destroy the husbande of the Wyfe?
The dreadful destinies approcht, the foode that last in lyfe
He tasted of before his death, theyr maysters bloud shall see,
The gubs of bloude downe dropping on the wynde shall powred bee.

By traytrous tricke of trapping weede his death is brought about,
Which being put upon his heade his handes coulde not get out,
The stopped poake with mouth set ope his muffled head doth hyde,
The mankinde dame with trembling hand the swerd drew from her side,
Nor to the utmost of her might it in his flesh shee thrast,
But in the gieving of the stroke shee stayed all agast,
Hee as it were a bristled Bore entangled in the net
Among the bryars in busshy woodes yet tryeth out to get.
With strugling much the shrinking bands more streightly he doth bind,
He stryves in vayne, and would slip of the snare that doth him blind.
Which catcheth holde on every syde. But yet th' entangled wreatch
Doth grope about, his subtle foes with griping hand to catch.
But furious Tyndaris preparde the Pollaxe in her hande,
And as the priest to sacrifice at Th'alter side doth stande,
And vewes with eye the Bullockes necke, eare that with Axe he smite,
So to and fro shee heaves her hand to stryke and leavell right.
He hath the stroke : dispatcht it is : not quite chopt of the head,
It hangeth by a litle crop : heere from the Carkasse dead
The spouting bloude came gusshing out : and there the head doth lye,
With wallowing, bobling, mumbling tongue : nor they do by and bye
Forsake him so : the breathlesse coarse Ægist doth all to coyle :
And mangled hath the gasshed corpes : whyle thus hee doth him spoyle,
She putteth to her helping hand : by detestable deede
They both accorde unto the kynde, whereof they doe proceede.
Dame Helens syster right shee is, and hee Thyestes sonne :
Loe doubtfull Titan standeth still the day now being donne,
Not knowing whether best to keepe still on his wonted way,
Or turne his wheeles unto the path of dyre Thyestes day.

THE SECONDE SCEANE

ELECTRA

O THOU whom of our Fathers death the onely helpe wee have,
Fly, fly, from force of furious foes, make hast thy selfe to save :
Our house is topsey turvey tost, our Stocke is cast away,
Our ruthfull realmes to ruin ronne, our kingdomes doe decay.
Who cometh heere in Chariot swift thus galloping a mayne ?
Brother, disguised in thy weede let mee thy person fayne.
O Bussard blynde, what dost thou meane from forrayne folke to fly ?
Whom dost thou shun ? it doth behove to feare this family.
Orestes now bee boulde, and set all shivering feare a side,
The certayne succour of a trusty friende I have espide.

THE THIRD SCENE

STROPHILUS. ELECTRA

WITH solemne Pompe I Strophilus forsaking Phocis lande,
Bearing a braunch of Paulme, that growes at Elis, in my hand,
Returned backe I am, the cause that wild mee heather wend,
Is with these gyftes to gratefie and welcome home my frend,
Whose valiaunt army skalde, and shooke the tattred Troyan walles,
Who wearied with the ten yeares warre, now flat on floore shee falles.
What wofull wight is this that staynes her mourning face with teares,
And drowned deepe in drousy dumpes oppressed is with feares ?
I know full well this damsell is of Prynces lynage borne.
What cause Electra hath this joyfull family to morne ?
ELE. By treason that my mother wrought, my Father lieth slayne,
And drincking of their fathers cup the chyldren doe complayne.
Ægist engroceth Castels got by fornication.
STR. A lack that of so longe a tyme, filicity is none.
ELE. I thee request even for the love my father thou doest owe,
And for the honour of the crowne, whose brute abrode doth growe
In every coast : and by the Gods that diversly doe deale,
Take into thy tuicion, convey away, and steale,

This poore Orest: such kinde of theft is piety in deede.
STR. Although that Agamemnons death doth teach mee to take heede,
Yet will I undertake the same, and with all diligence
Orestes shall I goe about with strength to have thee hence.
Prosperity requireth faith, but trouble exacts the same,
Have heere a pryce for those that doe contende and wage in game.
An Ornament with comely grace ordaynde to deck the brow,
And let thy heade be coverde with this greene and pleasaunt bow.
And cary this victorious triumphant braunche in hand.
God graunt this Paulme that planted was in fertill Pisa land,
(Where solemne games were celebrate Joves honour to expresse)
May both a savegarde bee to thee, and bring thee good successe.
Thou that bestryds thy fathers steedes, as he before hath done,
Goe stryke a league of amity with Pylades my sonne.
Now nimble Nagges let Greece heereof recording testify,
With headlong scouring course amayne this traytrous country fly.
ELE. Hee is escapte and gone, and with unmeasurable might
The Chariot horse with rayne at will doe scud out of my sight.
Now free from perill on my foes attendaunce will I make,
And offer willingly my head the deadly wounde to take.
The cruell conqueresse of her spouse is come, whose spotted weede
With sprinkels (signe of slaughter) doe beare recorde of her deede.
Her goary handes new bathde in bloude as yet they bee not dry,
Her rough and churlishe rigorous lookes the fact doe notify.
Unto the Temple will I trudge. Cassandra suffer mee,
Opprest with egall griefe, take parte of sacrifice with thee.

THE FOURTH SCENE

CLYTEMNESTRA. ELECTRA. ÆGISTHUS. CASSANDRA

O THOU thy Mothers Enemy, ungracious saucy face,
After what sorte dost thou a mayde appeare in publyque place ?
EL. I have wyth my virginity the bowres of Baudes forsooke.
CLY. What man is hee, that ever thee to bee a vyrgin tooke ?

EL. What your own daughter? CLY. With thy mother more modest should thou be.
EL. Doe you at length begin to preach, such godlines to me.
CLY. A manly stomacke stout thou hast with swelling hawty hart,
Subdued with sorrow learne thou shall to play a womans part.
EL. A swerd and buckler very well a woman doth beseeme,
(Except I dote.) CLY. Thy selfe dost thou haylefellowe with us esteeme?
EL. What Agamemnon new is this, whom thou hast got of late?
CLY. Hereafter shall I tame, and teach thy gyrlish tongue to prate.
And make thee know, how to a Queene thy taunting to forbeare.
EL. The whilst (thou Wyddow) aunswere me directly to this geare.
Thy husband is bereved quight of breath, his lyfe is donne.
CLY. Enquier where thy brother is, so seeke about my sonne.
EL. Hee is departed out of Greece. CLY. Goe fetch him out of hande.
EL. Fetch thou my father unto mee. CLY. Give me to understande,
Where doth he lurking hyde his head? where is he shrunke away?
EL. All plunge of perills past hee is, and at a quiet stay
And in another Kyngdome where no harme hee doth mistrust,
This aunswere were sufficient, to please a Parent just.
But one whose breast doth boyle in wrath, it cannot satisefy.
CLY. To day by death thou shalt receyve thy fatall destiny.
EL. On this condition am I pleasde, the Aulter to forsake,
If that this hand shall doe the deede, my death when I shall take.
Or els if in my throate to bath thy blade, thou doe delight,
Most willingly I yeelde my throate, and give thee leave to smite.
Or if thou will chop of my heade in brutishe beastly guise,
My necke a wayting for the wounde out stretched ready lies.
Thou hast committed sinfully a great and grievous guilt.
Goe purge thy hardned hands, the which thy husbande bloud have spilt.
CL. O thou that of my perills all dost suffer part with mee,
And in my realme dost also rule with egall dignity,
Ægisthus, art thou glad at this? (as doth her not behove,)
With checks and taunts the daughter doth her mothers mallice move.

Shee keepes her brothers counsell close conveyde out of the way.
ÆGI. Thou malipert and witlesse wenche, thyne elvishe prating stay,
Refrayne those wordes unfit thy Mothers glowing eares to vex.
EL. What shall the breeder of this broyle controll me with his checks,
Whose fathers guilt hath caused him to have a doubtfull name,
Who both is to his sister, sonne, and Nephew to the same ?
CLY. To snap her head of with thy swerd Ægist dost thou refrayne ?
Let her give up the ghost : or bryng her brother straight agayne :
Let her be lockt in dungeon darck, and let her spend her dayes
In Caves and Rocks, with painefull pangues, torment her every wayes.
I hope him whom she hidden hath shee will agayne discry,
Through being clapt in pryson strong and suffring poverty,
With yrksome and unsavory smells on every syde annoyde,
Enforst to weare a wyddowes weede, or wedding day enjoyde :
Put in exile and banishment when eche man doth her hate :
So shall she bee by misery compeld to yeelde to late,
Prohibyted of holsome ayre fruition to have.
EL. Graunt me my dome by meanes of death to passe unto my grave.
CLY. I would have graunted it to thee, if thou should it deny.
Unskilfull is the tyraunt, who by suffring wretches dy
Doth ende theyr paynes. EL. What after death doth any thing remayne ?
CLY. And if thou doe desyre to dye, the same see you refrayne.
Lay hands sirs on this wondrous wretch, whom being caryed on,
Even to the furthest corner of my jurisdiction,
Farre out beyond Mycœnas land in bonds let her be bound,
With darknesse dim in hiddeous holde let her be closed round.
This captive Spouse and wicked Queane, the Trull of Prynces bed
Shall pay her paynes, and suffer death by losing of her head.
Come, hale her on, that she may followe, that way my spouse is gon,
Whose love from mee entised was. CAS. Doe not thus hale mee on.
I will before you take the way, these tydings first to tell
Unto my countrey men of Troy beneath in lowest hell.

How overquelmed ships ech where, are spread the seas uppon :
And Micœne countrey conquerde, is brought in subjection.
He that of thousand captaynes was graunde captayne generall,
Come to as great calamity as Troy it selfe did fall,
Entrapped was by traytrous trayne, and whoredome of his Wyfe,
And by a gyft receaved of her, deprived of his Lyfe.
Let us not linger : on with mee, and thankes I doe you give.
I joy, that it might be my hap, thus after Troy to live.
Cly. Go to, prepare thy selfe to dye thou frantique raging wight.
Cas. The fransy fits of fury fell on you shall also light.

EURIBATES, added to the Tragedy by the Translator

Alas yee hatefull hellish Hagges, yee furies foule and fell,
Why cause yee rusty rancours rage in noble heartes to dwell ?
And cancred hate in boyling breastes to grow from age to age ?
Coulde not the graundsires paynefull pangues the childrens wrath asswage ?
Nor famyne faynt of pyning paunche, with burning thyrst of hell,
Amid the blackest streame of Sticks where poysning breathes do dwel.
Where vapors vile parbraking out from dampishe myry mud,
Encrease the paynes of Tantalus deservde by guiltles bloud,
Could not thine owne offence suffice Thyestes in thy Lyfe,
To file thy brothers spousall Bed, and to abuse his Wyfe ?
But after breath from body fled, and Lyfe thy Lymmes hath left,
Can not remembraunce of revenge out of thy breast be reft ?
What, yet hast thou not layde thy lips, to taste of Lethes floude ?
Now after death why dost thou come to move thy sonne to bloude ?
Coulde cruell Ditis graunt to thee thy pasporte backe agayne ?
To worke this woe upon the world, and make such rigour raygne,
That Clytemnestra is become the fifty sister dyre
Of Danaus daughters, that did once theyr husbands death conspyre.
Loe here how fickle fortune gives but brytle fading joy.
Loe, hee who late a Conquerour tryumphed over Troy,
Enduring many sturdy stormes with mighty toyle and payne
To sowe the seede of fame, hath reapt small fruite thereof agayne.

When as his honour budding forth with flowre began to bloome,
(Alas) the stocke was hewed downe and sent to deadly doome.
And they that of his victory and comming home were glad,
To sodayne mourning chaunge their myrth with heavinesse bestad.
The lusty pompe of royall courte is deade : (O doleful day)
The people mone theyr prynces death with woe and weale away :
With howling, crying, wringing hands, with sobs, with sighes, and teares,
And with their fists they beate their breasts, they pull and hale their heares.
And as the sheepe amased run, and rampe about the fielde,
When as theyr shepherd to the Wolfe his goary throate doth yeelde,
Even so as mad they rage and rave throughout Micœnas land,
Deprived of theyr Prynce, they feare the bloudy Tyrauntes hand.
While thus were woefull waylings hard in every place about,
The good Cassandra (come from Troy) to death is haled out.
Like as the Swan, who when the time of death approcheth nye,
By nature warned is thereof, and pleased well to dye,
Doth celebrate her funerall with dirge and solemne songe :
Even so the noble vyrgin who in woe hath lived longe,
Most joyfull goes she to her death with milde and pleasaunt face,
Stout boulstring out her burly breast with pryncely porte and grace.
Nothing dismayde, with courage bolde and chearefull countenaunce,
On stage ordeyned for her death shee gan her selfe advaunce :
As though she had not thyther come, to leave her lothsome lyfe,
As though she had not come, to taste the stroke of fatall knyfe.
But even as it in brydale bed her journey were to meete
Corebus deare, not having mynde of death, nor winding sheete,
When looking rounde on every side she tooke her leave of all,
From vapourde eyes of younge and olde the trickling teares doe fall.
The Greekes them selves to griefe are movde to see this heavy sight,
So pity pearst the headmans heart, that thrise aboute to smite
He stayde the smot : with shivering hand yet once agayne he tryed.
And from her shoulders stroke her heade. And thus the vyrgin dyed.
But now the Greekes another cause of mourning have in hand :
Orestes, Agamemnons sonne, is forst to fly the land.

Amonge olde rotten ragged Rockes there lies an ugly place,
A Dungeon deepe, as darke as hell, unknowne to Phœbus face.
An holow huge wyde gaping hole, with way still bending downe,
Whose mouth with venomous wythred weedes is hid and overgrowne,
Where stinking smels come belching out from filthy durty dyke,
Where Verment vyle doe creepe and craule, in hell is not the lyke.
Ilfavourde, foule misshapen bugges, doe lurke about this cave,
With dreadfull sounds, and roaring noyse within the pit they rave.
Even heather is Electra sent, in darckenesse deepe to lye,
In poverty, and comfortlesse without the lyght of skye,
Fast clogde with Yron boults and Chaynes, thus by her mother layde
In torments, till by her to death Orestes be betrayde :
Who (as Cassandra telleth) shall revenge his fathers death,
Depryve with swerd th'adulterour, and Mother both of breath.
So after all these bloudy broyle, Greece never shall bee free :
But bloud for bloud, and death by turnes, the after age shall see.

FINIS

THE NINTHE TRAGEDY OF LUCIUS ANNÆUS SENECA

CALLED OCTAVIA

TRANSLATED OUT OF LATINE INTO ENGLISHE

BY T. N.

THE ARGUMENT

Octavia daughter to prince Claudius grace,
To Nero espousd, whom Claudius did adopt
(Although Syllanus first in husbandes place
Shee had receiv'd, whom she for Nero chopt)
Her parentes both, her Make that should have bene,
Her husbandes present Tiranny much more,
Her owne estate, her case that she was in,
Her brothers death (pore wretch) lamenteth sore.
  Him Seneca doth persuade his latter love,
Dame Poppie, Crispynes wife that sometime was,
And eake Octavias maide for to remove.
  For Senecks counsel he doth lightly passe
But Poppie joynes to him in marriage rites,
  The people wood into his pallace runne,
Hir golden fourmed shapes which them sore spytes,
They pul to ground : this uprore now begunne,
To quench, he some to griesly death doth send,
But her close cased up in dreadful barge,
With her unto Campania coast to wend,
A band of armed men, he gave in charge.

THE SPEAKERS NAMES

Octavia.
Nutrix.
Chorus Romanorum.
Seneca.
Nuntius.
Agrippina.
Poppea.
Nero.
Præfectus.

OCTAVIA

THE FIRST ACTE

THE FIRST SCENE

OCTAVIA

NOW that Aurore with glitteryng streames,
The glading starres from skye doth chase,
Syr Phœbus pert, with spouting beames,
From dewy neast doth mount apace :
And with his cheerefull lookes doth yeeld
Unto the world a gladsome day.
Go to, O wretch, with ample Fielde
Of heavy cares oppressed aye,
Thy grievous wonted playntes recount :
Do not alone with sighes and howles
The Seaysh Alcyones surmounte,
But also passe the Pandyon foules :
More yrksome is thy state then theirs.
O Mother deare whose death by fits
I nyll lament but still shed teares,
My ground of griefe in thee it sits.
If that in shade of darksome denne,
Perceiving sence at al remayne,
Heare out at large, O mother then,
My great complayntes, and grievous payne.
O that inmortall Clothos wrist,
Had torne in twayne my vitall thred :
Ere I unto my griefe had wist
Thy waundes, and face of sanguine red.
O day which aye doth me annoy :
Since that tyme did I more desyre,
The feareful darknes to enjoy,
Than Phœbus fresh with fayre attyre.

I have abode the bitter hest
Of stepdame dire, in mothers place,
I have abode her cruell breast,
Hir stomake stout, and fighting face.
She, Shee, for spyte unto my case,
A doleful, and a grave Eryn,
To Bridegromes chamber spousall space,
The Stygian flashing flames brought in.
And thee, (alas) most piteous Syre,
With traytrous traynes hath shee bereft
Of breathing soule with poysoned myre :
To whom ere whyle, the world all left
Unvanquisht from the Ocean Seas
By martiall feats did freely yeeld :
And didst subdue with wondrous ease,
The Brittayne brutes that fledde the fielde :
Whom living at their propre swaye :
No Romayne power did earst invade.
Now lo (ful wel lament I may)
Thy Spouse deceypte thy prowes hath lade :
And now thy court and child of yore,
With homage serve a Tyrantes lore.

THE SECOND SCENE

NUTRIX

Whom so the glistering pompe of royal place,
With soden sight ynumd doth quite disgrace,
Who so at courtly fleeting ebbing blase,
Astonied sore, himselfe doth much amase :
Lo see of late the great and mighty stocke,
By lurking Fortunes sodayne forced knocke,
Of Claudius quite subvert and cleane extinct :
Tofore, who held the world in his precinct :
The Brittayne Ocean coast that long was free,
He ruld at wil, and made it to agree,

Their Romaine Gallies great for to embrace.
Lo, he that Tanais people first did chase,
And Seas unknowen to any Romayne wight
With listy sheering shippes did overdight,
And safe amid the savage freakes did fight,
And ruffling surging seas hath nothing dread,
By cruel spouses gilt doth lye all dead.
Her sonne likewyse more fiend then Tigre fierce,
Of naturall mother makes a funerall herse,
Whose brother drenched deepe with poysoned cup,
Pore Britannick, his senseles soule gave up.
Octavia sister and unhappy make
Doth sore lament her case for Britans sake,
Ne can her ruthful piteous sorrow slake,
Though Neros wrath do sore constrayne her grace
She nil esteemes the secrete closet place :
But boyling stil with equal peysd disdayne.
With mutuall hate gaynst him doth burne agayne.
My true and trusty love that I do beare,
In vayne I see doth strive to comfort her.
Revenging greedy griefe doth streight reprive,
T' appease her smarte the counsel that I give.
Nor flame of worthy breast doth once relent
But heaps of greefe, her courage do augment.
Alas, what griesely deedes for to ensue
My feare foreseeth : God graunt it be not true.

THE THIRD SCENE

OCTAVIA. NUTRIX

O staggering state, O peerelesse yll :
With ease Electra I repeate,
And call to mynd thy mourning will.
With watred eies like smarting sweat
Thou mightst lament thy father slain,
Stil hoping that thy brother myght
That deadly deede revenge agayne.
Whom thou O tender loving wight

Didst safely shield from bloudy foe,
And naturall love did closely kepe :
But Neroes dreaded visage loe,
Doth feare me that I dare not weepe,
Nor wayle my parentes ruthful case,
By cruell lot this slaughter cought :
Ne suffers mee this geniall face,
To dash with teares to dearely bought
With brothers bloud : who onely was
Myne onely hope in all my griefe,
And of so many mischieves, as
My comfort greate, and sole reliefe.
Now loe reservd for greater care,
And to abyde more lingring payne,
Of noble famous lineage bare,
A drouping shade I do remayne.
NUTRIX. My Ladyes heavye voyce mee thought
Within my listning eares can sounde,
And snaylish age in going soft,
Unto her thews is not ybounde.
OCTAVIA. O Nurse our dolours witnes sure
By curroll cheekes distilling rayne,
And heavy heartes complaynt endure.
NUTRIX. Alas, what day shall ridde of payne,
With care your welnye wasted heart ?
OCTAVIA. That sends this guiltles ghost to grave.
NUTRIX. This talke (good madame) set apart.
OCTAVIA. In rule my state theire destenies have,
And not thy prayers, (O matrone) just.
NUTRIX. The doune soft easy God shall geve,
Your troubled mynd a tyme I trust,
More sweete then ever you did live.
With fevell fayre as one content,
And glosed face, but onely please
Your man, and make, he will relent.
OCTAVIA. The Lyon fierce I shall appease,
And sooner tame the Tygre stoute,
Then mankynd Tyrantes brutish breast.

He spytes the noble raced rout,
Contemnes hygh powers, disdaynes the least :
Ne can wel use that princely weede,
Which venemous parent wrapt him in
By huge unspeakeable griesly deede.
Although that wight unthankful, gryme,
In Kingly throne that hee doth raygne,
Throughe cruel cursed mothers ayde :
Although hee pay with Death agayne
So greate a gift, it shal be sayde
And after fates in long spent age,
That woman wight shal have alwaye,
This eloge yet and saying sage,
That he by her doth beare the sway.
NUTRIX. Let not your ragious mynde so walke,
But doe compresse your moody talke.

THE FOURTH SCENE

OCTAVIA. NUTRIX

THOUGH much I beare that boyling brest do beate
And tollerably take divorcements threate,
Deathes only deadly darte, I see an end,
Of all my broyle and pinching payne can send,
What pleasant light to me (O wretch) is left,
My natural Mother slayne, and Syre bereft
Of breathing life, by treason, and by gilt :
Of Brother eake deprivde : with miseryes spilt :
And wayling overcome : kept downe with care,
Envyed of Make, which I dare not declare.
To mayden subject now, and now defied :
What pleasant light can me (O wretch) abyde,
With feareful hart suspecting always ought :
Because I would no wicked deede were wroughte :
Not that I feare Deathes griesly gyrning face,
God graunt I do not so revenge my case,

A better deede to dye : for to behold
The Tyrantes visage grimme, with browes uprolde
And with soft tender lippes my foe to kisse,
And stand in awe of beckes and noddes of his,
Whose will to please my griefe with cares yfirde
Since brothers death by wicked wyle conspirde,
Could never once vouchsafe for to sustayne,
Lesse griefe to die, then thus to live in payne.
His Empyre Nero rules and joyes in blood :
The cause and ground of death that Tirant wood.
How oft (alas) doth Fansie fondly fayne,
When slumber swete in pensive parts doth raigne,
And sleepe in eyes, all tyrd with teares doth rest,
I apprehend deare Brittans lively brest :
Ere whyle me thinkes his feble shivering hands
He fenseth sure with deadly blasing brandes,
And fiercely on his brother Neros face,
With sturdy stinging stroakes he flies apace.
Ere whyle thilke wretch recoyleth backe agayne,
And to my thewes for aide retyres amayne :
Him foming foe pursues with hast to have :
And whyle my brother I desire to save,
And in my clasped armes to shield him free,
His goary bloudied falchion keene I see.
The boysterous raumping fiend to tugge, and hale
Through out my shivering limmes, as ashes pale.
Forthwith a mighty trembling chattering quake
From weary lims all souple sleepe doth shake,
And makes me woeful wretch for to recount
My wayling sobbing sorrowes that surmount.
Hereto, put to that gorgeous stately Mouse,
All glistring bright, with spoyles of Claudius house
His parent deare in bubling boate did douse,
That wicked sonne, this fisking dame to please.
Whom yet escaping daungers great of Seas,
He fiercer freake than waves that scantly rest,
With bloudy blade hir bowels did unbrest.

OCTAVIA

THE FIRST ACTE

What hope of health, can me, O wretch, abyde,
That after them thilke way I should not ryde ?
My speciall foe, triumphant wise doth weight,
With naked nates to presse by lovers sleight,
Our spousall, pure, and cleane unspotted bed :
Gainst whom she burns, with deadly foode bloud red.
And, for a meede of filthy strumpets sport,
She causeth Make from spouse for to divort.
O auncient Syre, step forth from Limbo lake,
Thy daughters heavy troublous cares to slake :
Or your twygated hellysh porche unfolde,
That downe through gaping ground I may bee rolde.
NUT. O piteous wretch, in vaine, (alas) in vaine
Thou calst upon thy fathers senselesse sprite :
In whome, God wot, there doth no care remaine
Of mortall broode, that here doth take delight.
Shall he, thinke you, asswage your sory cheere,
Or shape you forth some sleight, t' appall your paine,
That could preferre, before his Brittan deere,
Th' imperiall throne, a straunge begotten swaine ?
And with incestiall love benummed quyte
His brother Germanicks daughter that could plyght,
And joyne to him in solemne mariage rites,
With woefull, and unlucky lovers lightes ?
Here sprang the roale of hurly burly great,
Here beastly venomous slaughter gan to sweate,
Here wylie treasons traines appeared first,
Here rules desire, and brutish bloudy thirst.
Syllanus first Prince Claudius sonne in lawe,
A bloudy mangled offring fall we sawe,
That in our graces Hymæneal bed,
Ymatcht with you, he might not couche his hed.
O monstrous slaughter, worthy endlesse blame :
In steade of gift unto that wanton dame,
A carkasse colde pore soule, and curelesse corse,
Sillane was given against his will perforce.
And falsly then attacht of traitors crime,
As one conspyring death in Claudius time,

With lothsome streakes spewde out upon the wall,
He all bedasht your fathers princely hall.
Eft stepped into servile Pallace stroke,
To filthy vices lore, one easly broke.
Of Divelish wicked wit this Princocks proude :
By stepdames wyle prince Claudius Sonne avoude.
Whome deadly damme did bloudy match ylight :
And thee, against thy will, for feare did plight.
Through which successe this Dame of corage fine,
Durst venture, mighty Jove to undermine.
Who can so many cursed kindes report
Of wicked hopes, and actes in any sort,
Or such a womans glosed guyles can name,
That raumpes at rule, by all degrees of shame ?
Then holy sacred zeale put out of grace,
Her stagring steppes, directed forth apace,
And sterne Erinnis in with deadly steps,
To Claudius Court, all desert left yleps.
And with hir dririe drakes of Stygian sort,
Hath quite distainde the sacred princely port.
And raging riven in twaine both natures lore,
And right to wrongs mishapen fourme hath tore.
That haughty minded dame first gave her make
A deadly poysoned cup, his thyrst to slake.
Straight wayes againe through vile unkindly touch,
Her Nero causde with him in hell to couch.
And thee, unhappy Britt, in all that broyle,
Till that of breth, and life he did dispoyle,
Thilk greedie bloudy tyraunt never stent :
Whose dolefull death for aye we may lament.
Ere whyle, unto the world the starre that shone,
And was the stay of princely court alone,
Now loe, light ashes easly puft aforne,
And griesly goast to grave with torche yborne.
Whom blessed Babe, thy stepdame did lament :
Nor from hir gushing teares, did scarce relent,
When as she gave eche trimme appointed parte,
And goodly portraide limmes with natures arte,

Of flaming stacke to be devoured quite,
And sawe the scortching fervent fire in sight
Thy naked joynts to ravin up a pace
And like the flittring God thy comely face.
Oct. Dispatch he me least with this hand he fall.
Nut. That power you nature graunted not at all.
Oct. But wondrous dolor, great and wrathfull yre,
And miseries will it graunt without desyre.
Nut. Nay rather cause your angry moody make,
With souple cheere his fury for to slake.
Oct. What, that he will by guilt once slaine before,
Alive againe my brother mee restore ?
Nut. Nay, safe that you may live and issue beare :
Your fathers auncient court for to repayre.
Oct. That court doth wayte another broode they say,
And poore Britts death tugges me another way.
Nut. Yet let the cities love unto your grace,
Your troubled minde confirme but for a space.
Oct. Their mindes so prest to pleasure me, I know
Great comfort brings : but do not slake my wo.
Nut. Of mighty power the people have bene aye.
Oct. But princes force doth beare the greater sway.
Nut. He will respect his lawfull wedded wife.
Oct. His mynion brave can not so leade her life.
Nut. Of no man shee esteemde. Oct. But dear to make.
Nut. She can not truely yet of wifehood crake.
Oct. Ere longe she shall a mother eke be made,
So farre therein I dare most boldly wade.
Nut. His youthfull heate at first in filthy love,
With lusty, crusty pangs doth boyle above :
Thylke corage quickly colde in lust apace
As vapour sone extinct in flame gives place.
But holy, loving, chaste unspotted spouse,
Her love endureth aye with sacred vowes.
That wanton first that there durst couch hir hed,
And tumbling stayned quite your spousall bed,
And being but your mayde hath ruled longe,
Hir soveraine Lord, with beauties grace bestong,

That pranked Paramour pert shal croutch with pain,
When she your grace shall see preferd againe.
For Poppie subject is, and meeke of spright,
And now begins her goastly tombs to dight :
Whereby she closely graunting doth bewray
Hir secret hidden feare eche other day,
That swift, unconstant, double winged lad
With cloute, before his blinded eyes, yclad,
That fickle brayned God, thunhappy boy,
Shall leave hir in the midst of all hir joy :
Although for beauty bright the bell she beare,
And goodly glistring garments new she weare,
And now do vaunt her selfe in gorgeous geere,
Shee shall not long enjoy this gladsome cheere.
Be not dismayde, Madame, for such like paine,
The queene of gods was forced to sustaine,
When to ech pleasaunt shape the heavenly guide,
And syre of Gods yturnde, from skyes did glyde.
The swannes white wings, to se how they could fadge
He did on him, and cuckoldes bullysh badge,
That God shone bright in Golden raynie showre
To Danaes brest through top of fortred towre.
The twinckling starres the twinnes of Læda bright,
Whom Pollux, some, and Castor, call aryght,
In large and ample space of starry scope,
With cristal glimmering faces shyne wyde ope.
And Semeles sonne, whom Bacchus we do call,
In heavenly byrthright doth himselfe ystall.
And Hercules that puissant Champion stoute,
His sturdy brawnes, his Hebe wyndes aboute.
Nor once regardes how Goddesse Juno fare :
Whose lowring stepdame now she is yframde,
That whyle on earth his prowes he did declare,
Agaynst that maryage, aye, was sore inflamd.
Yet loe her wise and closly couched greefe,
Debonaire face, obeisaunce to her leefe,
Causde him at length his mynd for to remove,
Through mortall feeres estraungde from Junos love.

OCTAVIA

THE FIRST ACTE

And now that mighty heavenly Goddesse great,
No more adred of mortall strumpets feat,
Aloft alone in cloudy bowre contentes
The thundring Lord, which now to her relentes.
Nor now with earthly Ladyes beauty bright
Yfyred, leaves his starry specked right.
Now madam sith on earth your powre is pight
And have on earth Queene Junos princely place,
And sister are, and wyfe to Neroes grace,
Your wondrous restles dolours great appease.
OCT. Nay, sooner shall the roaring froathy seas,
And mounting flashing flawes ymatch the skye,
And smoaking, stifling parching fyer drye
With dankish pooles agree and watrye fenne :
And griesly Plutoes filthy feltred denne,
With starbright heaven shal sooner coupled be,
And shyning light with glomy shades agree,
And with the cleere drye day the dewy night,
Than unto servile lore of husbande wight,
That brutish wyse in bloud takes his delight,
My heavy woeful mynd can I addresse,
Whyle brothers death my heart doth stil possesse.
O that of heavenly powers the prince and syre,
That shogges and shakes the earth with thundring fyre,
And with his wondrous, feareful, cursed crackes,
And straunge mishapen monsters which he makes,
Our feareful musing myndes doth sore amase,
Would coyne some cureles burning wildfyre blase,
To pelt and pash with thumping fyer bright,
That divelish pate, that cruell cursed wight.
We saw from heaven, with beames forthshoting farre
Doubtles a dreadful heary, blasing starre,
That spouted out a mortall fiery flake,
Whose force a princes bloud can only slake :
Even where that hayting carman sloe Boote
With chilling cold al starcke of frosen pole,
Doth guyde aright Charles whirling running rote,
In steade of night that never away doth role.

Loe now the open ayre in every streate
With doggish tyrantes breath is poysoned quite,
And dreadful starres some sodayne death do threate
To people rulde by wicked Neroes spright.
So sterne a freake, or mankynd tyrant stoute,
Not Tellus with the Gods displeasd brought out,
When mighty Jove neglected she uphorlde
Huge, ugly, monstrous Typhon to the worlde.
A sorer plague, a cleaner scouryng scourge,
With bloudy pawes that cityes boundes doth purge,
Is Nero dyre, this cruell cursed wyght,
That doth himselfe gaynst God and man ydyght :
And thrustes from sacred shrynes their quiet porte,
And goodly temples gay the sancted sort :
That cittyes dwellers puts from countries fort :
That hath bereft his brother of his lyfe,
And launcht his mothers sides with goary knyfe :
Yet doth this present lightsome day enjoye
And leades his lyfe, that doth us sore annoy.
O Father of heaven, in vayne why dost thou throwe
Thy great unvanquisht ratling thundring blowe
Uppon the whistling woods and ample seas,
With force of princely power thy wrath t' appease ?
On such an hurtful and pernicious streake,
Thy due and just conceyved yre to wreake.
Why stay thy mighty puissaunt braunds so long,
Ere thou fling downe thy ratling cracking throng ?
O Lord, that Nero once might pay the price
Of all his devilish deedes, and every vyce,
Th' whole wyde worlds tyrant sterne when he a stroke
Doth beare : which he overlades with burdnous yoke
Of princely syre yborne, but doth defame,
With beastly manners vyle his princely name.
NUT. Unworth he is your spousall chamber place,
But yet your destnies force, you must imbrace,
And wel abyde your fortunes crooked race :
Nor move unkyndly Neroes gauly yre.
One day perchaunce, there wil as I desyre,

Some God revenge your lamentable case :
And once I trust a gladsome day shal be,
When you shal joy a fresh in wonted place.
Oct. Ah, no, now, long this court (alas) we see
With heavy wrath of Gods displeased yre
Hath overcharged bene : which Venus dyre
With Messalinas monstrous ramping lust,
Shee first hath brought adowne into the dust.
Who madly maryed to prince Claudius grace,
But little myndful then of that same case,
And not regarding much thappoynted payne,
With cursed cressets maried once againe.
To which unlucky incestuall brydall bed,
That drofell dyre that furious slut Erin,
With hanging hayre aboute her hellish hed,
And gyrt with snakes with deadly step went in.
And flaming brandes from spousall chamber cought,
In both their blouds ybathd, hath quenched cleane :
And hath incenst prince Claudius burning thought
In bloudy thratling stroake to passe all meane.
My mother first of wretches all the most,
With stripe of deadly sword gave up her ghost.
And now extinguisht quite, left me forlorne,
With dolours pyning panges and mourning worne.
And after her in hellish teame doth hayle,
Unto the senseles soules of Plutoes jaile
Her make, and Brittannick her sonne that way :
And first this ruinous court did she betray.
Nut. Let be, Madame, with teares your face to dight :
Ne so renew your bitter wayling just :
Ceasse troubling now your parents piteous spright,
That payed hath the price of raging lust.

THE FIFT SCENE

CHORUS

God graunt the talke wee hearde of late,
To rashly trusted every where,
And blowne abroad through each estate,
No badge of truth that it may beare.
And that no fresh espoused dame,
Our Princes thewes do enter in,
But that Octavia keepe the same,
And that the seede of Cladius kin
May once bring forth some pledge of peace :
That to the world rest may redowne,
And wrangling stryfe may easly cease,
And Rome retayne her great renowne.
The peerlesse Princesse Juno hight,
Her brothers wedlocke yoke retaynes :
Why is Augustus sister bright,
Where like betroathed league remaynes,
From stately pompe of court reject,
What doth devoutnes her avayle ?
To sayncted syre who hath respectt ?
What doth her Virgins life prevayle ?
And Claudius now in ground ylayed,
Even wee to much unmyndefull be :
Whose worthy steme we have betrayed
Through feare that made us to agree.
In breast our elders did embrace,
The perfect Romayne puissaunce,
The true unstayned worthy race,
And bloud of Mars they did advaunce,
The proude and lofty stomackt trayne
Of lusty hauty mynded Kinges,
They could not suffer to remayne
Within this noble Cities winges.

And justly they revengd thy death,
O Virgin chast, Virginia pure,
Deprivde by sire of vitall breath,
That bondage thou mightst not endure :
And that his shameles brutish lust,
So good a meede might not enjoy :
Although by filthy force unjust
Thy chastity he would annoy.
Thee likewyse whom thyne owne right hande,
With sword did pearce, Lucretia true,
Who tyrantes rape could not withstand,
Did bloudy broyles and warres ensue.
And with her proude disdaynfull Make
Lord Tarquin ympe of cursed seede,
Correction due doth Tullia take
For her unkindly shameles deede,
Who on her Fathers mangled corse,
To mischiefe bent, and wicked bane,
The Carman shee to drive did force,
His cruell brusing wombling wane.
And quite agaynst all natures law,
Even from her owne dismembred syre,
The sacred rytes she did withdraw,
Denaying wonted burial fire.
This griefe our woeful age doth feele,
Through monstruous act agaynst all kinde,
When as in deadely crafty keele,
To Tyrrhen seas, and wrastling wynd,
The proude presuming Prince did put
His mother trapt in subtil sort.
The Mariners appoynted cut
The swelling Seas from pleasaunt port.
The clash resoundes with stroake of Ores,
The Ship out launcht apace doth spinne,
In surging froath aloofe from shores,
And ample course of seas doth winne.
Which glydyng forth with leusned plankes,
Inpressed streames with peysed weight,

The riftes do open closed crankes
That hidden were with secrete sleight :
And gulpeth up the leaking wave
The woeful roaring noyse and crye,
With womans shrikes themselves to save,
Do reach and beate the starry skye.
Then griesly present death doth daunce
Before their eyes with pyning Cheekes :
Whose deadly stroake and heavy chaunce
For to avoyde, then each man seekes :
On ryvened ribs some naked lie,
And cutte the beating waves in twayne :
And some theyr skilful swimming trye
To get unto the shore agayne.
The greatest part that sayled there,
By destnies dire to men prefixt,
In whirling swallowes drowned were,
The brinkes of Seas and ground betwixt.
Queene Agrippyne her garments rendes,
Shee teares her ruffled lockes of hayre,
Abundant blubbring teares she spendes
Through deepe distresse of faynting feare.
Who when no hope of health shee spies,
Enflamde with wrath, which woes appeasde,
O sonne, for so greate giftes, shee cryes,
Hast thou with such reward me pleasd ?
This keele I have deserved sure,
That bare and brought thee first to light :
Who empyre witles did procure,
And Caesars title for thy ryght.
Shew forth thy feareful spritish face,
O Claudius now from Limbo lake,
And of thy wyfe in wretched case,
Revenge and due correction take.
Thy deth I causeles did conspyre,
Which now I rue with woeful harte :
I dressed eake a funerall fyre
Unto thy sonne by deadly smart.

OCTAVIA

THE FIRST ACTE

Lo now as I deserved have,
Untombde go to thy guiltles Ghost,
Encloasd in seas in stead of grave,
And wrestling waves of Romayne coast.
The flasshing flawes do flappe her face,
And on her speaking mouth do beate,
Anone shee sinkes a certayne space,
Depressed downe with surges great :
Anone shee fleetes on weltring brim,
And pattes them of with tender handes :
Through faynting feare then taught to swim,
Approaching death and fates withstandes,
At length on troubled Seas displayde
Shee geving over working vayne
And tyrd with streames is weary layd,
Not able toyling strength to strayne
In close and secrete silent breastes,
Of mates with her to sea that yode,
In whom no feare of death there restes
True fayth unto theyr Queene abode.
Theyr Ladyes weather beaten limmes
To helpe, some freely venter dare,
Some in the combrous waters swymmes
And desperate daunger do not spare.
With cheereful voyce they comfort her,
Though drawling dragling limmes shee drew,
To lift her up with helpe they stirre,
And nummed corpes to strength renew.
What bootes it thee the death to shonne
Of roaring raging ravening waves,
From deadly sword of wicked sonne,
Alas pore wretch thee nothing saves ?
Whose huge and heinous cursed rage,
Agaynst all course of natures lore,
Our after slow beleeving age
Wil scarce beleeve it done before.
The devillish man repynde with griefe
When he his mother saved sawe,

From swallowing seas have safe releefe,
And that she vitall breath did draw,
He grudgde with griefe and in his heate,
He huger mischiefe heapes to this :
He doth not once delay his feate,
But headlong rashly caryed is
Upon her death. A souldiour sent,
Dispatcheth that he had in charge,
His Ladies breast his blade doth rent :
Shee yeelding up her soule at large,
From wretched corpes for to entombe
Her slaughter man she then besought,
That bloudy blade within her wombe,
That fyrst this woe to her had brought,
This, this accursed breast (quoth shee)
Which this unkindly monster bare,
From pinching payne may not be free :
Digge, slash the same, no mischiefe spare
When this with foltring tounge was sayde,
At last her sad and trembling ghost,
With latter sobbing sighes unstayd,
Through goryd woundes leaves vitall coast.

OCTAVIA

THE SECOND ACTE

THE FIRST SCENE

SENECA

N me with like consent why didst thou smile,
With glosed lookes deluding mee a whyle,
O fortune much of might and princely powre ?
To lift aloft to noble royall bowre ?
To the'nde that I to honours court extold,
From stately seate might have the greater fall,
And round aboute in every place beholde,
Such dreadful, threating daungers to us all.
I safer lay aloofe from envyes knockes,
Remov'd among the craggy corsicke rockes :
Where as my mynd there free at proper sway,
With leysure did repeate my studies aye,
A gladsome joy alone it was to viewe
And earnestly to marke the heavens so blew :
And sacred Phœbus double wheeled wayne :
And eake the worldes swift whirling motion mayne.
The Sunne so even his second course to keepe :
And Phœbes glyding globe so swiftly sweepe :
Whom wondrous starting starres encompasse round,
And to behold that shynes in every stound,
The glistring beauty bright of welkin wyde :
Than which in al the world nothing besyde.
Of all this huge and endles worke the guyde,
More wondrous nature framde that I espyde,
For all the bumping bignes it doth beare,
Yet waxing old is like agayne to weare,
And to be chaungde to an unwyldy lumpe.
Now prest at hand this worldes last day doth jumpe,

With boystrous fall, and tumbling rush of skye.
To squease and make this cursed kynd abye.
That springing once agayne, it may yeeld out
An other straunge renued vertuous route,
As once before it did, new sprong agayne,
What tyme Saturnus held his golden raygne.
That blamelesse, chast, unspotted Virgin cleere
A goddesse much of might clept Justice heere,
With sacred sooth sent downe from heavenly space,
At ease on earth did rule the mortal race.
That people playne knew not of warlicke feates.
Nor trembling trompets tunes that rendes and beates
The souldiers eares : nor clashing armour bright,
That warring wightes defend in field and fight.
Nor wonted was with walles to rampyre round,
Their open cityes set in any stound.
To each man passage free lay open than :
Nothing there private was to any man.
And then the ground it selfe and fertil soyle,
Hir fruitful bosome baard all voyd of toyle,
Into such bounden barnes a Matrone good,
And peaceable unto so just a broode.
But then an other second race arose,
Perceyved not to be so meeke as those.
A third more wyse and witty sort up startes,
Of nature forged fit, t' invent new artes :
As yet unspotted quite with filthy vyce.
Soone after thoe, they raungd with new devyce,
That boldly venture dare in scudding race,
Unweldy beastes for to pursue apace.
And mighty weying strugling fishes great,
With watry coats yclad with fishers feat,
With net in window wyse draw forth, and streeke
With craft of quill, the nibling fysshes cheeke.
And silly byrdes begylde with pyning trayne :
And light foote deare for lyfe that flyng amayne
Intangling gins entrapt, that safely hold,
And sturdy scouling visage buls controld,

On fleshye fillet neckes, make weare the yoake :
And earth ere that ungrubbed up that broake :
Which then turnd up with Plowmans shyning share,
In sacred bosome deepe, her fruits kept thare.
But now this age much worse then all the rest,
Hath lept into her mothers broken breast :
And rusty lumpish yron and massye Gold
Hath digged out, that was quite hid with mold.
And fighting fistes have armd without delay :
And drawing forth their bondes for rule to stay,
Have certayne severall joly kingdomes made,
And cities new have raysde now rulde with blade,
And fenseth eyther with their proper force
Straunge stoundes or them assaults the which is worse.
The Starry specked virgin flowre of skies,
Which Justice hight, that guilty folke discries,
Now lightly esteemd of mortall people here,
Each earthly stound is fled, and comes not neere
The savage mannerd route, and beastly rude,
With dabbed wristes in goary bloud embrude.
The great desyre of griesly warre is sprong :
And raping thurst of gold, it is not young.
Throughout the worlde a mighty monstruous vice,
Fowle, filthy, monstruous lust hath got the price,
A pleasaunt tickling plague, whom longer space,
And errour deepe have fostred up apace.
The heaps of vyce rakte up in yeares long past,
Abounding flowe in these our dayes at last.
And this same troublous tyme, and combrous age,
Oppresseth all men sore, both yong and sage.
Wherein those wicked wayes that be do raygne,
And cruell, raumping woodnes boyles agayne.
Lust strong in filthy touch doth beare a sway,
And Princes ryot now doth catch away
With greedy pawes, to bring it to decay,
Th' whole worldes uncredible wealth, without delay.
But loe, which staggring steppes where Nero flinges,
And visage grymme, I feare what newes hee brynges.

THE SECOND SCENE

NERO. PREFECTUS. SENECA

DISPATCH with speede that we commaunded have :
Go, send forthwith some one or other slave,
That Plautius cropped scalpe and Sillas eke
May bring befor our face : goe some man seeke.
PRE. I nill protract your noble graces hest :
But to their campes to goe am ready prest.
SE. Gaynst lynage naught should rashly poynted bee
NE. A light thing tis for to be just, I see,
For him whose heart is voyd of shrinking feare.
SE. A soveraigne salve for feare is for to beare
Your selfe debonair to your subjectes all.
NE. Our foes to slea, a cheftaynes vertue call.
SE. A worthier vertue tis in countries syre,
His people to defend with sword and fyre.
NE. It wel beseemes such aged wightes to teach
Unbridled springolles yong, and not to preache
Both to a man and prince of ryper yeares.
SE. Nay, rather frolicke youthful bloud appeares,
To have more neede of counsell wyse and grave.
NE. This age sufficient reason ought to have.
SE. That heavenly powers your doinges may allow.
NE. A madnes 'twere to Gods for me to bow,
When I my selfe can make such Gods to be :
As Claudius now ycounted is we see.
SE. So much the more because so much you may.
NE. Our power permittes us all without denay.
SE. Geve slender trust to Fortunes flattring face :
She topsie turvy turnes her wheele apace.
NE. A patch he is that knoweth not what he may.
SE. A Princes prayse I compted have alway,
To do that same which with his honor stoode,
Not that which franticke fancy counteth good.

NE. If that I were a meacocke or a slouch,
Each stubborne, clubbish daw would make mee couch.
SE. And whom they hate, with force they overquell.
NE. Then dynt of sword the prince defendeth well.
SE. But fayth more sure defence doth seeme to mee.
NE. Ful meete it is that Cæsar dreaded be.
SE. More meete of subjectes for to be belov'd.
NE. From subjects myndes, feare must not be remov'd.
SE. What so by force of armes you do wringe out,
A grievous worke it is to bring aboute.
NE. Well hardly then our will let them obay.
SE. Will nothing then but that which wel you may.
NE. We wil decree what we shall best suppose.
SE. What peoples voyce doth joyntly bynd or lose,
Let that confirmed stand. NE. Swordes bloudy dynt
Shall cause them else at me to take their hint.
SE. God sheeld, and far that facte from you remove.
NE. What then, why Senec, do you that approve
That we contemnde, despysde and set at nought,
With finger put in hole (ful wysely wrought)
Our bodies bloud to seeke should them abyde,
That they might us sometyme destroy unspyde ?
Their native countrey boundes to banisht bee,
Nor Plautius brest nor Scillas eake we see
Hath broke or tamd : whose cankred churlish yre
Shapes bloudy freakes to quench our bodyes fyre.
And chiefly when these trayterous absent clounes,
Such wondrous favour fynd in cityes bownes,
Which those same exiles lingring hope doth feede :
Suspected foes with sword we wil out weede.
And so Octavia shall that joly dame,
Continue after them their bloudy game,
And wend that way her nowne whyte brother went,
Such hye mistrusted thinges must needes be bent.
SE. It is (O Prince) a worthy famous thing,
Amids redoubted Lordes alone to ring :
And wysely worke your countries prayse to save :
And wel your selfe to captive folke behave :

From cruell brutish slaughter to abstayne,
And voyde of moode to wreake your angry payne :
And to the world a quiet calme to geve,
That al your age in peace their lives may live.
This is a Princes prayse without al cryme :
This is the path to heaven wherby we clyme.
So is Augustus prince and father cald
Of countrie first in starbright throne ystald :
Whom as a God in minsters we adorne,
Yet troublous fortune tossed him beforne
A great while long on lands and ruffling seas,
Until his fathers foes he could appease,
And through wars diverse course could quel them quite.
To you did fortune yeelde her power and might,
And raynes of rule without all bloud and fight.
And to your beck both land and seas hath bent
Grim deadly envye daunted doth relent.
The Senate Lordes gave place with free consent :
The battaylous route of knights with willing hartes
(That same decree from sager sires departes)
Unto the lay mens choyse do well agree.
Your grace the spring of peace they count to bee,
And chosen Judge and guyde of mortal stocke.
Your grace, your countreys sacred syre, doth rocke
And rule with princely gorgeous tytle bright,
The cyrcled world in rundel wyse ydight.
Which mighty mounting name to keepe so great,
This noble citty Rome doth you entreat :
And doth commend unto your royall grace
Her lively limmes in charge for your lives space.
NE. The gyft of Gods it is, as we discus,
That Rome with Senate sorte doth honor us,
And that the feare of our displeasure great,
From cankred envyous stomackes maketh sweat
Both humble talke and supplications meeke.
And were not feare all these would be to seeke.
Unweldy, combrous cityes, members ill,
That Prince and countrey both do seeke to spill,

To leave alyve (which swell, and puffed bee,
Bycause of lynage great, and high degre)
What madnes meere is it when as we may,
Even with a word, such freakes dispatch away ?
Sir Brutus sterne, his brawnes and armes did dight,
His soveraygne liege to slayne by force and might,
That erst had holpen him and geven him health,
And had endued him with princely wealth.
In brunt of raging warre undaunted out,
That vanquisht many people strong and stoute,
Prince Cæsar matcht by great degrees of power
To Jove, in stately chayre of starry bower,
By div'lish citizens wicked wyle was slayne.
What store of bloudy stiffling streames on moulde
Did tatred Rome, of her owne lims, beholde ?
He by his noble vertues worthy prayse,
Whom peoples common bruite to heaven doth raise,
August among the Gods ysayncted well,
How many noble breastes did he compel,
How many springoldes young, and hoary heads,
Each where disperst to lig in molded beds ?
How many men did he bereave of breath
Tofore proscript that were condemnd to death ?
When for the griesly feare of deadly dart
From propre home they were constraind to part
And flye Octavius force, and Lepidus might,
And not abyde sterne Marke Antonius sight,
Which then the ample world at once did guyde,
That into kingdomes three they did devyde,
To dumpish sadded syres, with heavy cheere,
Their childrens griesly cropped pates appeere,
Hong out beforne the Senates judgement seate,
For each man to behold in open streate :
Ne durst they once lament their piteous case,
Nor inward seeme to mourne to Claudius face.
The market stead with bloud from bodies spued,
And lothsome mattrie streames, is all imbrued :

And quite throughout their faces foule arayed,
The piteous gubbes of bloud drop downe unstayd.
Nor here did this same slaughterous bloudshed stay,
Phillyps Pharsalia gastly fieldes each day,
The cromming ravening foules, and cruell beastes
Long fed with gobbets bigge of manlye breastes:
Besyde all this, the cost he scoured quite
Of Sicill sea and ships to ware ydyght
With force of armes did win, and havocke made
Of propper subjectes slayne with his owne blade.
The rundle round of landes with mighty mayne
Of noble Chieftaynes stroake reboyles agayne.
Antonius overcome in Navale fight,
To Egipt poastes in shippes preparde to flight:
Not looking long to live nor hoping life.
Incesteous Egipt (through Antonius wyfe)
That worthy Romayne princes bloud did sucke:
And coverd lye their ghostes with durty mucke.
Long wicked, waged civil warre there stayed,
In Marcke Antonius grave with him played.
Augustus at the last of conquest greate
His dulled swords that wounded soules did beate,
In peaceable sheathes repos'd hath layd at rest:
And feare doth rule, and guyde his kingdome best
By ready force of armes at all assayes,
And Captaynes fayth he shieldes him selfe alwaies
Whom now his sonnes most worthy vertuous praise,
To heaven a consecrated God doth rayse,
And causeth all, in Churches for to place
The sacred Picture of Prince Claudius grace
And us the starry raigne of Gods shall bide
If first with dreadful sword about us wyde
We wype away what so our person stayne:
And found our court with worthy stem agayne.
SE. Your noble spouse, sprong forth of saincted peer
Of Claudius stocke, the starbright diamond cleere,
That Goddesse Juno wise her brothers bed
Partaking, pressed downe with buttockes red,

Your graces princely court shal garnish gay,
With wondrous heavenly fayre descended stay.
Ne. Incestuous maryed dames, from stocke and stem,
Detract all hope that we should have of them.
Nor us, could she once love that we could see,
Nor with our person once at all agree.
Se. In tender budding yeares, when love supprest
With blusshing hydes the flames of burning breast,
Scant playne appeares the love they bare indeed.
Ne. Thus wee our selves with hope in vaine did feede :
Although undoubted signes, as bodye wryed,
And frowning lookes, which we have oft espyed,
Her spyteful hating stomacke did bewray
Which shee doth beare, whom duty byndes t' obaye,
Which yet at last, big, boyling, grievous payne,
With death determined hath t' avenge agayne,
Wee have found out, for byrth and beauties grace,
A worthy make for such an Empresse place :
To whom that lovely Goddesse Venus bright,
And mighty Jove his spouse that Juno hight,
And goddesse fierce in boysterous warlike artes,
Geves place for bodyes seemly portrayd partes.
Se. Fayth, meeknes, manners mild, and bashfull shame
Of spouse, those ought an husband to reclayme.
The perles of judging mynd alone remayne,
Not subject once to any rulers raygne.
The passing pryde of beautyes numming grace
Each day appals, and bleamisheth apace.
Ne. What prayses woman wights have in them closd ?
All those in her alone hath God reposde,
And such a peerlesse peere, the guydes of lyfe,
The destnies would have borne to be our wyfe.
Se. O noble prince, such blynd unlawful love
(Do rashly credite naught) from you remove.
Ne. Whom Jove can not repell that rules the cloudes,
And pearcing raging floods, therein him shroudes,
And raungeth through the raigne of Plutoes pit,
And pulleth downe in welkin hie that sit

The mighty powers of heaven, the God of love ?
And can I then his force from me remove ?
SE. Swift winged love, mens fancy fond, in vayne
A mercy wanting God to bee, doth fayne :
And armes his handes with woundinge weapons keen
And bowes with burning brondes, for lovers greene :
Of Venus to be sprong they al accorde,
And blyndly forgde of thunders limping Lorde.
Bland love the myndes great torment sore appeares,
And buddeth first in frolicke youthful yeares.
Who while we drinke of Fortunes pleasaunt cuppe,
With laysie pampring ryot, is nestled up :
Whom if to foster up you leave at length
It fleeting falles away with broken strength.
This is in all our life (as I suppose)
The greattest cause how pleasure first arose,
Which sith mankind by broodyng bydeth aye,
Through gladsom love that fierce wild beastes doth sway
It never can from manly breast depart.
NE. This selfe same God I wish with all my hart
The wedlocke lightes to beare before our grace,
And fasten Poppie sure in our bed place.
SE. The peoples griefe might never yeeld to it :
Nor vertue can the same at all permit.
NE. Shall I alone to do, forbidden be
That every patch may do ? that grieveth mee.
SE. No tryfling toyes the people lookes to have
Of him that ought to rule with wisdome grave.
NE. It pleaseth us with daunted power to trye
If peoples rash conceived rage will flie.
SE. Seeke rather for to please and calme their moode.
NE. Ill ruled is that raygne where people wood,
Their subject Prince doth weld, as they thinke good.
SE. When nought that they require they can obtayne,
They justly then agrieved are agayne.
NE. That gentle prayers cannot win with ease,
By force to wring it out it doth us please.

SE. An hard thing tis the people not to have
That of theyr Prince which they do justly crave.
NE. And horrible 'tis a Prince to be constraynd.
SE. Let not your subjectes then so sore be raynd.
NE. Why then the common brute abroade wil be
How that the people have subdued mee.
SE. That no man trustes that is of credite light.
NE. Be it so, yet many it markes with deadly spyghte.
SE. With countrie peeres to medle it is afrayd.
NE. To quip and frump, 'tis nothing lesse dismayd.
SE. Your grace may easly couch that budding bruite
Let Sayncted sires desertes with pliant sute
Your graces mynd remove : let spouses age
And curteous bashfull shame disrumpe your rage.
NE. Leave off (I say) that we entend to grutch,
For now your talke our pacience moveth much :
I pray you let it lawful be to do,
That Senec geveth not advyse unto.
  And we our peoples wishes do defer,
While Poppie feele in wombling wombe to sterre,
The pledge of faythful love to me and her.
  Why do we not appoynt the morrow next,
When as our mariage pompe may be context ?

THE THIRD ACTE

THE FIRST SCENE

AGRIPPYNA

HROUGH paunch of rivened earth, from Plutoes raigne
With ghostly steps I am returnd agayne.
In writhled wristes, that bloud do most desyre,
Forguyding wedlocke vyle with Stygian fire.
Let Poppie, which these cressets coupled sure,
Unto my sonne be joynd in mariage pure:
Whom mothers griefe, and hand revenging wrackes,
Shal end with heave and hoe to funeral stackes.
I always do remember wel beneath
Where piteous, ghostly, crauling soules do breath,
Th' unkindly slaughterous deede, whiche to our spright
Yet unrevengd is grievous and of right:
And for the good I did a cruell prise,
That deadly framed ship in crafty wyse:
And due reward that he gave me agayne,
For helping him to rule of Empyres raygne:
And eake that night, when as I did bewayle
Both losse of shippe wherin we then did sayle,
And mates unhappye death, and whyle I thoughte
For this accursed deede to have besought
The Gods to trickling teares he gave scant tyme
But twice encreased hath his devillish cryme.
Quite slayne with sword, thrust through my bodyes boundes
And filthy layed through goary mattring woundes,
Delivered safe from seas, devouring sup,
In antique court my ghost I yeelded up.

Nor yet his cancred and unsatiate hate
For all this bloud doth Nero once abate.
That Tyrant dyre doth rage at mothers name,
And seeketh wayes my deedes for to defame.
Who threating death to them that doe withstand,
My shapes he dingeth downe in every land:
My princely tytles large hee scrapeth out
In every place, the whole wyde world aboute,
Which my unlucky parentes love did geve,
To much unto my paine whyle I did live,
Unto a boy to guyde, which now I rue.
My poysoned make my Ghost doth oft pursue:
And in my face with burning brondes doth flye.
He stayes a space with earnest talke hard by,
And threatneth sore, and doth impute his death
And tombe he should have had to mee beneath
And now desyres to have some factious wight,
That dare despoyle my sonne of breathing spright.
Let be, you shall have one to worke this cryme,
I do require no long delayed tyme.
Revenging spright Erin a death doth coine
Of life, that wicked tyrant to purloyne.
Sore smarting leaden strypes and shameful flight,
And pyning panges with thurst and hunger dight:
That Tantalus spungelike thursty mouth befurde,
And Sisyphus toyle shal passe, and Tityus burde,
And Ixions paynful wombling wheele aboute,
That teareth all his bodyes partes throughout.
Although that Tyrant proude and scornful wight,
His court with marble stone do strongly dyght,
And princelike garnish it with glistring golde:
Though troupes of souldiours shielded sure, upholde
Their chieftaynes princely porch: and though yet still
The world drawne drye with taskes even to his will,
Great heapes of riches yeeld themselves to save,
Although his bloudy helpe the Parthians crave,
And Kingdomes bring, and goods al that they have,

The tyme and day shall come when as he shall,
Forlorne and quite undone, and wanting all,
Unto his cursed deedes his life and more
Unto his foes his bared throate restore.
Alas, unto what ende is all my payne ?
Or in what case do now my vowes remayne ?
Whereto doth now thy rage and destnies spyte ?
Draw thee O Sonne, with brayne benummed quite ?
That to such monstruous heapes of ylles thy dame
(Whom thou with cursed mischiefe overcame)
Hir wrath should yeeld ? O that ere to the light
A sucking babe I brought thee foorth in sight,
And fedd thee fyne with pappe as princely borne,
The fierce, wild, savage beastes had rent and torne
My wombe and bloudy entrails all beforne.
Without all cryme, and wanting reasons pride,
Mine own deere dandling child thou shouldst have dide.
And fastned sure to me shouldst aye beholde
The quiet place where Ghostly soules be rolde :
And see thy graundsyres great of worthy fame,
And syre Domitius eake of princely name,
Whom now both shame and wayling doth abyde,
That whyle they dure from them shal never slyde.
For which both thee, O cursed Barne, they may,
And mee, that thee have borne geeve thankes for aye.
But why ceasse I, with hel to hyde my face,
Wyfe, stepdame, mother dire, in my life space ?

THE SECOND SCENE

OCTAVIA. CHORUS

Do not, alas, thus sore lament,
But rather yet your mourning stay,
Sith that the city whole is bent
To celebrate this joyful day :
Least your great love and favour both,
Which I do count to be most sure,

The more cause Nero me to loth,
And eake his bitter wrath procure :
And I fal out to be the ground
To you of many mischieves vyle.
This same is not the first deepe wounde
That I have felt now this good whyle :
Farre worse then this have I abode :
But of these troublous cares this day
Shall make an end I trust in God,
Although with Death he do me pay,
No man to see shall me constrayne
His bended browes knit furrowyse,
Nor step within the Chamber ragyne
Of mayde drest up in brydall guise.
Augustus sister I wil bee,
And not his wyfe as wont I was :
But onely paynes remove from mee,
And feare of death I wil not passe.
Yet canst thou piteous wretch once trust
Thy cruell husbandes father law,
Or these few thinges to have so just
Whyle mischieves yet in mynd are rawe ?
Now long reservd, until this day,
And these same maryage rytes be past,
Thou shalt poore wretch without delay,
A bloudy offring dye at last.
Why thus with teares disfigured sore
Thy wonted home dost thou behold ?
Make hast to shunne this deadly shore
And leave this slaughtrous Princes fold.
CHO. Lo see that day suspected long
And whispered Fame in all mens eares,
With glisteryng pompe of brydall throng,
To us pore wretches now appeares.
And Claudius broode Octavias grace,
From Neroes wedlocke place expelde,
Departed is, whose spousall space
Hath Poppie conquerour long tyme helde.

The whyle, our pyety couched lyes
Kept downe with heavy, combrous feare.
And slow revenging grief likewyse :
Where doth the peoples power appeare,
That brake the force of Princes great,
That conquerous city lawes hath framde,
That worthy men to honours seat
Preferd, that warre and peace proclaymd,
That savage people straunge did tame,
That Kinges and Princes caught in fight
Shut surely up in prison frame
To keepe them close from all mens sight ?
Loe, which wee cannot once abyde,
To see wher Poppies ymage trym,
Conjoyned unto Neroes syde
All glistring bright shynes very brim.
Let force of Armes pul downe that frame
And match with grounde that Ladyes face
Too likely carved to his name,
And snatch her downe from bedding place,
And let it forthwith flye with brandes,
With Dartes and Javelins fiercely flonge,
From pythy braunes and sturdy handes
Unto the princes courtly throng.

OCTAVIA

THE FOURTH ACTE

THE FIRST SCENE

NUTRIX. POPPEA

ROM out of spousal bower dismayd with feare,
Whither go you ? what secrets daughter deare
Unknowen, makes you to looke so drousely ?
Why spungelike lokes your face with tears from eye
That fell ? of truth the tyme desyred long,
And wished for by prayers, and vowes among
Hath shyned bright. Cæsars wedlock are you :
Your golden grace, wherof he tooke the view,
Him prisoner caught, and did him surely bynde,
So much the more, how much Senec his mynd
Did seeke to chaunge, and wild from love to weeld.
And Venus chiefe in love hath made him yeeld.
O in beauty passing all, what beds then downe
More soft have borne thy weight when thou with crowne
Didst sit in middes of court the Senate all.
At thy great beauty agast, thou didst appall.
Whylst thou the Goddes with perfume sendest fyne,
And sacred alters drencht with thankful wyne,
Thy head attyrd with veyle of yellow hiew
By Cæsars side thou wentst as princesse new :
When he aloft extold above the rest,
With hauty courage merily went to feast.
Like as kyng Peleus went sometymes to take
Queene Tethis, whom salt seas fome bred, his make.
Whose bridinge chambers, banquet wise ydrest,
The Gods vouchsafe to hallow with their hest,

Both they that rule in skyes and eake in Seas.
But tel, O Lady, tell, if it you please,
What sodayne chaunce doth shade your beautyes light,
What meanes your colour chaunge from red to white ?
What moves those trickling teares, how stands your plight ?
Pop. With dreames, and griesly sightes, this last night, Nurse,
My mynd was troubled sore, but frayd much worse.
For when sir Phœbe his weary course had ryd,
Whyle quiet restyng night each thing shadid,
My sences weary fel in slumber deepe,
Whyle Nero me within his armes did cleepe.
Resolving lims, at length gan sleepe discharge,
And long I rest not under quiets targe,
For loe, I saw a route that brought me feare,
Come to my chaumber with disheveled hayre :
The Matrons sage of Latin land did mourne,
And sounded shryking sighes as though forlorne
They were, the dolefulst wightes that live on ground.
And oft among the warlike trumpets sound,
I sawe my husbands mother teribly stand,
With threatning looke berayed with bloud in hand :
A light fyre brand she bare which oft she shooke,
And made mee goe with her through feareful loke.
When downe we came through op'ned earth shee led
The way, I after went with bowing hed,
And musing much therat, marke what I say :
My bed, me thought I saw, wherin I laye,
When first espousde I was to Rufe Chrispyne :
And hee me thought, with first sonne of his lyne,
With many following them agaynst me fast
Did come, and me to cleepe did swift his hast,
And as he wonted was he kist me oft,
Then rusht into my house with pace not soft
Amased Nero sore, in Chryspines breast
That hidde his faulchion kene : feare shakte of rest
From mee : I trembling stode with quivering feare,
And brest dismayd to speake made me forbeare.

Til now (O Nurse) I met with thee, whose trust
And fayth into these wordes have made me brust.
Alas, what threatneth mee eche griesly spright ?
What meanes of husbands bloud that doleful sight ?
Nu. The hidden sacred vayne that moveth swift,
Which fantasie we call by secret drift,
When we do take our rest doth shew agayne
The thinges both good and bad that broyle in brayne :
You marvel that you saw your make, and bower,
His ghostly funerall stackes, at that same hower
Round clasped close in armes of husband new :
Hereto, the beaten breastes with handes mov'd you,
And maydens hayre, on mariage day displayd :
Octavias friendes with heavy hartes bewrayed,
Amids hir brothers both and fathers hall
Their heavy cheere for her unluckye fall.
That dreadful blasing flame of fyre forborne
In Agryppynas hand your grace beforne.
Which you did follow streight declares renowne
To you, though envye stryve to keepe it downe :
The seat you saw beneath doth promise you
Your state to stand ful sure not chaunging new :
That Nero prince in Crispins throat did hyde
His sword, it telles that he in peace shall byde,
Unknowen to bloudy ruthful warre for aye.
Therfore (Madam) plucke up your hart I pray :
Receive both mirth and glee, cast feare asyde,
With joy and ease you may in bowre abide.
Pop. To temples hie where mighty Gods do dwell,
I wil repayre, and offringes to them fell
In humble wyse their heavy wrath t'appease,
And me of mighty sight and dreams to ease.
My second wish shal be, that this feare all
Uppon my foes as sodayne chaunce may fall.
O Nurse pray thou for mee, some vowes do make
To th' Gods, that ghostly feare his flight may take.

THE SECOND SCENE

CHORUS

If stealth discloasde by blabbing fame,
And lusty, pleasaunt, thankfull love,
Of Jove be true : who fourme did frame
Of swan to come from skies above,
And did enjoy the sweete consent
Of Ladye Ledas loves delight :
Who like a Bull his labour spent,
Through flowing floods to cary quite,
Europa slylie stolne awaye :
Hee will no doubt leave raygne of Skye
And Poppies love disguisd assaye.
If hee her soveraygne beauty spye.
Which hee might wel preferre before
Fayre Laedas sugred sweete delight :
And Danae whom hee wonne of yore,
Amasde with golden shoure so bright :
Let Sparte now for Helens sake
Of beauty bragging fame uprayse :
Admit the Trojan heardman make
Of gayned spoyle tryumphant prayse :
Fayre Helen here is stayned quight :
Whose beauty bredde such boyling yre,
That earth was matched even in fight
With Trojan towres consumde with fyre.
But who is this that runnes with feare opprest ?
Or els what newes bringes he in panting breast ?

THE THIRD SCENE

NUNTIUS. CHORUS

WHAT sturdy champion stoute doth joy with glee
Our chieftaynes royal bower safe to see,
Then to his court I counsel him to wend,
Gainst which the populus rout their force doth bend.

The rulers runne amasde to fetch the gard,
And armed troupes of men, theyr towne to ward.
Nor woodnes rashly cought through feare doth ceasse,
But more and more their power doth encrease.
CHO. What sodain rage doth beat their broiling braine?
NUN. The garisons great with fury astonde againe,
And sturred up for Queene Octavias sake
With monstrous mischiefe vile, their rage to slake,
They rumbling rush into the Pallace farre.
CHO. What dare they do, their counsailers who are?
NUN. Advaunce their Empresse old, subvert the new:
And graunt hir brothers beds as is hir due.
CHO. Which Poppie now with hole consent doth hold?
NUN. Yea that unbrideled rage in brest uprold,
Sets them agog, and makes them wondrous wood.
What ever ymage graven in marble stood,
If Poppies badge it bare, or if in sight,
It tended for to show hir beauty bryght,
Though it on heavenly altares brave did stand,
They break, or pull it down, with sword or hand.
Some parts with ropes sure tide, they trayle them forth
Which spurnd with durty feete, as though naught worth,
With filthy stinking myre they it all beray.
And with their deedes their talke doth jumpe agree,
Which mine amased minde, thinks true to bee.
For fierie flames they threat for to prepare,
Wherewith to waste the princes Pallace faire,
Unlesse unto their furious moode he give
His second wife, and with Octavia live.
But he by me shall know in what hard stay
The City stands: the rulers Ile obay.
CHO. Alack, what made you cruell warres in vaine
To move, sith prisoner love you can not gaine:
You can not him overcome, your fiery flame
He recketh not: his fyre overcomes the same.
He darkened hath those thundring thumps that shake
Heaven, Earth, Hel, sea, al things that makes to quake.

Yea mighty Jove, in heaven that weares chief crowne,
His flames from welkin hie hath brought adowne :
And you, not victors now, but vanquished,
Shall raunsome pay, the price of hearts bloud red.
Love pacient can not be, but hote in rage,
No easie thing it is his wrath t'asswage.
Achilles, worthy wight, that was so stout
To twang the Harpe he made in Ladies rout,
Prince Agamemnon sterne that boy benumd,
And rable rude of Greekes with love bronds bumd.
King Priams raigne he topsie turvie tost,
And goodly Cities great he chiefly lost.
And now my minde sore frighted stands agast,
What Cupides furious force brings us at last.

THE FOURTH SCEANE

NERO

Ah, ah, our captaines sloe dispatching coyle,
And our long suffring yre in such a broyle,
That streames of bloud yet do not quench their rage
Which thei against our propre person wage,
And that all Rome, with corses strewd about,
Those cruell villaines bloud, doth not sweat out.
  But deedes already done, with death to pay
A small thing 'tis, a greater slaughtrous day
The peoples cursed crime, and eke that dame,
Whom I did aye suspect, deserves the same.
To whome, to yelde those peasaunts would me make :
At last she shall with life our sorow slake,
And with hir bodies bloud shall quench our yre.
Then shall their houses fall by force of fyre :
What burning both, and buildings fayre decay,
What beggerly want, and wayling hunger may
Those villaines shal be sure to have ech day.
  Ah, Provender pricks that vile rebellious race
Ne can they once our favour well embrace,

Nor be content with peace in quiet state,
But broyling raumpe about with troubled gate.
Hereon with boldnesse straight, hereon they flie,
With harebraind rashnesse hedlong by and by.
  Well, they must tamed be with heavy stroke,
And downe be kept with peise of weighty yoke :
That they with like attempt do not arise,
Nor once cast up their deadly peasaunts eyes
Against our loving spouses golden lookes :
First punish them sure, then feare shal be their bookes
To teache them at their Princes beck t' obay.
But see at hand, whom fayth and vertue rare,
Lieuetenant chiefe of camps, appointed thare.

THE FIFTE SCEANE

PRÆFECTUS. NERO

THE vulgare peoples rash unruly rage
The slaughter of a fewe did sone asswage,
Which long withstode our valiant force in vain.
To tel your grace this newes, I come againe.
NERO. And is this then ynough, dost thou so well ?
O souldiour marke what doth thy captaine tell ?
Hast thou withheld thy hand from bloudy yre ?
Is this the due revenge that we requyre ?
PRÆ. The captaine guides of treason payd their hyre
By desperate death of bloudy sword in fight,
The route which sought with flaming fyre to light.
NER. Our royall Pallace great, who would assigne
Their Prince what he should doe : and pull in fine
Our mate from us, dissolving wedlocke bandes :
Whose hardy slaunderous tongs and wicked handes,
Hir princely grace reprochfully withstandes,
From due revenge are they dismissed free ?
PRÆ. Shall subjectes payne by griefe assigned bee ?
NER. It shall assigne which time shall never weare.
PRÆ. Which neither wrath may end, nor yet your fear :

NERO. Shee shall appease our hie displeased minde,
Who fiyrst our wrath deserved due to finde.
PRÆ. Declare whose death your moode doth most require,
Let not my hande be stayde from your desire.
NER. It seekes our sisters death and trayterous hed.
PRÆ. Those words through all my lims hath stiffnesse spred,
Opprest with griesly feare : NER. Us to obay
Stands thou in doubt ? PRÆ. On fayth why do you lay
So great a fault ? NER. Bycause thou sparedst our foe.
PRÆ. Deserves a woman to be termed so ?
NERO. If treason she begin. PRÆ. Is any man
So sure that hir accuse of treason can ?
NER. The peoples rage. PRÆ. Those madde unweldye wights
Who order could ? NER. Who could stir up their sprits ?
PRÆ. No creature as I thincke. NER. A woman could,
In whome a mind Dame nature hath upfould,
To mischiefe prone : shee armed hath hir heart
To hurt by wyles : yet strength shee set apart,
Least shee undaunted force with hir should beare :
But now hir slender power with doubting feare
Is quickly quaylde, or else with punishment,
Which hir condemned state to mischiefe bent
To late doth ende : away with grave advise,
Us with entreating seeke not to entyse.
Dispatch that we commaund on shipboorde borne,
Farre off to shore aloofe with dashing worne
Commaund shee be : that tunlike swelling brest
At length in storming stomack may take rest.

THE SIXTE SCENE

CHORUS. OCTAVIA

ALACK the peoples bitter love,
And dyre good will to many one,
Which, when they hoysted sayles above,
With pleasaunt blastes it made to grone,

And caried them from quiet shore,
That faynting, leaves them in the deepe,
And tumbling, raging waters rore.
  Cornelia piteous wretch did weepe,
And sore bewayle hir sonnes estate :
The peoples love did undoe them,
And wondrous favour bred them hate :
Great worthy peeres of noble stem,
Of high renowne for vertues prayse :
In fayth and eloquence did pas,
Their stomacks stout their fame did rayse :
With lawes eche one most excellent was.
  And Scipio, thee did Fortune yeelde
Unto lyke death, and curssed wracke,
Whom neyther honours pompe coulde sheelde,
Nor fenced house thy foes keepe backe.
Moe to repeate, although I coulde,
Pure present griefe forbiddeth sore :
Ere whyle to whom the people woulde
Her Fathers antique Courte restore,
And Brothers wedlocke once againe,
Now weeping, wringing hands poore wretch,
Unto hir cruell, deadly payne,
The armed souldiours doe hir fetch.
How safe doth poverty lye content,
In thetched house safe shrouded there ?
High raysed towers with blasts are bent,
Which often tymes them over beare.
Oct. Where pull you mee, poore wretch ? alas,
Into what banisht exiles place
Woulde Nero have mee for to passe,
Or Fortune bids, with frowning face ?
If now with faynting strength quite coolde,
And with my broyles all wearied ceasse,
And longer lyfe shee graunt mee woolde,
If that shee worke for to increase
My sorrowes great with deadly dart,
Why is she then so much my foe,

In country that I may not part,
And leave my life before I goe ?
But now no helpe of health I feele,
Alas I see my Brothers boate :
This is the same whose vaulted keele
His Mother once did set a flote.
And now his piteous Sister I,
Excluded cleane from spousall place,
Shall be so caried by and by :
No force hath vertue in this case,
No Gods there be my woes to wrecke.
The griesly, dreadfull drab Eryn,
Doth weld the worlde at nod and becke,
Who can lament my state, wherein
I am, alas, sufficientlie ?
How can Aedon duely playne
My smarting streames of teares that I
Do shedde ? whose wings I would be faine,
If destnies would them graunt, to weare.
Then would I leave my mourning mates,
As swiftly fled as wings could beare,
And so avoyde these bloudy pates.
Then sitting sole in shirwood shirle,
And hanging sure, by dandling twigge
With plaintive pipe I might out twirle
My heavy tuned note so bigge.
Chor. The mortall broode the destnies guide :
Themselves they nothing can assure,
That certainly doth stedfast bide :
Which our last day of life procure,
(Whereof we alwayes should beware,)
Much daungerous chaunces for to try :
Unto your troubled minde with care,
Now many saumples do apply,
Which your accursed court hath brought,
To bolden you in all your broyle :
For what hath more your troubles wrought,
What doth against you sorer toyle,

Than fortune doth ? the first of all,
Agrippas childe brought forth to life,
Whome we Tyberius daughter call,
By lawe, and eke Prince Cæsars wife,
Of many sonnes a carefull dame,
I cannot chose but now recount,
Whose worthy, glorious ample name
Throughout the world doth much surmount.
So oft with belly bolne that bare
Desyred fruicts and peaces pledge,
Ere long thou sufferedst exiles care,
Strypes, chaines, and boltes of yron wedge,
And mourning much, which so did frame,
That death they causde thee to abyde.
  So Livia, Drusus lucky dame,
In male kinde babes did hedling slyde
Into a cruell monstrous deede,
And death sore pearcing deadly dart.
  Hir mothers fates doth Julia speede,
To folow streight with all hir heart,
Who after longer wasted time
With bloudy fauchion kene was slaine,
Although for no just cause or crime.
Your mother eke that once did raigne,
Who then esteemd of Claudius well,
Did wisely weld his court at will,
And fruitfull was, as you can tell,
What could not her desire fulfill ?
Shee sometime subject to hir slave,
To death was put with souldiours blade.
What shee, that easly hope might have,
Toth skies, hir raigne to rise have made,
Prynce Neroes lusty Parent great ?
First tost with shipmans boysterous force,
Then torne with sword in Prynces heat,
Did shee not lye a senceles corse ?
Oct. Loe mee the tyrant stern will send
To yrcksome shades and hellish sprits.

Why wretch doe I the tyme thus spend ?
Draw mee to death you to whose myghts
False Fortune hath bequeathed mee.
I witnesse now the heavenly powre.
What dost thou bedlame ? leave to flee,
With prayer to Gods, who on thee lowre.
I call to witnesse Tartar deepe,
And sprytes of Hell revenging freakes
Of haynous facts, in Dungeon steepe,
And Syre whom death deserved wreakes.
I doe not now repyne to dye,
Deck up your Ship, and hoyse your Sayle,
On frothing seas to windes on hye :
Let him that guides the Helm not fayle
To seeke the shore of Pharian Land.
Cho. O pippling puffe of western wynde,
Which sacrifice didst once withstand,
Of Iphigen to death assignde :
And close in Cloude congealed clad,
Did cary hir from smoking aares,
Which angry, cruell Virgin had :
This Prynce also opprest with cares,
Save from this paynefull punishment,
To Dians temple safely borne :
The barbarous Moores to rudenesse bent,
Then Prynces Courtes in Rome forlorne.
Have farre more Cyvile curtesie :
For there doth straungers death appease
The angry Gods in heavens on hie,
But Romayne bloude our Rome must please.

FINIS

THE TENTH TRAGEDY OF
L. ANNAE. SENECA
ENTITULED HERCULES ŒTÆUS
TRANSLATED OUT OF LATIN INTO ENGLISHE
BY J. S.

THE ARGUMENT

Hercules havinge subdued the Sonnes of Euritus Kynge of Œchalia (who contrary to theyr promise, denied to geve their Sister Iole unto him) and having made conquest of the City and countrey thereabout, meant to sacryfice unto the Gods for his victory in that behalfe, and successe in bringing away, perforce, his beeloved Iole. For the solemne celebration whereof, he sent Lycas his servaunt, unto Deianeira his Wyfe, to fetche his Robe, which hee alwayes used when hee sacrifized. Deianeira dippinge and besprinckling the same Robe in the bloude of Nessus the Centaure, because she feared least her husband loved Iole better then he did her, (for Nessus being shot through, and slayne by Hercules, had perswaded and advised her that shee shoulde so doe, whensoever shee doubted that her husbands love were alienated from her to any other,) sent it unto him. Which Garment when Hercules had put on, the poyson wherein it was dipped, and washed, envenomed all his Vitall partes, and drove him into most intollerable tormentes. For remedy whereof hee sent to Apollo his Oracle at Delphos : from whence hee received aunswere, that hee should bee caryed unto Mounte Œtus, and there, that a greate fier shoulde bee made : and as for all other things, they should bee referred to the pleasure and direction of Jupiter. The fier being there made and kindled by Philoctetes, (unto whom Hercules bequeathed his Arrowes), Hercules went up into it, and was there burned. Whose boanes being afterward sought for and not founde, the standers by were fully perswaded that he was deified, and taken up into Heaven. When knowledge thereof was broughte unto Deianira, shee thinking her selfe to bee the cause of her husbandes tormenting death, strangled herselfe.

THE SPEAKERS NAMES

Hercules.
Alcmena.
Hyllus.
Nutrix.
Iole.
Chorus.
Philoctetes.
Deianira.

HERCULES ŒTÆUS

THE FIRST ACTE

HERCULES alone

O LORDE of Ghostes whose fyrye flashe (that forth thy hand doth shake)
Doth cause the trembling Lodges twayne of Phœbus Carre to quake,
Raygne reachlesse nowe : in every place thy peace procurde I have
Aloofe where Nereus lockes up lande Empalde in winding Wave.
Thwack not about with thunder thumpes, the rebell kinges bee downe,
The ravening tyrauntes Scepterlesse, are pulled from their crowne :
By mee all daunted is whereon, thy boults thou shouldst bestowe.
And yet O Father, yet the Heavens are still withhelde mee froe,
At all assayes I serve, as might an Impe of Jove behove,
And that thou ought to Father mee, my stepdame well doth prove.
Why dost thou linger in delay, is Heaven of us afraide ?
Seeme wee so awfull, fell, and fierce ? and wherefore are wee staide ?
And cannot Atlas boysteous backe on stouping shoulder tough,
Upholde the payse of Hercules, and heaven well inough ?
What is it sier ? what is it Jove that thee so much detarres ?
What may thee force keepe backe thy sonne from scaling of the Starres
For death hath let me passe againe from dungeon darke to thee,
When mischiefes fell and monsters all destroyde and spoyled bee
That eyther Lande, or Seas, or Ayre, Or hell engender coulde
Arcadian Lion none to raunge in salvage Nemea wolde.
The Stymphall Foule hath chased bin with Bowe, and Brasell boulte,
No nimble heart of Menalus doth lye in hill nor houlte

The Dragon daunting with his bloud hath goarde the goulden grove.
And Hydra hath his courage coolde, and Diomedes drove
Whose puffed paunches pampred were with stoare of straungers bloud
That scoarde the Coaste and barren bankes of cruell Heber floud
I slaughterd them, and that the force of foe might well bee seene,
I prowlde away the booties of the prowde Amazon Queene.
Of silent shades in glummy Goulphes the dreadfull doomes I saw
On Cerber black the Tartar Tike the sonne did shine with awe,
And he with steaming Goggle eyes hath glyed upon the soone :
Anteus yawnes, and gapes no more whose gasping breath is doone.
A front his alters Busir fell was knockt unto the grounde,
By him whose hande gave Gerion his deepe and deadly wounde,
And slew the mighty Bull that was to hundred heartes a dreade,
All noyous plagues I spoyled have that ever Tellus bread,
And daunted by my hand they lye : the Gods now neede not fret :
The worlde to aunswere Junoes yre, no monsters now can get.
Now show thy valiaunt sonne his sire, or set him in the clowdes,
Thou shalt not neede to bee my guide, my selfe will climbe the shrowdes.
Doe thou my passage but allow, and I shall finde a way :
But if thou dreade, that monsters more the earth engender may,
Hast on eache monster hideous, to shew it selfe in time,
Whyle Hercules hath his aboade beneath the heavenly Clyme.
For who encounter shall the fiendes ? who ist that Grecis hath,
That may be meete to bide the brunt of mighty Junoes wrath ?
My prayse hurtes not my health : my fame doth fly from land to land :
The ysy poale doth know mee, where the northerne beare doth stand :
The easterlings encombred with the gleede of scorching sunne :
The south, where Phœbe by crooked cleaze of Tropick Crab doth runne :
In every coast O Titan where thou dost thy selfe reveale,
Now I have met thee face to face, to thee I doe appeale.
Aloofe beyonde the compasse of thy light I set my foote,
And never coulde thy blaze so farre his glymsinge glory shoote.

HERCULES ŒTÆUS

THE FIRST ACTE

As I have forst the honour of my triumphes for to streatch,
The day it self hath had his stint, within my travells reatch
Dame Nature faylde, the worlde was shogd beside his center dew,
And ougsome night in shimmering shade from dungeon darck I drew
And cankred Chaos lodged aloofe encountred mee amayne :
Yet from the deepe I gat to ground, whence none returnes agayne.
Wee strave against the Ocean stormes, I balased the keele
Fraught with my waight, that wrestling waves could not compell it reele.
What heapes of hazardes tempted I ? through all the open ayre,
To qualify thy wedlocks wrath can mischiefe none repayre
The earth would loath such baggage bred as I would match by might,
Yea monsters none are to be founde, the fiendes doe shun my sight.
And Hecules for want of fiendes agaynst him selfe did rage
What elvishe creatures curst did I with naked arme asswage.
Was ever any pevish thing so big upon the ground
That coapt with mee, but that my hand alone did it confound.
Not hetherto from vermin vyle through faynting feare I leapt
In babish yeares, not when to me in Cradell layde they leapt :
Eache thing that was commaunded me, at ease I did obay :
Thus free from paynefull toyle to me there never past a day.
What vermin have I vanquished, no king commaunding it ?
My courage cloyes me more then all the wyles of Junoes wit.
But what avayleth me to rid mankinde of fickle feare ?
The Gods yet cannot raygne in rest : while up the world doth peare,
New rid of furious fiendes, it sees aloft in starry skies
The cruell creatures all, that earst on earth did sore aggrise.
Dame Juno hath transport the elves : The scorching Crab doth creepe
Abouth the burning zone, and loofe at Affrica doth keepe
The Tropick line : and Harvest far he feedes with parching heate :
To Virgo, Leo turnes the time, and in a reaking sweate,
He buskling up his burning Mane, doth dry the dropping south,
And swallowes up the flabby cloudes in fyry foming mouth.
The Urchins all are creapt to skies, and have prevented mee :
I Conqueror from Earth to Heaven, my travells all may see :

These gargle Faces grim on heaven, Dame Juno first did set,
As though thereof the terrour might to skies my passage let :
Although she scatter them in Skyes, or make the Heavens forlorne
More then the Earth, or hellike Goulphes, (wherby the Gods are sworne)
Yet roome for Hercles shalbe made, if after monsters quelde,
Or battells fought, or hellike hound in Chaynes as captive helde,
If all exploytes cannot prevayle in skies a place to gayne,
Then soukt up bee the midland Sea twixt Barbarie and Spayne,
That eyther shore may joyne in one, with channell none betweene,
There will I dam the running streame, that Sea shall none be seene.
Or as for Corinth out shot land that tweene two seas doth lye,
It shall give way to eyther streame, that through the same shall fly.
And when the seas on passage have, the Fleete of Athens towne
May floate in Channell new : thus shall the world turne topsidowne :
Let Ister turne his streame, and Tanaus flow another way :
Graunt Jove a placket, graunt, whereby the Gods upholde I may.
Discharge thy thunder dint, where I shall keepe due watch and warde,
If eyther to the ysy poale thou bid mee have regarde,
Or burning zone, heere let the Gods full safe all force defy :
Prynce Pæan purchast hath an house amid the cristall sky,
And well deserved he the temples of Pernassus hill,
For slaughter of a Dragon made ? how oft recovering still
In Hydra poyson Python lay ? with Bacchus Perseus strong
By lesse desert then Hercules, have crept the Gods among.
But all the East (a mighty coast) to bond is brought by him,
Whom Juno spightes, how stearne a bug was snaky Gorgon grim ?
What Impe is he, begot betweene my stepdame dyre and thee,
Whose praysed paynes have purchaste him a place in heaven to be ?
The heaven that on my shoulders I have bolsterd up I crave :
But Lycas, (partner of my paynes) dispatch our triumph brave.
Display in pomp the ruin of Euritus house and Crowne :
And for the sacrifice with speede strike yee the Bullocks downe,
Where as the Aare (that doth advaunce the Church of Cenci Jove.)
Lyes open to Euboea sea : that wrackfull wave doth move.

HERCULES ŒTÆUS

THE FIRST ACTE

CHORUS

The Gods in blisse that man doth countervaile,
That can at once both Grave, and glory gayne,
Death upon death the whilst doth him assaile
Whose wretched life is lingred on in payne,
With frowning fate in spurning spighte who strives,
And sets the Keele of gaping goulphe at nought,
Will not submit his captive handes to gives,
As dishe of dishonour in triumph to bee brought :
Like carefull caytife hee shall never droupe,
Whelmed in storming thoughts of sower annoy,
Whose stomacke scornes for dawnting death to stoupe,
Though seas amid the deepe in hoysted hoy
Drive him aloofe, when as a southern gale
Beates Boreas back, or eastern puffe agayne
Recoiles the western winde, and seemes to hale
From deepest sandes the surges torne in twayne.
The broken planckes to catche hee scrambles not
Of wracked barke, as one that hopes to have
Amid the channell deepe a landing plot,
When dismall death appeares in every wave
Hee cannot suffer shipwracke all alone :
With pined karrayne coarse, and streames of teares,
And with our country dust our heades upon,
Powldring our lockes, wee languishe out our yeares.
Neyther flashing flame, nor thumping thunder cracke
Will once dawnt us : O death thou dost pursew
Where fortune fawnes : but where shee worketh wracke,
Thou shunnest those that woulde thee not eschew,
Wee stand not in our razed countrey wall,
Whose ground shall now bee overgrowne (alas)
With bramble, and bryer, and down the temples fall :
While mucky sheepecotes are planted in their place.
And now the frostifaced Greeke (alas)
This way, this way, with all his drove of Neate
By so much of Æchalia must passe.
As heapt on ashes gloweth still with heate.

The Tessayle sheepherd sitting by the way
On jarringe Pype shall play his countrey ryme,
Singing wyth sighes alacke, and weladay,
Thus to bewayle the sorrowes of our time
Ere tyme shall roll the race of many a yeare,
It will bee askt, where earst the towne did stand?
O well was I, when as I lived a leare,
Not in the barren balkes of fallow land,
Nor in Thessalia on the foodlesse clives,
But now among rough Trachin craggy Rocks,
And ougly shrubs necessity mee drives,
Whose flaming toppes detarres the feeding Oxe.
And in the way lesse woods untrode before
All comfortlesse, afright and in a maze
Needes must I trot alone, that would abhorre
The salvage beastes, that on the mountaynes graze
But better lot (if any Dames may have)
They over Inach wambling streame shall row,
Or shrowd in Dirce Walles, where Ismen wave
With feeble force of shallow fourde doth flow.
The hawty Hercles mother heere was wed,
What Scythian crag, what stones engendred him?
What Rocky mountayne Rhodope thee bred,
Of Tyrant Titans race a cursed lim?
Stipe Athos hill, the brutish Caspia land,
With teate unkinde, fed thee twixt rocke and stoane:
False is the tale, wherewith thou bearst in hande,
Two nights for thee thy Mother deare did groane.
While lingring starres long lodged in purple sky:
The shepherd starre his course did enterchaunge
With the load starre, and up the Moone doth sty,
That couched Phœbe durst not the Welkin raunge,
No Launce can pearce his monsters ruggy skin,
The blunted Iron tryed it with thumping thwack,
And Steele is not so tough: on naked skin
A swerd was brast, and stones rebounded back.
The force of fate he utterly defies,
And toughly timbered as he is of lim

Hee doth contrive, how quarrells may arise,
That death might prove his febled force in him
The quaries coulde not enter to his flesh,
Nor yet the bowe with Scythian steule drawn deepe,
No nor the glaves, with which Sarmacians fresh,
Hot skirmishes in th'ysy Clyme doe keepe.
No nor the Parthian better Archer farre,
Then Creete, who parcht with Phaëtons soultring flame,
Under the Equinoctiall rayseth warre,
Gaynst th' easterling discomfetinge the same.
Hee with his body did batter downe the wall,
Of Oechalie : nothing may him withstande :
By valiaunt prowesse hee hath conquerd all :
Tis woon before, that hee doth take in hande.
The howgy Briar that fifty paunches had,
The hawty Giges with hundred armes likewise,
That clamb up Thassayle hills as Gyant mad,
When rebells rage woulde take from Jove the skyes,
Such steaming byes, such gastly visage foule,
Such Gargle face, such countnaunce glaring grim,
Wherewith stearne Hercles glowningly doth scowle,
Those Gyaunts had resembling playnely him.
Thus greatest blisse is prone to greatest bale :
There wants no woe whose cup wee have not taste,
Wee wretched women have with countnaunce pale.

IOLE

But carefull caytiffe I doe not bewayle forlorne
The sweeping flames, nor Idolles, wyth their tattred Temples torne :
Nor that the Fathers burne together with theyr Sonnes,
That Gods and men, that tombes and Church, at once to ruin runnes.
Upon the common care wee doe not powre our playnt,
For Fortune wills us turne our teares with other woes attaynt :
And thus my frowning Fate allotteth unto mee
Another kinde of wretchednes, that must lamented bee :

THE TENTH TRAGEDY

What shall I first beweepe ? Or chiefly what complayne ?
And to bewayle them all at once woulde mitigate my payne.
Alas that but on breast Dame Nature did mee frame,
That blowes agreeing to my griefe might bounce upon the same.
With weeping Sipill rocke, broose yee my balefull breast,
Or on Eridanus silent shore in sorrowes let mee rest,
Where as the mourning troupe of Nymphes doe hale theyr heares,
To wayle the death of Phaëton with showres of dropping teares.
Or els in Sicill rocke cause mee encoucht to dwell,
Where Scilla Hag with howling noyse, and barking big doth yell.
Or else in Lynnets shape let me tell on my tale,
And weepe with Adon in the woods, or turnde to Nightingale
As Lady Philomele, recordes with weeping lay
In shade of hawty Ismar hill upon a tender spray,
With soking sighes her griefe, O Gods : and mee addight
In shape, that may be suetable unto my playntiffe plight.
And of my piteous moane let craggy Trachin sounde,
Sith Myrra sawe the teares wherein Dame Venus eyes were drownde,
That shee for Adonis with smoky sighes did shed,
And Halcion might wayle at will her loving Ceyx dead :
The Lady Tantalis gat life to weepe alone,
And Philomele did chaunge her shape, and earnefully did mone
Her tender Itis death : (alas) why are not yet
With flickering Fethers fit for wynges my naked armes beset ?
O happy shall I bee, and happily bee bleast,
When in the woods as in an house I make my shrowding neast,
And sitting like a birde upon my countrey grounde
In dolefull harmony shall tune the cares that me confounde.
That thus the people fond may talke how they have seene
In piteous likenesse of a Byrde, the Daughter of a Queene.
I carefull caytiffe, I, beheld my Fathers fate,
When in the Courte a deadly club did Palt him on the pate,
And sprawling on the floore with braynes pasht out hee laye,
Alas if fates would let thy Coarse beshrynde in pit of Claye,
What flowing teares (O Syer) would I on thee bestowe ?
And coulde I brooke it Toxeus, to see thy death with woe ?

That wert unwaunde in yeares, and eake in pits unpaysde,
Upon whose naked Cheekes the pregnaunt sap no hayres had raysde.
Why should I parents deare your fates with teares detest,
Whom death with hand indifferent hath taken hence to rest :
My Fortune seekes my teares, due to myne owne distresse,
Now as a captive must I dawnce attendaunce more and lesse,
Upon my Ladyes rock : and twyst her threde yspoon.
Woe worth my beauty, for the which in dread of death I run,
And for thy sake alone my stock hath lost his lyfe,
Whyle that my syer Denyeth me to Hercles as his wyfe
And did for feare refuse his stepfather to bee,
But to our Ladyes balefull bower as Captives hence goe wee.

THE SECONDE ACTE

NUTRIX. DEIANIRA

HAT furious fits of ramping rage doth boyle in Womens brayne,
When in one roofe both wedded wyfe and Harlot doe remayne ?
Both Scylla and Charibdis gulfe no daunger like it have,
That raging roll on Sicill shore by heapes the wrastling wave.
No salvage beaste so bad there is, that betters not the same.
For bruite no sooner blew abroade the captive Harlots name,
And that the beauty of Iolas countnaunce shyned brym,
As doth the day when marble skies no filthy fog doth dim :
Or like the glimse of twinckling starre, that in the welkin bright
Displayes abroade his shooting beames amid the frosty night :
But Deianira Hercles Wyfe all bedlem like doth stande,
And scowleth as the Tiger wilde which couched on the sande
In shade of rocke doth shrowde his whelpes, and buskells up in haste,
Espying him that of his younge doth come to make the waste :
Or like as Menas overcharg with Bacchus licour sweete
With Ivy bunche on thurled Darte from place to place doth fleete
Shee makes a pawse, in doubt where to shee might derect her pace,
Then frantickly as on bestraught, shee fiskes from place to place
In Hercles house, thus was shee rapt in rage of flaming yre,
The house to narrow was to coole the despret dames desire.
Shee runneth in, shee trots about, shee makes a soddayne stay.
The mallady in frowning face it selfe doth playne display.
No galling griefe remaynes at heart. The teares gush from her Eyes,
Nor in on kinde of temper still in frensy fits shee fryes :

Hir glowning lookes with fury fell doe chaunge her former hew,
Now glaring stande her steaming Eyes, and palenesse doth ensew
The ruddy colour in her Cheekes: the anguish of her heart
Drives out her dolors deepe, to shew them selves in every part:
Shee languisheth, shee moanes for helpe, shee wayles her froward fate,
And all the house an Echo makes resounding her estate.
Loe headlong to and froe shee hies, and running still about
Goes mumbling, and the secrets of her minde shee mutters out:
Oh Juno Spouse to Jove, what part of heaven soever thou keepe,
Rayse up some salvage beast, agaynst lewde Hercules to creepe,
That I shall thinke sufficient: If any combrous snake
With breeding hee doe craule, more big in all the slimy lake,
That may not take a foyle: or if that ought doe yet remayne,
So ougsome, grisely, curst, and grim, so fraught with filthy bayne,
That hee may loathe to looke thereon, that may his sight appaule,
Undoe their Dennes, from hydeous hoales procure such vermin craule.
Or if that fiendes can none be founde, then conjure thou my ghost
To what thou list: this soule of myne can well abyde the most:
Some uncouth shape, some gastly face, such one bestow on mee,
Whereby the horrour of my pangues may countervayled bee:
My boyling breast cannot conceave the vengeaunce I woulde trye:
Why serchest thou the corners farre of landes aloofe that lye?
And turnst the world thus upside downe? why seekst thou harme of hell?
To trounce him, furious fiendes ynough within this breast doe dwell:
Make me thyne instrument of hate: his stepdame I will bee,
And thou mayest worke the overthrow of Hercules by mee:
Appoynct my hand to any thing. Why dost thou make delay?
Use thou my frensy, as the meanes to compasse his decay.
The mischiefe shall be brought to passe, what ever thou wilt crave:
Why stande yee musing still thereon? contrived all I have:
Thou mayst forbeare thy mallice now: my rancour shall suffice,
To bryng this wretche unto his ende, my selfe can well devise.
NU. My Foster gyrle, of raving mynde, these dreary playnts asswage,
Forbeare this heate, and brydell yet the rigour of thy rage:

Behave thy selfe for such an one, as men may worthy judge
The noble Spouse of Hercules. Dei. Shall Iole (slavish drudge)
Bring basterd brethren to my Babes ? of her that is a slave
Shall Jupiter the God of heaven forsooth a daughter have ?
The flashing flames and fighting floodes shall joyne togeather first,
The northern beare to Marble seas shall stoupe to quench his thyrst.
Yea vengeaunce, vengeance will I have, though on thy back thou wyeld
The boysteous heavens, and all the worlde doe peace unto thee yelde :
There is a thing shall stinge thee worse then Hydra hissing Snake,
The corsey curst of angry Wyfe. Doth any firy Flake
Upthrowne from Etnas boyling Foarge, so sowse the beaten skyes ?
More then all things that thou hast daunt, my ghost shall thee aggryse.
Shall thou prefer a servill Trull before thy wedded Wyfe ?
For feare of many monsters more I tendred still thy lyfe,
And now for to encrease my care, I see no monsters lurke,
And now steps in an hateful whoore, (which more my minde doth urke)
To cumber us, as ill as fiendes. O Father thou of might,
The shielde of Gods : and Titan thou, that bearst the Lamp of lyght,
I onely unto Hercules a loyall wyfe abod,
And to an Harlots use are turnde my prayers made to God :
The fruite of my felicity a Strumpet doth obtayne,
And for an Harlots love yee Gods have harde my prayers vayne :
Is Hercules returnde for her ? O griefe not yet content,
Devise some tearing torments, seeke some pangues, and punishment.
Let Juno learne of mee, what force a womans fury hath.
Shee knowes not how in deepe despight, to use her harming wrath.
For mee you did these battayles wage : for my sake Acheloe
Did let his streaming bloud amid his wamblinge waves to floe.
When snarling Adders shape hee tooke, and to the boysteous Bull
Hee gieving up his sloughty shape did bende his mallice full.
And thus thou foylde a thousand foes by conquest of this one :
Yet presently thou plunged art, and that by mee alone :

A prysoner now must be preferde before thy loyall wyfe.
Ile none of that : but even the day that first begins the strife,
And to our wedlock brings the breach, shalbe thy dismall day,
And knap in twayne the fatal twist where on thy lyfe doth stay.
What meaneth this ? my mynde relents. My mallice breakes his rage :
O wretched griefe why dost thou faynte ? thy spight wilt thou asswage ?
With fealty of a faythfull Wyfe dost thou thy conscience charge ?
Why lets thou not my boyling yre for to encrease at large ?
Why dost thou slake thy frying fits ? this mallady still survive.
Even now I able was with him for maistership to strive.
In deede I have not craved ayde : yet Stepdame Juno will,
To weilde my handes to worke his wracke, bee heere asistant still.
NU. What treachery entendest thou mad bedlem to commit ?
Thy husband wilt thou murder wreatch ? whose flickering fame doth flit
From east to west : whose bryght renowne the earth coulde not contayne
But raysde aloft, from marble Skies it doth rebounde agayne :
The mother Earth shall ryse in armes for to revenge his grave.
His former Stepsiers stocke heereby the overthrow shall have :
And all Ætolia royall bloud will feele an utterfall :
In quarrell of thy Hercules the worlde conspier shall.
Then silly wight how many plagues shalt thou alone abyde ?
But bee 't that from the face of man thou myght thy body hyde,
Yet Jove the lightning leames of heaven doth holde in armed hand,
Beholde the flying fyry flakes in ranckes all ready stand :
And threatning thunders thumping thicke doe bounce out all the day.
Deathes dungeon (that thou dost defy) full duely scaare thee may.
For there his Uncle umpyre sits : Myche where thou mayest unspyd
And every where thou shalt perceave the Gods to him allied.
DE. I graunt it despert deede, whereto dispayre now doth me drive
NU. Die sure thou shall. DE. And die I will, (as presently I live)
The loyall spouse of Hercules. And ere this night doe passe,
Day shall not see that Deianire a living Wydow was.

Nor of my spousall bed an whoore shall get the interest.
The dawning day shall sooner make the morning peere in West,
Unto the eastwarde Indians the ysy poale shall melt,
And freezing Scithian first shall fry with flames that hee hath felt
Of Phœbus fervent wheele ere mee Thessalia Trulls shall see
Divorst : my brydall blase shall with my bloud iquenched bee :
And eyther let him murdred bee, or take away my Lyfe,
So soothly let him count among the foyled fiendes his Wyfe.
Among Alcides labours let mee reckned bee as on.
His love in heart I holde, untill the utter gaspe bee gon.
Thus undivorst (not unrevengde) I will to Hercles tombe.
If Iole be with chylde by him, ile teare it from her wombe,
And rent it with these pawes of myne. Yea in the wedding place,
I flying at her fearce will set my tallantes in her face :
Let him not spare in raumping rage a sacrifyce to make
Of me uppon his wedding day, when he his Trull doth take,
So that I fallyng downe may light on Ioles senceles coarse :
He dyes a happy man that first hath quelde his foes by force.
Nu. O wretched wight why dost thou thus encrease thy fuming heate :
And feede thy fury wittingly least hap should thee defeate.
He loved Lady Iole, but whyle her fathers crowne
Stoode florishyng in royall state and were not battred downe,
And as unto the daughter of a King hee suter was,
But when from type of hawty pompe she did to thraldome passe
He shooke her of, hot love was coold, and now her bitter bale
Would not allow the wracked kele to beare to hie a sale :
Unleeful thinges that should be shund we gredely desyre,
But matters meeter for our state we seldome do require
The pytying of adversity doth oft enkindle more
The fervent fittes of love, and this perhappe doth urge him sore,
To see her reast of natyve soyle, it may his fancy touch,
Her hayre not tuct with tresses trimme, nor dect with golden ouche,
Perhaps the man with pitty prickt doth love her for her care.
Unto his noble hart to pitty prisoners tis not rare.
The sister deare of Priamus (fayre Lady Hesyon) he
Did cause to Thelamon the Greeke in wedlocke knit to bee :

Account how many wyves before, and maydens did he love,
And raung'd abroade to coole the rage that Venus brand did move.
Fayre Auge mayde of Arcadye ententive set to leade
Dianas daunce, by force of him did leese her mayden hed.
And yet no token could she shew nor pledge of any love,
What shall I speake of any more, or doth it mee behove
To prate what prankes he playd with fifty daughters in one night.
And yet how soone of such a pange he overcame the might,
He set much store by Omphale of Lidis land the Queene,
When like a guest on Timolus the mount he hath bene seene.
He was so prict with Cupids dart, and caught in Venus trap,
That tuckt in womans weede he sat with distaf in his lap
And spoon the flaxe with fombling fyst, and rudely thumbde the threde
And flong from him the lyons case the price of noble deede.
With tresses tricke on plaited lockes he wayled as a mayde
With myre his friseled poale was smeard, and curled bush was brayde,
Thus every where as fancy fitts, the fondling dotes in love.
But in such sort as easely he can the same remove.
DEI. But they whom fickle fansies fits have taynt, doe learne at last
In linke of love by tract of time to fix affiaunce fast.
NU. Trow yee that hee this captive queane, and on whom hee doe see
The daughter of his deadly foe, will more esteeme then thee ?
DE. As gladsome groves at Prime of spring in beauties pride are seene
When fresshest warmth the naked twigges doth clad in pleasant greene,
But when coulde Boreas boysteous blast the pipling puffes doth stop
Of southwinde sweete, rough wynter powles the naked busshes top :
The barewoode with misshapen stumpes doth shew a withered Face,
Even so my beauty marching forth a season on his Race
Still fades away, and evermore abates his glimsing glosse,
And what so ever was in mee, by care is come to losse.
And that which earst by fansy fed the greedy gazing eyes,
Is fallen away by bearing childe : so oft it droupes, and dyes.

And since I came to mothers state, I faded fast away,
And wrinckled age with furrowed face steps in with quick decay.
But yet this bondmaydes feauter fresh her sorrow better brookes,
Her comely countnaunce crazied is with leane and wanny lookes,
And yet for all her kark and care amid her deepe distresse,
Shee beares a glimse of beauty bryght, and favour nothing lesse.
Her heavy hap and frowning fate can nothing from her plucke,
Save Scepter from her royall hande by all this lowring lucke.
By meanes of this first faynting feare did lodge within my breast,
That makes mee wake the weary nightes, and leese my kindely rest.
In all mens eyes at first I seemde to be a blessed Wyfe,
And Ladies all at our estate repining very ryfe
Did wyshe my match in spite of fate what Stepsier shall I hope
As match in majesty to Jove within the heavenly coape ?
Deare fosterdame whom shall I make my feere in spowsall bed ?
Although Euryst that Hercules to all these toyles hath led,
Doe linke with mee in bridall bandes, my state shalbe impayrde.
Tis small worth to deserve to bee to kingly wedlock rayrde.
Nu. But Issue is the thing that doth in marriage kindell love.
De. And Issue is the thing that doth in marriage mallice move.
Nu. This while the bondmayde to thee for present shalbe braught.
De. Loe hee jetteth up and downe with pryncely port full haught,
And buckles fast about his Loynes the lively Lyons case,
Who doth invest the wretched with the right of kingly mace,
Deposing those from honoures type that late so lofty sat,
And pestereth his puissaunt pawes with huge unwieldy bat,
Of whose exploytes, and maarciall actes the Seres sing aloofe,
And all enclosde in Ocean sea thereof have perfit proofe
Is now become an amorous knight : the honour of his name
Doth nothing touch his conscience, to render once his fame.
Hee roveth through the worlde, as on that doth no whit esteeme,
Although that men as soone to Jove shall him unworthy deeme.
Nor like the man whose credit through the townes of Greece is greate.
Hee seekes to compasse his desier, to worke a Lovers feate.
With single Dames is his delight : If any him deny,
Then to attayne his lawlesse lust by rigour doth hee try.

With men hee fareth frantickly, to others smart and blame
Hee wins his Wyves, his folly frayle is cloackt by vertues name.
The noble City Oechalie is made a razed towne.
The Sunne twixt morne and even did set, in one day up, and downe.
One day did see it stand in state, the same did see it fall.
These bloudy broyles, and wasting warres of Love proceeded all,
As oft as parents unto him deny theyr daughters deare,
So oft I warrant them they neede his wrathfull fury feare.
So oft a man with Hercules shalbe at deadly foode :
As hee denies his stepfather to bee by joyning bloude.
If hee may not be sonne in law, then doth hee rage and rave :
Why doe these guiltlesse handes of myne still keepe him from his grave,
Till hee dissemble franticke fits, to bend his ayming bowe,
And deaths wounde on my chylde, and me with bloudy hands bestowe ?
Thus hawty Hercules was wont his wedlockes to devorce.
Yet nought there is, that lawe of guilt on him might have recorse,
Hee makes the worlde blame Juno, for the ills hee hath commit.
O rigour, of my rage why dost thou qualify my fit ?
Now must thou set thy hands on worke, too 't while thy hands bee hot.
Nu. Thy husband wilt thou slay ? De. Him whom his Leman lewd hath got.
Nu. But yet he is the sonne of Jove. De. And so Alcmenas sonne.
Nu. With stroke of steele ? De. With stroke of steele if it cannot bee donne,
Then for to bring his death to passe, ile set for him a snare.
Nu. What kinde of madnesse may it be that makes thee thus to fare ?
De. Such as my husband hath mee taught. Nu. Wilt thou thy spouse destroy,
On whom the stepdames spite yet had no power to work annoy ?
De. The wrathes of heavenly mindes do make them blest on whom they light,
So doth not spite of mortall men. Nu. Oh silly wretched wight
For beare thy rage, and feare the worst, mans force may not assayle
Him, that agaynst the power of hell, and death coulde once prevayle.

DE. Ile venter on the dint of swerd. NU. Thy wrath (deare foster child)
Is greater then the crime, that hath thy Hercules defilde.
With egall mallice measure faultes. Alas why dost thou bring
So great and sore a penalty upon so smale a thinge?
Let not thy griefe be greater then the sorrow thou sustaynes.
DE. Set you it light that with our wedlocke linkt an harlot raygnes?
Nay rather thinke it still to much, that doth thy sorrows breede.
NU. And is the love of Hercules revolt from thee in deede?
DE. 'Tis not revolt, deare foster Dame, fast in my bones it stickes:
But yre boyles hoate in burning breaste, when love to anger prickes.
NU. It is almost a common guise, that wedded wyves doe haunte,
Theyr husbands hearts by magicke Arte, and witchcraft to enchaunte.
In winter coulde I charmed have the woods, to make them sprout,
And forst the thunder dint recoyle, that hath bin boulting out.
With waltring surges I have shooke the seas amid the calme,
I smoothed have the wrastling waves, and layde downe every walme.
The dry ground gaped hath like gulphs, and out new springs have gusht,
The roring rocks have quaking sturd, and none thereat hath pusht.
Hell gloummy gates I have brast oape, where grisly ghosts all husht
Have stood and aunswering at my charme the goblins grim have scoulde.
The threefolde headded hounde of hell with barking throates hath houlde.
Thus both the seas, the lande, the heavens, and hell bowe at my becke.
Noone day to midnight, to and froe turnes at my charming checke.
At my enchauntment every thing declynes from natures lawe.
Our charme shall make his stomacke stoupe, and bring him more in awe.
DE. What hearbes doe grow in Pontus sea? Or els on Pindus hill?
To trownce this machelesse champion, where shall I finde the ill?
The magicke vearse enchaunts the Moone from Starry skies to ground,
And fruictfull harvest is thereby in barren winter found.

The whisking flames of lightning leames oft sorcery doth stay,
And noonetyde topsy turvy tost doth dim the dusky day.
And leave the welkin to the starres, and yet not cause him stoupe.
Nu. The Gods themselves by charme of love have forced bin to droupe.
De. Perhap hee shall be woon by one, and yeelde to her the spoyle.
So love shall be to Hercules the last and latest toyle.
By all the hoste of heavenly powers, and as thou seest mee feare,
The secrets that I shall attempt, in councell see thou beare :
Nu. What may it be, that thou woulde have me keepe so secretly ?
De. No broyle of blades, no privy cote, no fiery force perdye :
Nu. I you assure I can conceale, if mischiefe none be ment,
For then the keeping close of it is sure a lewde entent.
De. Then looke about if none be heere our councell to betray :
Looke rounde about, on all sides cast thy countnaunce every way.
(Nu. Beholde the place is safe inough from any listning eare.)
De. Beside the place of our estate there is a secret nooke,
A covert corner for our talke, that sonneshyne never tooke.
Neyther at morne, nor evening tyde, when Titans blaze doth quench,
And hee in ruddy westerne wave his firy wheeles doth drench,
There secret lyes the privy proofe of Hercules amorous thought,
Ile tell thee all deare foster dame : This witchcraft Nessus taught,
Whom Ixion engendred of a mysty groning clowde,
Where Pindus hauty hill his top among the starres doth shrowde,
And other stipe doth heave his Crest above the ryding rack
When Achelous over layde, with many a thumping thwack
Of Hercles club, did shift him selfe to every kinde of shape,
And triall made of all his sleights none served to escape,
At length he turnde him selfe into the lykenesse of a Bull,
And so was fowly vanquished in forme of horny scull.
(While Hercules being Conquerour did me his Wyfe enjoy.)
Returning home to Greece agayne, it hapned Even lake
To overflow the drowned marshe and chaunell to forsake,
And strongly streamde to seas hee runns, and swells about his bankes,
And Nessus usde to passe the poole, and search the croking crankes

As Ferryman demaundes his fare, and bare mee on his backe,
And wading forward brake the Waves and surges of the lake.
At length yet Nessus waded out unto the farther shore,
Yet Hercules had swam but halfe the river and no more :
And plyde it hard to cut the streame : but when espied had hee,
That Hercules was farre behinde, Madam (quoth hee) to mee,
(Be thou my booty, and my wyfe, and clasping mee about)
Away he flings, and Hercules besturres him mauger Wave :
Though Ganges gulph and Ister streame (quoth he) thou traytour slave
Might roon in on, yet shift to scape them both well coulde I make,
And in thy hast a shaft shall soone thy running over take :
And ere he spake the word, his arrow flew out of his bowe,
And wrought a wounde in Nessus ribbs, hee coulde no farther goe.
It sped him sure, to looke for death. Hee cried, well away.
The baggage running from the wounde reserved as hee lay,
And putting it into his hoofe the which undoyng, hee
In cutting yt with his owne hand, did geve it unto me.
And thus at latter gaspe he sayde, the witches have me toulde,
That love may charmed be by this, to have and keepe his hould.
The conning witch dame Michale did teach Thessalia dames,
Who onely forst the Mone to stoupe to her from heavenly frames.
Therfore (quoth he) at any tyme when hateful whores abuse
Thy spousall bed, or waveryng man do haunt to any stewes,
Then with this salve annoynt his shyrtes, and let it see no sonne,
But kepe it close in corners darke, the bloud then shall not shonne
His strength : and thus ful sodenly he left his talke with rest :
And deadly sleepe with senceles death his feeble lims opprest.
Thou Dame to whom in hope of trust my secrets all bewray,
Oh, that the poyson soakt into the vesture bright, it may
Preace through his limmes unto his hart, and sinke through every bone,
NU. I wil dispatch it all in hast, make thou thy earnest mone
Unto the God, whose tender hand his stedfast dartes doth weild.
DE. I thee beseech that art of earth and heaven in honour helde,
And thou that shakest burning boltes, thou curst and cruel boy,
Whose elvish weapons make thy mother feare thy sharpe annoy.

Now arme thy hand with speedy shaft not of the slender sort,
But biggest boultes, with which as yet thou hast assault no fort.
We neede no litle shaft that may styrre Hercules to love,
Bring cruel handes and force thy bow his depest draught to proove.
Now, now draw forth thy shaft wherwith thou caused cruelly
The burning breast of Jove by fyttes of fervent love to frye.
When as the God his thonderbolt and lightning layd assyde,
Gan boalne with bumpes on forehead big : and through the wave he hid,
And swam with Europ on his backe in shape of horny Bull.
Now powre downe love, and therewithall let Hecles hart be full.
If Ioles beauty kyndle heat and Hercles hart doth move,
Quench thou these coales, and force him glow with us in lawfull love.
Ful oft the thunder thumping Jove hath stouped to thy yoke :
And him that weildes the moary mace of blacke Averne to smoake.
Thy flames enforce, and eake the Lord of glummy Stigian lake :
But onely match thou Hercules, and of him triumphe take
O Jove, whose wrath more wrackful is then yreful Junoes might,
The charme is made in perfecte force is al our medcine right,
Wherein the shirt shal steeped bee that wearyed many wighte.
Whose handes on Pallas distaffe spoone the weary Web with payne.
And if for Hercules avayle shall drincke up all the bane.
And with my charme Ile strengthen it. But loe yee in the nick
Defte Lycas commeth heere at hand who will dispatche it quick :
But tell him not what force it hath least hee the guilt betray.
Dei. Alas that fayth to kinges dwells not in howses of estate :
Have Lycas heere this shirt, the which my handes have spun of late,
Whyle Hercules at random roves, and overshot with wyne
Doth rudely dandle on his lap the Lidiane Lady fyne.
Now doates hee after Iole : but this his boyling rage
That burneth in his breast I will with curtesy asswage.
For curtesy conquers canckred churles. See thou my spouse desire,
Hee spare the Shirt, untill hee set the Franckinsence on fire,
And offer up his sacrifice, and weare his Garlond gray
Of Popler boughes on wreathed lockes. And I will goe my way

To'th royall Gods, and will beseeke the cruell Cupids dame
Yee ladies and companions that with mee heather came,
Now force the fountaynes of your teares from watred eyes to roon,
To wayle our Countrey Calydon on every side undoon.

CHORUS

O Deianire deare daughter of our King
Oeneus late, to see thy frowning fates
Who after woe thus downe on thee to fling,
It irks our heartes, that were thy foster mates.
O woefull wight it pitieth us to see
Thy wedlock in this tickle state to bee.
Wee, Lady, wee that with thee wonted were
With flapping Oare on Acheloe to rowe,
When having past the spryng tyme of the yere,
With Channell smoth hee newely wexeth lowe,
And makes agayne his swelling surges calme,
And boobling runnes at Ebbe withouten walme.
Through weale and woe wee still with thee remayne,
And now what griefe so ever thou feare in mynde,
Account thou us as partners of thy payne,
For commonly when Fortune turnes the wynde,
And makes thee beare thy beaten Sayle but low,
Then friendship ebbes where it before did flow.
And who so guydes the sway of golden mace,
Though people thicke doe haunte his stately courte,
And in at hundred gates doe preace a pace,
Yea though that thou mayntaine so greate a port,
To garde thee with this garrison, yet shall
Thou scarcely finde one faithfull hearte of all.
In paynted porche, and gates of guilded bowers
The lurcking hagge Eryn her tuskes doth whet :
And sturring strife with quarreling face shee lowers.
The portly doares no sooner oape are set,
But treason black, pale envy, deepe deceight,
With privy knife of murther step in streight.

And when the Prynce appeares in open place,
To shew him selfe before his subjects sight,
Swelling despight attendeth on his grace :
As oft as dawning day removes the nyght,
And every time the sunne at West goes downe,
They looke another man should clayme the Crowne.
Fewe heartes love kinges, not few their kingly might :
The glorious shew of courtly countenaunce
Bewitcheth many : where one sets his delight
How next the king hee may him selfe advaunce,
That through high streetes hee may as lorde of rule
With lofty lookes, ryde mounted on his Mule.
Ambitious heate enflames his hawty breast.
Another would his greedy hunger staunch
With gubbes of goulde, (and though hee it possest)
Rich Arabie serves not his pyning paunch,
Nor western India (a worlde for to behoulde)
Where Tagus flowes with streames of glittring goulde.
The covetous charle, the greedy gnosse in deede,
In whom from cradell nature so it plantes,
No hourded heapes his endlesse hunger feede,
In plenty pines the wreatch, in wealth hee wantes.
Some other fondlings fansy thus doth guyde,
To fawne on kings, and still in courte to byde.
As one disdayning lyke a Country mome
And crooked clowne, the plowe to follow still :
Although the dingthryfte dayly keepe at home
A thousand drudges, that his lande doe Tyll :
Yet wantes his will and wissheth wealth therefore,
Onely to waste on other men the more.
Another claweth and flattreth fast the King,
By clymbing up to treade downe every wyght :
And some at least to blockam Feaste to bryng
And thus hee strives to arme him selfe with myght
In bloude : but of their ship doth Fortune fayle,
When safe they thinke to floate with highest sayle
Whom Moone at morne on top of Fortunes wheele
High swayed hath seene, at fulnesse of renowne,

The glading sunne hath seene his Scepter reele,
And him from high fall topsey turvey downe.
At morne full merry, blith, in happy plight,
But whelmde in woes and brought to bale ere nyght.
These sildome meete hoare hayres and happy dayes :
The Lord that lyes on stately crimsen bed
Sleepes more in feare then snoring drudge that layes
Upon the countrey clod his drowsy head.
In goulden roofes, and hauty courtes they keepe,
Whose dreadfull dreames doe make them starte in sleepe,
The purple roabes lyeth waking many a night,
And slombers not, when homely ragges doe rest.
O if as at a Grate espy wee might
The sorrows shrined in a Prynces breast,
What pangues, what stormes, what terrour, O what hell
In sighing heartes of prowde estates doth dwell?
The Iryshe Seas doe never roare so ruffe,
When wrastling waves and swelling surges ryse,
That hoysted are with sturdy northern puffe,
As fearefull Fansyes doe theyr myndes aggryse.
But hee sighes not, nor combred is with care,
Whom Fortune hath bequeath'de a slender share.
In woodden dishe and blacke beche Bole hee swills,
And heaves it not to mouth with quaking hand :
With homely fare his hungry Mawe hee fills,
And leares not backe for feare of those that stand
With naked swerdes : but Kings in goulden cup
Wyne blent with bloude (most dreadfull draughts) do sup,
In dainty dishe the poyson bayte is layde,
And treason lurkes amid the sugred wyne :
At every bit they quake, and are a frayde
The swerde will fall that hanges but by a twyne,
And ever as hee liftes his head and drynkes,
The rebelles Knyfe is at his throate hee thinkes.
Such flattring joyes these happy worldlinges have,
Their outwarde pomp pretendeth lusty lives,
When inwardely they drowpe, as doth the slave
That pines in pangues fast clogde in goulden gives.

Strive not in hast to climbe the whirling wheele,
For hasty climers oft in haste doe reele.
Meane dames defy both peareles and glittring spanges,
And goulden chaynes with rubies ryche beset,
Nor at theyr eares doe massy Jewelles hange
With turky stones : nor pranked prowde they jet
In murrey gownes : nor doth the wooll they weare
Of Crymsen dye the costly colour beare.
Neyther in Tissew, nor silken garments wrought
With needle, nor embroadred Roabes they goe :
And yet this state is free from Jealous thought,
Theyr wedding is not unto them theyr woe.
When thousand stormes in Ladyes hearts doe dwell
By wedlocke breach, that breedes their noysom hell.
Who so he is that shunnes the middle waye,
Shall never fynd fast footing any where.
The wilful lad that needes would have a day,
And wayghty charge of Fathers charyot beare :
While he from wonted wayes his Jades doth jaunce,
Amonge straunge starres they pricking forward praunce,
Enforcing them with Phœbus flames to frye,
Whose roaming wheeles refuse the beaten rutt :
Thus both himselfe, and all the Cristall skye
In peril of the soulthring fyre he put.
So hawty myndes that clymbe above their skill,
Do worke their owne decay and others yll.
While Dœdalus in flying through the ayre
Did keepe the midst betweene the skie and grounde
He could in safe to Italy repayre,
And gave no gulph his name by beyng dround.
But Icarus presumes to mount on hie,
And stryves above the fethered foules to flye,
And scornes the guyding of his fathers trayne.
And in his flight wil coape to lofty sonne :
Which molt his winges so downe he droppes agayne
Into the seas, whereby his name they woone.
Thus proud attemptes of hauty clyming hier
Receive shrewde falles to quit their fond desyre.

Let other mount aloft, let other sore,
As happy men in great estate to sitte.
By flattring name of Lord I set no store :
For under shore my little keele shall flitt :
And from rough wyndes my sayles fayne would I kepe,
Least I be driven into the daungerous deepe.
Prowde Fortunes rage doth never stoupe so low
As litle roades, but them shee overflyes
And seekes amid mayne seas her force to shew
On argosies, whose toppes do reach the skyes.
But lo, here comes our Lady Deianire,
Straught of her wits, and ful of furious yre.

HERCULES ŒTÆUS

THE THIRD ACTE

DEIANIRA. CHORUS

LAS through all my quiveryng joyntes a running feare doth rest,
My staryng hayre standes stiffe upright and in my quaking breast
Deepe terrour dwelles, and eake my hart, with dread amazde doth pant,
With swelling vaynes my liver beates, as when the wynd doth want
Asswagd in calmy day, and yet the raging Seas do rore
Whose wrastling waves were rais'd aloft by Southren blastes before.
So yet my wit be tocksicate, although my feare be gone:
Thus God turmoyles us when he meanes to cloy th' unhappy one.
Thus prowd attempts bedasht at length. Ch. Oh wretch, O carefull wight,
What mischiefe may it be wherwith thou art so sore affright.
Dei. The shirt with Nessus bane imbrewde no soner hence was sent,
And wretched woman that I am toth closet strayght I went.
(My mynd mistrusts I knowe not what, and treason doth surmyse)
And Nessus by the heate bewrayed, that taynted was the bloud:
The God foreshewed that here the force of all the treason stoode:
For by good hap the fomy glede no foggy clowde doth dim,
But with ful power of burning beames he shyned blasing brim.
Scant yet I can for feeble feare unlocke my fastned jawes,
The scorching heate doth drye away, and by up force it drawes
The soaked bloud that beyng layed amid the frying flame
And boyling heate of shyning sonne did shrinke before the same:
Wherein the shyrt was steept, and all the royall robe imbrewde:
I cannot shew the villany wherwith it was indewde:

For as the Easterne wynd doth force the winter snow to melt,
Or lukewarme South when in the spring from Mimas mount they swelt
As Lucas els that fronters on Ionian sea, a land
Doth breake the wave the beaten surge lies foaming on the strand,
Or by the warmth of heavenly heat the frankinsence doth drop,
So all the venim wastes away and melteth every croppe.
And while I wonder stil hereon the wonder shrynkes away
But with a froath it spottes the ground, and there the poyson lay,
It rotts the cloth : my woman boalne and sweld doth follow me,
And shakes her head, my sonne as one astonished I see :
And hying hether all in hast declare what newes ye bring.

HILLUS. DEIANIRA. NUTRIX

Go mother goe, seeke out aloofe yf place of bydyng dwell
Beyond the ground both goulfe and starres, beyond both heaven and hell,
Flye mother far beyond the boundes of Hercules his toyle.
DEI. A mischiefe great I know not what within my breast doth boyle.
HIL. Unto the royall temples of dame Junoes tryumph hie,
These will allow the sanctuary though other it denye.
DEI. What heavy hap is it that may annoy my guiltlesse ghost ?
HYL. Oh mother, O that diamond of the world, that piller post
Whom fate as Joves lieuetenaunt heare have placed for the nones
Is dead : and Nessus burning bane deveuers Hercles boanes.
The daunter of the brutish beastes he conquering knight before
Is conquerd now : he mournes, he wailes, what aske ye any more ?
DEI. We wretches love the order of our wretchednes to heare,
Tell me the state now of our stocke what countnaunce doth it beare :
O stock, O sylly wretched stocke now shal I be esteemd
A widdow now, a cast of now, and now a beggar deemd.
HIL. Thou dost not languish all alone for Hercules lyes dead :
For whom the eyes of all the world have cause their teares to shed.
Count not thy fate allotted thee alone : now all our kind
Do howle and mourne for him whom thou bewaylest in thy minde.

Thou suffrest greefe, the smart wherof belonges to every land
Although the sower tast therof first happen to thy hande:
Thou careful caytiffe dost not wayle for Hercules alone.
De. Speake, speake, how nigh to Deathward was my deare Alcides gon?
Hi. Death whom in his owne empyre hee had conquered before,
Did shrinke from him and fate durst not allow a deede so sore,
And Clotho she perhap put out her rocke with trembling arme
As one that hastning Hercles death did feare to do such harme.
O day, O dismall day, and shall even Hercules the greate
Passe thus to death and silent shades and to a worser seate?
(De. Is he thinke you already dead or may I dye before?)
Speake on, if yet he be not deade. Hi. Eubœa that doth rise
With hauty crest ringes every where, and Caphar rocke likewyse
Devydeth Hellespontus sea and turnes that side to south,
Wheras it bides the boysteous blastes of Boreas wyndy mouth:
Euripus bendes his wandring streame and windes in creakes about
His croked course seven tymes and doth as often breake it out:
While Phœbus drencht his werye teame amid the Westerne wave
Here on a rocke above the reach of cloudes a temple brave)
Of Cænæi Jove shew bright whyle all the beastes for sacrifice
At th' alter stoode, and through the woode the noyse began to rise
Of al the herd: then of he put the matterd Lyons case,
And likewyse did discharge him of his houge and heavy mace,
And easde his shoulder from the burthen of his quiver light.
Then tuckt in your attyre he shone among the people bright
With ougly lockes, and on the alter made the fier flame.
Receyve (quoth hee) these fruits (O syre) though fyer send the same
And not the harvest Sithe: but let with frankinsence good store
The fyer burne that far the riche Arabyan therfore
Doth gather out of Saba trees for Phœbus sacrifyce.
The earth (quoth he) is now at peace, so be both sea and skies
All beastes be conquered, and I am victor come agayne.
Lay downe thy lightning leames (O Jove) in feare thou nede not raign.
In middest of his prayers thus wherat I was agast,
Hee fell to sighes and grievous groanes, and al the skyes at last

With dreadful cryinge lowde he filles, Even as the braynsick bull
When with the axe in wounde he scapes doth fil the temples full
Of roaring noyse.
Or as the thunder throwne from heaven doth rumble in the skyes,
Even so the seas and starres of heaven doth Hercles shake with cryes.
Both Calpe clyve, and Cyclas yle wel hard his yellyng have,
Here Caphar rockes there al the woods therof an Echo gave.
Wee saw him weepe, the people thought his former franticke fyttes
Had now agayne as earst they did bereave him of his wittes.
His servaunts scatter then for feare, while he with flaming eyes
Al staryng standes, with streaming lookes among them all he pryes
For Lycas : him alone he doth pursew, who in his arme
With trembling hand the alter held and scaped al the harme
By dying first for faynting feare, and while Alcydes helde
The quaking Carkas in his hand, thou shalt (quoth he) be queld
And beaten with this fist of myne, O Gods eternall raygne,
Wretch Licas killeth Hercules, and hath his conqueroure slayne,
But to another slaughter yet : for Hercules agayne
Killes Lycas : thus the sacrifyce of Gods with bloud they stayne,
With Lycas thus his labours end throwne up to heaven they say,
That with his dropping bloud the cloudes he stayned all the way.
Even as the pitched dart of Gete with pith doth score the skyes,
Or as the whirling fling of Creete doth make the pellet ryse :
So swift he mounted up to heaven, but downe his body dropte,
And as his Carkas fel among the rockes his necke it chopt.
The grave prepared for their corps (quoth Hercules) bestill,
I am no brainsicke franticke man, but loe this despret ill
More noysome is then rage or wrath, it easeth much my will
To wrecke my rage uppon my selfe, his mallady he scant
Bewryes : but fareth franticklу : and he himselfe doth rent
His limmes, and ryflyng them, with mighty hand a sunder teares,
And strives to strip him selfe of all th' apparell that he weares,
And onely this was it, of all the thinges that I do know,
That past the power of Hercules yet standes he pulling so
And plucketh of his limmes withall the vesture doth not linne
To bring of lumpes of filthy flesh, the shyrt stickes to the skyne.

But what should ayle the poyson ranke none knoweth what nor whye,
And yet there is good cause therof: now grovelyng doth he lye
And beates his face agaynst the ground, to water now he hyes,
But water cannot coole his heate, and now to shore he plyes,
And for his sucoure seekes to seas, at length his men him catch,
We holding him (alas the whil'st were able him to match
Now in a keele amid the seas we launched were aloofe,
And Hercles payse was hosted with a litle southerne puffe.
My Ghost then left my careful coarse and darknesse dimd my sight,
Why stay I wreche? why doth this dreary deede make mee afright.
Her coapefellow dame Juno doth reclayme, and Jove his sonne,
The world must render him: then doe as much as may be donne,
And boare my body with a sworde, such sower sauce is dew
To her whose cursed caytiffe hand her love so lightly slew.
O Jove with fier and lightning flash destroy thy wretched Neece,
Let not thy mighty hand be armed with a slender peece:
Let brast the boult from skies wherewith thou wouldest Hydra burne,
If Hercles had not bin thy sonne thereof to serve the turne,
Strike mee with uncouth pestilence, and with such weapon smite
As may be farre more yrkesome plague then all my stepdames spite.
Drive forth these deadly dartes that earst young Phaëthon overthrew
When he full crancke in firy carte about the heavens flew:
For thus by slaying Hercules eake Nations slaine I have,
What neede thou Deianire of Gods a toole of death to crave?
Now trouble not thy stepsier Jove, thinke scorne may Hercles wyfe
To wishe for death, for to her heart her hand shall set the knyfe.
Dispatch then quickly with the blade, yet let thy blade alone,
For who with weapon endes their lyfe tis long ere they be gon:
I wilbe headlong hurled from a rocke as hie as skies.
The Oeta hill this shalbe it, where first the sonne doth ryse,
Thence will I throwe my body downe, the edge of brasten rocke
Shal cleave my corps, and every crag shall geve a broosing knock.
My hand shall hang torne by the way, the rugged mountayne side
Shall with the gushing bubbles of my dropping bloud be dyde.

On death were vengeaunce small, though small yet may it be delayde.
What despret death I should attempt it makes my heart dismayde :
Alas, alas, that Hercles swerd within my chamber stucke,
Then well were I if for to dye on that it were my lucke :
It is inough if one right hand doe bring us both to grave.
Come neare, come neare yee Nations, now let all people have
In redinesse both stone and fier the same to throw at mee :
Now hold your hands, and take yee to your tooles for I am shee
That of your succour spoyled you now cruell Kaysars may
All uncontrolled tyrantlike, in kingdomes weilde the sway,
Now every mischiefe may start up, and not rebuked bee.
The alters now shall up agayne that wonted were to see
A bloudy offring like him selfe in kinde that offer should.
Thus have I made the guilty gap to let in bloudshed boulde,
I render you to tyrants kings, bugges, beasts, and grysely divells,
By taking him away that should revenge you of these evilles.
O spouse thou of the thunderer and can you yet forbeare,
Wilt thou not fling thy flames from heaven as did thy brother deare ?
Dispatch me hence sent up to Jove, wilt thou not me destroye ?
The greatest prayse that thou might winne then shalt thou not enjoy,
Nor lusty tryumphe : I am she that beare the name to be
The daughter of the man that would in prowes coape with thee.
NU. Why wilt thou stayne thy stocke which hath untaynted bene before ?
This il procedes of ygnorance although it be ful sore :
Hee is not gylty that committes the gylte not with his will.
DE. Wel may hee erre of ignorance that savoreth his ill
And spares himselfe : my selfe of death most worthy I do deeme.
NU. He doth condemne himselfe to dye that needes wil guylty seeme.
DE. Death can deceive no one but such as innocentes may bee.
NU. Wilt thou forsake the gloryous sonne ? DE. The sonne forsaketh mee.
NU. Wretch wil thou cast away thy life ? DE. Yea though it be to death,
I follow wil my Hercules. NU. He hath both life and breath.

DE. When he perceaved him overmatcht he hastned his decay.
NU. Wilt thou forgoe thy sonne, and eake prevent thy dying day ?
DE. Her selfe hath lived long ynough who buryed hath her childe.
NU. And wilt thou follow on to death thy spouse ? DE. Yea Ladies mild
Before their husbandes use to dye. NU. Thy selfe thou dost accuse
Of guylt if thou condemne thy selfe. DE. No gylty one doth use
To take revengemente of themselves. NU. But those are pardoned still
That do offend of ygnoraunce and not of pevish wil
Who wil condemne the deede hee doth ? DE. Ech man doth seeke to shun
His lot when spite of frowning fate against him seemes to runne.
NU. And he for whom thou languishest, with arrow slow his wyfe
Hight Megara, and did destroy his tender childrens life.
When as a braynsicke beast in hand he tost his knartye mace,
That squeasde the snake in Lerna lake before his fathers face.
He played thryse the murtherer, himselfe yet he forgave
And for the haynous gylt hee did when frenzy made him rave
He purgde himselfe in Cynips spring toward the Southerne poale
And in the water bath'd his hand againe to make him hoale.
Now whether wilt thou caytiffe wretch, why dost thou dam thy handes ?
DE. In condemnation of these the ghost of Hercles standes,
I meane to plague the treachery. NU. Your Hercules wel I know,
Perhap he wil be heare agayne and mayster al his woe :
Then shall your slaked greefe unto your Hercules geve place.
DE. They say the serpents poyson doth devower him apace,
The poyson of his wicked Wyfe his lusty lims destroyes.
NU. And think yee it to bee the serpents bane that him annoyes,
That hee cannot escape who bare the brunt of it alive,
And how to pare of Hydraes heads he coulde full well contryve
When as the victour stoode with grinning teath amid the moode,
And all his body slaverde fowle with venomous spit and bloude,
And shall the Centaur Nessus goare agaynst the man prevayle
That made the pithy strength it selfe of Nessus for to quayle ?

DE. In vayne yee rescue her that is of purpose set to dye,
Therefore I have determinde with my selfe this lyfe to flye,
And long inough hee lyved hath that may with Hercles dye.
NU. I doe beseech thee humbly for this gray and hoary head,
And for these pappes that as thy Mother have thee nourished,
Remove the fervent fits that rage within thy boyling breast,
And suffer not these despret thoughtes of death in thee to rest.
DE. Who woulde perswade a wretch to live, he hath a cruell heart,
And though that death be unto me a great and grievous smart,
Yet unto other some it is an easing of their payne.
NU. O wreatch excuse thy handy worke, and say at last agayne,
T'is ignoraunce that did the deede, and not the willfull Wyfe.
DE. It will be quit whereas th' infernall fiendes shall stint the stryfe
And quit my guilty ghost : my conscience doth my handes condem.
But Pluto Prince of glummy goulph shall purge from slaughter them :
Before thy bankes I will appeare forgetfull Lethes Lake,
And being then a dolefull ghost my husband will I take.
But thou that wields the scepter blacke of darke infernall skies
Apply thy toyle : the haynous guilt that none durst enterpryse,
This ignoraunce hath overcom, Dame Juno never dare
To take away our Hercules. Thy plunging plagues prepare,
Let Sisiphs stone on my neck force my stouping shoulders shrynke,
And let the fleeting licour from my gaping gums to synke.
Yea let it mock my thyrsty throate when as I meane to drynke,
And thou that rackes Ixion King of Thessayle O thou Wheele,
My haynous handes deserved have thy swinging sway to feele,
And let the greedy gripe scratch out these guts on eyther side,
If Danaus pitchers cease : by mee the rome shalbe supplide.
Set open hell, take mee Medea as partner of thy guilt.
This hand of myne, then both of thyne more cruell bloud hath spilt
More then thou did as in respect of mother to thy chylde.
Or loking to thy brothers ghost whose gore hath thee defylde,
Have with the Lady thou of Thrace for such a cruel wyfe,
And the Althe that burnt the brand of Meleagers life.
Receyve thy daughter now, denye me not thy babe to bee :
Why such a one should quayle by you, some reason let us see :

THE THIRD ACTE

Ye honest matrons that enjoy the groves of holy wood
Agaynst me shut the heavens, or such whose handes with husbandes blood
Have bene imbrewde, if any of the fifty sisters dyre
Defying honest duty all that wedlocke did require :
But desprat dames with goary blades stood armde : in me let them
See and allow theyr bloudy handes that other wil condem.
I wil go get my selfe among the troupe of cruel wyves
But they wil shunne such gylty handes as shred their husbandes lives.
O valiant spouse, a guiltlesse ghost, but gylty handes I have,
Ah silly woman, woe is me, that given light credite have :
O traytor Nessus while I ment by Centaures subtil charme
To draw from Iole Hercles love my selfe sustayne the harme.
Hence Phœbus, hence, and thou O flickring life of her that lackes
Her Hercules and givest day to wretches in their wrackes.
This is a dismal day : to thee Small penaunce yeld I will
And life with all : my woeful fate shal I continue stil
Deferryng death, O spouse that of thy hand I may be slayne,
And doth their any sparke of life yet in thy breast remayne ?
Or can thy hand yet draw the bow Sarmarcian shaft to cast,
Do weapons cease, and have thy feble handes given up at last
Thy bow ? but if thy hardy wyfe to thee a toole may reache
I long to perysh of thy hand, myne hower yet wil I stretche.
Like gyltlesse Licas mangle me, disperse in other townes
My corpes, and hurle me to a worlde beyond the travayles bownes.
Trounce mee like monster Arcadie or ought that did rebell,
And yet thou shalt do nought but that becommes an husband wel.
Hɪ. I pray you mother spare your selfe, forgeve your fatal lot,
If ye offend of ygnoraunce, then blame deserve yee not.
Dᴇ. If thou regard true honesty, thy wretched mother slay.
Why trembleth thus thy feareful hand, why lokest thow away ?
Such sinne shalbe a sacrifyce, why dastard dost thou feare ?
I spoylde thy father Hercules, this hand, this hand aleare
Hath murdred him wherby I have done thee a more despyte
Then joy I did in that my wombe did bring thee first to light.
If yet thou know not how to kill, then practise fyrst on me.
If as thou like within my throate thy blade shal sheathed bee,

Or if to paunch thy mother soone thou meane to take in hand
To yeeld her dreadlesse ghost to thee thy mother still shall stande.
It shall not wholly be thy deede, by thee it shall be done,
And caused by my wil to be. Art thou Alcides soon
And art affrayd ? so shal thou never great exployts atchieve,
Nor passe the worlde such feats of armes and sleightes for to contrive.
If any monster should be bred thy fathers courage shew,
And to it with unfeareful arme, for overchargde with woe
My breast lies bare unto thy hand. Stryke, I thy gylt forgeve,
The fiendes infernall for their sinne thy soule shal never greeve.
What yerking noyse is this we heare, what hagge here have we fownde
That beares aboute her writhen lockes these ugly adders wound,
And one her yrksome temples twayne her blackysh finnes do wagge.
Why chase ye mee with burning brandes Megera filthy hagge ?
Alcides can but vengeance aske, and that I wil him get.
But have the judges dyre of hell for yt in counsell set
But of the dreadful dongeon dores I see thunfoulding leaves
What auncient sier is he that on his tatred shoulder heaves
Th' unweildy stone that borne toth top agayne doth downward reele,
Or what is he that spraules his lims uppon the whirling wheele ?
Lo heare stood ougly Tisiphon with sterne and ghastly face,
And did demaunde with steaming eies the manner of the case.
O spare thy strypes Megera spare, and with thy brandes away,
Th' offence I did was ment in love, but whether do I sway ?
The ground doth sinke, the roofe doth cracke, whether went this raging route,
Now al the world with gasing eyes stand staring me about,
On every side the people grudge and call for their defence.
Be good to me O nations, whither shall I get mee hence ?
Death onely is my roade of rest, there may my sorrowes byde,
I do protest the fiery wheeles that Phœbus charyot guide.
That heare I dye and leave the worlde, thers Hercles yet behynde.
Hi. Away she runnes agast : aye me, shee hath fulfylde her mynd,
For purposed she was to dye and now remaynes my wil
For to prevent her that by force her selfe she shall not kill.

O miserable piety, if I my mother save
I sin agaynst my father then, but if unto the grave
I let her goe, then toward her a trespas foule there lyes.
And thus (alas) on eyther syde great mischiefe doth aries,
And needes her purpose must be stayde Ile hie and take in hand
To stop her despret enterpryse and mischiefe to withstand.

CHORUS

Full true the ditty is that holy Orpheus sang,
On Thracian harpe with sounde whereof the Rocks of Rodop rang,
That nothing is creat for ever to endure.
Dame Natures byrdes each on must stoupe when death throwes out the lure.
The head wyth Crispen lockes, or goulden hayres full :
In time hath borne an hoary bush, or bin a naked scull.
And that which tract of time doth bring out of the grayne,
Olde Saturne sharps his Syth at length to reape it downe agayne.
Though Phœbus ryse at morne, with glistring rayes full proude,
Hee runnes his race, and ducketh downe at length in foggy Clowde.
Toth Gœtans Orpheus sang such kinde of melody,
And how the gods themselves were bounde to lawes of destiny.
The God that doth the yeare, by egall partes dispose,
Howe fatall webbe in every clyme are dayly spunne he showes.
For all thinges made of moulde the grounde agayne will gape,
As Hercles preacheth playne by proofe that nothing can escape.
For shortly shall ensue discarge of Natures Lawe
And out of hande the gloming daye of doome shall onwarde drawe,
Then all that lies within the scorching Libicke clyme,
The poale antarticke of the South shall overwhelme in tyme.
Poale articke of the North shall jumble, all that lyes
Within the Axeltree, whereon drye Bores blasinge flyes
The shiverynge Sunne in Heaven shall leese his fadyng lighte,
The Pallace of the frames of Heavens shall runne to ruin quight.
And all these blockish Gods some kynd of Death shall quell,
And in confused Chaos blynde they shall for ever dwell,

And after ruin made of Goblin, Hegge, and Elfe,
Death shall bringe finall destenye at last uppon it selfe.
Where shall be then bestowde the world so huge a masse,
The beaten hye way unto hell is like away to passe,
To leade unto the Heavens that shall be layed flatt :
The space betwene the Heaven and earth, inough thinke ye is that?
Or is it not to much for worldly miseryes :
Wher may such heaps of sinnes be lodgd what place above the skyes
Remaynes, but that the sea with Heaven and lowest Hell,
Three Kingdomes cast in one are like within one roofe to dwell?
But hark what roaring crye thus beates my fearefull eare,
But lo its Hercules that yelles, tis Hercules I heare.

HERCULES ŒTÆUS

THE FOURTH ACTE

HERCULES. CHORUS

RETYRE, retyre thy breathing breastes, O Titan blasing bright,
Unfold thy mysty mantle blacke of dim and darkesome Night :
And dash this dreary day wherin I Hercules must die,
With blemish black of filthy fogge defyle the griesly skye :
Prevent my stepdames naughty mynd. Now should I have resignde,
(O Father) my inheritaunce of Plutoes dungeon blynd :
Heaven frames should here and there be brast, and eyther poale should crack,
Why sparest thou the starres and letst thy Hercles go to wracke ?
Now Jove loke round aboute the heavens, and if thou can espye
On gyant heave the Thessaill clives agaynst thassalted skye
Unburdned be Enceladus of hugye Ofir hill,
And hurled be on Hercules the mighty mountayne still,
Prowde Pluto shall unbarre the gates of blacke and glummy cave
Yet maugre all their might (o Father Jove) I wil thee save
From fury of thy foes, and set thee up agayne in skyes,
Yet lo Jove, loe, hee that on earth thy thunderdint supplies,
And for to be liuetenaunt of thy boultes on earth was borne,
Is sent to burning Limbo lake in tormentes to be torne.
The sterne Enceladus agayne in ramping rage shal ryse
And hurle the weighte (that now doth croude him downe) against the skies,
Thus by my death they shal presume to conquer heaven all,
But ere that day uppon my corse compel the heavens to fall,

Breake downe, breake downe, the welkin that thou suffrest to decay.
CH. O sonne of thunder thumping Jove no shadowes do thee fray,
Now Ossa mount of Thessalie shal Pelion hill downe crush
And Athos pilde on Pindus toppe his bushy hed shall push
Among the starry skies therby above the craggy rockes.
Typhoëus up shal clyme, and thumpe with store of battryng knockes
Juarmen stone in Tyrren sea from thence eake shall be beat
The smoaky forge of Ætna mount, that glowes with stewing heate,
Enceladus not overthrowne yet with the thunder cracke
Shal hew the mountayne syde in twayne, and truve it on his backe,
The signes of heaven shal follow thee, and goe with thee to wracke.
HER. I that returnde from dennes of death, and Stigian streame defyed
And ferryed over Lethes lake, and dragd up, chaind, and tyde
The tryple headded mastiffe hownd, when Tytans teeme did start
So at the ougly sight that he fel almost from his cart.
Even I whose pith the kingdomes three of Gods ful wel have knowne
Lo yet myne end I daunted am by death and overthrowne,
But yet no bloudy blade agaynst my rived rybbes doth crash,
It is no rock that unto death my brused bones doth pash,
Nor as it were with Osir hill that cloven were in twayne,
Nor with the sway of all the mountayne falling am I slayne.
The glaring eyed giant grym doth not now squeaze my coarse
With paise of Pindus rock and thus not feling enmyes force
I conquerd am and yet alas this coarsse frets me more.
O feeble force of man : he whom no might could match before
Withouten any conquest made doth end his latter day,
Without exployt or feat of armes my selfe I passe away.
O mighty umpier of the world and all ye Ghostes above
That witnes how in quarell good my right hand ever strove,
O all ye landes, O earth alas, may it your mercy please
To spoyle the spiteful sting of death that dauntes your Hercules.
Fy, fye, what shame is it to us what filthy fate we have ?
A woman prowde shall boast her bane brought Hercles to his grave,
Then what are they whose mortall mayme Alcides weapon gave
If thus with sway invincible my fatal wheele do run
And neede must on this shameful rocke my fatall twist be spunne :

As by a womans cursed hand my bloud should thus be shed,
Yet Junoes mallice might have powrd this vengeance on my head,
So might a womans deadly hand have brought me to my beere :
But yet a woman weilding sway amid the welkin cleare.
But this seemde overprowde attempt for Gods to take in hand
The paples dame in Scithia borne where pight on hie doth stand
The Apeltree whereon the underpropped poales do sway,
It might as well have bene her hap to take my breath away.
What womans might may maister me Queene Junoes hatefull foe
Fye stepdame fye the fowler shame by this to thee doth grow.
Why dost thou triumph in this day ? why did dame Tellus breede
Such parlous bugges thy humour ranck of colour hoate to feede ?
A mortall womans peavishe spight doth passe thy rancour rough,
Thou sayst thou cannot have revenge on Hercules inough :
Then are wee twayne that passe thy power the Gods may blushe for
shame
To see their mallice overmacht by such a mortall dame
Would God the ramping Lyons pawe that noyed Neme woode,
Had fillde his greedy mounching Jawes with plenty of my bloude :
Or while the twining snakes had hembde mee in by hundreds thick,
Why might not Hydra swallow up my wrinched body quick ?
Why was it not the centaures hap my silly flesh to gnawe ?
Or that I bounde on Tantalis rocke shoulde gape with greedy Jawe ?
In vayne to catch the fleeting foode when deepe from Tartar soyle,
Where at the Gods aggrized were, I did purloyne the spoyle.
And from the darck infernall Styx I gat agayne to light,
Of Ditis dungeon all the stops and stayes I conquerde quight.
Death shranke from mee in every place that I a noble knight
At length might ende my dayes in shame, and in dishonour spoylde
Oh Jove the creatures terrible thou knowst that I have foylde
The threfolde shapen mastiffe curre whom up I draggde in chayne,
Hee starting from the sonnewarde coulde not hale mee back agayne.
The sheepherdes churlishe rabble that aloofe in Iber bee
Under the Spanishe fervent clyme coulde never maister mee.
Nor serpents twayne that unto mee in tender cradell creapt.
Aye woe is mee that valiant death so oft I overleapt :
What honour shall I dye withall ? Ch. Beholde how death and hell
Cannot appaule the verteous mynde that of deserving well.

By guiltlesse conscience warrant hath the death that doth him spoyle,
Irkes not as thus of such an one to take this filthy foyle.
If with this torment life were lost, his mynde should much be easde,
As with unweildy Gyauntes sway hee had his body squeasde.
Or Titans burden with his monsters all he woulde abyde.
Or wishe of raging Gyants rent in pieces to have dyde,
And if thy dolefull death because that monster none is left.
Who may be worthy thought by whom Alcides life bee reft ?
But thine owne hand to doe the deede. HE. Aye me and wellaway,
What Scorpion scrapes within my Mawe ? what crailing Crab I say
With crooking cleaze to comber mee, from scorching zone returnes,
And hoat within my boyling bones the seathing Marowe burnes.
My River whilom ranke of bloude my rotting Lunges it tawes,
And teareth them in shattred gubs, and filthy withered flawes.
And now my Gall is dryed up, my burning Lyver glowes,
The stewing heate hath stillde away the bloude, and Jove hee knowes
My upper skin is scorcht away and thus the Canker stronge
Doth eate an hole that get it may my wretched Limmes amonge,
And from my frying Ribs (alas) my Lyver quite is rent.
It gnawes my flesh, devowers all, my Carkas quite is spent,
It soakes into the empty bones, and out the juyce it suckes
The bones by lumps drop of while it the joyntes a sunder pluckes.
My corpulent Carkas is consumde of Hercules every lim
Yet stauncheth not the festring rot that feedeth fast on him,
O what a tingling ache it is that makes mee thus to smart,
O bitter plague, O pestilence that gripeth to the heart.
Loe Cities, loe what now remaynes of Hercules the great.
Are these the armes that did with stripes the roaring Lyon beate ?
And in Nemea wood did teare him from his bary case.
Might this hand bend the bow from cloudes the Stimphall foule to chase ?
Are these the shankes that coapt the heart who shifting pace full oft
Did beare his braunched head ypranckt with garlond gay aloft ?
Was Calpe craggy clive of these my feeble clowches broake ?
To rayse a dam in seas that did their foamy channell choake.

Had these armes pith the breath of Kings, of Beastes, and bugs to stop ?
Or might these shoulders tough the payse of heaven underprop ?
Are these the lusty Lims and Neck that shrank not at the payse ?
Are these the hands that I agaynst the weltring heavens did rayse ?
Alas whose handes shall now perforce from hence hell Jaylour leade ?
Alas the noble courage earst that now in mee is deade.
Why call I Jove my Father great of whom my stock should ryse ?
Why by the Thunderer make I my challenge to the skyes ?
Now, now Ampitrio is my sier all men may it avouch.
Come out thou murreyn fowle that dost within my bowells couch.
Why dost thou thus with privy wound my carefull Carkas foyle ?
What gulph under the frozen Clyme in salvage Scithian soyle
Engendred thee ? what water Hag did spawne thee on the shore ?
Or stony Calpe Rock in Spayne that borders on the Moare ?
O yrksome ill, and art thou not the Serpent that doth sting
With crest on ougly head, or els some other lothly thing,
Or spronge of Hydraës bloude, or left heere by the hellick hound.
Art thou no plague ? and yet a plague in whom all plagues abound ?
What gastly countnaunce cariest thou (alas) yet let me know ?
What kinde of mischiefe may thou be that dost torment mee so ?
What salvage sore, or murreyn straunge, or uncouth plague thou bee ?
With open combat face to face thou should encounter mee.
And not thus ranckle in my flesh, nor soake into the sap,
By sowltring heate within my bones thy boyling bane to wrap,
And in the mid thereof to fry the Maroe that doth melt.
My jagged skin is ript, and out my smoaky Bowells swelt.
From bursten Paunch my selfe doe flea the skin with grasping pawse,
And from the naked boanes doe teare the mangled flesh by flawes,
I searched for thee through my Mawe, yet further dost thou creepe,
And festring farther in my flesh hast gnawne an hole more deepe.
O mischiefe match to Hercules, what griefe coulde make mee greete ?
Whence flow these streames of trilling teares that down my cheekes do fleete ?

The time hath bin no plunging pangues could cause our courage quaile,
That never use with cristall teares our anguish to bewayle.
Ah, fy, I am ashamde that I should learne these teares to shed :
That Hercules in weeping wise his griefe hath languished :
Who ever saw at any day in any time or place
All bitter brunts I bare with dry, and eake unreky face ?
The manhoode that so many ills hath maistred heretofore,
Hath yeelded onely unto thee, to thee thou Cankar sore,
Thou first of all hast strayndе the teares out of my weeping eyes,
Thy gargle face thy visage wan that doth mee sore aggrise.
More towgh then mossy Rockes, more hard then Gads of sturdy steele,
Or roaming streame of Simplegade, whereby this smart I feele
Hath crusht my cracking Jawes, and wronge the streaming teares from me.
O wielder of the Welkin swifte, loe, loe the Earth doth see
How Hercules doth weepe and wayle, and to my greater payne
My Stepdame Juno sees the same, beholde, beholde agayne
My Lunges doe fry, the scorching heate prevayleth more and more.
Whence fell this thunder Boult on mee that burnes in mee so sore ?
CH. Who stoupeth not when griefe doth gal ? more tough then Aem of Thrace
Whas whilom hawty Hercules, and did no more gieve place
Then doth the marble axelltree, his Lims hee now doth yeelde
To paynefull pangues : and on his Neck his aking heade doth wielde,
And tossing still from side to side, hee bendes with hugy sway,
And oft his noble heart doth force his trilling teares to stay.

HERCULES. ALCMENA

O FATHER wyth thy heavenly Eyes, beholde my wretched plight
For never Hercules till nowe did crave thy hande of might,
Not when as Hydraës fruictfull heads about my Lyms were wounde,
Nor when I lockt in Lakes alow fought with th' infernall hownde,
These hideous fiends I foylde, with kings, and tyraunts prowde likewise,
Yet in these broyles I never lookt for succour to the skyes.

This hand did still avouch the bowe, no thunder for my sake
Did glitter in the holy heavens, this day hath bid mee make
Some suite to thee, and of my boones yet heeres the first and last,
One onely Thunder boult I crave at mee O Jove to cast.
Count mee a Giaunt of my selfe, I can no lesse devise,
While Jove I thought of promise true, I spaarde the starry skies.
Bee thou eyther a cruell sier, or pity if thou have,
Yet lend thy sonne thy help, and get the glory of my grave :
Preventing this my dreary death, of this if thou doe skorne,
Or that thy hand abhorre the guilt, from Sicill clive suborne
The soultring Giaunts that in hand high Pindus mount can weilde,
Or Ossa that it hurlde on mee I may therewith bequeilde,
Brast up hell Gates, and let Bellone scourge mee with Iron rod,
And let in armes encounter mee thy mighty Martiall God,
My brother I acknowledge him but by my stepdames side,
And Pallas thou my sister eake, let at thy brother slide
A thirling Darte. O stepdame myne with humble suite I crave
A wounde of thee that womans hand may bring mee to my grave :
Why dost thou feede thy fury nowe as one whose wrath were ende
And satisfied ? what seeke yee more ? I stoupe, I yeelde, I bende.
Thou seest Alcides humbly layde, where as unto this day
That ever I entreated thee, no Land, no Beast can say,
Now doe I neede thy deadly wrath to rid mee of my payne,
And now thy rankour is appeasde, thy hate is quencht agayne,
And thus thou sparest mee my life when as I wishe to dye :
O Earth will none make mee the fier wherein my bones may fry ?
Nor reach a blade to Hercules, convay yee all from mee ?
So let no country Monsters breede when I shall buried be,
And let none wayle the losse of mee if monsters more aryse,
God send another Hercules to succour Earth and skyes.
But as for mee on every side ding out my broosed brayne,
And crash with sturdy stroke of stones my cursed Scull in twayne
And rid my torments : wilt thou not ? O worlde to mee unkynde,
And are so soone our benefits forgotten in thy mynde.
Een to this hower with bugs and beasts thou had bin over layde
Had not I bin : good people cause his torments to bestayde
That succored you : time gives you leave to recompence my payne,
If yee with death will guerden mee, I aske none other gayne.

AL. Where shall I wretched mother of Alcides wishe to bee ?
Where is my chylde ? where is my sonne ? If sight deceave not mee,
With gasping mouth and panting heart loe where hee sprawling lyes.
Where as (alas) in raging heate of boyling fits hee fryes,
Hee grones, all is dispacht, deare childe let mee Alcides myne
Embrace thy pining lims : with kisse enfoulde my armes in thyne.
Where are the lims ? where is the neck that bare the skies alone ?
What thus hath mangled thee that all thy corps is waste and gone ?
HE. I am your Hercles mother deare, whom thus yee see here lost,
Acknowledge mee all though God knowes I seeme but as a ghost.
Why doe you turne your face away and mourning visage mylde ?
Are yee ashamde that Hercules should counted bee your chylde ?
AL. What world hath bred this uncouth bug ? what land engendred it ?
Or els what monstrous mischiefe may on thee triumphing sit ?
Who ist that conquers Hercules ? HE. By treason of his Wyfe
Thou seest how wretched Hercules do leese his lothed Lyfe.
AL. To overthrow my Hercules, what treason hath the might ?
HE. That which a wrathfull Dame doth seeke to ease her of her spight.
AL. How hath this pestilence gotten to thy Lims and bleeding bones ?
HE. Into a Shyrt the woman had convayde it for the nonce.
AL. Where is the Shyrt for nothing but thy naked corps I see ?
HE. The vesture by the poyson ranke devowred is with mee.
AL. And can such poyson be contrived ? HE. I thinke within my guts,
That hideous Hydra hissing Snake his slowghy body puts,
A thousand plagues of Lerna Poole within my Bowelles rampes :
What raging heate is this that drives up all Sicilia dampes ?
What Clime of Hell forbids the day to passe the boyling zone ?
O Mates amid the greedy gulphes and pooles let me be throwne.
What Ister can my Carkas coole ? no not the Ocean mayne
Of these my stewing vapours may the raging quench agayne ?
(Al moysture of my limmes in these my fits are fryde away)
The juyce wil sone be soaked up, what president of hel
Let me returne from under grounde agayne with Jove to dwell.

He ought to have retaynd me still, receive me once agayne
Into thy dungeon darke that hel may in this pickle playne
Behold the man that conquerd yt, no booty bringe I will
Away with me : why dost thou quake for feare of Hercles still ?
Set on me death coragiously for now I may be kilde.
AL. Now strut thy tender tears that down thy cheekes so long have trild,
And mayster this thy mallady, compell thy sorrowes stoupe.
And shew that in these plunging panges Alcides did not droupe,
And as it hath bene earst thy guyse force death and hel to shrinke.
HER. If ougly grested Caucasus in chayne of yrone linke
Should bynd me as agroning pray the greedy grype to feede,
Yet from myne eyes it should not strayne a broken teare indeede
If wandring Symplegads would me with eyther rocke assaile,
To byde the brunt of double wracke my courage would not quayle.
Let Pindus tumbled be on me, houge Aemus let me have
Or Athos rocke in Thracian seas that breakes the weltring wave,
And bode the boultes of thondring Jove although thunweildy masse
Of all the world should fal on mee and might be brought to passe
That Phœbus flaming apeltree should burne uppon my grave,
No uncouth crye should force the mynd of Hercles thus to rave.
Let meete a thousand savage beastes and rent me al at once
Let Stymphal foules with houling hoarse lay strokes uppon my bones
Or scrowling bul on thother syde strike on with head and horne
Or els of other serpentes wilde let al my partes be torne
With roring earthquakes, hougy lumpes be puffet uppon me,
With griping greefe let all my limmes to nothing pyned bee.
Although I be to pouder crusht I wil with pacience peace
In spite of beastes or brusing blowes my sighes and teares shal seace.
ALC. It is not sonne the womans bane that in thy bones doth boile,
But festring teares and broosing knockes of thy continual toyle,
The wrinches old with aking panges begin to smart anew.
HE. O where is death, where is hee now ? of all that I do rew :
Can any witnes what it is ? let death now bend his bow.
A naked hand is stronge ynough to make mee stowpe ful low,
Let any wight in al the worlde attempt to set on mee
I warrant him, approch let him, Ah wretched might I bee.

ALC. This wayward agony hath take his perfit wits away.
Have hence his tooles, and eake his shaftes for daunger hence convay.
His ruddy gills that glow like fier some mischiefe doe pretend.
To shrowde my selfe (alas) into what corner shall I wend ?
This mallady a frensy is, this onely is the meane
To conquer Hercules, why then doe I as doting queane
Thus fall to teares and seeke to shrynke, may bee that hee will have
Alcmenas hand to give the stroke to bring him to the grave.
But dye he in a Murreynes name, ere I for cowarde will
Such deadly penaunce bee enjoynde, that on my doings still,
His haynous hand may vaunt it selfe, loe how the pangues full deepe,
With struggling ceast, doe binde the purple vaynes with deadly sleepe,
And beating sore lift up and downe his faynt and panting breast :
If I O Gods of this my noble Childe bee dispossest :
Be gracious yet, and for the worlde some lusty champion save.
Rid his annoy and let his limmes agayne theyr courage have.

HYLLUS. ALCMENA. HERCULES

O DISMALL day, O anguishe, O the heaper up of ill,
Joves Sonne is slayne, his Daughter dyes, his Nephew lyveth still.
First by the Stepdames treason is the Sonne to ruin brought,
The Daughter likewyse trapt in traynes, and thereby come to nought.
What hoary head in chaunge of tunes, or teanour of his age
Hath seene that Fortunes frowning Face hath sturd such stormy rage ?
One dolefull day bereaveth mee (alas) of parents twayne,
But least I speake to spite the Gods, I will somewhat refrayne.
I lost a Father, Hercules this onely I complayne.
AL. O noble Impe of Hercules, (alas) my Nephew deare,
That dost of wretched Alcmens Sonne the lively feature beare,
Refrayne my chylde thy wayling woordes, this quiet sleepe perhap
Will overcome these plonging fits. But loe ! loe in my lap

Hee doth begin to strive agayne, his fits begin a fresh,
Sleepe gieving up the feeble ghost to ranckle in the flesh.
He. What meaneth Thrachin craggy crest to shew before myne eyes ?
Or now forsaking man am I advaunst above the skies ?
Why do the heavens provyde for me ? the father Jove I see,
And eake my stepdame Juno dire appeased now with me.
What heavenly harmony is this that soundeth in myne eare ?
Dame Juno calles me sonne in law, I se the pallace cleare
(Of christal skies and beaten rakes of Phœbus flaming wheele)
I see the dumpish moary denne of glowming lady night
Here he commaundeth darknes dim to shew it self in sight.
What meaneth this, who is it that the heavens agaynst me sparres ?
And am I thus O father myne brought downe againe from starres ?
Even now Appolloës sowltring car did fume about my face
So nie I past the pinch of Death, lo Thrachin top in place
Who brought me backe to ground agayne, beneath me earst it lay
And al the world was under me, thou smart wert worne away,
Thou forcest me confesse the same. Ah mercy, mercy now,
In stead of farther vengeance do these humble wordes allow.
Lo Hillus, lo thy mothers giftes such presentes shee preparde :
Ah, might my trunchion punch her puddinges once as whilom farde
The haughty Ladye Amazon wel trounsed for her pride
On thedge of ysy Caucasus afront the mountayne syde.
O noble lady Megara were thou my wretched wyfe,
When rapt in rage of franticke fittes, I reft thee of thy life,
Geve me up my batt and bow in hand, my wrestes I wil imbrew,
And force ye all your brages on me with blemish blacke to rue.
Thus let of Hercules exploytes a woman be the last.
Hi. Forbeare O Syre thy hateful threates, she hath it, all is past.
The vengeance that ye seke on her already hath her spedd.
With wound received at your hand my mother lieth dead.
(Her. O blynded anquish : dye she should of Hercles furious hand)
Thus Licas hath his marrow lost, the heate of burning brest
Wil have me on the breathlesse coarse for to revenge the rest :
Why doth shee not yet fele her force both let her want a grave
And on her cursed flesh to feede let beastes her carkasse have.

HIL. The silly woman was more woe then ye that bide the smart.
Ye wil release some part hereof for pitty in your hart.
For greefe of you with her owne hande, alas her selfe she slew,
Thus more then ye do aske of her, she doth her doyng rewe.
Yet is it not your Wyfes misdeede that brought you to this plight,
No nor my mothers traytrous hand hath wrought this deepe deceit
This treason Nessus did contrive whom yee did pay his hire,
With arrow shot into his Ribs for rape of Deianire.
Thus father with the Centaures bloud your shyrt was sore embrewde,
At Nessus hand the vengeaunce of your deede thus have yee rewde.
HE. Hee hath his will: all is dispatcht, our Fates themselves display.
This is the day of death to mee. Thus earst to mee did say
A charmed Oake, and all the wood that range with yetling noyse
Of Parnass hill the Temples shooke, and thundred out this voyce:
The dead mans hand whom thou before hast slayne,
O Hercules shall murther thee agayne.
Thou having mot the space of gulph and grounde,
And deapth of hell, heare shall thou bee confounde.
I therefore doe bewayle no more, such should our ending bee,
That Hercles conquerde after him no man alive may see.
Now let mee dye a manly death, a stout and excellent,
And meete for mee: this noble day shall valiauntly bee spent.
Fell all the Timber on the grounde, hew down all Œta wood,
Let coales devower Hercules, let fyer fry his bloud.
But ere I dye thou noble Impe of Pëans royall race,
This dolefull duety doe for mee: See that an whole day space
My funerall fier flaming burne. And now my tender Hill,
The last peticion of my mouth make unto thee I will.
Among the captive Ladies, one there is, a noble Dame,
Of royall bloud, Euritus Chylde, Iole is her name:
Accept her to thy spousall Bed, whom victour I unkinde
Have trayned from her native home, and but my heart, and mynde
Poore silly mayde I gave her nought, and now shee shall mee lose.
Loe thus the wretched woman wailes her still encreasing woes.
But let her foster that she hath conceaved as Joves ally,
And childe to mee: bee 't thyne by her that earst begot have I:

And as for thee deare mother myne, your dreary dole forgoe,
Your Hercules shall live : doe not vayne teares on him bestowe :
My manhoode made a strumpet thought a Stepdame unto thee,
But if that eyther Hercles byrth shewe her unsure to bee,
Or be a man my sier or els be falsified my kin.
Now let Joves jugling cease, and let my mothers slaunder lin,
I have deserved a father well that have advaunst so hye
The glory of the rolling heavens, of nature framde was I.
To worke the wondrous prayse of Jove, and Jove him selfe doth Joy
To have the name of Hercules, begetting such a boy.
But pardon now my strayned teares, but you as Jove his niece
Shall as a stately matrone bee among the Dames of Greece.
Though Juno with the thunderer in spousall chamber lyes,
And in her heavenly hand doth weilde the scepter of the skies,
When ever bare shee such a Babe, and yet though heaven she hould
In heart agaynst a mortall man she fosters mallice oulde,
For spighte that borne of womans womb be counted thus I should.
Goe Titan goe, run out thy Race, thee onely I forsake.
I that went with thee foote by foote nowe to th' infernall lake,
And Ghostes, I do yet with this prayse to' th pit down will I passe
That Hercules of open foe yet never foyled was,
But hee in open combats brought his conquests all to passe.

CHORUS

O Titan crownd with blasing bush whose morning moystures make
The moone her foamy bridell from her tyred teame to take,
Declare to th' Easterlinges whereas the ruddy morne doth ryse,
Declare unto the Irishmen aloofe at western Skies :
Make knowne unto the Moores annoyed by flaming axentree,
Those that with the ysy Wayne of Archas pestred bee,
Display to these that Hercules to th' eternall ghostes is gone,
And to the bauling mastiffes den from whence returneth none.
With dusky dampe of filthy fog O Titan choake thy blaze,
With lowring light of wanny Globe on wofull wordlings gaze,
And let thy head bee muffled up with cloudes and darknesse dim
For Hercles sake, when shall thou finde, or where the like to him?

(O wretched worlde to whom wilt thou henceforth thy woes complaine,)
If any scattring pestilence on earth shall be renewde,
By venom ranck, from poyson mouth of scaly Dragon spewde :
If any Bore of Arcadie shall comber all a wood,
And teare the travelers flesh with tuske embrewed in goary blood :
If any champion rough of Thrace with heart more hard in breast
Then are the ysy rockes, where as the frozen Beare doth rest,
Shall trample thicke his stables fowle with bloud of slaughterd men,
When people quake for feare of warre, who shalt assist them then?
If wrathfull Gods for vengeaunce will some monsters to be bread?
Loe nowe enfebled all of force his karkasse lyeth dead,
Whom Natures moulde had made a match to thundring Jove in strength
Hale out (alas) and let your playnt be hearde to townes at length.
Let women beat their naked armes, and wring their trembling handes,
Untrusse their hayre, and from theyr locks pluck of their binding bands.
Boult up, and lock the Temple gates of Gods, and oape bee none
But despret Junoes Chapple doares. O Hercles thou art gone
To Lethes lake, and streame of Stix, from whence no keele agayne
Shall bring thee backe : O silly soule thou goest to remayne
Among the grisely goblins grymme : from whence thou whilom came
With triumph sooner daunted death, and conquest of the same.
With gastly face, and karrayne armes, and neck that yeeldes to waight,
Thy ghost returnes, but Carons boate then shall not have her fraight,
As balased with thy onely payse, and yet shalt thou not byde
Among the rascall sprites, but sit on bench by Eacus side,
And with the Judges twayne of Creete as Umpier there to bee,
Appoynting paynes to soules that maye to their desartes agree.
From slaughter hold your guiltlesse hands, bath not your blades in bloud,
Yee states, that beare high sayle on earth, and floate in worldly good :
It merits prayse a mayden swerd undipt in goare to beare,
And while thou rayne, to keepe thy realme from cruell doings cleare.
But vertue hath a pryviledge to passe unto the skies,
To th' top of frosen Apell tree O Hercules wilt thou ryse?
Or where the sunne with scorching blaze his burning beames doth rest?
Or wilt thou bee a shyning starre amid the lukewarme west?
Where Calpe Rocke is heard with roaring noyse of wrastling wave?
What place amid the azur skye entendest thou to have?

What place shall be in all the heavens from hurley burley free?
When Hercules amid the starres shall entertayned bee?
Let Jove appoynt thy byding from the ougly Lion farre,
And burning Crab: least thou with grysely countnaunce do them skarre,
And make the trembling starres in heaven for feare to breake aray
And Titan quake: while spring doth prank with flowers the tender spray,
Then hasty winter strip the trees of all their braunches greene,
Or sudden Summer deckt with leaves in busshy woods be seene.
And from the trees the Apples fall, the harvest being doone:
No age on earth shall wipe away the fame that thou hast woone.
As farre as Sun or Stars can shyne, thy glorious name shall goe.
Amid the botome of the Sea first Corne shall sprout and grow,
And brackish Seas his waters salt to water fresh shall chaunge,
And fixed starre of ysy beare from Clime to Clyme shall raunge,
And sink into the frozen poole agaynst his kindly sway,
Ere people cease the honour of thy triumphes to display:
O soveraygne Jove wee wretched wightes this boone of thee doe crave,
No monstrous beastes, no noysome plagues, hereafter let us have:
With bloudy champions let the earth encombred bee no more:
Cast downe the hauty sway of Courtes: if ought annoyaunce sore
Shall cloy the earth, a champion to bee our shylde wee crave,
Whom as an honour of the Crowne his ruefull realme may have.
(That stil will keepe his swerd from being taint with guiltlesse bloud.)
But loe what meanes this rumbling noyse? loe Hercles sier doth grone,
And sigheth for his sonne: is it the Gods that wayle and mone?
Or is it Junoes fearefull shrike, whom Hercles doth aggrise,
That seeing him for feare shee roares, and runneth from the skyes?
Or els did Atlas faltring feete with feeble sturring stumble?
And shrinking from his tottring waight thus force the Gods to rumble?
Or scared he the wauling ghostes, the which to feare he drave?
Or Cerberus brast his gingling Chaynes with buskling in his cave?
It is not so: but loe where Philoctetes doth appeare,
And Hercles famous shaftes to him bequeathed doth hee beare.

THE FIFT ACTE

NUTRIX. PHILOCTETES

F Hercules most heavy haps good youngman make reporte
How did hee beare it at his death? Ph. In such a chearefull sorte
As no man lives. Nu. And could he with so sweete and merry looke,
The scorching panges and torments of his ending fier brooke?
Ph. That there was any heate at all his face did not bewray,
Who prov'de that power might force al things to stoupe and to obay,
That under sonne untamed be. Nu. Where did the noble knight,
Among the wrastling waves of sea display his matchlesse might?
Ph. That mischiefe witch all only yet the worlde knew not before,
Even fier hath bin conquered as beastes, and monsters more
Among the toyles of Hercules the fier is crept in.
Nu. Declare us how the flaming force of fier coulde hee win.
Ph. As soone as hee with smarting hand the Oeta hill had grypte,
And forthwith from the braunched Beeche the shrinking shade was wipte:
And felled from the stump it lyes, a Pyne tree hee bendes,
That crakes the clowdes, and down from skyes his hawty head he sendes,
The Rocke did totter ready for to reele, and with the sway
It tumbleth downe, a little grove withall it beares away.
A spreading Oake of Chaon big, whose leaves did ever rush,
And dimde the sunne, and did beyonde the woode his braunches push,
It being hewde doth crack, and eake in twayne the wedges knappes:
The steele startes back and thus the toole of Iron bides the rappes,

And flyes out of the Logge, at length at roore it shogde and shooke,
And falling downe full lythily the overthrow it tooke.
Forthwith the place lost all his light, the byrds scard fro their nest
Doe soare about the cropped wood, and holes wherein to rest,
And chirping with their weary winges about the plot they flicker
In every tree the ringing strokes were multiplied thicker.
The holy Oakes in hugy hand the Iron Axe did feele,
No timber on the stallen stocks might scape the hewing steele,
Thus all the wood upon a pile is heapt, and one by one
The Logges are layde as hygh as heaven that Hercules thereon
Might have a narrow roome his burning bones for to bestow.
On Pynetree top, and towghest Oake the fier begins to glowe,
And on the stumped willowe flamth, and thus the forrest wyde
Doth make the Kill : the Popler wood all Hercles blocks doth hyde.
But as the puissaunt Lyon when his fits doe vexe him sore,
Lies wallowing on his back, and through the forrest lowde doth rore,
So fareth hee, who woulde have thought hee had to burning gon ?
As one that climbs to heaven, not fier, he was to looke upon
When up he stept on Oeta mount and gazed on his kill.
Being layde aloft he brake the blocke, so heavy was hee still
The shyves yet coulde not beare his wayght : he calling for his bow
Did say to mee, have Philocktet, on thee I it bestow,
This same is it that Hydra with his swarming heads did know.
This did fetch downe the stimphall foules, and all that wee have
daunt,
Goe thou with this, let victory and happinesse thee haunt,
For never shall thou shute agaynst thy foes with these but speede,
If at a byrde amid the clowdes thou aame shee dies indeede.
These certayne shaftes shall bring thy marke down from the azur
sky,
Thys bow shall not deceave thy hand, full oft I did it try,
And made it meete to beare a shaft, and cast his leavell dew.
Thyne arrowes shall not fayle thyne aame if that thou nock them
trew,
I aske but only this of thee, put fier to the Stack,
Bestow on mee my funerall flame to bryng me to my wrack.
This knarry Club (quoth hee) the which no hand shall ever tosse
Shall onely with his Hercules in fier goe to losse,

This also (quoth hee) shouldst thou have if thou could weild the
same,
Beside his maister let it lye to help towarde the flame,
And then beside him down hee layes the Lyons hayry skin
To burne with him : the shaggy case hid all the pyle within.
The people sobde, and none there was but sorrow straynde his teares.
The mother mad for egar griefe her breast all bare shee beates,
And naked downe toth Navill steade displayes her tender teates,
And languishing with wringed hands her naked dugges shee beates
And cryeth out upon the Gods, on Jove himselfe shee calles,
Her shriking rang through all the place so womanlike shee yalles.
Be still (quoth hee) good mother : force your showres of teares to
cease :
Your dreary dole disgraceth much the death of Hercules.
Wayle secretly unto your selfe : why make ye Juno glad,
To se that you a weeping day with store of teares have had ?
(It doth her good to see her bawdes to stand with weeping eyes.)
Forbeare, forbeare your malady, tis deadly sinne for yee
To teare the teates, and rent the wombe, that first did foster me.
And as he blustred giving gruntes, when earst he led in chayne
The hownd about the townes of Grece what tyme he came agayne
Tryumphing over conquerd hel defying Plutoes might
And dreadful desteny : so on the fyre he lay upright.
What conquerour ever sat in coatch with such a chereful grace ?
What tyrant did controll his folke by law with such a face ?
How husht was al thing at his death ? himselfe he could not weepe,
And also we had cleane forgot the wound of sorrowes deepe.
None doth lament him at his death, now were it shame to wayle :
Alcmen (whom nature ought to move) her teares now do her fayle,
And thus as yll as was the sonne the mother stoode almost.
Nu. But at his burning did hee not call on the heavenly host,
Remembring Jove to heare his suite ? Ph. As on in depe dispayre
He lay, and staryng up so rould his eyes into the ayre
To spye if Jove lookt downe to him from any turret hye.
Then with his handes displayd to heaven (quoth he) where so thou
lye,
And lokest downe to se thy sonne, this same, this same is hee,
Whom one day ecked with a night engendred hath to thee.

If East and West, if Scithia, and every burning plot
That parched is with glowing glede at Phœbus fier hot,
Doth sing my prayse ? and if the earth ful satisfyde with peace,
If languishing and wayling woords in every towne doe cease,
If none their alters do imbrew with any guiltles gore,
Then Jove let my uncaged spirite have heaven for evermore.
As for thinfernall dennes of death they do not me detarre,
Nor scouling Plutoes dungeon darck, but Jove I do abhorre
Unto those gastly Goblins as a silly shade to goe,
Sith I am he whose conquering hand gave them their overthrowe.
Withdraw these foggy clowdes of night, display the glimsyng light
That Hercles broyld with flying flames the Gods may have in sight,
And if thou do denye (O syre) the starres and heaven to mee,
To geve me them agaynst thy will thou shalt constrayned bee :
If glutting griefe do stop thy speach, the Stygian goulphes set oape,
And let mee dye, but first declare within the heavenly coape,
That thou accepst me as thy sonne : this day it shal be wrought,
That to be raysd aloft to starres, I may be worthy thought.
Thou hast doone litle for me yet : it may be doubted well
Whether Jove did first beget his sonne, or damnd him first to hell.
And (quoth he) let my stepdame see, how wel I can abyde
The scorching heate of burning brandes : for fyer then he cride,
And sayth to me O Philoctet in hast uppon me throw
The burning logges, why quakest thou ? dost dastard thow forslow,
For feare to this wicked deede ? O coward, peasant slave,
Thou art to weake to bende my bow, unmeete my shaftes to have.
What aylest thou to loke so pale ? and as thou seest mee lye
With cherefull looke couragiously do thou the fier plye.
Behold me wretch that broyle and burne, my father opes the Skyes
And unto me sonne Hercules come, come away he cryes.
O father Jove (quoth he) I come : with that I waxed pale
And toward him a burning beame with might and mayne I hale :
But backe from him the billets flye and tumbling out they leape,
And from the limmes of Hercules downe falleth all the heape.
But he encrocheth on the fyre as it from him doth shrinke,
That many mountaynes whole were set on fyer a man would thinke :
No noyse was hard, and all was husht, but that the fyer did hisse
In Hercles glowing paunch when as his liver burning is.

If boysteous gyant Typhus had amid this fire bene throwne,
These torments would have straind his teares and forst him sigh and grone,
Or tough Euceladus that tost a mountayne on his backe.
But Hercles lifted up himselfe amid his fyres all blacke,
With smoake besmeard his corps halfe burnt in shivers, gubs and flawes,
And downe the throate his gasping breath and flames at once he drawes.
Then to Alcmen he turnd himselfe : O mother myne (quoth hee)
Should ye so stand at Hercles death ? should you thus wayle for me ?
And thus betwene the fire and smoke, upright and stiffe he standes,
And neyther stoupes nor leanes awrye, but moves and stirs his hands
With al his lively gestures still, and thus he doth perswade
His mother leave the languishing and mourning that she made,
And did encourage all his men t' encrease the fyre than
As though he were not burning, but would burne some other man.
The people stoode astonished, and scant they would beleeve
That fire had any force on him, or that it did him greeve,
Because his chereful looke had such a majesty and grace,
And never wilde us meve the fyre that he might burne apace.
(And now when as he thought, he had endured pangues ynough,)
And stoutly bode the brunt of death, the blocks hee doth remove,
That smothering lay, to make them burne : then downward doth he shove
And where the stewing heate did chiefely scorch, and burne most hot,
That way he thrusts his frying lims, and thether hath hee got.
(With steaming countnaunce unapaulde his mouth now doth he fill)
With burning coales, his comely Bearde then blazde about his cheekes :
And now when as the sparkling fier unto his visage seekes,
The flame lickt up his singed hayre, and yet he did not winke,
But open kept his staring eyes. But what is this ? my thinke
Alcmene cometh yonder as a woefull wight forlorne,
With sighes and sobs, and all her hayre befrounced, rent and torne,
And beares the remnaunt in her Lap, of Hercules the great.

ALCMENA. PHILOCTETES

LEARNE Lordings, learne to feare and dreade th' unweildy fatall force,
This little dust is all thats left of Hercles hugy coarse.
That boysteous Giaunt is consumde unto these ashes small,
O Titan what a mighty masse is come to nought at all.
Aye me an aged womens lappe all Hercules doth shrowde,
Her lap doth serve him for a grave, and yet the champion prowde
With all his lumpe fills not the roome. Aye mee a burthen small
I feele of him to whom whole heaven no burthen was at all.
O Hercules, deare chylde, O sonne the season whilom was
That thou to Tartar pits and slugguish dens aloofe didst passe
For to repasse : from deepe of hell when wilt thou come agayne ?
Not to purloyne the spoyles thereof, or bring from captive chayne
To life thy friendly Theseus. But when wilt thou returne
Alone ? can flaming Phlegethon thy ghost in torments burne ?
Or can the mastiffe Dogge of hell keepe downe thy woefull sprite ?
Where then might I come see thy soule and leave this loathed light ?
When shall I rap at Tartar gate ? what Jawse shall mee devower ?
What death shall dawnt mee ? goest thou to hell, and hast no power
To come agayne ? alas why do I wast the day in teares and playnte ?
O wretched lyfe why dost thou last ? thou shouldest droupe and faynt,
And loath this dreary daye : how can I beare to Jove agayne
Another noble Hercules ? what sonne may I obtayne
So valiant to call mee thus (Alcmena mother myne) ?
O happy spouse Amphitrio, twyse happy hast thou bene
In entring at the dennes of death, and through thy noble sonne
The Devils at thy presentes quake to see thee thether come.
Though thou but forged father wert to Hercules of late,
Whether shall old beldam goe whom many kinges do hate ?
If any prince remayne with blody breast and murdring mynde,
Then woe to mee : if groning babes be any left behynd,
That sorrow for theyr parentes deathes now, now for Hercles sake
Theyr mallice let them wrecke on mee, on mee dyre vengeance take.

If any young Busiris be, I feare the Persians sore
Wil come and take me captive hence in chaynes for evermore.
If any tyrant feede his horce with gubbes of straungers flesh,
Now let his pampred jades unto my Carkasse fall afresh.
Perhap dame Juno coveteth on me to wrecke her yre,
And on us of her burning breast wil turne the flaming fire :
Her wreckful hand doth loyter now sith Hercules is slayne,
And now to feele her spurning spyte as harlot I remayne.
My valyant sonne is cause of this my wombe shall barrayne be,
Least I should beare another child as hardy as was hee.
Oh whether may Alcmena goe ? or whether shall she wend ?
What countrey or what kingdomes may my careful hed defend ?
Where may I couch my wretched coarse, that every where am knowne ?
If I unto my native soyle repayre among myne owne,
Euristeus is of Argos lord thus woefully forlorne.
I wil to Thebes where I was wed, and Hercules was borne :
And where with Jove I did enjoy dame Venus deare delight.
O blessed woman had I bene and in most happy plight,
If Jove with flash of lightning leams and blasing flakes of fyre
Had smolthred me as Semele was sowst at her desyre.
Would God that Hercles whyle he was a babe had rypped bene
Out of my wombe, then wretchedly I should not this have seene
The pangues and tormentes of my sonne, whose prayse doth countervaile
Even Jove : then had I learnd that death at length might him assayle,
And take him from my sight : O child, who wil remember thee ?
For now unthankfulness is great in men of each degree :
(That for thy sake I do not know where entertaynd to bee)
The curtesie of the Cleonies I wil attempt and trye,
Whom from the Lyon rescewde he and made the monster dye.
Or shal I too th' Archadians go where thou didst slea the boare ?
Where thy renowne remaineth ryfe of great exploytes before,
The parlous serpent Hydra heare was slayne, there fel he dead,
That with the flesh of slaughtred men his greedy horses fedde :
And yonder were the Stimphall burdes compelde to leave the skye,
And tamed by the handy toyle, now doth the Lyon frie,

And belketh stiffling fumes in heavens whyle thou liest in thy grave.
O if mankynd but any sparke of thankful nature have
Let all men preace to succour mee Alcmene thy mother deare.
What if among the Thracians I venter to appeare,
Or on the banckes of Heber floud ? thy prowesse every where
Hath succoured all these soyles : for earst in Thrace thou did put downe
The fleshy moungers of the King and put him from his crowne :
By slaughter of the salvage prince the people live in peace.
Where diddest thou denye thy helpe to make tormoyling cease ?
Unhappy mother that I am, a shryne where may I have
To shrowde thy coarse ? for all the world may strive aboute thy grave.
What temple may be meete to shryne thy reliques safe for aye,
And hallowed bones ? what nations unto thy ghost shal pray ?
O noble sonne what sepulchere what hearse may serve for thee ?
The world it selfe through flying flame thy fatal tombe shalbe :
Who taketh here this payse from me his ashes which I beare
Why loath I them ? imbrace his bones keepe stil his ashes here,
And they shall be a shield to thee, his dust shal thee defend,
To see his shadow, princes prowde for feare shal stoupe and bend.
Ph. O mother of noble Hercules forbeare your dreary playnt :
His valiant death thus should not be with femal teares attaynt.
Ye should not languish thus for him, nor count him wretched man
In dying, who by noble mynd prevent his destny can.
His chevalry forbyddeth us with teares him to bewayle :
The stately stomacke doth not stoupe : they sigh whose hartes do fayle.
Alc. (Ile mone no more : behold, behold, most wretched mother I)
Have lost the sheild of land and seas, where glittring Phœbe displayes
With whirling wheeles to foamy gulphes, and red and purple rayes
The losse of many sonnes I may lament in him alone.
Through him I lifted Kings to crowne, when crown my selfe had none
And never any mother livde, that neded lesse to crave
Of Gods, then I. I asked naught while I my sonne might have

What could not Hercles tender love like on me to bestow ?
What God would once denye to graunt, or what he held me froe,
Twas in my powre to aske and have. If Jove would ought denye,
My Hercules did bring to passe I had it by and by.
What mortall mother ever bare and lost so deare a sonne ?
Earst downe the cheekes of Niobe the trilling teares did runne,
When of her deare and tender brattes she wholly was bereven,
And did bewayle with strayned sighes her children seven and seven :
And yet might I compare this one (my Hercles) unto those,
And I in him as much as shee in all her impes did lose.
The mothers that are mourning dames do lacke on hed and chefe,
And now Alcmene shalbe shee deprivde of all releefe.
Cease woeful mothers cease, if that among you any are
Constrayne to shed your streaming teares by force of pensive care :
Ye Lady whom lamenting long of women fourmed rockes,
Geve place unto my gluttyng greefe, beat on with burning knockes
Ye handes uppon my riveled breast, alas am I alone
Enough for such a funerall to languish and to mone,
Whom al the world shallshortly neede ? yet streach thy feble armes
To thumpe uppon thy sounding breast thy griefe with doleful larmes,
And in despyte of al the gods powre out thy woeful crye,
And to receive thy flowing teares thy watry cheekes applye.
Bewayle Alcmenas woful state : the sonne of Jove bewayle,
Whose byrth did cause the dusky day in kindly course to fayle,
The East compact two nightes in one : Lo, lo, a greater thing
Then glorious day the world hath lost. now let your sorrowes ring,
Yee people al whose lowring lordes he draw to dennes of death
Theyr blades (that reekt with guiltles gore) he put into the sheath.
Bestow on him your Christall teares, which he deserved well :
Howle out ye heavens, ye marble seas, and goulphes with gronings yell.
O Crete Deare darling unto Jove for love of Hercles rore,
Ye hundred cityes beare your armes : my sonne for evermore
Is gone among the griesly ghostes and shimmering shades of hell,
Lament for him ye woeful wightes, that here on earth do dwell.

HERCULES ŒTÆUS

THE FIFTH ACTE

HERCULES. ALCMENA

Why Mother wayle you mee as tost in torments hoat of hell ?
Or plonged in panges of death, sith I among the Spheares doe dwell ?
Forbeare, forbeare to moane for mee, for vertue opened hath
To mee the passage to the Starres, and set mee in the path
That guides to everlasting Lyfe, whence coms this dreadfull sounde ?
Whence roares this thundring voyce, that doth against mine eares rebound,
And biddeth mee to stint my teares ? I know it now I know,
The darksome dungeons daunted are, and Dennes of Lakes alow.
O Sonne art thou returnd to me from Stygian gulph agayne ?
And can thou twise of ougly death the conquest thus obtayne ?
And brast the balefull prisons twise, of glum and gastly night.
Against th' infernall fyrrpes foorce prevayling thus by might ?
May any scape from Acheron ? Or dost thou scape alone ?
Hath hell no power to holde thy sprite, when breath from breast is gone ?
Or els hath Pluto baalde thee out, for feare least thou alone
Should cloyne his Scepter from his hand, and pluck him from his trone ?
For I am sure I sawe thee layde upon the burning trees :
And from thy Corps the flame and sparkes agaynst the welkin flyes :
That sure thou wast to poulder burnt, and feeble lyfe was lost :
But sure the deepes and pits of hell did not lock up thy ghost.
Why were the devills afrayde of thee ? why quaked Ditis grim ?
And did thy noble ghost seeme such a gastly bug to him ?
He. The dampy dikes of Cocitas coulde not keepe me from light.
Nor Carons fusty musty Barge transported hath my sprite.
Now Mother mourne no more : once have I seene the Hags of hell,
And all the stearne and steaming fiendes in dungeons deepe that dwell.
That mortall moulde I tooke of you to nought the flames have fryed :
Heaven hath the substaunce that I tooke of Jove : in fier yours died.

And therefore pawse your playntive teares, which parents use to shed,
When wretchedly they wayle their sonnes, that dastardly are dead.
Thus vulgar varlets weepe : loe vertue hopes the Starres to get,
But faynting feare stil dreames on death : from heaven where I am set,
You heare my voyce : Euristeus now shal byde the deadly push
With charyot sway his cracked scull ye shal on sunder crush.
Now must I hence advaunce my Ghost up to the rolling skyes,
Once more I daunt the devilles, and do the goblins grim aggrise.
Alc. But stay awhile my sonne : he fades and shrinketh from my sight,
Advaunst he is among the starres : doth this my charmed Spirite
Dote in a traunce ? or do I dreame that I have seene my sonne ?
A troubled mynd can scante beleve the thinges he seeth done,
But now I see thou art a God possessing heaven for aye :
I see it sure. I will to Thebes thy triumphes to display.

CHORUS

Lo vertue scapes the gastly shades of hell,
Ye noble peeres that shyne in vertue bright
Dire desteny cannot constrayne you dwell
Among the glowming glades of ougly might,
Nor sinke your fame in loathsome lakes of spyte :
But when deaths day drawes on the gasping howre,
You purchast glory shall direct your right
To fynd the passage to the heavenly bower.
When flesh doth fall, and breathing body dies
Then (Fame the child of Vertue) doth arise :
But sluggish sottes that sleepe their dayes in sloth,
Or geve their golden age to loathsome lust,
Them and their names the wretches bury both,
When as their bones shall shryned be in dust :
The clay shall cover their carkases forlorne,
As though such kaytiffes never had bene borne.

But if that ought of memory they have,
In thafter age it shalbe filthy shame.
The gnawing wormes torment not so in grave
Their rotten flesh, as tounges do teare their name,
That dayly kild to further mischiefe lives.
Lo both the fruites, that vice and virtue gives.

FINIS

Ovid.

Omne genus scripti gravitate Tragœdia vincit.